The Renaissance fresco, *Original Sin and Expulsion from the Garden of Eden,* depicted on the cover and throughout this book, is from the ceiling of the Sistine Chapel at the Vatican Palace in Rome. The frescoes were painted by Michelangelo di Lodovico Buonarroti Simoni (1475–1564), universally considered to be the greatest artist who ever lived. The painting of the Sistine Chapel was commissioned by Pope Julius II, and the ceiling depicts nine scenes from the book of Genesis in the Old Testament, including the famous *Creation of Adam.* Michelangelo painted the frescoes during the years 1508–12, but it took him a total of only twenty months to complete this masterpiece. To paint the ceiling, Michelangelo had to lie flat on his back on scaffolding built high above the floor, a difficult and painstaking task. The recent restoration of this work has highlighted Michelangelo's distinctive technique and the brilliance of color he used to create one of the most famous and beautiful works of art in the world.

Holy Sex

God's Purpose and Plan for Our Sexuality

Terry Wier
with Mark Carruth

W *Whitaker House*

Unless specifically noted otherwise, case histories described herein are composites of many people with similar problems.

HOLY SEX

ISBN: 0-88368-587-6
Printed in the United States of America
Copyright © 1999 by Terry Wier and Idealogic, Inc.
Cover Photo Credit: Scala/Art Resource, NY

Whitaker House
30 Hunt Valley Circle
New Kensington, PA 15068

Library of Congress Application Pending

1 2 3 4 5 6 7 8 9 10 11 12 13 / 10 09 08 07 06 05 04 03 02 01 00 99

Dedication

I dedicate this book to God my Father, to Jesus Christ my Savior,
and to the Holy Spirit, who urged me to author this work.

To my wife, Phyllis, for walking with me in the dark places
where few women have dared to go.

To Paul Johansson, Vice President of Elim Bible Institute,
for lighting the fire.

To Pastor Jim Cymbala of The Brooklyn Tabernacle
for opening the door.

I especially dedicate this to all of those who have suffered
in silence the shame and guilt of sexual bondage,
not even knowing if there was freedom for them.
I pray that the Lord will use this book as an instrument
of healing and deliverance for those people.

A portion of the royalties from the sale of this book will go to support
Isaiah Ministries, where there is a place of honor for all.

Isaiah Ministries
Therapeutic Living Center
2703 North Fitzhugh
Dallas, Texas 75204

Special Appreciation

To John and Yvonne Vazquez for all the years of nights on the streets of New York City and for all the souls they brought into the Kingdom of God. Most of all for standing by us in the midst of the storm.

To Mark Carruth who gave two and a half years of his life in full-time research on this project. He documented with passion every detail of the revelation that God has given me with clinical precision and accuracy.

To Fernando Zamora who labored in love to design the interior of the book.

To Odessagraphs for the cover design and overall art direction.

To the editorial staff at Whitaker House for their excellent work in the final execution of this project and to Bob Whitaker, Sr., for his vision and willingness to publish this book.

Contents

Foreword

The most widespread and troublesome issues facing the Church today are sexual in nature: adultery, divorce, premarital sex, homosexuality, to name just a few. It seems that every family has at least one member who has been caught up in one of these problems. Yet these are the topics least discussed from the pulpit and least understood by most Christians.

Every denomination has formulated a doctrinal position on these issues. Some have updated their doctrine over the years in response to social changes. But then we must ask why this was necessary. Has God changed? Has the Bible changed? Has human nature changed?

Some denominations are proud of maintaining their orthodoxy. But has their doctrinal purity prevented their members from falling into the same sexual problems as our society as a whole? Statistics (which we will examine in Chapter 8) show this not to be the case.

Many Christians have become confused by the false messages about sexuality with which our society bombards us each day. Yet the response from many churches is only an awkward and embarrassed silence concerning sexual matters. As a result, many Christians do not know God's answers for the sexual problems with which they are struggling. Some can no longer clearly distinguish right from wrong with regard to sexual behavior.

I believe what the Church today is lacking is a deep understanding of God's overall design and purpose for sexuality. We have lost the vision of what God intended human sexuality to be. Thus, the chief goal of Part I of this book is *reestablishing the holiness of sexuality.*

How often do *you* think of *sex* each day, and how often do you think of sex as something *holy* instead of something shameful and dirty?

Our sexuality is intended to be holy—set apart to accomplish God's purposes. Sex is an essential part of His plan, not only in bringing more children into this world, but in teaching us about God Himself. Far from being a continuous source of shame, our sexuality was intended to reveal important aspects of the nature and character of God. As the Apostle Paul taught, "this is a great mystery" (Ephesians 5:32 NKJV) through which God has chosen to reveal deep truths about the relationship He desires to have with humanity, both individually and collectively, and as His bride.

In my study of the Scriptures concerning sexuality, I have begun to see the outlines of a fundamental principle that I call *God's Law of Sexual Union*. As you come to understand this principle, you will see how the many Scriptures on sexuality fall into place around it in beautiful order. You will also see that everything that modern medical science is discovering about sexuality confirms this principle, and that scientific discoveries support every biblical commandment for proper sexual behavior. (You see, God gave us these commandments to protect us, not to spoil our fun.)

You will also discover that God has a higher spiritual purpose for marital union. There exists a much greater level of fulfillment to be enjoyed that few Christians today have even heard about, much less experienced.

Having this beautiful vision of God's plan for sexuality restored to our minds is foundational for having a fulfilling marriage. But it is also essential for bringing hope and healing to those of us who are struggling with sexual sins and problems, such as divorce, adultery, and shameful and out-of-control desires or practices.

This is the focus of Part II: *Confronting Sexual Problems in the Church Today*. It is written for hurting people, for those who have fallen into sexual sin and the problems surrounding it, for those whose sexuality has been damaged by the sins of others, and for those who have been bearing heavy burdens of guilt and shame about their sexual problems.

It is also written for those who wish to help the hurting. I meet so many pastors and leaders today who are desperately searching for solutions to the sexual problems that are tearing their people apart.

However, before we can even begin to resolve the tangled mess of sexual problems, the dark clouds of ignorance, fear, and shame surrounding this subject must be dispersed. These forces have long prevented many of us from even wanting to think about, much less discuss, sexual matters. Our viewpoint is in need of a drastic readjustment. We must learn to look at these issues from God's viewpoint. His love, His truth, and His compassion must fill our hearts. He must first free each of us from wrong attitudes before He can use us to help others.

As Christians we must no longer retreat from learning the truth and speaking the truth about sexual issues. Our society is increasingly filled with information about sex. The media shower us with messages about sex. Yet, despite their claims of objectivity, most of the sexual messages they deliver are either outright lies or distortions of the truth. In many instances, even scientific research has been twisted to support false concepts of sexuality.

This is the result of the efforts of those whose aim is to completely destroy God's plan for marriage and the family by encouraging *total and unrestrained sexual indulgence*. This effort is driven and controlled by demonic forces. They have deceived and gained influence over the minds of many highly educated and respected leaders. Through them they are producing disastrous changes in our society.

I call this agenda *the Kingdom of Sexual Perversion*. It is really nothing new, as its influence can be traced through ancient times all the way back to Babylon. But it is essential that we come to understand the spiritual forces behind it, how it is working in modern society, and how we can fight it—because our families and friends are at risk.

> I CALL THIS AGENDA *THE KINGDOM OF SEXUAL PERVERSION.*

I believe one of the keys to eliminating the influence of the Kingdom of Sexual Perversion within the church is for every Christian to develop a basic understanding of the roots of sexual problems: how they develop, how they can be cured, and how they can be prevented.

As a Christian counselor, I work with so many clients who were raised in "good" Christian homes (even pastors' homes) and who have been in church every Sunday as far back as they can remember. Yet they are struggling to overcome deep-seated, lifelong sexual problems. This is so tragic, because most of these types of sexual problems begin in childhood or adolescence, *and that is when they can be most easily treated or prevented.*

Yet, because so many churches have had a tradition of awkward silence on sexual matters, parents are not being taught how to ensure their children will develop a healthy sexuality, or how to tell when a child is not developing normally. Many teenagers are not being taught how to avoid the dangers of sexual experimentation or how to manage their sexual feelings. Few are extending help and reassurance to those teens who find, to their horror, that they seem to have some abnormal sexual desires. Many young couples are not being taught how to build strong and successful marriages.

When the Church has been silent, Christians have remained ignorant. Too many have fallen prey to the deceptions of the Kingdom of Sexual Perversion. The casualties are all around us.

The divorce rate is as high (or even higher, according to one survey) within the church as outside of it. Christian teens are having premarital sex at record levels. Christian women are leaving their husbands and children to move in with female lovers. Christian men are announcing to their families that they have joined the "gay" community. Christian people are startled to hear of the instances where children have been molested at church by church workers.

This all has to stop.

Rather, it must *be* stopped, in our families and in our churches, by the concerted efforts of informed Christians—those who are prepared to change the way things are today, and who are ready to call a halt to religious *business as usual*. In the last chapter of this book, I describe how every Christian, every parent, and every church can begin to break free from the influence of the Kingdom of Sexual Perversion and protect themselves and their families.

Fundamental to this effort is replacing ignorance with knowledge, deception with truth. That is what I have aimed to do in writing this book. However, to accomplish this, I will need to speak very plainly and frankly about sexual matters. Many sensitive, serious, and even explosive issues must be discussed. There are sure to be pages that some people will find difficult to read and topics about which some would prefer not to think.

But I challenge you not to quit reading. Just file those troublesome things away temporarily on a mental shelf. I believe that truth is incredibly powerful, much more powerful than falsehood. Truth has the power to change us in ways that falsehood never could. Moreover, truth will endure the test of time.

If you find yourself reading about sins with which you are struggling, do not allow yourself to feel hopeless. Please bear in mind that *God always has a solution* to every problem we are facing. *He is with you and He is for you*, not against you. He never intended guilt or shame to be a permanent condition.

God has a purpose for our sexuality that is much greater than most of us have imagined. He has a plan for us to follow so that we can fulfill His purpose. Within these pages, I hope to lay a foundation for you, based upon the Word of God, for a fundamental understanding of God's purpose and plan for our sexuality.

His Word contains simple truths, but these truths are so powerful that—when we truly understand them, believe them, and act upon them—they will change our lives forever.

Part I

Reestablishing the Holiness of Sexuality

In the Beginning
Was the Word

One of the biggest issues we all must wrestle with at some point in our lives is not only "What do I believe?" but "*Why* do I believe what I believe?" For Christians, the foundation for what we believe is the written Word of God. Not only is the Bible the most influential book ever written—having changed the course of world empires over thousands of years—but we have put it to the test in our own lives and found that it is true. What it says, works.

To that foundation we can add what we learn about God from His creation. The Apostle Paul says in Romans 1:20 that God's invisible attributes can be understood from the way He designed the world around us. In this book, we will be studying both God's written Word and His creation to help us understand His purpose and plan for our sexuality.

As we read the Bible, God speaks to us, showing us how our sinful thoughts and actions—those things we are doing that hurt Him, or hurt ourselves, or hurt others—are in conflict with His plans and purpose for our lives. He wants us to stop doing these wrong things—to repent. But we often choose to continue in our old ways because they give us some pleasure, even though we know they are harmful. Some of us just ignore His voice, which makes our hearts become hardened and insensitive toward Him. Some of us look for excuses that will justify our sin and make it seem not quite so bad. Some of us even try to convince ourselves that He does not really mean what His Word plainly says. We are particularly prone to use these defenses when God deals with us about our sexual sins, which often seem so powerful and pleasurable.

There are even some theologians, pastors, and teachers today who claim to be Christians but who teach others to disregard what the Bible clearly says about some sexual sins. Often these are sins in which they themselves are involved, such as adultery or homosexuality. This is sad, but it is nothing new. The New Testament authors reveal that this same attitude was found in some church leaders of that time.

The Apostle Peter spends at least a third of his second letter (2 Peter 2) warning the churches about these false teachers who encourage Christians to commit sexual sins. In Revelation 2:20-23, Jesus addressed a woman in the church at Thyatira who was teaching that it was acceptable for Christians to indulge in sexual sins. He urged her and her followers to repent, but warned that He would punish them, even to the point of cutting their lives short, if they did not.

Eventually, you will encounter some of these false teachers and their arguments. To some of you who are having a difficult struggle with sexual sins, it will be so tempting to believe them when they urge you to quit fighting and give in to those desires. When that temptation comes, here are some principles you will need to remember if you truly want to understand what the Bible says about the subject:

1. God wrote the Bible so that all could read His words and understand them.

God has even promised that He will explain His words to you through His Holy Spirit.

Jesus said:

> I have told you these things while I am still with you. But the Holy Spirit will come and help you, because the Father will send the Spirit to take my place. The Spirit will teach you everything and will remind you of what I said while I was with you. (John 14:25-26 CEV)

The Apostle John said:

> I am writing to warn you about those people who are misleading you. But Christ has blessed you with the Holy Spirit. Now the Spirit stays in you, and you don't need any teachers. The Spirit is truthful and teaches you everything. So stay one in your heart with Christ, just as the Spirit has taught you to do. (1 John 2:26-27 CEV)

So if someone tries to convince you that a verse in the Bible does not really mean what you think it means, be careful! Pray and ask the Father to show you what it means through His Spirit who lives in you. If your heart stays close to Him, you will not be deceived.

2. God the Father, Jesus Christ, and the Holy Spirit are one. They agree about everything.

Some false teachers try to paint an image of God the Father as fearsome and harsh, but Jesus as loving and accepting. They try to show a conflict between what God the Father said in the Old Testament and what Jesus said in the New Testament. They argue that if Jesus did not comment about a particular sexual sin, then it must not have been very important to Him; therefore, we can ignore any other Scriptures that do address it. They try to make us believe that certain Scriptures written through others, such as the Apostle Paul or the Apostle John, are less important, as if they were not really God's words, but just men's words. All of these arguments are contrary to what the Bible teaches us about itself.

This is how the gospel of John describes the relationship between Jesus and the Father:

> In the beginning was the Word, and the Word was with God, and the Word was God. He was in the beginning with God. All things were made through Him, and without Him nothing was made that was made. . . . And the Word became flesh and dwelt among us, and we beheld His glory, the glory as of the only begotten of the Father, full of grace and truth. (John 1:1-3, 14 NKJV)

We must remember that Jesus, God's the Son, was working in harmony with God the Father from the very beginning. Every place in the Bible where you see "God said," you should try to picture Jesus saying it, because when those words came out of God's mouth, Jesus was also speaking. Thus, anything that the Bible says about human sexuality, from Genesis to Revelation, should be understood as coming from Jesus Christ. He is the *living* Word of God.

Jesus said of Himself:

> Do not think that I have come to abolish the Law or the Prophets: **I have not come to abolish them but to fulfill them.** I tell you the truth, until heaven and earth disappear, not the smallest letter, not the least stroke of a pen, will by any means disappear from the Law until everything is accomplished. (Matthew 5:17-18 NIV)

Jesus knew the Old Testament very well. It formed the basis for His teaching. When He referred to Old Testament Scriptures, it was always to expand and deepen our understanding of them. We must assume that if He did not teach on certain Old Testament themes, it was because they needed no further explanation.

God used many different men over the span of many centuries to write the books of the Bible, but it is all God's Word. Christians know this is true because, when we read the Bible, God's Spirit speaks to us through it in a way that is different from any other book.

Remember this principle:

> Everything in the Scriptures is God's Word. All of it is useful for teaching and helping people and for correcting them and showing them how to live.
> (2 Timothy 3:16 CEV)

3. God wrote the Bible for all time. It is as applicable today as it was when it was first written.

Some false teachers say that things are so different today from when the books of the Bible were being written that many Scriptures are out-of-date and do not apply to the modern world. To refute this claim, we should read what God says about Himself:

> I am God, and there is none like me. I make known the end from the beginning, from ancient times, what is still to come. I say: My purpose will stand, and I will do all that I please. (Isaiah 46:9-10 NIV)

God exists outside of time and space, so He can see the end of something before it even begins. Every word in the Bible was known to God before the world was even created. The Bible is unlike any other book that has ever been written because it is as much about the future as about the past. It contains prophecies that have been fulfilled in recent history, such as the restoration of Israel as a nation, which occurred in 1948. But it also contains prophecies about our future—prophecies that many of us may yet see come to pass during our lifetimes.

As you read the life stories of those who lived in Old Testament times, you soon realize that they acted just as people do today. They lied, cheated, killed each other, and rebelled against God—things we also tend to do. Their clothes, customs, and language may have been different from ours, but their nature was the same. Human nature has not changed at all since Adam and Eve first rebelled against God, and since Cain murdered his brother Abel. Paul explains in 1 Corinthians 10:11 why the Old Testament records so many life stories of these ancient people:

> These things happened to them as examples and were written down as warnings for us, on whom the fulfillment of the ages has come. (NIV)

The Old Testament speaks very plainly about the sexual sins of the people of that day and the consequences they suffered. This now gives us the golden opportunity to learn from their mistakes so that we do not repeat them.

4. God's truth brings freedom into our lives, not bondage.

I have done my best to validate every point and verify every fact in this book. Yet when I am searching for the truth about an issue, I always rely on a promise Jesus gave His followers:

> If you keep on obeying what I have said, you truly are my disciples. You will know the truth and the truth will set you free. (John 8:31-32 CEV)

To me, this means that if you are doing your very best to obey what Jesus taught, then He will reveal even more truth to you. He will show you the very things you need to know to set you free from any remaining fears, hang-ups, sins, bondages, problems, or addictions that are troubling you.

But this promise of truth and freedom is based on a continuing *relationship* with Him. When we learn some new truth from Him, we must put it into practice. Then we can go back and ask Him a question, learn a little bit more, and adjust our behavior accordingly. This is what it means to be His *disciple*. If you truly want to find freedom in your life, then you must seek to develop this type of *interactive* relationship with Him. If you are living as His disciple, then you do not need to fear being deceived. You can trust Him to show you the truth about any matter.

Ultimately, the evidence of real truth is that it sets you free. It does not bring you into further bondage.

5. *What you choose to believe is ultimately a reflection of who you are.*

Belief always involves making a choice. We all prefer to think that we hold to a particular belief only because it is true—that is, we have examined the facts and are convinced that they fully support our belief. But hidden deep within our hearts is often a multitude of other factors that may influence what we choose to believe. Few people take the time or expend the effort to really search their hearts to determine what these deeper motivations are.

The answer to the question, "*Why* do you believe what you believe?" reveals a lot about the kind of person you are on the inside.

Here are some common influences on belief that affect all of us from time to time:

> • You may believe something because you were taught it as a child by people whom you loved and respected. You have never questioned that belief, because that would be too much like doubting and disrespecting those who taught you.
> • You may believe something because your friends or loved ones believe it so strongly. You feel that if you were to

question or reject it, those relationships would be put at risk.

• You may believe something because it makes you feel better about yourself. If that belief were ever challenged, it could seriously shake your self-image and self-confidence.

• You may choose a belief because you feel it gives you permission to do something you want to do very much, even though another part of you feels guilt or shame about doing that very thing.

All of us are influenced at some point in our decision-making by motivations such as these. Yet none of these reasons for belief are good enough. We all know that, ultimately, the only good reason for choosing to believe something is that we have determined to the best of our ability that it is *the truth*.

We all make decisions about what is true or false every day of our lives. We rightly put considerable effort into making good decisions. Is that salesperson telling you the truth about the product you are buying? Is that politician telling you the truth about what he or she will do once elected? However, it is a tragedy when people who can make a good decision about the best car to buy do not apply those same skills when making decisions with far greater consequences.

In Summary

Sexuality is one of the most central and powerful forces affecting all of our lives. What we choose to believe about sexual matters and the actions we take based on those beliefs can result either in some of the greatest joy and fulfillment to be found in this life, or in tremendous sorrow and pain.

We each have the power of choice concerning our own beliefs and our own behavior. That is why God will hold each of us responsible for the choices we have made. And the more truth we know about right and wrong, the more responsibility we bear for our actions (Luke 12:47–48).

As you read this book, examine your own beliefs about sexuality in light of the facts discussed herein. If you are not convinced of a point, then, by all means, investigate it further on your own. Yet, in all honesty, be willing to change your beliefs and behaviors if you see that they conflict with what is true and what is right. God expects nothing less from us.

One Flesh—God's Law
of Sexual Union

*In this chapter, we will be touching on issues that are highly sensitive for many people: fornication, adultery, and divorce. If your life has been impacted by any of these things, please bear in mind that I am not condemning you for what happened. I do not mean to focus on the question of guilt or "who did what to whom." I only want you to gain a deeper understanding of the underlying forces of sexuality at work, so that you can see **why** the Bible says what it does about these things.*

Let us first examine what the Bible says about the origins of human sexuality:

God said, "It is not good that man should be alone; I will make him a helper comparable to him." . . .

And the Lord caused a deep sleep to fall on Adam,
and he slept; and He took one of his ribs and closed
up the flesh in its place. (Genesis 2:18, 21 Fenton)

Notice that God's primary purpose here is to create a companion
for Adam. He does not even mention bearing children.

Adam then says with obvious pleasure:

This is now bone of my bones and flesh of my flesh;
she shall be called Woman, because she was taken
out of Man. (Genesis 2:23 Fenton)

God goes on to say in Genesis 2:24:

Therefore, a man shall leave his father and mother
and be joined to his wife, and they shall become one
flesh. (Fenton)

This passage is foundational to understanding God's purpose for
our sexuality.* *God designed sex so that man and woman can become one.*
Notice the beautiful symmetry illustrated here—that which was taken out
of man returns to him. Man is completed in woman and woman is completed in man. There is a union spoken of here that is much deeper than a
mere physical act.

Jesus quotes this same passage when teaching on marriage and
divorce:

"Haven't you read," he replied, "that at the beginning the Creator 'made them male and female,' and
said, 'For this reason a man will leave his father and
mother and be united to his wife, and the two will

---

* The importance of Genesis 2:24 is shown by the fact that it is quoted by both Jesus and Paul
as the basis of their teachings on sexuality. (Matthew 19:5, Mark 10:7-8, 1 Corinthians 6:16,
Ephesians 5:31)

become one flesh'? So they are no longer two, but one. Therefore, **what God has joined together,** let man not separate." (Matthew 19:4-6 NIV)

Notice that Jesus here makes an even stronger statement about sexual union by saying "what *God* has joined together." What an incredible statement! How many of us have considered that the joining that occurs in sexual union is an *act of God?* This fact alone should cause us to develop a greater respect for the awesomeness and holiness of sex.

God's Law of Sexual Union

Most of us think of marriage as the occasion when a man and woman make their vows in a wedding ceremony and receive a marriage license from the state. But Jesus does not mention vows, a marriage ceremony, or a license in this passage. What He is saying is that God designed *sexual intercourse* to be the force that actually marries (joins) a man and a woman together into one. I like to call Genesis 2:24, *God's Law of Sexual Union.*

Just as God designed the universe to operate in accordance with the law of gravity, so He designed human beings to function in accordance with the Law of Sexual Union. He created us with a deep-seated drive for union with the opposite sex that causes us to leave our families of origin and set out on a quest to find a mate. When we do find a spouse, the Law of Sexual Union binds us together more deeply and completely than we were ever joined to our parents and provides the foundation for a new family.

It is essential for us to distinguish this Law of Sexual Union from the *moral* laws given to guide our behavior, such as the Ten Commandments. The Law of Sexual Union is a *natural* law comparable to the law of gravity. You can choose to break a moral law, but you cannot break a natural law. Natural laws determine the consequences of our physical actions.

God's plan is for these natural laws to benefit us. Nevertheless, once they have been set in motion, we must bear the consequences, whether they are good or bad. For example, whether you fall off a cliff by accident, are thrown off the cliff by an adversary, or your rope breaks while you are climbing the cliff, the consequences are the same. You will fall until you hit something, with a force determined by the law of gravity. In a similar way, no matter what your reasons are for sexual intercourse with someone (even if it happens against your will), that act sets in motion the Law of Sexual Union, which joins you to that person as "one flesh." You may choose whether or not to violate God's *moral* law by having sex with someone other than your spouse, but you cannot escape the consequences of God's *natural* Law of Sexual Union that are set in motion by sexual acts.

We tend to think of sexual intercourse as a physical act that involves only our bodies. But because we are constructed of three parts that intermingle—spirit, soul, and body—the physical act of sexual intercourse ultimately affects us in all three areas, producing spiritual, mental, emotional, and physiological consequences.*

Have you ever noticed the peculiar fact that in all of the ceremonies ordained by Old Testament law, there is no mention of a marriage ceremony? Evidently God did not feel that it was necessary to add a ceremony to complete what His Law of Sexual Union accomplishes. Though there are descriptions of local marriage customs and celebrations in the Old Testament, the people of that time understood that the act of sexual intercourse was the only act that could create a marriage covenant between a man and a woman, as far as God was concerned. Even today, the laws in most countries acknowledge that a marriage is not legally enforceable and can be annulled if the couple has not had sexual intercourse, even if there has been a wedding ceremony and a marriage license has been issued.

Divorce and the Law of Sexual Union

Divorce has long been one of the most controversial topics within the Church. But if we look at divorce in the light of God's Law of Sexual

---

* Note: The law of gravity can also affect you in all three areas if you hit the bottom of the cliff with enough force to kill you, thus separating your spirit from your body!

Union, we can better understand what the Bible teaches about it.

In Matthew 19:6, quoted above, Jesus is teaching on divorce when He says, "What God has joined together, *let man not separate*." He clearly distinguishes here the act of God-ordained sexual union, which joins a man and woman, from the legal actions of men that would attempt to undo that union.

What do you think would happen if your city council passed a resolution rescinding the law of gravity on the first Saturday of every month within the city limits? Absolutely nothing! Man's civil laws have no effect whatsoever on God's natural laws.

Even so, a society may create laws that establish the civil duties of a husband and wife through a marriage contract, permit the contract to be dissolved under certain circumstances, and even determine how their property will be divided. But the laws of men can neither create nor undo the "one flesh" union that has come about through the operation of God's Law of Sexual Union. Human law has no jurisdiction at that level.

Looking further in the same passage, we read:

> "Why then," they asked, "did Moses command that a man give his wife a certificate of divorce and send her away?" Jesus replied, "Moses permitted you to divorce your wives because your hearts were hard. **But it was not this way from the beginning.** I tell you that anyone who divorces his wife, except for marital unfaithfulness, and marries another woman commits adultery." (Matthew 19:7-9 NIV)

(In the parallel passage in Mark 10:12, Jesus applies this principle to the wife also: "And if she divorces her husband and marries another man, she commits adultery." [NIV])

Jesus is saying two profound things here.

First of all, *divorce was never part of God's original plan for humankind.* Yet divorce was permitted under Old Testament law. (Perhaps this was because God saw it as the only means of preventing hard-hearted spouses from breaking a more serious commandment: "Thou shalt not kill" [Exodus 20:13].) However, this does not mean there were no negative consequences. Through the prophet Malachi, God expressed His feelings about divorce:

> You cry noisily and flood the LORD's altar with your tears, because he isn't pleased with your offerings and refuses to accept them. And why isn't God pleased? It's because he knows that each of you men has been unfaithful to the wife you married when you were young. You promised that she would be your partner, but now you have broken that promise. Didn't God create you to become like one person with your wife? And why did he do this? It was so you would have children, and then lead them to become God's people. Don't ever be unfaithful to your wife. The LORD God All-Powerful of Israel hates anyone who is cruel enough to divorce his wife. So take care never to be unfaithful! (Malachi 2:13-16 CEV)

Jesus' second point is more shocking: *divorce is actually a form of legalized adultery.* This makes sense only when we understand that the Law of Sexual Union is a natural law, which operates at a different level than the Law of Moses. Because God's original plan was for marriage to last for a lifetime, He never designed a mechanism to separate the "one flesh" union created through sex—it ends only at the death of one's spouse. Even though an Israelite woman had received a "certificate of divorce" from her husband under the Law of Moses, she remained joined to him by the natural Law of Sexual Union until either one of them remarried. At that point, the Law of Sexual Union would begin to unite the new couple, and adultery of the original union would occur. Of course, Jesus allowed for the situation in which adultery had already been committed by one spouse and served as grounds for divorce.

Adultery and the Law of Sexual Union

To help us better understand the Law of Sexual Union, we need to further examine the greatest danger it presents: adultery. The conventional and legal definition of adultery—having sexual relations with someone other than your spouse—is too limited. As we have seen, though man's laws do not view divorce and remarriage as adultery, Jesus does. He goes even further, saying:

> You have heard that it was said, "Do not commit adultery." But I tell you that anyone who looks at a woman lustfully has already committed adultery with her in his heart. (Matthew 5:27-28 NIV)

This passage is taken from the Sermon on the Mount where Jesus was teaching on how the Old Testament law is inadequate to produce true righteousness. What He says here about adultery gives us a profound insight into the nature of "one flesh" union. By saying that a decision of the heart to desire another woman sexually is an act of adultery, He is revealing to us that "one flesh" union is not just a union of bodies, but also *a union of hearts*. The truth is that adultery begins in the heart long before it is expressed in a physical way.

It is only recently that science has examined this situation and confirmed what Jesus is saying here. What a wife feels intuitively about her husband's wandering eye has a scientific basis. Researchers studying the effects of pornography found that both men and women, after viewing nude pinups, such as those found in *Playboy* or *Playgirl*, rated their spouses as less attractive than before and reported feeling less in love with them.[1]

Any book on marriage counseling contains examples of people who have fallen into adultery in one way or another. But I have found there is a similar thread of events that can be traced in every story. It begins with one spouse failing to meet the other's deepest emotional or sexual needs for some reason, whether knowingly or unknowingly. This creates an emotional/sexual deficit in one spouse and weakens the marital union in that area. However, the Law of Sexual Union continues to work, driving each to seek what they lack to be complete. So, the spouse who is lacking starts looking—looking for someone else to meet that need.

For example, the husband may suddenly notice that a woman at work is being particularly nice to him and seems to understand him so much better than his wife. He begins to look forward to their times together and rearranges his schedule so he can work with her more often. He likely does not even see the connection between the problems in his marriage and his sudden attraction to this woman. Unless this chain of events is interrupted by an outside force—or a sudden realization of guilt and shame—they may very well end up in bed together.

Let us look at the consequences of this adulterous situation as it pertains to the Law of Sexual Union. Even before the husband begins a sexual relationship with this coworker, his wife has been experiencing the pain of a weakening relationship with her husband as he develops a deepening emotional bond with the other woman. She is finding that more of her emotional needs go unmet as her husband invests more of his emotional energy in the other woman. The purity of their marital relationship has already been "adulterated" at this point. The union of their hearts is being disrupted by the husband's deepening emotional involvement with another woman. He has a divided heart.

The husband may have been happy with the adulterous situation at first because the needs his wife had been neglecting were at last being met by his lover. But he soon finds himself torn between the desire to further unite with his lover and the remaining bond he feels with his wife. The other woman is enjoying the completion she feels in her sexual and emotional union with this man, but she cannot help resenting the bond he still has with his wife, while wanting him all for herself. Even if he divorces his wife and marries her, she will never possess him as fully and completely as his first wife did, because some part of him will always belong to his first wife. After the divorce, his first wife must suffer the pain of being rejected by her husband and perhaps years of living in loneliness. Even if she does eventually remarry, her new husband will be in the same predicament as the other woman was—never possessing his spouse fully and completely because, in her heart, she still has a bond with her first husband. This tragedy is compounded if the couple had children. Researchers have only begun to document the terrible emotional damage that divorce inflicts on children.

This group of mixed-up, cross-connected, unhappy, and ultimately unsatisfied people illustrates what adultery is all about. This explains why God is so opposed to it. The drive for sexual union is a powerful motivator of human behavior; it *must* be strong to form a strong family unit. However, the consequences are disastrous when people disobey God's instructions for managing this powerful force.

. . . SHE WILL NEVER POSSESS HIM AS FULLY AND COMPLETELY AS HIS FIRST WIFE DID . . .

We now have a more complete picture of what adultery really is. *Adultery occurs when you allow someone other than your spouse to meet your deepest emotional or sexual needs, whether in thought (fantasies), word, or deed.* As you continue to receive what you need from the other person, a bond develops between you. This weakens the original bond between you and your spouse, since you no longer depend on your spouse to meet that need. Even if the adulterous relationship does not begin with sex, it will always head in that direction because the Law of Sexual Union is at work, seeking to join a man and woman as "one flesh." But the real crux of adultery is not the illicit relationship with the "other woman" (or man), it is the damage inflicted in *the tearing apart of the God-created union of the spirits, souls, and bodies of a husband and wife.*

Fornication and the Law of Sexual Union

The word *fornication* comes from a Latin word meaning *to visit a brothel.* This is the word the translators of the King James Version chose to translate the New Testament Greek word *porneia*. *Porneia* is used throughout the New Testament to refer to any type of heterosexual intercourse which takes place outside of a marriage relationship. This includes premarital sex, extramarital sex, patronizing a prostitute, and so forth. *Promiscuity* is the modern word with the closest meaning: *to have casual sex with multiple partners.*

We all know fornication is sinful, but learning *why* will deepen our understanding of the Law of Sexual Union. The Apostle Paul provides most of the biblical teaching on this issue, particularly in 1 Corinthians 6:

> Now the body is not for fornication, but for the Lord; and the Lord for the body . . . . Know ye not that your bodies are the members of Christ? shall I then take the members of Christ, and make them the members of an harlot? God forbid. What? know ye not that he which is joined to an harlot is one body? for two, saith he, shall be one flesh. But he that is joined unto the Lord is one spirit. Flee fornication. Every sin that a man doeth is without the body; but he that committeth fornication sinneth against his own body. What? know ye not that your body is the temple of the Holy Ghost which is in you, which ye have of God, and ye are not your own? For ye are bought with a price: therefore glorify God in your body, and in your spirit, which are God's. (1 Corinthians 6:13, 15-20 KJV)

I do not believe many Christians really understand the fundamental truth Paul is explaining here. If they did, we would not have such widespread fornication in the church today. When Paul says that your body is the temple of the Holy Spirit, he is not making a beautiful analogy. He is describing reality:

> The body is not for fornication, but for the Lord;
> and the Lord for the body.

Your bodies are the members [*body parts*] of Christ.

Your body is the temple [*dwelling place*] of the Holy Ghost . . . ye are not your own.

Shall I then take the members [*body parts*] of Christ, and make them the members [*body parts*] of an harlot?

These statements speak of a profound spiritual truth concerning our union with God that we need to grapple with until we truly understand it.

Due to the influence of ancient Greek philosophy on the development of our religious traditions, we tend to view our spirits as belonging to God, but see our bodies as inherently evil and belonging to this world. Not so! When we experience the new birth Jesus spoke of in John 3:3 and enter the Kingdom of God, not only our spirits but also our *bodies* become joined to God in the profound way that Paul here describes. Our *bodies* become the dwelling place of the Holy Spirit. Our *bodies* become joined to Christ. Our *bodies* are no longer our sole possession, but the Lord is now sharing them with us so that He can accomplish His work here on earth. Paul compares this union of our bodies and spirits with the Lord to the sexual union of a husband and wife. (See also Ephesians 5:30-32.)

Religious tradition has so twisted the common view of God that many now believe He spends most of His time in heaven, busy with grand pursuits that have little to do with our life on earth. Only on Sundays or special holidays does He peer over the edge of a cloud to see who is gathering in the beautiful buildings below that have been dedicated to Him. These traditions teach that God has the legal right of ownership of our bodies, but that He is not at all interested in them until they have been resurrected and made perfect.

Such religious ideas are flatly contradicted by the Apostle Paul in 2 Corinthians 6:16:

For ye are the temple [or *dwelling place*] of the living God; as God hath said, I will dwell in them, and
walk in them; and I will be their God, and they shall
be my people. (KJV)

This passage is not speaking of life after the resurrection, but of life
here on earth today. If you are a Christian, then God has made His home
in your body, and that is where He belongs! He wants to walk around with
you on this earth, sharing your body with you, helping you to do His work.
This statement may shock many of you: *there is no scriptural evidence that
God's presence abides in your church building or that He ever enters there
except when the building is filled with believers who bring Him along with
them in their hearts.*

Do you want to feel the presence of God every day? Do you want
His power to flow out through your hands and heal sick people? Do you
want His love to flow out of your eyes and melt the hearts of the lost people around you? Then start reminding yourself each day that He is living
with you *in your body* (1 Corinthians 6:19). Give Him opportunities to use
your body to do His work. Stop making Him withdraw to the depths of
your spirit to get away from the evil things you are doing with your/His
body.

Are you dragging "your body . . . the temple of the Holy Spirit"
(v. 19) to see R-rated movies? Are you watching violent, depressing, disgusting television programs? Are you swallowing mouthful after mouthful
of unhealthy food that you know is going to make His body weak and sick?
Do you use His lips to curse at someone who cuts you off on the freeway?
Are you filling the lungs He has given you with filthy cigarette smoke? Are
you becoming drunk with alcohol? Are you putting dangerous and illegal
drugs into your bloodstream? Are you looking at pornographic pictures
with the eyes He has given to you? Are you forcing His "temple" to endure
the experience of your having forbidden sex with someone?

This principle, *"The body of a Christian is God's home,"* helps us
to better understand the awesome consequences of entering into an intimate

relationship. One example, given in 1 Corinthians 7:14, says that a Christian's unbelieving spouse is "sanctified" (set apart for God) through the marriage relationship. We can now see how this is possible. A Christian is joined to God through spiritual rebirth *and also* to his/her spouse through their covenantal union. Thus, the power and grace of God can envelop the unbelieving spouse through the body and soul of the Christian spouse. This gracious influence occurs even though the unbelieving spouse does not yet know God in his/her spirit.

However, if a Christian has sexual intercourse with someone other than a spouse, the unthinkable happens. Since our bodies are already joined to Jesus Christ, we are actually joining the body that is rightfully His in a sinful "one flesh" union with that other person, even a prostitute (1 Corinthians 6:15–16). Paul gives us a very serious warning about defiling or corrupting our bodies, which are now God's home:

> Know ye not that ye are God's temple, and the Spirit of God dwells in you? If anyone corrupt the temple of God, God shall bring corruption to him; for the temple of God is holy, which ye are. (1 Corinthians 3:16-17 Berry)

In Summary

The issues of marriage, adultery, and divorce have been some of the most inflammatory and divisive throughout church history. Each Christian tradition has developed its own formal statement of doctrine on these issues that has changed slowly over time, due to social forces. Each reader undoubtedly has his or her own beliefs about these issues. These also may change over a lifetime of experience.

The problem with formal doctrinal positions is that they are often abstractions, having to do with somewhat legalistic interpretations of Scriptures, or the historical statements of church fathers. The problem with personal beliefs is that they are highly subjective and shaped by one's own life experiences—not a good basis for building toward an understanding of a universal, eternal truth.

What I am attempting to do within these pages is to refocus our attention away from legal abstractions and personal opinions and get us back to looking at reality, both spiritual and natural. We must learn to ask, "What are the facts?" In the following chapters we will look at some very interesting facts that have been uncovered concerning the physical, mental, emotional, and spiritual effects of sexual union.

Notes.
1. Dolf Zillman and Jennings Bryant, "Pornography, Sexual Callousness, and the Trivialization of Rape," *Journal of Communications* 32 (1982): 15. "Pinups and Letdowns," *Psychology Today*, September 1983.

III

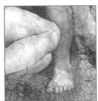

How the Law of Sexual Union Affects Our Bodies

We have studied what the Bible teaches about the Law of Sexual Union. However, it will benefit us to examine the details of sexuality to see how the Law of Sexual Union actually operates as it joins bodies, souls, and spirits. Though we will be discussing each area separately over the next three chapters, keep in mind that a person's spirit, soul, and body are closely interconnected, so that each part has a great influence on the others.

The human body has been the subject of much concentrated and fruitful study over the past hundred years. Though our knowledge of it has been greatly expanded, allowing much success in treating many diseases, there is still much more to be discovered. We hear of new medical breakthroughs almost every week. In the field of human sexuality, many amazing facts have recently been uncovered that demonstrate the reality of the "one flesh" union we have been studying.

We see perhaps the most literal manifestation of the term "one flesh" when a sperm cell from the husband fertilizes his wife's ovum to produce an embryo. These two separate cells become, literally, *"one flesh,"* *one new body.* But there is much more involved in reproduction than just a single act of intercourse. To produce a healthy baby requires that both the husband's and the wife's bodies cooperate in many ways.

There are several forces that act to coordinate the bodies of a couple. One is *pheromones*—scents released by our bodies that cause changes in the bodies of those around us. Not many people are aware of the fact that we have a special organ in our nose, called the *vomeronasal organ,* whose only purpose seems to be to detect these pheromones. Moreover, the nerves leading out of the vomeronasal organ are wired directly to the sexual centers of the brain. Thus, these pheromones have a definite sexual purpose. They are signals with sexual meanings.

Pheromones have been studied extensively in animals down to the level of insects. They have been found to be essential to normal sexual functioning. For most animals, if the ability to detect pheromones is blocked, they will be unable to mate or rear their young. However, human sexuality is much more complex than that of any animal. There are obviously many more factors at work in our decisions about whom to marry and when to have children. Nevertheless, pheromones have been found to play a subtle but important role in our sexual behavior.

For example, it has been discovered that when a woman is regularly exposed to a man's sweat, a pheromone in his sweat causes her menstrual cycle to become more regular. This regularity is believed to make her more likely to conceive. At the same time, a husband's testosterone levels become synchronized with his wife's monthly cycle. This means that his sex drive will peak right at the time when she is most fertile—again, making conception more likely. This synchronization is believed to be controlled by pheromones released by the wife's body.[1]

Clearly, the husband's and wife's bodies are acting as one body, "one flesh," by communicating and synchronizing with each other through pheromones. However, when a man and woman start having sex, a new level of communication between their bodies begins: their immune systems begin conversing.

When a husband's seminal fluid is first introduced into his wife's reproductive tract, it initiates a series of important changes in her immune system. Seminal fluid contains compounds that temporarily suppress her immune system, which soon learns to recognize and accept his sperm instead of mistaking them for infectious bacteria. This is important because sperm can live in the female reproductive system for up to five days. This means that if a couple is having intercourse once or twice a week on average, the wife will be carrying living cells from her husband in her body almost continuously for the rest of their married life. If this adaptive process fails, the wife becomes allergic to her husband's sperm. This can cause her great discomfort, and she will be unable to conceive by him.

This adaptive process is also essential for a safe pregnancy and for bearing healthy children. When a woman becomes pregnant, the child within her contains a mixture of genetic material from both her and the father. If her immune system has not yet learned to recognize and accept the father's genetic characteristics, then there is a very real danger that it will react to the embryo as to a foreign invader, producing a dangerous condition called *eclampsia*. This causes her blood pressure to rise to dangerous levels, which can result in kidney damage, brain hemorrhaging, and death. Her immune system may even attack her unborn child.

It has been shown that regular exposure to her husband's sperm for at least a year in advance of her first pregnancy protects a woman from eclampsia. However, in the case of a woman who becomes pregnant through a brief affair with a man other than her husband, she is at greater risk for eclampsia because her body has adapted to her husband's genes, but not those of the other man.[2] The same is true for a woman who has a series of sex partners and becomes pregnant by one of them.

These are examples of how men's and women's bodies, when joined by sexual union, behave as "one flesh." At a level far below conscious thought or control, the pheromone systems and the immune systems are sending chemical signals back and forth to regulate and coordinate their bodies as they prepare to conceive a child. This is a relatively new area of research, so there is likely much more yet to be discovered.

Since "the life of the flesh is in the blood" (Leviticus 17:11 KJV), perhaps the most serious and potentially life-altering union that occurs during sexual intercourse is the mingling of bloodstreams. The new plague of AIDS (*Acquired Immune Deficiency Syndrome*) over the past two decades has focused public attention on sexually transmitted diseases (STDs). Yet the media have consistently failed to tell people the full truth about the risks they are taking when they have a sexual relationship with someone.*

During their search for the cause of AIDS, researchers found *hundreds of unidentified viruses* in people's bloodstreams and in the blood banks. They have not yet identified all the diseases these viruses cause, but some researchers suspect that many are *slow viruses*—that is, they produce few noticeable symptoms until many years after infection. Slow viruses are suspected of being responsible for many types of cancer and some degenerative conditions—such as Multiple Sclerosis, Parkinson's, Alzheimer's, Chronic Fatigue Syndrome, and arthritis—that may not flare up until many years after infection. Because of this, many surgeons now recommend that anyone considering surgery "bank" his or her own blood and that of immediate family members in advance. The public blood supply presents too many unknown risks.

It is likely that some of these slow viruses are handed down in families from one generation to the next, causing the same diseases in many generations. One example is the HTLV family of viruses found worldwide, but concentrated in certain countries, such as Japan and Africa. These viruses have been shown to cause lymphoma (cancer of the lymph system) and leukemia that arise only during the latter decades of life. Some families studied have carried these viruses for many generations, since they pass from mother to child. Those who marry into these infected families can also become infected.[3]

A more familiar example of a slow virus is *mononucleosis,* or "Mono," as it is commonly known. "Mono" (or "the kissing disease") is

---

* See Appendix B for a summary of the latest findings on the dangers of STDs.

considered by many North Americans to be a normal and unavoidable adolescent rite of passage. However, not only can this disease have life-threatening complications when a person is first infected, but the virus that causes it (*Epstein-Barr*) is now known to remain in the white blood cells for life and can cause lymphoma as a person grows older.[4]

Many people do not realize that white blood cells and infectious agents from our bloodstream permeate all bodily fluids, such as saliva, tears, semen, and vaginal fluids. When you exchange bodily fluids with another person (even when kissing on the lips) you are also exchanging blood cells, viruses, bacteria, and perhaps unknown infectious agents yet to be uncovered. Even condoms do not provide full protection against some of these viral diseases, such as genital herpes, hepatitis, or the Human Papilloma Virus, which is now believed to be the cause of 95% *of all cases of cervical cancer.* Many viral STDs can be transmitted *simply by skin-to-skin contact*, particularly through the membranes of the mouth and genital region. They can also be passed on by an infected person *who has no visible symptoms.*

> MANY VIRAL STDs CAN BE TRANSMITTED SIMPLY BY SKIN-TO-SKIN CONTACT.

We receive our bloodstreams from our parents. If our ancestors obeyed God's commandments for sexual purity, then they have passed on to us a pure bloodstream. But if any of them transgressed His commandments of sexual purity, then it is possible that they contaminated their own blood and that of all their descendants with viral diseases that can cause much suffering and an early death. By having sexual relations with only one infected person, you can permanently infect your own body with a virus that will bring the curse of a disease on all your descendants.

Most people do not realize this fact. When you have sex with someone, with regard to STDs, you are having sex with every sex partner they have ever had, and every sex partner any of their sex partners have ever had, and so forth. Researchers have calculated some averages on this. For example, if you have had just six sexual partners in your lifetime, and each of them had just six partners, then you have been exposed to the STDs of not just six partners, but of *63 people*. For nine sexual partners, you would have been exposed to the STDs of *511 people*,[5] and so on. The numbers grow much faster than simple multiplication.

The people living in New Testament times did not understand that germs cause disease, nor did they know just how many different sexually transmitted diseases existed. Yet God understood these things. He gave us all a very specific warning about the damage we would inflict *on our bodies* if we dare to commit fornication:

> Flee fornication. Every sin that a man doeth is without [outside] the body; but he that committeth fornication sinneth against his own body. (1 Corinthians 6:18 KJV)

Do you see now how serious the act of sexual union is? It causes your bloodstream to be mingled with that of your sex partner. You are taking on any blood-borne diseases that the other may have. If you contract a disease through an act of fornication, then your body will suffer for it with pain, sores, infertility, internal damage as various organs are eaten away, and perhaps even a considerably shortened life span. You have sinned against your own body.

The days of "free love," when everyone thought a shot of penicillin would cure any STD, are long gone. But, in truth, those days never existed and never will. Most sexually transmitted viruses are incurable. In addition, viruses and bacteria have demonstrated that they can and will continue to develop resistance to every new drug that comes along. Scientists have not even begun to comprehend the long-term effects of the hundreds of viruses and new infectious agents (such as *prions**) that are found in the human bloodstream and are being passed around so casually.

We now know that the phrase "keep yourself pure for marriage" has an all-too-literal biological meaning. Yet, if you truly want to keep yourself pure and uninfected, it is not enough just to remain a virgin. You

---

* See Appendix B.

must also refrain from kissing anyone on the lips, other than your spouse (or spouse-to-be).

Americans are not accustomed to thinking this way, but this is the truth. When your romance has reached a point where you start kissing each other on the lips, then you have already made a serious commitment, whether you know it or not. By kissing someone on the lips, you are really saying: "Babe, whatever you've got—herpes, mono, slow viruses—I don't care. I want it, and I am willing to bear the consequences for the rest of my life just for the pleasure of kissing you!" That is one serious commitment!

Throughout human history, virginity has been highly prized. Even today, traditional cultures hold it in high esteem. Sadly, among "modern" young people, being a virgin on your wedding day is no longer considered a sign of virtue. It is a sign that you must be unattractive or have something wrong with you.[6] Even the threat of AIDS has had little effect on the rise of teen promiscuity.[7]

But now, medical science has proven traditional cultures to be quite wise in their reinforcement of virginity and marital fidelity. For the sake of your children yet to be born and all their descendants, not only should you marry a virgin, but it would be best to look for a spouse who comes from a godly lineage, someone whose ancestors valued virginity and obeyed God's commandments for sexual purity. Otherwise, you increase your risk of marrying into a disease-ridden family and passing on those diseases to all your descendants.

Notes.

1. Harold Persky, *Psychoendocrinology of Human Sexual Behavior* (New York: Praeger, 1987), 108–111.

2. G. A. Dekker, P. Y. Robillard, and T. C. Hulsey, "Immune Maladaptation in the Etiology of Preeclampsia: A Review of Corroborative Epidemiologic Studies," *Obstetrics and Gynecology Surveys* 53 (6):337–82 (1998).

3. Kazunari Yamaguchi, "Human T-lymphotropic Virus Type I in Japan," *The Lancet* 343 (8891): 213–4 (1994).

4. Issebacher Braunwald et al., eds., *Harrison's Principles of Internal Medicine*, 11th ed. (New York: McGraw-Hill, 1987), 699–703, 1555.

5. "Most People Underestimate AIDS Risk from 'Phantom' Sex Partners," *AIDS Weekly*, 18 July 1994.

6. The 1992 National Health and Social Life Survey showed that only 22% of American women and 16% of American men, ages 18–29, thought premarital sex was wrong. E. O. Laumann et al., *The Social Organization of Sexuality: Sexual Practices in the United States* (Chicago: University of Chicago Press, 1994), 507.

7. Robert T. Michael, John H. Gagnon, Edward O. Laumann, and Gina Kolata. *Sex in America: A Definitive Survey* (Boston: Little, Brown, 1995), 95.

IV

How the Law of Sexual Union Affects Our Minds

Before examining how the Law of Sexual Union affects our minds, there is a major issue that we must first address: Where does the body end and the mind begin? As Christians, we realize that we have a body, soul (thoughts and emotions), and spirit designed by God to operate in beautiful unity. However, humankind is no longer in the state of perfection enjoyed by Adam and Eve in the Garden of Eden. Thus, our inward unity is no longer in its original, perfect balance.

Indeed, the writers of the New Testament spend a great deal of time showing us how unbalanced the human spirit, soul, and body have become in their fallen state. Apart from God, the spirit is inert or "dead." The body and soul constantly fight each other for control. When we accept Jesus Christ as our Lord, and God's Spirit first enters our being, we experience spiritual "rebirth."* However, this is just the beginning of the road

---

* Spiritual rebirth, or being "born again," is explained more fully in Appendix A.

to full spiritual maturity. There are still many battles to be fought and lessons to be learned just within our own selves.

A large part of what we must learn on the way to spiritual maturity is how to regain the proper balance between the spirit, soul, and body, so that the spirit rules the soul and the soul rules the body. To achieve this, we must learn to distinguish the true origins of our many feelings, desires, and impulses. Do they come from the body, the soul, or the spirit? The Apostle Paul was particularly expressive about his own struggle with this difficult situation:

> For in my inner being I delight in God's law; but I see another law at work in the members of my body, waging war against the law of my mind and making me a prisoner of the law of sin at work within my members. (Romans 7:22-23 NIV)

Nowhere is this drama played out more explicitly than in the area of sexuality. The sex drive is a very powerful force that originates in the body, yet its influence extends into the mind. We are all aware of the power of sexual fantasies and the influence they can have on our behavior. Yet most people are confused about the whole issue of sexual desire, especially when trying to decide what is right or wrong, innocent or evil.

The Origins of Sexual Desire

To begin with, we must understand that the initial force of sexual desire comes from the body. The level of the hormone *testosterone* in the bloodstream (in both men and women) determines how much sexual interest and desire we feel at any given moment. A doctor can administer a drug that cancels the effect of this hormone, causing a person to quickly lose all interest in sex, along with most of his ability to participate in it. At this level, sexual desire is innocent of any sinful or shameful associations. It is essentially no different from hunger pangs.

However, if you have ever gone without food for more than a day or two, you know what eventually happens. You begin to have food fantasies. I am not talking about feeling a pain in your stomach and wishing you could eat a cracker to make it go away. I am talking about all-out, technicolor, fantasy banquets consisting of your favorite foods—freshly grilled steaks, mounds of mashed potatoes smothered in gravy, and a triple fudge ice cream sundae with a big piece of pecan pie on the side. At night you may dream endlessly of feasting, only to awaken with a gnawing hunger.

This situation shows how the body and mind can interact in quite subtle ways. Your stomach has sent a signal to the pain centers of your brain, which you feel as hunger pangs. If you choose to ignore them, the level of fuel continues to drop, and your cells release chemical cries for food. These hormonal signals begin activating other parts of your brain causing you to have "lustful" fantasies about food.

These food fantasies are certainly understandable in a hungry person, but let us pause to consider them further to see if there are some situations where they might actually be considered immoral.

Have you ever wondered why you fantasize about some foods, but not others? Obviously, you have a history of experience with eating different kinds of food. Your taste preferences have been developing since childhood. Perhaps you have a favorite food—raw oysters, for example—that someone else could not force himself to eat, even if he were starving. Perhaps he had an unpleasant experience with raw oysters as a child.

You might also have a real passion for some foods the doctor has said are bad for you. He has warned that if you continue to eat them, your cholesterol and blood pressure will go up, which will shorten your life span. In this situation, you know that indulging your fantasies of forbidden foods weakens your willpower. If you give in and eat them consistently, you will be taking years off your life for mere moments of pleasure.

If you are fasting for a serious purpose—such as to spend the time in prayer or in preparation for medical treatment—you would not want to break your fast before your goal had been accomplished. Indulging in food fantasies, and dwelling on them, might overcome your better judgment and willpower at some point so that you give in and eat, resulting in eventual shame or embarrassment.

Now, what if during your fast you accidentally come across a Swiss Colony* catalog? What effect do you think thumbing through its pages will have on you? As you turn each page, a new array of beautiful, delectable treats is laid out before you: sumptuous sausages, rich cheeses, a 15-layer chocolate torte with raspberry creme filling. You know that your doctor would not recommend that you eat any of these things, but their 800 number is listed on every page. You suddenly realize that a box of treats could arrive on your doorstep by tomorrow afternoon. Or, now that your passion for chocolate has been stirred up, you might just go ahead and eat the chocolate cake you have in the refrigerator. As you drift off to sleep that night, you may even find images from the catalog being woven into your dreams.

What if you found yourself starving and stranded in the wilderness with a group of other survivors? If your willpower is weakened from dwelling on food fantasies, might you be tempted to steal from the food rations that are keeping everyone alive?

The lessons these scenarios have to teach us about sexual lust should be obvious. Like hunger, sexual desire begins in the body, but it is given shape and focus in the mind. Sexual fantasies come uninvited because of surges in hormone levels. Thus, there should be no guilt attached to the initial experience of sexual thoughts and feelings.

(This fact should be reassuring to most men. Research has shown that men in their twenties and thirties experience surges of testosterone about every fifteen minutes. Other studies have shown that this is just about how often men think about sex. So, frequent sexual thoughts are just something with which men must learn to live.)

When Does Sexual Desire Become Sinful?

Similar to food preferences, our minds determine the object of our sexual desire based on experiences we have had, both good and bad,

---

* Swiss Colony is a major mail-order distributor of gift foods and desserts.

stretching from the recent past all the way back to childhood. At a very deep level, below our conscious control, the brain learns to associate certain images with sexual feelings. So when hormone levels rise in the blood, the brain pops up the images it has learned to associate with sexual feelings on your mental "view screen." This also works in reverse. If you look at images your brain has associated with sexual feelings, those feelings will begin to stir in your body.

People often have sexual dreams during the night that are beyond their control. The content of these dreams may be troubling. They may reveal some issues with which your mind is wrestling. Yet, the major stimulus for these dreams is believed to be surges in hormone levels. So we should not feel guilty about things we cannot control.

Some people are troubled by abnormal sexual desires and images. Like an aversion to certain foods, these abnormal desires can arise from disturbing childhood or adolescent experiences (including traumatic experiences that were not at all sexual when they occurred). It is essential that we understand that there is still no guilt or immorality associated with the initial experience of even abnormal sexual desires. The brain at some point has just made a mistake in associating these abnormal images with sexual feelings. The good news is that these abnormal desires can be corrected through therapy, although sometimes it involves considerable time and effort.

THE PLACE WHERE SIN FIRST ENTERS IS WHEN WE MAKE A CHOICE.

The place where sin first enters is when we make a choice to continue fantasizing when we know it is wrong, when we choose to focus our desire on someone we cannot rightly have. This is why Jesus said, "Whoever looks at a woman to lust for her has already committed adultery with her in his heart" (Matthew 5:28 NKJV). Although our body signals its desire for sex by having our brain flash sexual images through our imagination, we can still learn not to pursue those thoughts. We can idle the engine instead of racing it.

It is quite proper for a couple in love to adore and fantasize about each other. The Song of Songs in the Old Testament is an example of this very thing. But when you fantasize about someone you see on the street, you are desiring someone who is likely destined to be another's spouse, not yours. It is comparable to the desire to steal someone else's food to satisfy your own hunger, or to steal his or her money to spend on your own pleasure.

Alas, as many people have discovered, indulging in such forbidden sexual fantasies eventually weakens your willpower so that you are more likely to give in to temptation, perhaps becoming sexually involved with someone to whom you are not married. As we have seen, such behavior has many destructive consequences.

Viewing pornography (or even R-rated movies and advertising images) can be harmful for these same reasons, but there are even more negative consequences. First of all, pornographic images are artificial. Like the treats from Swiss Colony, which never taste quite as good as they look, these images raise your expectations so high that you are sure to be disappointed by real-life sexual experiences. Even if you were to marry a model from a photo spread, you would soon find she had extra wrinkles, moles, bulges, implants, and spots that were airbrushed out of the final images.

As you look at pornographic images, your brain is storing all those images in a file marked "SEX." The next time your body signals it wants sex, your brain has a whole pile of new images to project on your mental "view screen," whether you want to see them again or not.

For some people, a pornography "hobby" can quickly become an addiction (which we will examine in more detail a little later). Even worse, researchers have discovered that fantasizing about pornographic images containing abnormal sexual practices (such as depictions of rape or sex combined with violence) can induce those abnormal sexual desires in previously normal people.

The nature of sexual lust, much like hunger, is to consume. It is a desire to consume another's body to satisfy your own need. But people are not just objects to be consumed. Anyone who seeks sexual union only to satisfy lust—as a hungry man devours food—is living at an animal level. God has so much more in store for us.

Sexual Attraction and Bonding

Sexual lust may begin with the body, but the fulfillment of sexual desire involves our minds and emotions at a very deep level. Sexual union between a man and woman results in a powerful emotional bond between them, the richness of which has been mined for centuries by countless poets and singers. This strong emotional bond between a husband and wife helps them to withstand the stresses and pains of life, particularly the struggles of raising children.

As most single adults will admit, the drive to seek out a mate is one of the strongest motivators of human behavior. When a man and woman choose each other and become husband and wife, the strength and quality of their relationship should become the emotional foundation for the remainder of their lives.

The quality of this marital bond also has a great impact on the emotional health and development of the children. Children raised by parents who are deeply committed to each other have a good preparation for becoming secure, loving adults. But children who have been subjected to their parents' bitter conflicts become greatly handicapped in their emotional development and in their ability as adults to develop healthy, stable relationships with the opposite sex.

The emotional bond between a husband and wife begins with what most of us call "falling in love." Though almost everyone experiences this state at some point in their lives, it is still not completely understood from a scientific standpoint. However, researchers are beginning to unravel some of its mysteries and are finding that it is not only a state of mind, but also a state of brain and body, in ways that can be measured in a laboratory. The study of the connection between the mind and the body, and how they interact, is one of the hottest areas in medical research today.

What causes us to be attracted to a particular person? The leading theory holds that, through our experiences during childhood and early adolescence, each of us develops a list of attributes for the opposite sex that we consider ideal. This list is called a *lovemap*.[1] Such list-making is mostly subconscious, but it incorporates all of our experiences with the opposite sex (both good and bad), including our opposite-sex parent, our school friends, people we see on TV or in movies, and so forth. Our lovemap may specify physical features, personality traits, or even status symbols, such as wealth or popularity.

Certain features—such as facial symmetry, healthy skin, and V-shaped bodies (for men)—are considered attractive across all societies. These features undoubtedly indicate good health and perhaps good genes. Men seem to be initially most attracted to a woman's physical appearance. Women seem to be initially most attracted to men who are slightly taller than they, and who are financially secure.

When we finally meet a person who closely matches our secret list, "Mr. (or Miss) Right," we feel strongly attracted to him or her, as if by some magnetic force. "Love at first sight" is what some call this experience, especially if each matches the other's lovemap to a similar degree. It often seems to include a great deal of wishful thinking. There is a strong tendency to "read into" the other person those qualities that you are looking for, but that may not actually be there. This explains why we can quickly "fall out of love" when we really get to know the other person and find out they were not all they seemed to be, or we wished them to be.

Some very recent studies indicate that pheromones also play a role in romantic attraction. Women have been shown to be able to smell compounds secreted by men's bodies that men cannot detect. In one study, swabs were used to collect sweat from male volunteers. Female volunteers were then asked to sniff the swabs and rank them in order of attractiveness or "sexiness." It was discovered that the samples each woman preferred were from the men whose immune system proteins were most different from her own. Having parents with very different immune system proteins is believed to give children the advantage of a much stronger immune system. So it is true after all that the right "chemistry" can be an important part of romantic attraction.[2]

If testosterone is "the lust hormone," then oxytocin is "the bonding hormone." Oxytocin is found in all animal species and is released whenever an emotional bond needs to be formed, such as between a mother and her young, or in a mating pair who need to work together to raise their offspring. In humans, oxytocin has been found to produce feelings of emotional intimacy and a desire for affectionate touch.

Both testosterone and oxytocin occur in men and women, but as you might expect, men have a much greater flow of testosterone and women have a much greater flow of oxytocin. In both men and women, oxytocin is released whenever someone, such as a friend or relative, touches you affectionately. Women also experience a great peak of oxytocin as they are giving birth. They experience additional flows of oxytocin each time they nurse their child, and so does the nursing infant. This seems to strengthen the mother/child bond. Both men and women experience a release of oxytocin after having an orgasm, but its effect is greater in women. This may very well explain the desire to cuddle and be close after sexual intercourse, which typically is stronger in women than men. Women also experience highs and lows of oxytocin during the menstrual cycle, which may explain their seemingly mysterious shifts from wanting frequent cuddling to not wanting to be touched.[3]

As a couple begin to spend more time with each other, even in a casual dating relationship, they inevitably begin to touch more frequently—holding hands, kissing, and hugging. As they do these things, they are causing their bodies to release more and more oxytocin, which produces an emotional high and strengthens their emotional bond. This seems to cause a couple to become addicted to each other's touch. If they cease to touch for a period of time—because of travel or just being too busy—both will experience withdrawal symptoms, including depression, lovesickness, and a longing to touch each other again. Yet the longer they go without touching, the weaker their bond grows.

Addicted to Love?

So what really happens when two "fools fall in love"? For centuries, that peculiar state of mind has been the exclusive domain of study for poets and other artists. But now that the scientists have gotten their hands on it, we will never see it quite the same way again.

Anyone who has ever been in love knows what a peculiar state of mind it creates. When you are with your beloved, you feel as if you are floating on air. Problems diminish and the whole world seems glorious. You lose interest in other pleasures, your appetite diminishes, and you feel less need for sleep.

Yet when you are separated from your beloved, minutes become like hours, hours like days. All the things you once enjoyed seem dull and tasteless. You find yourself thinking of your beloved so frequently that it takes great mental effort to concentrate on daily tasks.

Even worse, if anything threatens you with the permanent loss of your beloved, you are cast into the depths of despair. You will sacrifice anything and everything to be with him or her. Many are the well-known stories of lovers who risk the loss of all their possessions, the rejection of their families, and even their own lives, to be together.

More than one thoughtful person over the years has observed that this delirious, ecstatic, obsessive, and often tormented relationship between lovers is quite similar to the relationship between a drug addict and his drug of choice. Similar behaviors have been noted in addicts, particularly those addicted to some type of stimulant, such as "crack" cocaine or amphetamines.

These drugs cause users to get "high," which is a state in which they feel extreme pleasure and a sense of well-being. They will do anything to stay that way. In this condition, they lose interest in food, sleep, and other pleasurable and necessary activities. When they come down off their high, they cannot think of anything else but how to get more of the drug and get high again. Most addicts eventually give up their careers, their friendships, their families, and everything they own in pursuit of the drug. They repeatedly choose to put their health, safety, and freedom at risk for just one more high. If they ever try (or are forced) to stop using the drug, they must endure a period of severe withdrawal, suffering through great mental and physical anguish and depression.

As expected, researchers have now confirmed these suspicious parallels between addicts and lovers. By dragging lovesick couples into the laboratory, they have identified a number of changes in brain activity and hormone levels associated with the state of being "in love." (Researchers call this state *limerence*.) Besides the elevated levels of oxytocin already mentioned, a hormone called phenylethylamine (PEA) has been found at high levels in lovers' brains. It is believed that PEA acts as a natural amphetamine, a natural version of "speed" or "meth." This is thought to be the most important agent in producing that "lover's high": a giddy, excited feeling and a loss of interest in food or sleep. If the level of PEA suddenly drops—say when you and your lover are apart—this would also cause feelings of mental anguish and depression.[4] Other chemicals called *endorphins* and *enkephalins* are also found in lovers' brains and act as natural opiates, relieving pain and giving a sense of well-being.

Seeing that God designed us with the natural capacity to become "addicted" to a mate should give us an entirely new perspective on some issues. No wonder falling in love involves such powerful and overwhelming feelings! Your brain is getting itself "high" when your lover is around. If you break up with someone to whom you are "addicted," you will experience painful withdrawal symptoms. However, we should not think falling in love is bad because of this association with addiction. God designed us with the capacity to fall in love. So it is a *good* thing, if we use wisdom. Addiction of any other kind is a bad thing for this very reason: *it is a false form of love.*

This may very well explain how people can become psychologically addicted to illegal drugs and why the pull of these drugs is so powerful. Researchers have long wondered why drug abusers—even after years of being "clean" and no longer physically addicted—still feel a mental craving for their drug of abuse. The answer may very well be that the drug produced chemical changes in their brains similar to those experienced in a state of limerence. Essentially, the drug hijacked the chemistry of love, and they "fell in love" with the drug. The memory of their drug use then acquires the same powerful, wistful pull that anyone would feel when he or she remembers someone once deeply loved and then lost.

This process could also explain other types of psychological addiction, such as addiction to pornography. As a man responds to a fantasy figure in a photograph and acts out sexually, his PEA level rises. He soon finds that he is in love with a piece of paper. But, of course, a piece of paper cannot trigger all the other components of sexual attraction and satisfaction that a real woman can. So the high quickly wears off and he must seek a new image to achieve that same high again. This begins an endless cycle that can become quite costly.

These little-known components of attraction also help explain how couples, who had always been good friends but had never felt any romantic attraction to each other, can suddenly fall in love. Their lovemaps may have been incompatible at first. Neither matched the other's image of an ideal mate, so they did not initially feel any romantic attraction. Yet over time, as they expressed friendly affection toward each other, the oxytocin released strengthened their emotional bond. As they spent time together in friendly pursuits, they each had the opportunity to be influenced by pheromones in the other's sweat. Even sharing secrets with each other and giving and receiving emotional support in difficult times builds an emotional bond. If both have healthy sex drives and are not physically repulsive to one another, these other attractive forces can eventually overpower their incompatible lovemaps, PEA kicks in, and they fall in love.

Western culture has taught us that falling in love should be a prerequisite for marriage. However, in many cultures of the Near and Middle East, a couple are not expected to fall in love until *after* they marry. This belief is still held and practiced in these cultures today—even among college-educated professionals—because *it works*, as it has for centuries.

In the Eastern tradition, a potential couple are first introduced through a network of relatives and friends. Professional matchmakers are often used, with the goal of finding a spouse who will be the most compatible. The families of the couple are often friends, or have friends in common, who can vouch for the good upbringing and high morals of each.

After corresponding for a while and meeting a few times in the presence of chaperones, they can determine whether they are truly compatible, whether they meet each other's standards, and whether they share common goals and values. This is considered a sufficient foundation for a good marriage, so the wedding is quickly arranged. After the couple has married and moved in together, the forces of attraction begin their inexorable work and—unless one discovers something unexpected and totally revolting about the other—they fall in love, as planned and on schedule.

This approach to courtship and marriage seems quite strange to Western minds, but it has worked quite well for millions of people over the centuries. (Of course, we are not talking about "forced marriages" where one party has no choice in the matter.) Curiously, some of these Easterners have been educated in the West and have tried our "dating game" method of mate selection. Yet, ultimately, many of them reject it for a more "traditional" matchmaking courtship and marriage.

The explanation I have often heard is that Western-style dating is just not a good way to find a compatible spouse. You typically pick up someone you do not know in a bar. Each person is putting on an act, trying to impress the other. All the focus is on physical attraction and sensuality. You do not really get to know the other person until after you are married, and by then it is too late. So, many of these Easterners conclude it is preferable to have a professional pick your ideal mate.

Perhaps the growing popularity of computer dating services and matchmakers reflects a dawning awareness of this truth. Studies of lasting marriages have concluded that the partners tend to show great similarities in age, class, intelligence, education, beliefs, personality, and even physical attributes. These are also the characteristics of lasting friendships.

Modern Western culture teaches us that when we "fall out of love," it is time to move on to someone else. This is another example of our shallow preoccupation with mere physical sensation and sensuality. Researchers who have studied couples over a period of many years have found that the levels of PEA in their brains do gradually diminish over time. They eventually lose that giddy, PEA-induced high when they are with each other. However, by that time, their relationship should have grown deeper in other ways. Yet for couples who are having serious problems at this time (which averages around the four-year mark), the loss of that "special feeling" may be just the thing that convinces them they should end their marriage. Curiously, many couples report in their later years that they learn to rekindle that romantic feeling they had when they first met. This seems to happen when they renew the very activities they enjoyed together when their relationship first began: going on dates, making frequent expressions of love, and spending more time cuddling.

This information on how the biological and emotional components of romantic attraction work should give many singles a new sense of caution when dating and choosing a lifetime partner. With American dating practices, it is far too easy to set in motion the physical, sexual mechanisms that lead inexorably to deepening emotional and physical bonds. Before you realize it, you can give your heart away to someone based only on an initial physical attraction and a period of intimate contact—with little consideration of whether your personalities, values, and goals are truly suited for building a life together.

The First Time

A much stronger degree of bonding occurs when a couple first has sex (either intercourse or some other type of mutual genital contact leading to orgasm). For most people, the experience of sexual union with a loving spouse produces the greatest physical pleasure that they will ever find in this life. It also provides the foundation for the most intense emotional relationship they will ever know. Researchers call this intense bonding effect the *pleasure bond*.

It seems that God designed us, and all animal life, to respond to and learn from pain and pleasure. All animals seek to avoid experiences that have been painful and seek to repeat experiences that have been pleasurable. In God's design, pleasurable things are good and painful things are bad. We do not see this principle violated in nature, except when humans start trying to circumvent nature, such as misusing drugs.

When you discover that your mate is the source of the greatest pleasure you have ever known, you will naturally want to keep him or her around as long as possible, and keep doing whatever it was that felt so good! This is the reason that a good sexual relationship is so important to a good marriage. No matter what painful difficulties life may throw at you, you can depend on each other for mutual enjoyment and refreshment.

Not only does sexual pleasure bond you to your mate, but research has also shown that the pleasure you both experience actually prolongs and improves the quality of your lives. These are some of the benefits that have been found to result from sexual union:

- It improves your mental attitude, decreasing feelings of depression
- It can relieve chronic pain for hours
- It strengthens your immune system

But another powerful factor besides pleasure may be at work. Many counselors and psychologists who specialize in helping those with sexual problems have observed, from working with thousands of clients, that a person's first experience of sexual intercourse has a very powerful and lasting effect on his or her sexuality. It is believed that your first experience of sexual intercourse becomes indelibly stamped on your brain in a process called *imprinting*.[5]

In those animal species that mate for life, the first act of intercourse between a courting pair causes a surge of hormones in their brains that imprints the sight and smell of their mate so that they will remain faithful to each other. These hormones also cause the male to be aggressive in protecting his mate from the advances of other males—what we would call "jealous" behavior. Many researchers believe a similar hormonal process also occurs in humans to produce an imprinting effect.[6] (We humans certainly have the same sort of jealous behavior.)

This imprinting process could well explain why promiscuous people always remember their "first time" as something special, even if they have had so many sex partners they cannot remember them all. This also could explain why people who were molested as children are troubled by those memories for the rest of their lives, unless they receive help. Nevertheless, God's purpose for imprinting is evident. Your first sexual intercourse should be with your spouse so that each of you becomes indelibly imprinted on the other's brain, forming a lifelong mental and emotional bond.

In addition to these fairly obvious effects of sexual union, there is now evidence that even more subtle mental processes are at work to reshape a husband and wife into an efficient team. One study has found that, as the marriage relationship develops, spouses will often subconsciously agree which of them should do which task. For example, though a husband and wife may both have been good cooks before marriage, over time one tends to become much better at cooking. Both may have been equally good at managing their finances when single, but after marriage, one will gradually take over all the bookkeeping.

When the couples being studied were asked why each partner seemed to have set aside some abilities, they could not explain it. All they could remember was that they had agreed that each person should do the tasks at which he or she was best. Just how couples adapt to each other and cooperate subconsciously has not yet been fully explored. There are likely many more effects of this mental union yet to be uncovered.

The negative side of such a tremendous union of minds and hearts is what occurs when the union is broken through death or divorce. Mortality statistics now confirm what folk wisdom has long held. When a couple is deeply in love and one of them dies, the other is more likely to die soon after of "a broken heart." Research has shown that the death of a spouse affects the survivor by depressing the activity of the immune system, thus making him or her more susceptible to contracting an infectious disease or even cancer. This again illustrates how closely interconnected our minds and bodies are. Emotional pain can cause physical illness; people really can die of a broken heart.

Being divorced is as devastating as being widowed, and may even be worse. Though a couple may feel hatred toward each other, they are still joined in so many ways by the Law of Sexual Union. Not only do divorcing couples bear the pain of all the emotional wounds they have inflicted on each other, but they still must also endure a lengthy process of separation, which researchers have found is quite similar to bereavement. In contrast to the mentality of the 1970s, which produced the quick and easy "no-fault" divorce laws we have today, there is now a building consensus that divorce is terribly damaging—not only to both partners, but also to their children—and should be considered only as a last resort. This is why there has been a movement in several states to enact new marriage laws that require couples who wish to divorce to go through marriage counseling and a waiting period.[7]

Notes.

1. John Money, *Lovemaps: Clinical Concepts of Sexual/Erotic Health and Pathology, Paraphilia, and Gender Transposition in Childhood, Adolescence and Maturity* (New York: Irvington, 1986).

2. Richard E. Jones, *Human Reproductive Biology,* 2nd ed. (New York: Academic Press, 1992), 382–383.

3. A thorough explanation of the effects of hormones on our romantic feelings is given by researcher Theresa L. Crenshaw in *The Alchemy of Love and Lust: How Our Sex Hormones Influence Our Relationships* (New York: Putnam, 1996).

4. Ibid.

5. Prendergast, William E. *The Merry-Go-Round of Sexual Abuse: Identifying and Treating Survivors,* (New York: The Haworth Press, 1993), 58–74.

6. Theresa L. Crenshaw, *The Alchemy of Love and Lust: How Our Sex Hormones Influence Our Relationships* (New York: Putnam, 1996), 93–105.

7. Louisiana passed a law in 1997 allowing "covenant marriages." Couples choosing to enter into covenant marriages will not be granted a divorce until they have submitted to marriage counseling and a two-year waiting period.

How the Law of Sexual
Union Affects Our Spirits

In order to examine how the Law of Sexual Union affects our spirits, we must venture into less-charted waters. We must leave the biologists and psychologists behind because many of them think that, since they cannot get the human spirit to show up under a microscope, it must not exist. We must also leave behind the common wisdom of our materialistic society, which thinks having a "spiritual experience" means watching a glorious sunrise, enjoying the sounds of a majestic symphony, or being moved by eloquent poetry. These are indeed wonderful experiences, but they involve primarily our aesthetic senses—our thoughts and emotions—not our spirits.

We have seen how sexual union can create a link between bodies so that they begin to function as one. We have also seen how sexual union creates a lifelong bond that joins minds. It should then come as no surprise to find that sexual union also joins spirits. If you are a married Christian with some degree of spiritual maturity, you may already have sensed this special spiritual link between you and your spouse, though you may not have fully understood what you were sensing.

Some Spiritual Basics

To understand the spiritual aspects of sexual union, we must first establish some basic facts about the human spirit, the answers to such questions as: *What is the spirit? Where does it reside? How does it function?* I have found that most Christians in Western nations know a great deal of doctrine about spiritual matters, yet have very little practical understanding or experience of spiritual realities in their daily lives.

We can gain some understanding of the human spirit by studying human experiences. It has become popular among the news media to report on the "near-death" experiences of those who have died on an operating table, but who were eventually revived. These survivors typically report being sucked through a tunnel. They find themselves floating near the ceiling, no longer in pain, looking down on the scene below as the doctors work frantically to revive their dying bodies. Some of them have reported catching a glimpse of a wonderful realm filled with light and love. Others have reported encountering hideous beings that tried to drag them down to a horrible place.[1]

I believe it is reasonable to use these experiences to conclude several things about the human spirit:[2]

1. Your spirit exists in a spiritual world (or dimension) that is very close to the physical world around us, yet separate. Just as your body has senses that inform your mind of the *physical* world around you, so your spirit has senses that can inform your mind of the *spiritual* world around you. Thus, your mind can receive information from both worlds. You can see with your biological eyes, and

you can see with your spiritual eyes. You can hear with your biological ears, and you can hear with your spiritual ears.

2. Though your spirit exists in the spiritual world and your body exists in the physical world, your spirit and body are tightly and intimately joined together to produce the real you. Where your body goes, your spirit goes. What your body does, your spirit does. When you touch someone with your physical hand, you are also touching that person with your spiritual hand. But if your body becomes so damaged that it can no longer maintain its union with your spirit, then your spirit separates from your body in a process we know as "death."

3. Animals have physical bodies, but no spirits. Angels and demons are spirits, but have no physical bodies. Only humans have both a spirit *and* a body and thus live in two worlds at the same time. This is what makes us such amazing creatures! This is also what makes our lives so very complicated.

If these things are true, then why are so many people today seemingly unaware that they even have a spirit? It is because they exist in a condition the Bible refers to as "spiritual darkness," "spiritual blindness," or "spiritual death."

Perhaps in noticing how closely our spirits are related to our physical bodies, some have wondered, "Does my spirit need to eat to survive? If so, what does it eat?" We all realize that our bodies need a regular supply of food to provide energy, allow growth, and repair damaged cells. Without food, we will grow weak and eventually die. The situation is quite similar with our spirits.

God designed your spirit to receive the energy it needs to function *directly from Him*. We might compare it to a

ANIMALS HAVE PHYSICAL BODIES, BUT NO SPIRITS.

branch of a tree receiving its nourishment from the trunk (John 15:1-8). If the branch is broken off from the trunk, it withers away. Likewise, if your human spirit is separated from God and is unable to draw the spiritual strength it needs from Him, it grows weak, shrivels up, and becomes inactive. It is essentially "dead" in the sense that it does not function, though it does not decay like your body would.

The Bible teaches that each of us is born into this world with our spirits in this state of spiritual death. Our spirits are separated from God and inactive. But God has a plan to bring our spirits back to life. Jesus explained this to a religious leader of His day named Nicodemus:

> Jesus answered and said unto him, "Most assuredly, I say to you, unless one is born again, he cannot see the kingdom of God." Nicodemus said to Him, "How can a man be born when he is old? Can he enter a second time into his mother's womb and be born?" Jesus answered, "Most assuredly, I say to you, unless one is born of water and the Spirit, he cannot enter the kingdom of God. That which is born of the flesh is flesh, and that which is born of the Spirit is spirit. Do not marvel that I said to you, 'You must be born again.' The wind blows where it wishes, and you hear the sound of it, but cannot tell where it comes from and where it goes. So is everyone who is born of the Spirit." (John 3:3-8 NKJV)

Jesus here explains that being born in a physical body ("born of water") is not enough for you to perceive the kingdom of God, which exists in the spiritual world. At birth you are physically alive, but spiritually dead (inert). It is only when God's Holy Spirit causes your spirit to come alive ("born of the Spirit") that you can begin to experience and participate in the spiritual events that take place in God's kingdom. You begin to react to what your spiritual senses pick up, which is something others may not understand. You develop spiritual abilities you did not know even existed.

What happens through this spiritual birth is that our spirits become joined to God's Spirit. As the Apostle Paul said, "He who is joined to the Lord is one spirit with Him" (1 Corinthians 6:17 NKJV). God's Holy Spirit takes up permanent residence in our bodies and we become His home (1 Corinthians 3:16).

Sadly, there are some Christians who experienced this spiritual birth many years ago, yet they still remain unaware of their own spirits and how they function in daily life. They have not yet learned how to distinguish the voice of the Holy Spirit from their own thoughts, or even from the voices of evil spirits trying to lead them astray. The Apostle Paul explains the source of this problem in his letter to the Romans, in chapters 6 through 8, where he describes the difference between "walking in the flesh"—living life with all our attention focused on ourselves and the *physical* world around us—and "walking in the Spirit"—living a life of daily fellowship and communication with the Holy Spirit, where our attention is focused on the *spiritual* world around us. (In 1 Corinthians 2:13–3:4, Paul further explains the differences between "natural" or "carnal" (fleshly) Christians and "spiritual" Christians.)

This lack of sensitivity to spiritual things can be a sign of spiritual immaturity in new Christians. Much as infants need time to grow, they are still learning how to listen and respond to the voice of the Holy Spirit. But to see someone who has been a Christian for many years, yet is still insensitive to spiritual things, is a great tragedy. Some of these people are afraid of having any kind of spiritual experience at all. It seems too "spooky." Others seem to have absorbed the materialistic, antispiritual tone of modern society, so they are skeptical and critical of those who claim to have had spiritual experiences.

This tragedy happens only when Christians continually and deliberately choose to walk in the flesh instead of walking in the Spirit. In so doing, their connection with the Holy Spirit weakens and their spirits cannot receive the nourishment from Him that they need in order to thrive. As Paul explains in Romans 6–8, those who walk in the flesh tend to fall into the same sins over and over again. They know what they are doing is wrong. They may even hate what they are doing, but they do not stop. Unfortunately, this describes many Christians today who are struggling with sexual sin.

Another basic principle we need to examine in order to understand how sexual union affects our spirits is that of *spiritual touch*. Throughout the New Testament, there are many examples of how God chose to minister to someone through human touch. In his earthly ministry, Jesus often laid His hands on sick people so that they could be healed by God's power. The early church leaders followed His example in the "laying on of hands" when they prayed for the sick, or imparted a spiritual gift or spiritual authority.

I am sure many Christians have wondered why the Bible so often emphasizes physical touch when ministering God's power to others. When we understand how the human spirit is so closely integrated with the human body, we can better understand how spirits can also touch when we hug someone or lay a hand on someone's shoulder.

Realizing that God's Holy Spirit is living in us—joined with our spirits—you can see how, if you are praying for those in need of God, it would be so easy and natural for the power of His Spirit to flow out through your spiritual "hand," through your physical hand, and into their bodies and spirits as you are touching them. Many people are somewhat afraid of supernatural experiences or of encountering God's awesome power. But what could be more gentle than experiencing God's love and power through the warmth of a friend's touch as he is praying for you or giving you a hug?

Maybe you have experienced touching someone's spirit with your spirit, but just did not realize what was happening to you. Christian friends have reported to me that sometimes, when they lay their hand on a friend's shoulder, as their friend responds to them in love, they feel a sudden rush of warm energy back through their hand and arm as their spirits touch.

Some people seem to have picked up the peculiar idea that their prayers gradually wend their way to heaven, bounce off a few clouds, and are played back by God on His answering machine. He then dictates a reply to an angel, who mails it back through the celestial post office, and you receive the answer in a few months (or years). Some, hoping for faster service, will address their prayers to particular saints or angels they believe are in charge of the department within the heavenly bureaucracy that specializes in their type of request.

Can you see how such childish fantasies are rendered unnecessary when we realize that God's Holy Spirit is living in each of us, always ready to help us, speak to us, and move through us to touch others and meet their needs?

A Husband and Wife Have a Spiritual Union

We have examined the forces at work in the bodies and minds of husbands and wives that create a union between them. We have also seen how spirits can join through intimate touch and prayer. However, there is a special spiritual union beyond this that is established between a man and woman through their sexual union. Paul describes it in this way:

> But I want you to know that the head of every man is Christ, **the head of woman is man,** and the head of Christ is God. (1 Corinthians 11:3 NKJV)

> For the **husband is head of the wife,** as also Christ is head of the church. (Ephesians 5:23 NKJV)

Paul is describing here a deep spiritual mystery, which undoubtedly has many layers of meaning yet to be uncovered. Certainly, there has been much debate about the implications of these verses. But the point that is most easily established here is that a special spiritual relationship exists between a husband and wife. They are spiritually joined into one, as inseparably as your head is joined to your body! Yet each has a different role in the family. There is also a clear implication that spiritual direction and spiritual authority for the family rolls down from God, through Christ, and through the husband.

Many Christian couples have experienced the practical effects of this spiritual relationship. Spouses often report that they have a special awareness of each other's needs and problems when separated, even across great distances. They often report a special awareness of temptations or spiritual attacks directed at their mate and the ability to minister to each other through prayer like no one else can. Most Christian couples have learned from experience that being in a state of disharmony with their spouse also seems to disrupt their relationship with God.

The Secret to True Sexual Fulfillment: Spiritual Sex

THE SECRET TO TRUE SEXUAL FULFILLMENT: SPIRITUAL SEX Over the centuries, Christians have been taught by some religious leaders that sex between a husband and wife is unholy, sinful, carnal, necessary only for reproduction, a hindrance to spiritual development, a distraction from serving God, and so forth. What a terrible bunch of lies! As we have seen, sexual union was designed by God to orchestrate an incredibly complex and powerful array of forces that join a husband and wife into one. But what is still missing for most couples is an understanding of the spiritual dimension of sexual union.

Here is what typically happens when a Christian couple has been taught some wrong attitudes about sex and are not aware of its spiritual dimension:

> Since childhood, they have both been taught
> that sex is "unspiritual" and "dirty." Beginning with
> their honeymoon, the wife has been somewhat reluc-
> tant to have sex with her husband. She sees it as an
> unpleasant but necessary duty that she must perform
> for him (much like cleaning the oven). He really

enjoys their times of sexual union, but for some reason never feels completely satisfied. Before marriage, he had an active fantasy life and struggled with an addiction to pornography. After a few years of married life, he finds himself getting bored with the same old bedroom routine, so he tries to get his wife to try some new activities. She reluctantly participates but lets him know that she is making a great personal sacrifice. Some wives, at this point, might even begin rationing their sexual favors based on their husband's good behavior.

There are many good Christian marriage manuals that address the problems of wrong attitudes about sex, poor lovemaking techniques that leave the wife unsatisfied, rationing of sex by one spouse, and adulterous sexual fantasy. But there is a deeper problem underlying all these others: *not finding true sexual fulfillment because of a failure to recognize and participate in the spiritual aspect of sexual union.*

In this example, the husband is thinking of sex only in terms of physical lust for a woman's body—a basically selfish attitude. He is not thinking of touching his wife's spirit with his. He does not realize sex can be a holy act. To his wife, sex is a dirty chore because she dislikes her husband's lustful attitude toward her. So her mind and spirit retreat from him until the incident is over. The husband soon develops a wandering eye and a renewed fantasy life, since the nature of lust is that it eventually gets bored and needs new material.

Many marriage manuals would recommend at this point that the wife buy a new negligee and the couple learn some new lovemaking techniques. But that is only an effort to keep lust alive for a little while longer. Fulfilling lustful desires is never enough to bring true satisfaction. What this couple needs is to learn how to touch each other's spirits during sexual union. Even if they eventually become skilled enough to give each other the ultimate in physical stimulation, they still have not gone "all the way"—to a joining not only of bodies and souls, but also of spirits.

John and Paula Sandford, pioneers in the field of biblical counseling through prayer and the gifts of the Holy Spirit, have taught more (and more eloquently) on the spiritual aspects of sexuality than anyone else I know. Here is how they describe the incredible intimacy that can occur when Christian couples experience spiritual union during sexual union:

> Some couples have testified that while they were hugging and caressing the other, it seemed as though they could feel their own hands stroking their own chest through the other! Some men have testified to being exhilarated by great swirls of loving energy flowing from their wife's breasts, filling them with exalted love and cherishing for her.[3]

Enjoying each other's bodies is thrilling. Feeling tender emotions of love is wonderful. But the embrace of your spirit by the spirit of your beloved is what provides true satisfaction in sexual union.

Yet there is still another level of spiritual depth available in marital union. We have seen that a typical Christian couple has the attitude that their sexual union is somehow unclean and unholy. This causes their hearts to withdraw from the Holy Spirit while they are being sexual because they think, "Surely God does not want to be involved in this nasty business." They do not yet understand that this very act of union is a key element of God's plan for extending His kingdom in the earth. He even wants to participate! This can happen when a couple learns to reach out with their spirits and touch the Holy Spirit dwelling within the other.

The Sandfords have described this event beautifully:

> The glory of marital sex happens by the fact that the Holy Spirit sings the love song of creation, for example, through my spirit to Paula and through Paula's

spirit to mine. Our spirits alone cannot fully enrapture us to and in each other. But God can and does. When His Spirit flows through mine to her and hers to me, we are blessed and fulfilled and caused to love and cherish each other more than words or actions can express.[4]

Husbands, can you fathom loving God with your spirit as you make love to your wife and enjoying His presence in her, loving you back? Wives, can you receive Jesus as your spiritual Husband, loving you through the body, soul, and spirit of the man you married? Can you grasp the reality of what is taking place? With every caress, every touch, you are expressing your love not only to your spouse, but also to the Holy God who created you, gave His life for you and to you, gave you to each other, and now lives within each of you. Do you see how understanding this truth must forever change the way you think about, look at, and approach your spouse? Do you see now that having sex with your spouse is a carnal act *only if you fail to touch his or her spirit with yours or fail to acknowledge the Holy Spirit within him or her?*

> WITH EVERY CARESS, EVERY TOUCH, YOU ARE EXPRESSING YOUR LOVE, NOT ONLY TO YOUR SPOUSE, BUT ALSO TO THE HOLY GOD WHO CREATED YOU.

Spiritual Sex: God's Secret Weapon

Not only is this sexual and spiritual union surely the most pleasurable and fulfilling experience we can have on this earth, but it is an essential element of God's plan for extending His kingdom in the earth today through the spiritual *principle of agreement*. Jesus taught us this principle:

> Again I say to you that if **two of you agree** on earth concerning anything that they ask, it will be done for them by My Father in heaven. For where **two or**

three are gathered together in My name, I am there
in the midst of them. (Matthew 18:19-20 NKJV)

Jesus is teaching us that spiritual agreement is important for two
reasons:

1. *The prayer of agreement.* Jesus makes a promise of incredible
power here. If two Christians agree in prayer about anything in accordance
with God's will, the Father *will* bring it to pass. The first thing Jesus taught
us to pray is, "*Our Father which art in heaven, hallowed be thy name. Thy
kingdom come. Thy will be done in earth, as it is in heaven. Give us this
day our daily bread. . . .*" (Matthew 6:9-10 KJV). Notice that this is a joint
prayer of agreement. He did not say "*My* Father . . . give *me* today *my* daily
bread." Thus, the prayer of agreement is the means God has chosen to
cause His kingdom to be extended and His will to be done in the earth.

2. *Agreement brings the manifested presence of God.* The gathering of at least two Christians who call on the name of Jesus brings the manifested presence of the Lord around and among them in a special way that
is different from the way He lives inside them each day. The Greek word
mesos used for "in the midst" has the sense of being "between" or
"among," which implies that His Holy Spirit is flowing out of each person
present and filling the space surrounding them.

Since Christians praying in agreement are such an important channel for God's power to be released in the earth, where could we find a
stronger example of this than a Christian couple who are joined in the ultimate union of body, soul, and spirit? Because of the time they spend together daily, they have many opportunities to pray together, thus continually
releasing the presence of God into their home. Yet how many Christian
couples are aware of the tremendous strategic importance of their unity,
not only for the protection and blessing of their whole family, but in the
battle between God's kingdom and Satan's kingdom?

Because of this great potential, we can now see why Satan seeks to
destroy as many Christian marriages as he can—if not through outright
divorce, then through some form of mental and emotional strife that breaks

their unity and diminishes their effectiveness in prayer. If Satan cannot convince a couple to divorce, he achieves the same result if he can get them to fight continually and hate each other for the rest of their lives.

The Apostle Peter explains:

> If you are a wife, you must put your husband first. . . .
> If you are a husband, you should be thoughtful of your wife. Treat her with honor, because she isn't as strong as you are, and she shares with you in the gift of life. **Then nothing will stand in the way of your prayers.** (1 Peter 3:1, 7 CEV)

Today, it is all too common for a Christian couple to spend all their time and energy raising their children, volunteering at church, and building toward their financial goals. Yet they end up neglecting each other. Because they are spending all their time on good things—even spiritual things—they may feel they are making a necessary sacrifice. What they may not realize is that everything they are building rests on the foundation of their unity. If that unity is destroyed, then their children, their ministry, and their finances will all suffer the effects. I have seen far too many Christian marriages end in disaster for this very reason: *they lost their unity*.

In our 27 years of building a business and then a ministry together, my wife and I have had to fight this battle for unity many times. We have often felt overwhelmed and exhausted by the effort required to minister to all the hurting people who come to us for help. But, again and again, we have seen that when our unity weakens, then our ministry suffers. We have learned through experience that a strong, *spiritual* sexual relationship is an effective means of maintaining our unity and provides a source of physical, mental, and spiritual refreshment. We have found that having sexual union following our times of prayer together seals our mutual vision and purpose with a love and unity that is powerful and sustaining. Because we invite the Holy Spirit into our union, He breathes new life into our relationship.

To put this all in perspective, in order to fulfill His purposes in the earth, God has a great desire for Christian couples with strong marriages. A good, *spiritual* sexual relationship is absolutely essential to maintaining the unity of a marriage against all the forces that could potentially destroy it.

Spiritual Consequences of Sexual Sin

We have examined the reality of the spiritual union that is created between a husband and wife through sexual union. But what happens spiritually when people become involved in fornication or adultery? More specifically, what are the spiritual consequences of the Law of Sexual Union that result from a *sinful* sexual union?

Christians know that any time we sin it breaks our spiritual fellowship with God. As a Father, He has promised to discipline us when necessary. But how many of us know that sexual sins can bring *even more serious* spiritual consequences, such as *spiritual fragmentation* or *demonic infestation*?

1. Spiritual Fragmentation

Many Christian prayer counselors who work with people suffering from sexual bondages of various types have discovered that their clients often have "spiritual ties" (some call them "soul ties") with former lovers. These spiritual ties, which are quite distinct from any remaining mental or emotional bonds, are the tattered remnants of the spiritual union created through their sexual union with these lovers. Such ties may manifest themselves as a heightened awareness of the other person's needs, feelings, or activities, even when separated from them by a great distance. There may be a feeling that one's spirit is continuously searching for the lost lover. There may be an inability to feel fully joined and committed to one's spouse. If there are ties to many former lovers, this can produce a feeling of being divided spiritually into many scattered fragments. This condition can only be cured by asking God to divinely separate any spiritual links that exist and to restore the person's spirit to wholeness.[5]

2. Spiritual STDs (Sexually Transmitted Demons)

Another spiritual consequence of sexual sin is what I call *spiritual STDs (Sexually Transmitted Demons)*. Though I do not believe that demons are necessarily involved in all sexual problems, I have counseled many people over the years who have shown clear evidence of an evil supernatural influence at work, in addition to the purely natural explanations for their sexual problems. I have found my experiences to be in general agreement with the published reports of other prayer counselors who also deal with sexual problems, such as the Sandfords and Leanne Payne.[6] So, while the information I am presenting here may be shocking or unbelievable to some, I believe it reflects the current consensus of those ministers who have learned how to deal with the demonically afflicted by using the special abilities* or "gifts" given through the Holy Spirit.

SEXUALLY TRANSMITTED DEMONS

Every person needs to heed this sober warning: *those who participate in sexual sins are exposing themselves to a very real threat of demonic oppression or even demonic possession.* We know that demons are actively involved in encouraging people to commit any and all types of sin. However, it seems that sexual sin—more than any other type of sin except occult practices—opens a spiritual doorway, or breaches some type of God-ordained protective barrier, which allows demonic access to the bodies, souls, and even spirits of the persons involved. These demonic "infections" can produce symptoms in the spirit, soul, and body simultaneously. *Table*

---

* The Apostle Paul mentions the "discerning of spirits" in 1 Corinthians 12:10 (NKJV). This is a spiritual ability imparted by the Holy Spirit to enable Christians to perceive the presence and activity of spiritual beings—demons and angels. This gift is absolutely necessary for every pastor or counselor because it enables a person to distinguish problems that are mental and physical from those that are caused by demons, who often mimic physical and mental symptoms. If you are involved in counseling others, you should ask God to develop this gift in you. As Paul says in 1 Corinthians 12:31, "Earnestly desire the best gifts" (NKJV).

> ## Table 5.1
> ### Some Typical Symptoms of "Infection"
> ### with a Sexually Transmitted Demon
>
> **Spiritual Symptoms**
>
> - Hearing, seeing, or sensing demonic spirits
> - For Christians: an inability to sense or hear the Holy Spirit
>
> **Mental/Emotional Symptoms**
>
> - An uncontrollable compulsion to repeat a sexual sin, in spite of the risks of catching a disease, being arrested, being publicly exposed, losing your job, or destroying your marriage
> - Unrelenting negative feelings, such as depression, anxiety, fear, and unrelieved guilt
> - Obsessive and disturbing thoughts that you cannot silence
>
> **Bodily Symptoms**
>
> - Unusual, unpleasant, or disturbing sensations in your body
> - Unexplained pain that does not respond to medication
> - Symptoms of disease that do not respond to medical treatment
>
> *Note: Some of these symptoms can have causes other than demonic ones. Having just one of these symptoms does not mean you have a demonic infestation. But having one or more in each category is a strong indication that you might. I recommend seeking help from a reputable Christian counselor who has broad experience in dealing with mental, emotional, and spiritual problems, and expertise in deliverance.*

5.1 lists some of the more common symptoms that may be seen. While most of these symptoms individually can have other causes, if several of these suddenly appear after involvement in sexual sin, it is a good indicator that a demonic infestation has occurred.

Let us compare the risks of catching sexually transmitted demons to that of catching sexually transmitted diseases. Some promiscuous people seem to have quite a number of sexual experiences before becoming infected with a curable sexually transmitted disease. Other less fortunate ones become infected with an incurable STD, such as HIV, during their very first sexual encounter. I have seen a similar range of risk for contracting sexually transmitted demons. Some individuals I have counseled have lived with serious sexual sin for years, yet seem to have only a mild case of demonic oppression that clears up after repentance and prayer. However, the most disturbing cases I have seen involve apparently mature Christian people who were raised in a Christian home. A sudden exposure to pornography or a brief sexual encounter can turn their lives into a nightmare of demonic activity, compulsive sexual sin, and mental torment that often destroys their ministry, their family, and all the other good things they had in life.

Just as an innocent victim of rape can become infected with a sexually transmitted disease, there have been documented cases where innocent victims of rape or molestation were subjected to a demonic infestation. Often, the demon does not manifest itself until some time after the attack. Based on the cases I have seen and the reports of others, it seems evident that if the emotional damage produced by the attack is not treated and healed through timely counseling, it can fester into hatred and bitterness. A demon may enter during the initial attack, or this emotional wounding may make the victim vulnerable to a demonic infestation that can occur much later. This might be compared to what happens in our physical bodies when a wound does not receive proper attention and eventually becomes infected by any bacteria that happen to be present.

> **RAPE OR MOLESTATION . . . MAKES THE VICTIM VULNERABLE TO A DEMONIC INFESTATION.**

Many of the most serious cases of actual demonic possession seem to result from a history of sexual violence, particularly ritual sexual abuse. Dr. Rebecca Brown, who leads a ministry for former Satanists, has described a common practice among Satanists of introducing demons into unwilling victims through rape.[7] Their victims are often children, who are dedicated to Satan through hideous rituals involving various forms of torture and multiple rapes. I myself have counseled people who as children were subjected to possession rituals involving homosexual gang rape by adherents of the Santería* cult. As a result, they came under the control of demons.

There has been much speculation about the different means of contracting sexually transmitted demons and what should be considered "risky behaviors." One commonly accepted explanation for what occurs is that the spiritual union created between two individuals through sex is like a bridge that allows demons to cross from one person into the other. If you choose to have sex with a demonically infested person, or even if you are subjected to rape, some of their demons may cross over during the union and take up residence in you without your knowledge or consent.

But how does a sexually transmitted demon invade the first person it infests? Also, how do we account for cases of demonic infestation that have resulted from solitary types of sexual sin, such as voyeurism or viewing pornography? Another possible means for demonic invasion may be that the very nature of sexual activity, particularly orgasm, lowers our natural defenses against a spiritual invasion. Being in a state of intoxication, where your reasoning powers cannot function, is often reported to facilitate demonic invasion. Confirming evidence for this is found in the many reports of demonic infestation occurring during intoxication with drugs or alcohol. There are also many religions where intoxicants are deliberately ingested in an effort to contact demons.

When we consider the high levels of drug and alcohol abuse in North American society coupled with the high incidence of sexual immorality, we can easily understand why reports of demonic infestation are on the rise. Even Christians are risking contact with demons if they engage in these types of risky behaviors.

Recall that the essence of sexuality is seeking union of body, soul, *and spirit* with a mate. Your spirit must lay down its defenses, open up the doors, and come out of its bodily "castle" in order to meet your spouse's spirit halfway and unite. If you are involved in sexual activity outside of a

---

* Santería is a religion that combines elements of Catholicism with African witchcraft and demon worship. It has spread throughout the Americas. The main goal of their rituals is to invite possession by particular demons they call *orishas*.

marriage relationship—particularly if it involves some form of sexual perversion—then you are laying down your defenses and opening up your spiritual doors in Satan's territory. You may think you are just enjoying a moment of physical pleasure with your body, not realizing that your spirit is actually reaching out for spiritual union. Perhaps this vulnerability or "openness" of the human spirit during illicit sexual activity is what attracts any demons that happen to be in the neighborhood and enables them to invade at that moment.

Pornographic Materials Are "Cursed Objects"

I frequently counsel Christians who have come under demonic influence through the use of pornography. Few Christians understand the real dangers involved with pornography because they are ignorant of the biblical principle of *cursed objects*.* This principle is well understood by those who have been involved in the occult. A cursed object is any object that has been made under the direction of a demon or dedicated to a demon for its use. This includes things such as idols, amulets, charms, items used in occult rituals, fortune-telling paraphernalia, and so forth. Demons commonly congregate around these objects and use them as tools to ensnare and control people. There are many reports of Christians who have encountered such objects and treated them lightly—until they found themselves under serious demonic attack that did not end until the object had been destroyed.

I believe there is strong evidence to suggest that pornographic materials should also be classified as cursed objects. There is much agreement among psychologists and counselors that pornography plays a central role in the development of many forms of sexual perversion, such as serial rape and child molestation. It typically becomes addictive. Obviously, this

---

* "You shall burn the carved images of their gods with fire; you shall not covet the silver or gold that is on them, nor take it for yourselves, lest you be snared by it; for it is an abomination to the LORD your God. Nor shall you bring an abomination into your house, lest you be doomed to destruction like it. You shall utterly detest it and utterly abhor it, for it is an accursed thing" (Deuteronomy 7:25-26, NKJV).

is a tool used by demons to ensnare and control people. It should also be evident that pornographic materials are made under the direction of demons. The pornographic industry worldwide is run by well organized criminal groups. It is apparent to many in Christian ministry that, as with any other cursed object, demons congregate around pornographic materials and lie in wait for the opportunity to invade those who pick them up. As the victim becomes sexually aroused, he begins to fantasize about the pictures and lets down his defenses. Then the demonic trap is sprung, and his soul is invaded.

No one who truly grasps the extreme spiritual danger presented by pornography will be tempted to own it or view it. The Old Testament clearly teaches that the presence of such a "cursed object" in your home brings a curse on your household, holds back God's blessings, and is an open invitation to demonic activity. Children seem to be particularly vulnerable. I have counseled Christians whose entire sexual development was perverted just by an accidental glimpse of "hard core" pornography during childhood—typically these were materials purchased and hidden by their father or another male relative. Many of these Christian children began to be oppressed by demons as a result of that brief exposure and have suffered torment for many years.

Though every Christian has the God-given authority to drive out demons, truly ministering to persons with sexually transmitted demons requires more than just a quick prayer for deliverance. Not only must the demon be driven out, but the damage it has caused to the person's sexuality must be repaired. The emotional wounds and weaknesses that allowed it to maintain control must be healed. The victim must come to a place of true repentance for any sinful attitudes and actions that allowed the demonic infestation to occur. He should also be taught the basic principles of spiritual warfare so he can fend off any attempts that the demon might make to return.[8]

Spiritual Causes of Sexual Sin

We have seen that sexual sin always brings definite spiritual consequences. Why? Because sexual acts involve our spirits, not just our minds and bodies. However, this close link between sexual and spiritual matters can also work the other way. There are some sins and weaknesses of the human *spirit* that can lead Christians into sexual sin. Sadly, widespread ignorance of this important principle seems to be a major cause behind much of the sexual sin that has become so common in the Church today.

We know that our bodies, even if strong and healthy, have limitations and vulnerabilities that can get us into trouble if we fail to take proper care of them. Should this not also be true of our spirits?

It is particularly troubling to many, both inside and outside the Church, when seemingly mature Christian leaders get caught in sexual scandals. It has caused many to doubt the keeping power of God and to question the genuineness of a fallen leader's entire ministry. Yet if a well-known minister suffers a heart attack due to an unhealthy lifestyle—too much stress, overeating, lack of exercise, and a poor diet—we do not blame God or question the genuineness of the person's ministry. Failing to take care of the body God has given us *is* a sin. The consequences can end our life on earth prematurely. But everyone understands that a minister who has a heart attack just made some poor choices and is reaping the consequences, so he receives our sympathy. *We need to start viewing those Christians who fall into sexual sin with this same level of understanding and sympathy.*

> **WE NEED TO START VIEWING THOSE CHRISTIANS WHO FALL INTO SEXUAL SIN WITH THIS SAME LEVEL OF UNDERSTANDING AND SYMPATHY.**

Over the years, I have counseled many Christians and Christian leaders who have fallen into various types of sexual sin. Some had their sexual development damaged during childhood through incidents such as molestation. Some had just failed to take proper care of their marriage relationship. But many had first fallen victim to spiritual forces, of which they were completely ignorant, that led them step by step into sexual sin. In many cases, demonic forces became focused upon them *specifically because they were trying to minister to someone else who had a problem*. Being well-intentioned, but ignorant of the spiritual forces at work, they failed to take the proper precautions and stumbled.

(Please understand, we are examining here some of the reasons that Christians fall into sexual sin. However, these explanations in no way justify sinful acts. We still have a choice of doing right or wrong. We will still have to answer to God for our actions. And our actions still have unavoidable consequences.)

What are these spiritual forces to which even mature Christians seem to be vulnerable? I see three major problem areas: *spiritual adultery, spiritual defilement,* and *demonic seduction.*

(I will give just a brief overview of spiritual adultery and spiritual defilement because they illustrate aspects of how the Law of Sexual Union affects our spirits. A fuller treatment of these is found in Chapter 11.)

1. Spiritual Adultery

John and Paula Sandford were the first to identify and describe a common type of sin they named *spiritual adultery.*[9] This sinful condition occurs when either a husband or wife achieves a depth of spiritual (and subsequent emotional) intimacy with someone outside of the marriage that should have been reserved only for his or her spouse.

Spiritual adultery often leads to physical adultery. This seems to be an example of the Law of Sexual Union operating in reverse. A close spiritual relationship between a man and woman pulls them inexorably toward a deepening emotional bond and eventually into a sexual relationship—unless something intervenes with enough force to wake them up to the sinful nature of what is going on between them. Ignorance of this very principle is the root cause underlying the adultery that has destroyed so many ministries. It explains how two mature Christian people with the highest aspirations, whose lives are committed to serving God, can still be blindsided by forces they do not understand and begin an affair that destroys everything they have worked so hard to achieve.

Even if a spiritually adulterous relationship never culminates in physical adultery, it is still wrong because it is a betrayal of the mutual trust, honesty, confidentiality, and emotional intimacy that belong between a husband and wife. Each should be the other's best friend, prayer partner, and confidant, so they rightfully feel betrayed if they find another competing for that special position.

We need to understand that there is a definite spiritual dimension to spiritual adultery that goes beyond the emotional or physical relationship. In looking at the spiritual dimension of marriage, we saw that a husband and wife have a special spiritual link that can make them aware of each other's feelings and needs. It seems that with spiritual adultery, there is a similar spiritual link established between one spouse and another person outside the marriage. Women tend to be more sensitive about spiritual matters than men, so it is often the case that a wife will sense this spiritual link between her husband and another woman and be troubled by it although she may not be able to put what she feels into words. If she tries to tell her husband what she is sensing about this other woman, he will often respond with righteous indignation because he, in truth, has had only the purest of motives in his dealings with the lady. She may be a colleague in ministry, a member of their home prayer group, or a new believer who needs teaching and encouragement. But his mind is unaware that, through their times of prayer and sharing, her spirit has latched onto his and formed a deep attachment. This spiritual link is beyond any merely emotional or physical attraction that may or may not exist between them, and it represents a very real threat to his marriage.

Spiritual adultery seems to be a particular danger for Christians, since we have so many opportunities for developing spiritual and emotional intimacy with others through praying together, counseling, or just sharing heart-to-heart. Such intimacy is generally a good thing, for we cannot effectively disciple or counsel others without a relationship of mutual love and trust. Joining in prayers of faith toward a common goal requires that our spirits touch and unite together in the Holy Spirit. We all need good friends who know our hearts and can agree with us in prayer. We cannot truly fulfill God's purpose for our lives without developing these spiritually intimate relationships with others. However, we can and must exercise wisdom and due caution in any relationship where there is some danger of spiritual adultery.

The situation requiring the greatest caution is obviously a man and a woman working closely together or spending time alone together, while at least one is married to someone else. We have seen the multitude of ways through which the Law of Sexual Union can work to unite our minds and bodies, even before we are fully aware of what is happening. Even those who have not been spiritually reborn can fall into adultery through such forces. But when you add the spiritual relationship required of two Christians working in ministry together—joining their spirits in intercessory prayer, or one ministering to the spiritual needs of the other—the situation becomes even more precarious.

If they are both single, then they are in an ideal situation for falling in love. But even in that case, if they let these forces sweep them off their feet, they may later find that their personalities are not really compatible for the lifetime partnership of marriage. However, if one or both is already married, then practical steps must certainly be taken to defuse the situation.

The message here is *not* to stop ministering to needy people and avoid all close friendships. We just need to become more *aware* of what is going on in our own hearts by getting feedback from God and from others. As Jeremiah says, "The heart is deceitful above all things, and desperately wicked; who can know it? I, the LORD, search the heart, I test the mind" (Jeremiah 17:9-10 NKJV). And "in the multitude of counselors there is safety" (Proverbs 11:14 NKJV).

2. Spiritual Defilement

Spiritual defilement occurs when we are affected by another person's sinful condition through spiritual contact with them. This is another rarely recognized way in which spiritual forces can directly influence our sexual feelings. We have all experienced how another's thoughts and feelings can affect us through his or her spoken words and facial expressions, causing us to change our minds or our moods. When we accept that the human spirit is just as real as the body or mind, then it seems quite reasonable that our spirits could also be influenced by contact with another's spirit.

Christians are often in situations where they can be affected by another's spirit. Even in casual conversations with others, there may be some degree of spiritual contact. Have you ever met someone for the first time and felt uneasy about him in a way you could not quite put into words? He may have been well-dressed, well-spoken, and good-looking, but you just could not trust him. After he left, you may have even felt so disgusted you wanted take a shower just to get the "gunk" off that he seemed to have transferred to you. I have met people like this and only later learned that they were scoundrels, liars, con artists, or enthusiastic practitioners of gross immorality. Nothing in what they did or said gave them away. They could not have been so "successfully" wicked had they not developed exceptional skills in deceiving. Yet a renewed spirit can perceive the evil that is within them.

But I should emphasize here that this disgusting feeling, which goes beyond spiritual discernment, is not given by God's Holy Spirit. He and His gifts are pure and holy. We feel dirty and defiled by these people because our spirits have contacted theirs in some way. Perhaps because we are too inexperienced in spiritual matters to know how to avoid doing so, or because they are using their spirits (in league with any demons living in them) in an attempt to deceive and manipulate us. Afterward, we need a spiritual cleansing by the Holy Spirit to get rid of the spiritual defilement they have left with us.

The greater our spiritual contact with another person, the greater our risk of spiritual defilement by them. Whenever we are ministering to another in some way—encouraging, comforting, teaching, counseling, or praying with them—not only are feelings expressed and thoughts exchanged, but there is a spiritual interchange taking place as well. God's Holy Spirit is certainly present, but so are our own human spirits.

3. Demonic seduction

The spiritual defilement that can come from contact with demons moves to an even deeper level with *demonic seduction*. Demonic seduction is more than just being tempted by a demon to commit a sexual sin. It differs from demonic infestation, although it can result in that. Demonic seduction involves direct sexual contact with a demonic spirit.

In certain circumstances it is possible for a demon to take on the appearance of a beautiful woman (*succubus*) or man (*incubus*) in order to seduce a person while he or she is asleep and to induce the experience of having sexual intercourse or being raped in the victim. For many who fancy themselves "well educated," this is no more than a fable from the Dark Ages. Yet many ancient and modern cultures have recorded incidents of this type.[10]

All the clients I have dealt with who have experienced demonic defilement of this type have had a background of occult involvement or pornographic influences, which made them spiritually vulnerable to this type of attack. People who willingly give in to such temptations come under heavy bondage and delusion and, in addition, can bring bondage upon those around them. Other counselors have reported cases where rape or childhood molestation made someone susceptible. These cases almost always require extensive counseling combined with intercessory prayer to set the individual free.

In Summary

This discussion of the spiritual aspects of sexuality no doubt contains much that some readers will find challenging. However, there are really no new doctrines presented here, just an exploration of some practical *consequences* of commonly accepted Christian doctrines—such as the existence of the human spirit, the reality of demons, God's Spirit living within us, praying in agreement, and so forth.

Real Christianity is about meeting the needs of others, and that is often a risky, messy business. We should not withdraw from needy people out of fear; we just need to use wisdom. Just knowing what risks are present and being prepared to take some simple steps in advance to fend off potential problems is all that is really necessary. When our lives are truly submitted to the lordship of Jesus Christ and we are willing to work with Him, He will provide the training, resources, guidance, and protection we need in order to be successful.

This has necessarily been just a brief overview of these topics. If you are in any way disturbed or confused by what you have read, I would recommend that you study these subjects further through the sources referenced in the endnotes.

Notes.

1. Maurice S. Rawlings, *To Hell and Back* (Nashville: Thomas Nelson, 1993). This noted cardiologist relates the firsthand afterlife experiences of many patients he has resuscitated.

2. These same facts about the human spirit can be found by studying passages in the Bible that refer to the structure and functions of the human spirit. However, it would take more space than I have available to present all of the necessary passages.

3. John and Paula Sandford, *Healing the Wounded Spirit* (Tulsa: Victory House, 1985), 116.

4. Ibid., 117.

5. John and Paula Sandford have written extensively on this subject in several of their books. Some examples can be found in: John L. Sandford, *Why Some Christians Commit Adultery* (Tulsa: Victory House, 1989), 24-26, and Paula Sandford, *Garlands for Ashes: Healing Victims of Sexual Abuse* (Tulsa: Victory House, 1988), 72-73.

6. Leanne Payne, who has been a pioneer in healing prayer for those who are struggling with sexual perversions, describes her approach to dealing with demons of sexual perversion in Chapter 14 of *The Healing Presence* (Westchester, IL: Crossway Books, 1989).

7. Rebecca Brown, *Prepare for War* (New Kensington, PA: Whitaker House, 1992), 213-226.

8. There are many good books on ministering to demonically infested people. The most thorough and practical one I have seen is by John and Mark Sandford, *Deliverance and Inner Healing* (Grand Rapids: Revell, 1992). I highly recommend it.

9. John Sandford addresses these, and many other forces that lead Christians into sexual sin, with great depth and insight in *Why Some Christians Commit Adultery* (Tulsa: Victory House, 1989). I am indebted to both him and Paula for broadening and refining my understanding of these issues through their writings and seminars.

10. For more information, see the following books: Rebecca Brown, *He Came to Set the Captives Free* (New Kensington, PA: Whitaker House, 1992), 64, and John and Mark Sandford, *Deliverance and Inner Healing* (Grand Rapids: Revell, 1992), 247-249.

VI

The Relationship

We have examined many aspects of the Law of Sexual Union and how it operates. But we need to reach a deeper level of understanding by asking, "Why did God choose to create us as sexual beings, male and female?" and "What is the ultimate purpose of this powerful principle of sexual union?"

To begin, let us revisit the creation of humankind:

> Then God said, "Let us make humankind in our image, according to our likeness; and let them have dominion over the fish of the sea . . . ." So God created humankind in his image, in the image of God he created them; male and female he created them. (Genesis 1:26-27 NRSV)

Here, God the Father, God the Son, and God the Holy Spirit, in Their relationship of heavenly harmony and perfect love, are having an intimate discussion about their plans to create humankind. God is in perfect agreement with Himself (They are in perfect agreement with One Another*) that humans should be made like Him (Them) "in our image, according to our likeness."

So how did God create humanity in His own image? As both *a man and a woman*. It seems that to produce a full expression of His divine nature, God found it necessary to create both a man and a woman. In the creative act, God chose to divide up some of His many attributes between the man and the woman. The man received those aspects of God that we call *masculine* while the woman received those aspects of God that we call *feminine*. Thus, God Himself was the Author of these two complementary principles, the masculine and the feminine, that permeate all our human relationships, our arts, and our languages.

The concept that God has both masculine and feminine traits may, at first glance, be troubling to some Christians. While it is true that the Bible never refers to God as a female, some Scriptures do use feminine imagery in referring to Him, for example, as a mother in Isaiah 66:13 and as a woman in labor in Isaiah 42:14.

Perhaps the most significant revelation of a feminine aspect of God in Scripture concerns the nature and role of the Holy Spirit. Jesus referred to the Holy Spirit as the Helper (*parakletos*, Greek for "one who comes alongside to help," John 14:16) while Eve is called Adam's helper (*ezer*, Hebrew for "aid" or "help," Genesis 2:18).

When God deals with us through His Holy Spirit, He is gentle with us, sensitive to our needs, comforting us and nurturing us. These are all attributes we might call "feminine." Of course, these attributes were part of God's nature long before He created woman. We just tend to think of them as feminine because women seem to have been given more of His abilities in these areas than men. (Men often have to "work at it.") Since the Holy Spirit existed before Eve, it might even be more accurate to say that being gentle, sensitive, comforting, and nurturing is "Holy-Spiritual"

---

* This passage is one of the strongest indications in the Old Testament of the plural nature of God.

behavior rather than "feminine" behavior. Nevertheless, the key principle here is that *the masculine and feminine must both be combined* to give us a glimpse of the full image of God.

Let us look now at the details of the creation of both the man and woman to see what we can learn:

> Then the LORD God formed man from the dust of the ground, and breathed into his nostrils the breath of life; and the man became a living being. . . .Then the LORD God said, "It is not good that the man should be alone; I will make him a helper as his partner." So out of the ground the LORD God formed every animal of the field and every bird of the air, and brought them to the man to see what he would call them; and whatever the man called every living creature, that was its name. The man gave names to all cattle, and to the birds of the air, and to every animal of the field; but for the man there was not found a helper as his partner. So the LORD God caused a deep sleep to fall upon the man, and he slept; then he took one of his ribs and closed up its place with flesh. And the rib that the LORD God had taken from the man he made into a woman and brought her to the man. Then the man said, "This at last is bone of my bones and flesh of my flesh; this one shall be called Woman, for out of Man this one was taken." Therefore a man leaves his father and his mother and clings to his wife, and they become one flesh. And the man and his wife were both naked, and were not ashamed. (Genesis 2:7, 18-25 NRSV)

Some Christian traditions over the centuries have misinterpreted these verses on the creation of humankind as saying something like this:

God created a man, Adam, as the perfect expression of His nature. Then God said, "Oops, I almost forgot! If we are going to have any more of these magnificent male creatures, we will need some way for him to reproduce. Let Me see now . . . why don't I create a female for that purpose? She can have his babies and be his servant." This misinterpretation has often been used as justification by those who want to treat women as "second-class" persons, not created in the "full" image of God.*

Nothing could be further from the truth. I believe God formed Adam first, then Eve, in order to teach Adam some important lessons about his wife.

First, God had to convince Adam of his need for a wife. "Then the LORD God said, 'It is not good that the man should be alone; I will make him a helper as his partner.'" But God knew that just telling Adam of his need for a wife would not be sufficient. He would have to be shown. So God paraded all the animals before Adam to let him name them. Through this process Adam could see that they all had mates, that it was the normal thing to have a mate, and that he was the only creature without a mate. He could also see that none of the animals would make a suitable mate for him.

By this point, Adam probably felt quite sharply his need for a companion. God had made him notice the fact that he was alone. He could see that he was a misfit bachelor compared with all the other creatures. He had also spent quite a bit of time scrutinizing the animals for their "wife" potential and was not at all pleased with his options. If God had not come up with something better, it was beginning to look like he might soon be saying, "Yes, dear," to a female gorilla.

Now that God had Adam in a properly appreciative frame of mind, He set about creating Eve. Recall that God created Adam and the animals from dirt, but He did not create Eve in this manner. If He had made Eve from dirt, Adam might have received the wrong impression: that

---

* In this exposition of the creation of humanity I am indebted to the efforts of many women Bible teachers over the years, including Marilyn Hickey and Fuschia Pickett, who have been bold pioneers in correcting centuries of misogynistic exegesis. They have, indeed, broadened my perspective on this subject.

Eve was just another type of animal, very different from himself, created just to serve him. So, to ensure that Adam did not make this mistake, God put him under anesthesia and fashioned Eve from a part of Adam's own body. Adam clearly understood what had happened because he said, "This at last is bone of my bones and flesh of my flesh; this one shall be called Woman, for out of Man this one was taken." Immediately following is the first statement of the Law of Sexual Union: "Therefore a man leaves his father and his mother and clings to his wife, and they become one flesh."

Through this elaborate scenario, God taught Adam that Eve was not an inferior being, but his equal and a missing part of him that he required to be fully complete—because she was taken out of him and yet was to become one with him again.

Verse 25 makes an important point by immediately referring to Adam and Eve as "the man and his wife." We have already studied how the act of sexual intercourse brings about a "one flesh" union between a man and woman and how it is the only basis for God's definition of marriage. For verse 25 to refer to Adam and Eve as man and wife is a clear indication that they must have had intercourse—no doubt, shortly after God introduced them.*

Have you ever wondered why God created a husband and wife as the first humans? He could have created a pregnant woman who would then have had many children; He could have created a whole nursery full of infants and raised them Himself. But He did not do so. When He said, "Let us make humankind in our image," He fulfilled His plan by creating not just the perfect man and the perfect woman, but *a husband and wife.* The only possible reason for this is that *a husband and wife are the most accurate expression of His divine nature.*

---

* There is certainly nothing to support the quaint notion that they remained virgins until they disobeyed God and were exiled from the Garden of Eden. Such ideas stem from erroneous religious traditions that associate even marital sex with sinfulness. Adam and Eve were in a state of sinless perfection, and they had sex in that state or they could not have been "man and wife."

Ways That a Husband and Wife Reflect God's Image

Let us examine some of the ways in which the union of husband and wife reflect the image of God.

1. The masculine and feminine are integrated through marriage.

As we have seen, God divided up some of His attributes, or character traits, between Adam and Eve to create what we now call *masculine* and *feminine*. Yet God did not just create the ideal man and the perfect woman to remain separate expressions of His masculine and feminine sides. They were designed to become a new unity—that "one flesh" union we call *husband and wife*. Only in this way could they reflect a *whole and complete* image of God.

For any husband and wife to have a successful marriage, their separate masculinity and femininity *must be integrated*. As they learn to harmonize their often conflicting masculine and feminine perspectives and work together as a team, they reveal a new strength and beauty much different than they had as singles. As their marriage matures, they learn how to complement each other. In this way, they reflect more completely the image of God.

2. The union of a husband and wife teaches us about the Trinity of God.

A husband and wife are both triune beings of spirit, body, and soul. Though still distinct as persons, through their sexual union they have been joined spiritually, physically, and mentally/emotionally into one new whole. They were originally separate from each other, but they have joined to become a family and are working to build a life together. They can now accomplish more together than they could have separately.

This reflects in some ways the mystery of the Holy Trinity. We know that God is One. Yet He has different Personalities who love each other, who interact, who are separate yet still enjoy a perfect union. In the

Bible, God is sometimes presented as a Team or Family who work together in continuous harmony and fellowship. Jesus illustrated this when He said, "The Son can do nothing of Himself, but what He sees the Father do" (John 5:19 NKJV) and, "The Helper, the Holy Spirit, whom the Father will send in My name, He will teach you all things" (John 14:26 NKJV).

3. A husband and wife share the Godlike power of creating children and caring for them.

Let us look at an idyllic marital scene:

> A husband and wife are lying in bed together one cool spring morning, their arms wrapped around each other, their faces touching—just enjoying their love.
>
> The woman says, "Honey, I had such a wonderful dream last night. I dreamed we had a house full of kids. In fact, there were twelve of them! The older boys all had dark hair and eyes just like yours and were helping you manage the cows and tend the fields. The older girls were helping me in the kitchen and taking care of the little ones. We were all so happy. The house was just full of laughter!"
>
> Her husband replies with a start, "Twelve kids? Listen, woman! We haven't even had our first one yet. But you're right. It would be a lot of fun to have a little tyke following me around. I could teach him to play baseball and football and . . . ."
>
> "Honey," she interrupts while snuggling closer, "let's go ahead and start a family. I know we agreed we would wait until our finances were better, but we had such a good year last year, and this year is looking

good already. We could afford just one little baby. What do you say? Pretty please?"

He replies, "You sweet thing! When you look at me like that I want to give you all the babies you want. Come here!"

Let us compare this familiar scene with the scene in heaven described above in Genesis 1:26-27, where God is planning the creation of humanity. Can you see the similarities? God, the Holy Trinity, wrapped up in sweet communion with Himself on the morning of Creation, is planning to fill His world with children who resemble Him and follow Him around, wanting to do what He does and learning to help Him with his work. So, in a tremendous act of love, He gives birth to a man and woman, husband and wife, who together are much like Him.

Like the Trinity, this couple also enjoys being wrapped up in each other's company for endless hours, giving each other pleasure, enjoying fellowship, and making plans together. Indeed, they are so much like Him that they also want to fill their house with their own little babes, who will follow their parents around and learn to do as they do. Just as He created this couple, God has given to them the awesome, Godlike power to create other human beings like themselves, *whenever they choose*, through an act of their love. This is a power that not even angels possess. Having borne a child, the parents are then charged with the responsibility of learning how to be a father and a mother to this new person and raising the child to full maturity.

We often see some of the roles of the Trinity played out in a traditional family. To take one example, Dad (like God the Father) lays down the guidelines for proper behavior for his children and the consequences that will result if they transgress. Mom is in agreement with Dad because she was involved in formulating the guidelines and communicating them to the children (like Jesus, the Living Word of God). But when the children do transgress, she (like Jesus) often intercedes with Dad on their behalf that he not be too hard on them. When the children must be disciplined, Mom (like the Holy Spirit, the Comforter) is there to comfort them and let them know they are still loved.

In this way, the parents learn firsthand something of what God must feel in His dealings with us. Also, as children have these loving experiences with Mom and Dad, it prepares them for understanding how God wants to relate to them as they mature, whether He disciplines them in love, as God the Father, or comforts them, as God the Holy Spirit.*

Sex is essential to these three ways of expressing the image and likeness of God. Far from the dirty, fleshly, unholy activity that some religious people have made it out to be, sexual union within marriage is holy. It is a significant way in which we reflect the divine nature of God. The pleasure and intimacy of the sexual union between a husband and wife exemplify the loving union the Father, Son, and Holy Spirit have enjoyed throughout eternity. Sex was not intended only for making a baby, as some have imagined, but also for the Godlike experience of two becoming one.

Not only did God invent sex, but from the frequency with which He mentions it throughout the Old and New Testaments, He seems to care about it as much as we do. Those who have read through the Bible may recall just how frequently God uses sexual language and metaphors to describe His relationship with humankind.

Why does God talk to us in such blatantly sexual terms? As we have seen, sex is something He designed to make us more like Himself. Since sexuality is a common ground of experience for us all, God can use familiar sexual concepts and language to explain spiritual realities that otherwise might be hard for us to grasp. In God's wise plan, by getting married, having sex, and raising children, we all can come to better understand Him and the relationship He wishes to have with us.

Let us look more closely at some of the ways in which God has used the language of sex to explain Himself to us.

---

* This scenario may no longer occur in some modern American families, but a study of family life in societies throughout history shows that this indeed is quite typical for the rest of the human race.

God as the Husband, Israel as His wife

A recurrent theme in the writings of the Old Testament prophets is that God had chosen the Jewish people to be His wife, and He loved and cared for them as a husband should. Because they so frequently turned away from God to worship the false gods of neighboring countries, the relationship between God and Israel is often pictured as stormy: an unfaithful wife is divorced by her wounded Husband; eventually, she repents, He forgives her, and they are reconciled.

> The LORD All-Powerful, the Holy God of Israel,
> rules all the earth. He is your Creator and husband,
> and he will rescue you. You were like a young wife,
> brokenhearted and crying because her husband had
> divorced her. But the LORD your God says, "I am
> taking you back! I rejected you for a while, but with
> love and tenderness I will embrace you again."
> (Isaiah 54:5-7 CEV)

Chapter 16 in the book of Ezekiel is a poignant passage where God reveals His feelings toward the Jews who were living in Jerusalem at that time. He describes His initial love for them in rescuing them like a baby who had been abandoned and then raising them to maturity to be His bride:

> I passed by you, and saw you flailing about in your
> blood. As you lay in your blood, I said to you, "Live!
> and grow up like a plant of the field." You grew up
> and became tall and arrived at full womanhood;
> your breasts were formed, and your hair had grown;
> yet you were naked and bare. I passed by you again
> and looked on you; you were at the age for love. I
> spread the edge of my cloak over you, and covered

your nakedness: I pledged myself to you and entered
into a covenant with you, says the Lord GOD, and
you became mine. (Ezekiel 16:6-8 NRSV)

(The last sentence of this passage, beginning with "I spread the
edge of my cloak over you," is a poetic way of describing marriage and sexual union.)

But instead of trusting in God, they began to make treaties with
other nations for protection and to worship their idols. God viewed this as
adultery of the marriage relationship and prostitution of what belonged
only to Him:

But you trusted in your beauty and used your fame
to become a prostitute. You lavished your favors on
anyone who passed by and your beauty became his.
You took some of your garments to make gaudy
high places, where you carried on your prostitution.
Such things should not happen, nor should they ever
occur. You also took the fine jewelry I gave you, the
jewelry made of my gold and silver, and you made
for yourself male idols and engaged in prostitution
with them. . . . And you took your sons and daughters whom you bore to me and sacrificed them as
food to the idols. Was your prostitution not enough?
You slaughtered my children and sacrificed them to
the idols. . . . You adulterous wife! You prefer
strangers to your own husband! Every prostitute
receives a fee, but you give gifts to all your lovers,
bribing them to come to you from everywhere for
your illicit favors. (Ezekiel 16:15-17, 20-21, 32-33
NIV)

(Notice that God considers the children they had sacrificed to be *His* children, children He had entrusted to them, and whom He loved as dearly as any earthly father would.)

Jesus Christ as the Bridegroom, the Church as His Bride

A much broader vision of this same theme is revealed in the New Testament. Jesus Christ is presented as the Bridegroom, and those He has redeemed from all of humanity—past, present, and future—are to become His bride, the Church. The Apostle Paul often referred to this grand concept in the letters he wrote to the churches:

> For I am jealous over you with godly jealousy: for I
> have espoused you to one husband, that I may pres-
> ent you as a chaste virgin to Christ. (2 Corinthians
> 11:2 KJV)

In one letter, while teaching on this theme, Paul does something quite surprising. Instead of just reiterating the Old Testament example of how the relationship between a husband and wife illustrates our relationship with God, he does the reverse. He uses the relationship between Jesus Christ and the Church to teach Christian husbands and wives how better to relate to each other. Some commentators have tried to interpret the spiritual marriage between Christ and the Church as just a poetic allegory. But Paul evidently viewed it as a very real relationship, so real that he could use it to give every Christian some practical pointers on how to make their own marriages work better:

> Be subject to one another out of reverence for Christ.
> Wives, be subject to your husbands as you are to the
> Lord. For the husband is the head of the wife just as
> Christ is the head of the church, the body of which
> he is the Savior. Just as the church is subject to

Christ, so also wives ought to be, in everything, to their husbands. Husbands, love your wives, just as Christ loved the church and gave himself up for her, in order to make her holy by cleansing her with the washing of water by the word, so as to present the church to himself in splendor, without a spot or wrinkle or anything of the kind—yes, so that she may be holy and without blemish. In the same way, husbands should love their wives as they do their own bodies. He who loves his wife loves himself. For no one ever hates his own body, but he nourishes and tenderly cares for it, just as Christ does for the church, because we are members of his body. "For this reason a man will leave his father and mother and be joined to his wife, and the two will become one flesh." This is a great mystery, and I am applying it to Christ and the church.
(Ephesians 5:21-32 NRSV)

Just so no one will miss what he is saying here, Paul restates the Law of Sexual Union in verse 31, calling it "a great mystery" (which we are attempting to explore in this book), and then *specifically applies it to Christ and the Church.*

Now, I want you to really grasp what is happening here. The Apostle Paul, writing under the direct inspiration of the Holy Spirit, is teaching us about this holy, exalted, glorious, spiritual relationship between us and Jesus Christ. So, out of all the glorious and holy things in heaven and earth, what example does the Holy Spirit choose to explain this concept to us? *The sexual relationship of a husband and wife.* Talk about the "holiness of sexuality"! Sex is at *the very center* of God's plan for teaching us about our relationship with Him.

Here is a further example from Paul's letter to the Roman church:

Therefore, my brethren, you also have become dead
to the law through the body of Christ, **that you may
be married to another;** to Him who was raised from
the dead, **that we should bear fruit to God.** (Romans
7:4 NKJV)

The Church is not in some loveless, sexless marriage with her Husband. This is a passionate, intimate, "one flesh" love relatiuonship, and Jesus wants to get us "pregnant"—in other words, enable us to bear spiritual children and to bear the fruit of the Spirit.

"Born Again" Is a Sexual Term

I realize many Christians get nervous when anything of a sexual nature is discussed, even when it is mentioned in the Bible. Most would become more than a little uncomfortable if their pastor got up to preach one Sunday morning and said, "To become God's child, you need to have God's sperm (His Word) impregnate your heart. If you are truly His child, then you will not continue to sin, because God's sperm (His Word) is now a part of you."

Yet this pastor would be saying exactly what the Bible says:

No one who is born of God will continue to sin,
because God's seed [Greek: *sperma*] remains in him;
he cannot go on sinning, because he has been born
of God. (1 John 3:9 NIV)

The New Testament authors used the Greek word *sperma* to refer either to human sperm, the children that resulted from those sperm, or even a grain of wheat that is planted in the ground. They certainly did not know the details that we know today about genetics and DNA. But they knew enough from experience to understand that a husband's sperm was necessary for his wife to conceive a child, and that his sperm imprinted his characteristics on their child. This is the very metaphor God has chosen to explain to us the process of spiritual rebirth necessary for us to become His children.

How can someone be "born again"? Jesus told the Jewish leader Nicodemus:

> Most assuredly, I say to you, unless one is born again, he cannot see the kingdom of God. . . . Unless one is born of water and the Spirit, he cannot enter the kingdom of God. That which is born of the flesh is flesh, **and that which is born of the Spirit is spirit.** (John 3:3, 5-6 NKJV)

Furthermore, we are told in 1 Peter:

> For you have been born again, not of perishable seed, but of imperishable, through the living and enduring word of God. (1 Peter 1:23 NIV)

As these verses make clear, God's Word is like His spiritual sperm. Knowing what we do today about genetics, we could even say that, like the genes carried in the head of the sperm, *God's Word carries God's characteristics.* So, for you to be "born again," God's Word, His sperm, must be implanted in your heart by the Holy Spirit. If your heart chooses to receive His Word, a new spirit will be birthed within you. Then, as your reborn spirit grows, it will begin to manifest the characteristics of your Father God that are encoded in your new spiritual "genes." This is why John can say with confidence, "No one who is born of God will continue to sin, **because God's seed remains in him;** he cannot go on sinning, because he has been born of God" (1 John 3:9 NIV).

Are you beginning to see how essential it is for us to understand God's design for sexuality if we are to truly understand the spiritual truths He desires to teach us?

The Believer's Love Affair with God

The central theme of the Bible is God's desire and plan to have a relationship with each of us. This often seems like such a difficult concept for us to grasp. How do we even begin to relate to an all-knowing, all-powerful, omnipresent, eternal, spiritual Being? What kind of relationship does He desire to have with us? What kind of relationship is even possible between a human and such an awesome and incomprehensible Being who is so far above us in every way?

In reading through the Bible, from the Old to the New Testament, we see a progression in the type of relationships God invites humans to have with Him. The traditional Jewish approach to God, illustrated throughout the Old Testament, is as a servant approaching his Master. Jesus greatly expanded this relationship with His disciples when He called them His "friends" (John 15:15 NKJV).

Yet the highest expression of the relationship God desires to have with us is not Master to slave, Friend to friend, or even Father to child; it is Husband to wife, a marriage relationship. We see this in the grand culmination of the Bible story presented in the book of Revelation. The redeemed of all humanity are presented in splendid perfection to Jesus Christ to be His wife for all eternity (Revelation 19:7-9; 21:9-27).

Many Christians have become accustomed to thinking in a very abstract and "spiritual" way about this marriage relationship that God desires to have with us. They have no trouble believing that a glorious wedding feast will take place at the end of time. But there is so much more to this spiritual marriage relationship than that future culminating event.

What about our personal relationship with God today? The Scriptures we have been studying so far (such as Ephesians 5:21-32, quoted above) speak as if we were *already married* to God. While it is true that the heavenly marriage celebration described in the book of Revelation is the ultimate fulfillment of God's plan for humanity, many Scriptures make it plain that those who believe in Jesus Christ today are already in a "one flesh" union with Him. As Ephesians 5:30 states, we are already "members of his body" (NRSV).

In Chapter 2, we reviewed the Apostle Paul's explanation of why fornication is wrong:

> The body is not meant for sexual immorality, but for the Lord, and the Lord for the body . . . . Do you not know that **your bodies are members of Christ himself?** Shall I then take **the members of Christ** and unite them with a prostitute? Never! Do you not know that he who unites himself with a prostitute is one with her in body? For it is said, "The two will become one flesh." **But he who unites himself with the Lord is one with him in spirit. . . . The wife's body does not belong to her alone but also to her husband. In the same way, the husband's body does not belong to him alone but also to his wife.** (1 Corinthians 6:13, 15–17; 7:4 NIV)

It is quite obvious here that the marriage of Jesus and the Church is not something that will begin at some distant point in the future: it has *already begun.* Paul is speaking about life here on earth *today.* In God's eyes, each individual Christian is *now* in a "one flesh/one spirit" marriage with Jesus Christ. From His standpoint, our bodies are no longer ours alone but must be shared with Him—just as a husband and wife no longer have sole ownership of their own bodies but must share them with their spouse.

Most Christians are comfortable with the imagery of being "born again" to describe our relationship with God. This comparison was used by both Jesus and Peter to help us understand what happens to us when we first begin our relationship with God. But *the new birth is just the beginning of our relationship*. Fewer Christians feel as comfortable with the imagery of marriage to describe our *continuing* relationship with God, perhaps because marriage involves sexual union. Yet, as we have seen, the concept of our being married to God is used throughout the Bible and has much to teach us about a *mature relationship* with Him.

We saw earlier in Ezekiel 16:6-8 a description of how God's relationship with the Jewish people changed over time. I believe this passage also illuminates for every Christian how our relationship with God changes as it matures. At first, He must rescue a suffering infant, then care for a child as she grows into womanhood. Only when she has become a young woman, ready for mature love, does God take her to be His wife.

So many of us desperately need to grow up spiritually! We need to reach spiritual maturity so that we can begin this mature phase of our love relationship with God. An infant may love his parents to the full extent he is able, but such a love relationship is very imbalanced. It is based primarily on the parents' love—their meeting the infant's needs and always being there to comfort and answer his every cry. How different his infantile love is from the love his parents have for each other, or the love he will someday feel for a young woman as he reaches maturity. If such a child fails to mature mentally because of some disorder, his parents will still love him and care for him, even though he would continue to express a childish form of love for them. Yet, as we all recognize, this would be less than ideal.

When the Holy Spirit first penetrated your heart and impregnated you with the sperm of the Word of God, your spirit was reborn. But that was just the beginning of a never-ending love affair Jesus wants to have with you.

The Song of Songs is a beautiful poem in the Old Testament, describing the romantic love between a king and his bride. This work has been interpreted by both Jews and Christians over the centuries as speaking of God's love for the nation of Israel and for the Church. Going even further, Christian leaders from many centuries and many lands have taught that this love poem has a deeper message. It describes the love affair that God desires to have *with each person* who will seek Him.[1]

Here are just a few passages from this poem that speak of the passionate intimacy of mature romantic love:

> Let him kiss me with the kisses of his mouth—
> for your love is more delightful than wine.
> Pleasing is the fragrance of your perfumes;
> your name is like perfume poured out.
> No wonder the maidens love you!
> Take me away with you—let us hurry!
> Let the king bring me into his chambers.
> (Song of Songs 1:2-4 NIV)

> You have stolen my heart, my sister, my bride;
> you have stolen my heart
> with one glance of your eyes,
> with one jewel of your necklace.
> How delightful is your love, my sister, my bride!
> How much more pleasing is your love than wine,
> and the fragrance of your perfume than any spice!
> Your lips drop sweetness as the honeycomb, my
> bride; milk and honey are under your tongue.
> The fragrance of your garments is like that of
> Lebanon.
> (Song of Songs 4:9-11 NIV)

> How beautiful you are and how pleasing,
> O love, with your delights!
> Your stature is like that of the palm,
> and your breasts like clusters of fruit.
> I said, "I will climb the palm tree;
> I will take hold of its fruit."

May your breasts be like the clusters of the vine,
the fragrance of your breath like apples,
and your mouth like the best wine.
May the wine go straight to my lover,
flowing gently over lips and teeth.
I belong to my lover,
and his desire is for me.
Come, my lover, let us go to the countryside,
let us spend the night in the villages.
Let us go early to the vineyards
to see if the vines have budded,
if their blossoms have opened,
and if the pomegranates are in bloom—
there I will give you my love.
(Song of Songs 7:6-12 NIV)

Who is this coming up from the desert leaning
on her lover? . . .
Place me like a seal over your heart,
like a seal on your arm;
for love is as strong as death,
its jealousy unyielding as the grave.
It burns like blazing fire,
like a mighty flame.
Many waters cannot quench love;
rivers cannot wash it away.
If one were to give
all the wealth of his house for love,
it would be utterly scorned.
(Song of Songs 8:5-7 NIV)

Can you imagine yourself expressing such passionate feelings of love toward God and He toward you?

Three Essentials of Marital Love

We need to understand three important aspects of marital love to see how they illuminate the mature love relationship God desires to have with us.

1. Passion

> For love is as strong as death. . . .
> It burns like blazing fire,
> like a mighty flame.
> (Song of Songs 8:6 NIV)

The foundation of any great romance is always a passionate desire for one's beloved. You will do whatever it takes to be with the one you truly love above all others. Examples of the heights such passion can reach are celebrated in the folklore of every culture. Stories are often told of lovers who sacrifice everything to be with their beloved. Some even end their own lives if their union becomes impossible, rather than live on without the other.

God has always had just such a passionate love for us. He has given each of us so many gifts and blessings in His steadfast pursuit of our hearts. Jesus has already laid down His own life out of His love for us. But God is looking for a passionate response from *us*. He is waiting and watching for us to leave the selfishness of childhood behind and enter spiritual maturity, when our passion for Him will awaken.

His first and greatest commandment was given to us through Moses and was reiterated by Jesus. It reveals just how passionately He desires our love:

> "And you shall love the LORD your God with all your heart, with all your soul, with all your mind, and with all your strength." This is the first commandment. (Mark 12:30 NKJV)

117

We can see such a passionate desire for God expressed in the poetry of the book of Psalms:

> As the deer pants for the water brooks,
> So pants my soul for You, O God.
> My soul thirsts for God, for the living God.
> When shall I come and appear before God?
> (Psalm 42:1-2 NKJV)

> Whom have I in heaven but You?
> And there is none upon earth that I desire besides
> You. (Psalm 73:25 NKJV)

> My soul longs, yes, even faints for the courts of the
> LORD; my heart and my flesh cry out for the living
> God. (Psalm 84:2 NKJV)

Other Scriptures encourage us to have this kind of passionate desire for God, but with one requirement: God will reward us with His presence only if we seek Him earnestly with our whole being.

> You will seek me [God] and find me **when you seek
> me with all your heart.** (Jeremiah 29:13 NIV)

> And without faith it is impossible to please God,
> because anyone who comes to him must believe that
> he exists and that **he rewards those who earnestly
> seek him.** (Hebrews 11:6 NIV)

2. Intimacy

> Let us go early to the vineyards . . .
> there I will give you my love.
> (Song of Songs 7:12 NIV)

In a loving marriage, your mutual passion for each other drives you to seek time alone together where you can become more intimate, where the two of you can become one. This is a time of tremendous mutual pleasure and satisfaction, as you come to fully know and enjoy one another. You express your deepest longings for each other. You adore each other. You worship each other.

This observation may be startling to some, but allow me to explain what I mean. *The expression of intimate, affectionate marital love is truly a form of worship.* Some people tend to think of worship as an ethereal religious emotion that should be expressed to God in a formal way, such as through a carefully composed hymn or prayer. Yet we often use this word informally in a romantic context, such as, "He *worships* the ground she walks on." This romantic aspect of worship is even acknowledged in the traditional wedding vows: "With this ring I thee cherish, with my body I thee *worship.*"

Well, what does the word *worship* really mean? *Worship* (from the Anglo-Saxon *worthship,* meaning "to attribute worth") in its most general sense means "giving special honor or devotion to someone, expressing the worth or value that another has to you, performing acts of devotion, or expressing intense love or admiration for someone." Although the meaning of this word has changed over time to mean mainly the reverence we show toward God, modern dictionaries still specify that *worship* can mean "to intensely love or admire a person."

The Apostle Paul further blends these two ideas of worship—worship that belongs to God and worship that belongs to a spouse—as he teaches us about the necessary differences in the relationships that single and married Christians have with God:

> An unmarried man is concerned about the Lord's affairs—how he can please the Lord. But a married man is concerned about the affairs of this world—how he can please his wife—and his interests are divided. An unmarried woman or virgin is concerned

about the Lord's affairs: her aim is to be devoted to the Lord in both body and spirit. But a married woman is concerned about the affairs of this world—how she can please her husband. (1 Corinthians 7:32-34 NIV)

We know that God will not permit us to worship any other gods (Exodus 20:3). That is adultery of our relationship with Him, and His passion for us makes Him very jealous of our love. But we see here that He permits married Christians to divide their worship—their concern, interest, attention, efforts to please, and acts of devotion in body and spirit—between Himself and a spouse. A single Christian is married only to God "in both body and spirit," but a married Christian is married both to God and to his or her spouse, so there must be some compromises.

Paul described an example of such a compromise earlier in this passage. In speaking of a couple's obligation to meet each other's sexual needs, he made one exception:

Do not deprive each other except by mutual consent and for a time, **so that you may devote yourselves to prayer.** (1 Corinthians 7:5 NIV)

The only reason to take a break from spending time in your earthly spouse's arms is so you can spend that time in your heavenly Spouse's arms.

We have been studying how God designed marriage to teach us about the kind of relationship He desires to have with us. But there is still one more aspect of this relationship we need to explore. If we are truly in a "one flesh" marriage with Jesus Christ, so that our spirits and bodies are one with Him (1 Corinthians 6:13, 15-18), if we truly have as passionate a love for Him as He has for us, *then how and when do we "have sex"?* Every married couple must have sex, because that is what creates a marriage in the first place. That is how they satisfy their longing and passion for each other. That is how they express their mutual love and affection.

Well, if loving, affectionate sex between a husband and wife represents a way that they worship each other, then what does our loving, affectionate worship of God represent in our relationship with Him? The answer should be obvious.

Through sex, a husband and wife *express* their love for each other with all their heart, soul, mind, and strength, thus fulfilling one of their greatest desires in this life. Likewise, through worship, you can express your love for God "with all your heart, with all your soul, with all your mind, and with all your strength" (Mark 12:30 NKJV), thus fulfilling *His* great desire and, ultimately, yours as well.

> **THROUGH WORSHIP, YOU CAN EXPRESS YOUR LOVE FOR GOD.**

Worship is the fulfillment of the first and greatest commandment.

True worship requires that there be *intercourse* between God and us. The word *intercourse* means "the communication or exchange of ideas and feelings." A husband and wife are said to have *sexual intercourse* when the intimate affections exchanged between them have a sexual component. Our worship of Jesus Christ is not "sexual" intercourse,* but it is certainly intercourse. It involves the most intimate expressions of love, flowing back and forth. It is a loving communion between you and Jesus, Jesus and you.

We really need to start looking at worship in this new light. Worship is so much more than going through the motions of singing a few hymns on a Sunday morning. True worship is offering your whole being to your Husband for His pleasure and fulfillment as you learn to yield, respond, and take pleasure in His touch.[2] If you have ever felt the touch of the presence of God, then you know what I am talking about. If you have not yet experienced His touch, then seek Him with all your heart. Reach out to love Him with all your heart, soul, mind, and strength, and you soon will.

---

* I want to make it quite clear that I am in no way referring to Christians really having sexual intercourse with a spiritual being that claims to be Jesus Christ. This is a type of demonic deception that has reportedly happened to some. For a discussion of this, see Chapter 5, the section titled "Demonic Seduction."

3. Bonding and Fruitfulness

> Who is this coming up from the desert
> leaning on her lover?
> (Song of Songs 8:5 NIV)

When sexual union has been achieved between a husband and wife, a powerful bond is established between them. Their spirits, souls, and bodies are sealed together. This "one flesh" union is the goal and result of all the passion and intimacy that preceded it. There will also be fruit from this union. Children will be conceived and born.

Similar things happen when a Christian becomes intimate with God. He has always held us firmly in the bond of His love. Yet when we learn to have intimate communion with Him, it changes our hearts' response to Him. Our love for Him and attachment to Him are greatly deepened. We will bear fruit from receiving His Word implanted in us: the fruits of the Spirit—"love, joy, peace, longsuffering, kindness, goodness, faithfulness, gentleness, self-control" (Galatians 5:22-23 NKJV)—and spiritual children, those who receive from us the good news about Christ.

One passage quoted above from the Song of Songs speaks of the Beloved as wearing fragrant perfumes: "Pleasing is the fragrance of your perfumes; your name is like perfume poured out. No wonder the maidens love you!" (Song of Songs 1:3 NIV). We all know that if a woman spends hours in the arms of her lover, then whatever cologne he is wearing is going to get all over her, and she will carry his scent with her wherever she goes.

> For we are to God the aroma of Christ among those
> who are being saved and those who are perishing. To
> the one we are the smell of death; to the other, the
> fragrance of life. (2 Corinthians 2:15-16 NIV)

Jesus has His own glorious fragrance in the spiritual realm. As you spend hours in His arms, His fragrance will permeate you, so that you will begin to smell like Him. This fragrant perfume comes from the *anointing* (meaning "to rub with fragrant oil") of the Holy Spirit. Wherever you go, people will begin to react to you as they would to Him. Demons will begin to react to you like they would to Him, because when you walk into a room, *they can smell Him all over you.*

As your bond with Jesus deepens, it becomes the strong, mature kind of love that faith requires if it is to reach its full potential. There is a certain minimum amount of faith required to initially seek after God. You must believe that He, indeed, exists and that He will answer your call (Hebrews 11:6). But the faith that works through love (Galatians 5:6) is much more powerful, because it comes from a firsthand, experiential knowledge of His nature and His character. You know *what He will do* because you now know *who He really is.* This kind of love, and the faith that comes with it, is strong enough to bear fruit—to have spiritual children and raise them through any kind of hardship (Hebrews 11).

Jesus said, "For where two or three come together in my name, there am I with them" (Matthew 18:20 NIV). When your church meets each week, a special presence of Jesus is there with you. That is the time for the bride of Christ to become intimate with her Husband. As she worships and adores Him, her deepest longings are satisfied, her love for Him is strengthened, and she receives His seed—His Word—into the center of her being. The Holy Spirit is there to bring the Word to life and cause her to become "pregnant." In due time she will give birth to spiritual fruit.

Now, a woman who is too busy to spend time in her husband's embrace may be accomplishing many wonderful things, but the one thing she cannot do is have his babies. Inevitably, her union with him will also weaken. I think this should signal a warning to many churches today. I see so many churches working so hard at so many things. Yet we need to ask ourselves, if we spend all our time in a constant whirl of activities among ourselves, and if our meetings do not center around quiet, intimate times with Jesus, what will be the result?

The church at Ephesus had a multitude of good works, yet Jesus rebuked them because they had forsaken their "first love"—*Him!* Even if we are bearing spiritual fruit or spiritual children, we must ask ourselves, "Are they His kids? Do they have His genes?" Or have we been spending time in the arms of other lovers? The end of a sexless marriage is almost always barrenness, coldness, adultery, and divorce.

When I counsel single men and women, they often share with me their great longing for a mate. Some have searched for years, yet still have not found the right person. More than a few have done some foolish things because of the overwhelming power of their desires. We would all agree that the emotional and sexual need for a mate is one of the most powerful longings we can experience.

But I ask you to consider, how long has God been waiting for fulfillment in the arms of His wife? How great is His desire for our love? I believe it very likely that one reason God designed us to feel the pull of such powerful sexual passion is so that we can get an idea of the power of His passionate desire for us.

"The Spirit which He has caused to dwell in us yearns jealously over us" (James 4:5 Weymouth). He is indeed a passionate, jealous Lover. And each of us has the power to give Him what He so longs for, or to turn away from Him while we pursue other things, other loves.

Unmarried Christians need to finally and fully understand this fact: you are not "single"; you are married to Jesus. You are already in a "one flesh" and "one spirit" union with your Lover that is going to last for all eternity. But you have a choice. You can either begin to explore and enjoy the rich fulfillment and contentment that can be found in your Husband's arms, or you can resist His affectionate advances while you pursue other lovers. If your Lord chooses to share you with another spouse for a few years of marriage on this earth, well, that is a wonderful thing. But if not, you have the opportunity to get a head start on enjoying "the real thing" for which earthly marriage is only a training ground.

For thousands of years the Jewish people performed sacrificial rituals—life-and-death dramas whose express purpose was to explain God's long-term plan to redeem humanity through the sacrifice of Himself in the person of Jesus, the Messiah. These rituals were a pattern, a type, a foreshadowing of that which was to come, and they have now ceased since their purpose has been fulfilled.

For an even longer period—since Adam and Eve—men and women have been joining in marriage. Though it certainly offers many practical benefits for this life, marriage is also a pattern, a type, a foreshadowing of that which is to come. Its deep purpose is to teach us about God's ultimate plan for humanity.

Jesus said:

> The people of this age marry and are given in marriage. But those who are considered worthy of taking part in that age and in the resurrection from the dead will neither marry nor be given in marriage, and they can no longer die; for they are like the angels. (Luke 20:34-36 NIV)

Like the Jewish system of rituals, marriage will also end when its purpose has been fulfilled. Its symbolism, its role as a training exercise, will be replaced by the real thing—the final and complete fulfillment of God's eternal, burning passion to be united with humanity.

Notes.

1. Watchman Nee, Theresa of Avila, and Madame Guyon are just a few examples of renowned Christian teachers who have taught the Song of Songs as lessons in developing an intimate relationship with God. A good introduction is *The Song of Songs* by Watchman Nee (Fort Washington, PA: Christian Literature Crusade, 1965). Another more recent book on this subject is *Passion for Jesus* by Mike Bickle (Lake Mary, FL: Creation House, 1993).

2. This deeper understanding of the importance of corporate worship as a time of intimate communion between Jesus Christ and His bride is becoming more widely recognized. Here are some good resources for studying this subject further: Vivien Hibbert, *Prophetic Worship* (Dallas: Cuington Press, 1999); Ruth Ward Heflin, *Glory: Experiencing the Atmosphere of Heaven* (Hagerstown, MD: McDougal Publishing, 1990); Tommy Tenney, *The God Chasers* (Shippensburg, PA: Destiny Image Publishers, 1998).

PART II

CONFRONTING SEXUAL
PROBLEMS IN THE CHURCH
TODAY

VII

The Kingdom
of Sexual Perversion

Although the purpose of this book is to address the sexual problems that exist in churches today and to renew our vision of what God intended sex to be, it is essential that we come to recognize and understand those forces that are working to oppose God's purpose and plan for human sexuality.

In the first part of this book, we have studied how God's Law of Sexual Union is the foundation for a marriage between a man and a woman, enabling them not only to have children, but also to raise them within the nest of the loving relationships that we call a family. As history proves, families have formed the basis of every society ever known. Nuclear families, consisting of a husband, wife, and children, are joined into extended families through a rich network of relationships between grandparents, aunts, uncles, cousins, and in-laws. Intermarriage among many extended families who live in the same locale for generations eventually produces a clan or tribe. Groups of tribes then form states and nations.

So we can see that any forces that work to destroy the marital bonds between husbands and wives, or hinder young men and women from forming those bonds, are attacking the very foundation of human society.

We have also studied how God designed human sexuality and the family to reveal important truths about Himself and the relationship He desires to have with us. Since the dawn of Creation, God knew that no matter how far people retreated from His presence or how much they might forget of the words He had spoken, yet, within His plan for marriage and family, everyone would have the opportunity to learn the following basic lessons.

Through a mother we learn of God's tenderness and nurturing love; through a father, God's loving protection, provision, and discipline; through a spouse, what it is like for God to love us so intensely that He desires for us to become one with Him; through our children, how God could love us so much that He would even lay down His own life for us so that we might live.

Viewed in this light, we can see that any force that seeks to destroy normal human sexual development and its loving expression through marriage and family is an attack against *the very revelation of the knowledge of God Himself*. Every child who grows up without a loving father and mother, every youth whose developing sexuality is damaged through some trauma such as molestation or pornography, every young adult involved in a series of sexual relationships outside of marriage—these have all been hindered in his or her ability to approach or understand God, and to fully enjoy the loving relationship with Him that He so desires and that we all need so desperately.

So what exactly is *sexual perversion*? The most obvious meaning is *any sexual problem or practice that destroys marital bonds or prevents people from forming healthy marriage relationships*. But at its core, *sexual* *perversion is **anything that opposes the knowledge of the intimacy of the Godhead's relationship or His relationship with us**.* (It has taken me years of study to formulate this one principle.)

In today's society we see many forces at work to destroy marriage and family, including those that would even undermine normal heterosexuality and its expression within marriage. But unless we realize that there is a monumental spiritual evil orchestrating and driving these forces—attacking not only society's foundation of healthy families, but also the very capacity of humankind to know and love God—then we are missing the full truth of what is happening. We will, therefore, be ill-equipped to do battle against these destructive forces in our own families, churches, and communities.

There is truly a war going on, not just between sexual holiness and perversion, not just between moralists and libertines, but between God and Satan—and humanity is the great prize.

> And there was war in heaven. Michael and his angels fought against the dragon, and the dragon and his angels fought back. But he was not strong enough and they lost their place in heaven. The great dragon was hurled down—that ancient serpent called the devil, or Satan, who leads the whole world astray. He was hurled to the earth, and his angels with him. . . . Exult therefore the heavens, and you who are sheltered in them! Woe to the earth, and to the sea!—because the Devil has descended to you, in great fury, knowing that his time is short. (Revelation 12:7-9, 12 Fenton)

As this passage illustrates, Satan and his minions rebelled against their Creator and were rejected by Him. Having lost their original place in heaven and their relationship with God, and being destined to eternal torment, they hate humanity with a fierce passion fueled by their hatred of God and their jealousy of His great love for us.

So it is no wonder that, in the time they have left to wander this earth, they are using every means available to destroy humanity, not only by trying to make life on earth as miserable as possible, but by drawing away as many of us as they can to share their own fate—an eternal banishment from the presence of God—thus robbing God of His beloved children.

Satan and his demons are evil beings of great power, yet we do not see them marauding openly and destroying people directly through supernatural means. In studying the Bible and the record of human history, we see that God's laws do not permit such acts. Instead, Satan is limited to working upon us through an appeal to our minds, using a variety of deceptions, lies, and temptations. It is with good reason that Jesus called him the "father of lies" (John 8:44).

Like a puppet master, he can act on the stage of human history only by turning people into puppets, each one pulled along and manipulated by strings of deception. It is only through his human puppets, then, that we see his plans for the destruction and damnation of the human race put into effect—through human mouths and human hands. Yet when these strings of lies are cut through by the truth, then his power to cause us to harm ourselves, our families, and our societies is broken.

Human nature is certainly corrupt enough on its own. But being basically self-centered, it does not knowingly attempt to destroy itself, its own culture, or those it loves. To do so, it must be subverted through some form of deception and manipulation. This is why it is so vital for us as Christians to know and unashamedly declare the full truth about the sexual problems our society is facing.

As we consider the vast array of ideas, messages, trends, opinions, leaders, and movements that are working to attack and destroy healthy sexuality and family life, we must not lose our perspective on the spiritual forces operating behind the scenes.

We are not fighting against humans. We are fighting against forces and authorities and against rulers of darkness and powers in the spiritual world. (Ephesians 6:12 CEV)

It should come as no surprise that Satan has recruited a great number of talented, educated, and powerful people to serve as his spokespersons. Since he is neither omnipotent nor omnipresent, if he is to influence great masses of people, he needs all the help he can muster. In fact, he needs an entire army of beautiful, articulate, charming, and charismatic individuals who are able to hold the public's attention while they communicate his deceptive messages or model a destructive lifestyle. He needs highly respected men and women with expertise and authority whose words can shape public policy. He needs talented artists who can construct works of great beauty that conceal devastating lies. He needs highly educated people of great intelligence who can construct elaborate systems of half-truths and deceptions that can be used to justify anything and deceive just about anyone. He needs highly successful businesspeople to "make things happen" and fund the whole operation.

These are Satan's modern-day "prophets of Baal." They include many of our finest entertainers, artists, writers, media personalities, advice columnists, educators, researchers, politicians, businesspeople, and even some religious leaders. These are all being deceived and manipulated by demonic forces in such a way that, under the illusion of fighting for a noble cause, they will gladly use every resource they have available to undermine and obliterate the knowledge of God's purpose and plan for marriage and family, replacing sexual morality and normality with every possible perversion. This great army of demonic manipulators, their human puppets, the carefully constructed falsehoods they proclaim, and the millions of souls they hold captive—this is *the Kingdom of Sexual Perversion.*

The Ancient Kingdom

For millennia the Kingdom of Sexual Perversion existed openly, its demonic origin apparent to all. In the Old Testament law God found it necessary to give quite an extensive list of forbidden sexual practices, evidently because these were so common in the nations surrounding Israel at that time. Both Old and New Testament passages reveal that perverse sexual practices were often part of pagan rituals of worship to demon gods. Priests and priestesses of these pagan religions often served as prostitutes for these obscene rituals.

The ancient Greek and Roman civilizations provided fertile ground for popular cults, known as *mystery cults*, which traced their origins back to ancient Babylon. Their gods, such as Aphrodite and Dionysus, were the gods of sex and fertility. They worshipped images of the naked human body and of the sex organs. Their sacraments were sex acts, and their religious services were orgies.

It was against this background that Jesus founded the first-century church. Many of the first believers were, no doubt, converted from among the mystery cults. That is why it is not at all surprising to see from the New Testament writings that sexual sin was a considerable problem in the churches of that day; they lived in a society that was permeated by it.

As Christianity spread across Europe, it was opposed by the native pagan religions. Like all known primitive societies, the European tribes sought to appease and receive favor from the spirits that lived around them (these were, in reality, demons posing as demigods). Like the mystery cults, a great number of their rituals centered around sexual themes and perverse sexual practices as a means of ensuring the fertility of their crops, flocks, and families. We see vestiges of these rites in traditions that are still being practiced today in Europe and America, though the original meaning has been lost.

Surely everyone has heard by now that Easter, which is named after the Babylonian fertility goddess *Ishtar* (*Oester*, in German), was originally a pagan fertility celebration that was appropriated by the church. That is why the holiday is associated with eggs and rabbits. These were elements used in the pagan rituals. The Old Testament mentions *ashtoreth*, which were large phallic pillars used in the worship of Ishtar. Yet, how many people realize American and European children today still dance around such ashtoreth poles in a dim echo of ancient rites? The custom of dancing around May poles is descended directly from such pagan fertility rituals. *A May pole is an ashtoreth.*

The key point here is that *the origin of the Kingdom of Sexual Perversion is found in false religion.* Yet, in today's modernized, rational, scientific culture, religion is out of favor. So, Satan has had to adapt his tactics. The Kingdom of Sexual Perversion has had to take on a new secularized form.

The Modern Kingdom

The modern Kingdom of Sexual Perversion has been designed to harmonize with Western culture's highest secular ideals of "self-fulfillment" and "freedom of the individual." It is based not on magical rites, but on government-granted rights. For example, the right of free speech is used to protect pornography. The right of personal privacy is used to protect abortion and every conceivable sexual act. The right of personal freedom is used to mandate that divorce be made simple and convenient. The right of equality is used to grant special privileges to those who identify themselves as gay or lesbian.

As if all this were not enough, over the past few decades, some who control the entertainment industry, the media, and the academic community have invented a new fundamental moral principle and have been exerting all their efforts to convert every American to their point of view. Since Americans seem so obsessed with their "rights," this new moral principle is being presented as a fundamental human right, the right of *Total Sexual Indulgence.* Simply stated, it is this:

> *Any and all types of sex acts between any group of consenting individuals are entirely good and are to be encouraged. Every sexual desire should be indulged to the fullest. Anything that interferes with the exercise of this basic human right can and should*

be eliminated by any means necessary. Anyone who criticizes or in any way tries to discourage others from practicing total sexual indulgence must be punished.

This is the central creed of the modern Kingdom of Sexual Perversion. This is what makes it a new secular religion, where sexual indulgence is the ultimate and universal good. Those who follow this creed are saying, in effect, that *sexual lust is their god*, because it is given first consideration when making other moral decisions.

An illustration of just how accepted this principle of Total Sexual Indulgence has become can be found in the recent sexual scandal involving President Clinton and a young intern. What is so disturbing about the whole incident is not that President Clinton had an adulterous affair, but that he believed he was entirely justified in lying to a grand jury and to the American people about it because of his "right to privacy." Indeed, he believed he was justified to such an extent that he should be exempt from the legal penalties for perjury. What is even more horrifying (if the polls are to be believed) is that the overwhelming majority of Americans *agreed with him,* condemning those who had dared to breach his sexual privacy and had tried to fulfill their legal duty to prosecute him for perjury.

SEXUAL LUST IS THEIR GOD.

One of the most perverse consequences of this corrupt creed is that the "sanctity" of sexual indulgence is given precedence over the sanctity of human life. Clear proof of this consequence in action can be gleaned from current events.

Abortion provides perhaps the most obvious example. Since the advent of "abortion rights," men and women have been given the freedom to indulge in promiscuity while aborting any inconvenient "products of conception" that result. But medical science has advanced so far since *Roe vs. Wade* that we are now seeing incredible and completely illogical consequences. Infants born three to four months premature are kept healthy, at great cost, in special incubators. Yet, just down the hall, infants of exactly the same age with no medical problems whatsoever are delivered, killed, and thrown in the trash in so-called "partial-birth abortions."

Thus, the recent rash of teenage moms (and dads) who have had their babies in secret, killed them, and then dumped them in the trash should really not surprise us. Many times these were not "troubled" teens, but popular, church-going, "good kids" who were just acting on the moral principle they had been taught: a child is just a lump of tissue unless it is "wanted."

These teens are not truly being prosecuted for murder, but for exposing the hypocrisy of our abortion laws. If these teen moms had only asked a doctor to deliver and kill their babies even a week earlier, everything would have been fine. (No doubt, some charity would even have volunteered to pay for it.) Killing healthy babies is completely legal in America today, if it is done the "right" way. So, to their minds, having the baby in secret and killing it themselves was no different morally. It just saved them the cost and embarrassment of going to an abortion clinic. Sexual shame also played a great role in these dramas because these girls did not want their parents to know they had been having sex.

Another area in which we see Total Sexual Indulgence exalted over the value of human life is in the academic, governmental, and media responses to the problem of sexually transmitted diseases (STDs). As we have already seen, the true dangers of STDs are far greater than most Americans realize.* We like to think of ourselves as the most educated and informed society on earth. Yet, in this area, most remain ignorant and terribly at risk. Why? Because the media and public agencies have chosen, again and again, to minimize and suppress the terrible truths researchers have uncovered about STDs. Instead of giving us the harsh truth, they bombard us with misinformation and seductive ad campaigns for "safe sex" techniques (now renamed "safer sex" after the hypocrisy of the original label became too obvious). These campaigns encourage promiscuity while merely reducing the risk from "very high" to "moderately high" that

---

* See Appendix B for a summary of the latest findings on the dangers of STDs.

people will contract an incurable or deadly disease. It is as if they were to produce an ad campaign saying, "Practice safer Russian roulette. Never load the gun with more than one bullet."

It would seem that preserving the current climate of "sexual liberation" and preventing sudden outbreaks of chastity is far more important to media moguls and opinion leaders than protecting Americans from a lifetime of suffering or an early death from STDs.

The Perversion of Science

A characteristic of modern society is our almost worshipful awe of science and medicine. Science has provided us with the tremendous wealth, luxury, and technological prowess that we enjoy today. Medicine has become the only hope for many against the onslaught of aging, disease, and death. Yet the principle of Total Sexual Indulgence has also infiltrated and subverted the scientific and medical communities, proving that its dark hold over the human mind is much stronger than a mere concern for scientific truth.

"PRACTICE SAFER RUSSIAN ROULETTE. NEVER LOAD THE GUN WITH MORE THAN ONE BULLET."

To spread this doctrine, any form of misrepresentation or distortion seems permissible. Some scientists distort the implications of their research. The media consistently report only information that supports this doctrine and suppress any information that might cause the public to question it.

The infamous Kinsey sex surveys, done in the 1940s, are the premier example of how this is done.

Kinsey was a zoologist who deeply believed that every form of sexual perversion (including pedophilia and his own homosexuality) was normal, healthy, and to be encouraged, while heterosexuality was the only abnormal sexual practice. His stated agenda was to radically change American society so that the principle of Total Sexual Indulgence would become the norm. His chosen tool for accomplishing this agenda was to publish the results of surveys purporting to show that sexual perversion was already widespread in American society and thus was "normal."

His publication of *Sexual Behavior in the Human Male* and *Sexual Behavior in the Human Female* were widely acclaimed as heralding a new era of sexual freedom. These books made startling claims, such as that 10% of Americans are homosexual, and 36% of American men have had same-gender sex.* These claims were soon reprinted in every textbook on human sexuality and trumpeted by those in the media who also wished to advance the cause of "sexual liberation." Even today, these claims continue to serve as the unquestioned authority for many popular works on human sexuality and as justification for much misguided public policy.

However, for decades, many in the academic community have known that Kinsey's work is nothing more than a massive deception, a piece of "social engineering" designed to fool the public and change the prevailing morality. Though he advertised them as such, Kinsey knew his surveys were not at all representative of the American public. To get the results he wanted, he deliberately recruited people who had a disturbed sexuality. He advertised for homosexuals and those practicing other perversions. At least 25% of his surveys were conducted with prisoners, many of whom had been convicted of sexual offenses. Perhaps the most horrifying fact to come to light is that he *deliberately recruited active child molesters and trained them to record and report the sexual responses of the children they molested.* Documents show that even infants were forcibly masturbated by these men to observe and record their sexual response. Of course, Kinsey believed that sex between adults and children was a learning experience for the child and entirely beneficial.[1]

Because of his total disregard of scientific and statistical principles, Kinsey's results are now regarded as *meaningless* by those who research American sexual behavior today. However, they must carefully word their opinions, since he and the Kinsey Institute he founded are still so highly regarded by the uninformed. So, we still see new textbooks and news articles

---

* The best and most recent figures for these behaviors are given in Chapter 8.

making erroneous claims about American sexual behavior and advancing the cause of Total Sexual Indulgence, all based on Kinsey's research.

Why does such deception continue? The facts about Kinsey's research errors have never been hidden. Many of his own colleagues severely criticized his work on these very grounds while it was still being done in the 1940s. The continuance of this flagrant deception is just more evidence of a massive conspiracy among our academic and media elite to lead Americans down the path of sexual license, using every means available, including the promulgation of outright lies disguised as scientific fact.

Since the "sexual revolution" of the 1960s, the latest campaign for this conspiracy is to make the practice of homosexuality a normal and even preferred status in our society. Following in Kinsey's steps today are quite a number of "scientists" who have proven they are willing to do anything, including compromising scientific principles, to advance their agenda of social change. Many of those who have published research claiming to prove that homosexuality is entirely biological and completely unchangeable are actually gay political activists posing as scientists. They earnestly believe that the best hope for finding public acceptance of their own gay lifestyle is to prove that it is something over which they have no control—it is just the way evolution made them. Since these people know no god but science, they turn to their god seeking approval and absolution for their sexual abnormality. Their own colleagues have dismissed their findings, yet the press is still eager to print front-page stories based on their discredited research, claiming the proof for "gay genes" and "gay brains" is just around the bend.

Such overwhelmingly biased publicity has had its desired effect. This campaign is now essentially won. Only some mopping up of scattered pockets of resistance remains to be done. Public opinion and prevailing political forces have now been directed to give homosexuality the same legally protected status as race, gender, disability, and *religion* in every public and private arena.

The effects of this victory are rapidly spreading. Researchers dare not even propose research projects that might cast doubt on the foregone conclusions of the homosexual agenda. Professors have had their careers threatened if they dared to question the spurious research that provides the foundation for this agenda. Employees of large corporations have already been fired or demoted, not because they expressed hatred or contempt toward lesbians and gays, but because they stated their honest belief that homosexual behavior is morally wrong and treatment is available for those who wish to change. Psychologists and psychiatrists—who have had a long tradition of treating sexual perversions such as homosexuality—now risk censure by professional organizations and the threat of legal action if they dare to treat someone who asks for help in getting rid of unwanted same-sex desires.

One of the most significant political victories, soon to have widespread effects, is an executive order signed by President Clinton in May of 1998. By placing sexual orientation in the same category as race or disability, this order requires government agencies, government contractors, state and local governments, and all who receive federal money to prove they are not discriminating against those who label themselves gay or lesbian by taking "affirmative action," which means instituting hiring preferences and quotas. Enforcement of this order is in the hands of Elaine Kaplan, a lesbian activist appointed by Clinton to head the Office of Special Counsel, which has the power to investigate and prosecute those it deems not in compliance with the order.

Perversion 101

Even now, in public schools across the country, teachers are being trained by gay activists to recognize youth who may be unsure of their sexuality and support them as they try to figure out whether they prefer sex with boys, girls, or both.[2] According to an organizing manual published by a coalition of gay activist groups working to change public schools, (called P.E.R.S.O.N., Public Education Regarding Sexual Orientation Nationally), "The struggle for equal LGBT [Lesbian, Gay, Bisexual, Transsexual] rights must move into the K-12 classrooms. This is where information is conveyed and attitudes formed."3

A similar organization, called the Gay, Lesbian, and Straight Education Network (GLSEN), has been quite successful with a more subtle approach. They claim they are not promoting homosexuality in the schools, but only trying to prevent hatred and persecution of homosexual youth by educating teachers and students about *"homophobia,"* which means *an unreasonable hatred or fear of homosexuals*, through "gay sensitivity training." However, a close examination of their literature shows that their ultimate goal is to have homosexuality presented to school children, beginning in kindergarten, as an equally acceptable alternative to heterosexuality. Along with other gay political groups, they apply the label "homophobic" to anyone who opposes their agenda, even for religious reasons. Their programs teach children that "homophobic" is the moral equivalent of "racist."

The National Education Association (NEA) has fully supported these groups' agendas for the public schools, having "passed a resolution supporting the celebration of Lesbian, Gay, Bisexual History Month in October, promoted diversity training for students, backed the introduction of [Gay/Lesbian] issues into the curriculum, and changed its previously heterosexist language."4

Within the next few years, any public school teachers who refuse to fully support and participate in such perversion indoctrination programs will undoubtedly find themselves out of a job.

This is the *new* "new morality" parents need to be concerned about—that "gay is OK" and "bi is better." According to this view, adolescence is a time for learning and new experiences, so whatever children want to do sexually is just great. In fact, they *need to experiment* by having sex with both boys and girls to see which they like best. That way, they can choose a sexual and cultural identity from among the choices presented to them by our public schools: gay, lesbian, bisexual, transsexual, or straight. For the "lesbigay" youth of today, there are support groups, special programs, and special schools designed to provide them with lesbian/gay/bi/trans role models, teach them the principles of lesbian/gay/bi/trans culture, and even help them learn the sexual practices common among those with their chosen sexual identity.

It is tragic that teens with disturbed sexuality are being encouraged in their perversion instead of being offered therapy. This new morality teaches them that "lust is destiny." There is no hope for change. The only way to be happy is to give in to all your desires, not fight them.

However, there is also a great danger in this message for heterosexual teens, since early sexual experiences have lifelong effects. Heterosexual teens *can* learn to enjoy homosexual behavior and can even become addicted to it. Though they may not lose their heterosexual feelings, they do lose their initial disgust toward homosexual behavior, so that it becomes a temptation.

As always, public school officials and teachers will tell the children that their parents are uninformed and prejudiced. As we have already seen with premarital sex, birth control, and abortion, whatever the children decide, the political, legal, and educational systems will too often support them—and help them to act against their parents' beliefs and wishes.

Yet, despite all these "advances," those who advocate total sexual indulgence have shown they will not be satisfied until our whole society is in a state of total sexual perversion.

Total Sexual Perversion

The campaign to officially "normalize" homosexuality achieved its first major victory in 1973 when the American Psychiatric Association decreed that homosexuality was no longer a disorder unless a person felt negatively about his homosexual feelings *(ego-dystonic homosexuality)*. This strengthened the efforts to make homosexuality socially acceptable, legally protected, and now, actively encouraged among school children. In 1994, the American Psychiatric Association made significant changes to its diagnostic manual (DSM-IV). Many feel that these modifications have begun a similar normalizing process for *all sexual perversions, including pedophilia.*[5]

According to noted conservative psychiatrist Dr. Jeffrey Satinover:

> Now, in order for an individual to be considered to have a paraphilia—these include sadomasochism, voyeurism, exhibitionism, and, among others, pedophilia—the DSM requires that in addition to having or even acting on his impulses, his "fantasies, sexual urges or behaviors" must "cause clinically significant distress or impairment in social, occupational or other important areas of functioning." In other words, a man who routinely and compulsively has sex with children, and does so without the pangs of conscience and without impairing his functioning otherwise is not necessarily a pedophile and in need of treatment. Only the man who suffers because of his impulses is a pedophile requiring treatment.[6]

The current consensus among all major American associations of health care professionals is that any therapist who attempts to help someone overcome homosexual feelings is committing an unethical act. It is fast reaching the point where those who still offer this type of therapy risk censure by their professional organizations and loss of their licensing and privileges. They may even open themselves up to lawsuits. The official position now is that therapists should only treat such people to free them from their *guilt* about same-sex desires and *to help them overcome any inhibitions, such as religious beliefs, that keep them from acting on such desires.*

Following the twisted logic now laid out by DSM-IV, such a policy toward the treatment of all sexual perversions seems inevitable. It may be only a matter of time before even pedophiles are treated only to help them overcome their *guilt* for being sexually attracted to children, not for the attraction itself. This may seem unbelievable and incomprehensible to many of us who wonder, "What about the damage sexual molestation does to the children?"

Amazingly enough, while there is a wealth of evidence from the therapists who treat molested children that molestation is quite harmful, there is no unanimity on this among psychologists and psychiatrists. Over the years, numerous papers have been published questioning the harmfulness of molestation. Some have actually claimed that a child may *benefit* from being molested.

A major review of all the "evidence" on this topic was published by an official journal of the American Psychological Association in 1998.[7] The authors' conclusion was that any psychological harm to children resulting from sexual abuse was very slight and most likely was caused by negative attitudes about the abuse within the child's family. If the child had "willingly" participated and "enjoyed" the sexual activity, no harm would result.[8] Two authors of this study have previously made known their pro-pedophilia views in other publications.

This certainly clears the way for treating child sexual abuse as a minor offense in the future, and there is no doubt that this paper will soon be used to defend pedophiles in court. A small but vocal group of psychiatrists and psychologists are busy making the case for this very thing.[9]

For example, Dr. John Money—world-renowned sexologist, professor emeritus at Johns Hopkins University, recipient of numerous honors from the American Psychiatric Association—has given us his views on "adult-child sex":

> If I were to see the case of a boy aged ten or eleven who's intensely erotically attracted toward a man in his twenties or thirties, if the relationship is totally mutual, and the bonding is genuinely totally mutual *then I would not call it pathological [unhealthy] in any way.*[10]

THIS CAMPAIGN TO LEGITIMIZE ALL SEXUAL PERVERSION . . .

This campaign to legitimize all sexual perversion, including pedophilia, is just one example of how even the most educated and sophisticated people can become no more than puppets, deceived and manipulated by demonic forces pulling at their strings. They can easily defy all logic—except the perverse logic of the principle of Total Sexual Indulgence.

In Summary

It should come as no surprise to spiritually aware Christians that the issues and forces we must confront today are essentially no different from those faced by the New Testament believers or the Israelites in Old Testament times. Though customs and lifestyles have changed over the centuries, human nature has not changed at all.

We must learn to perceive the spiritual realities beneath the surface of events. Those same demonic powers that designed the ancient mystery cults and used them to enslave our ancestors still roam the earth today. They are still seeking the forms of worship to which they have become accustomed, yet they must deal with our secular, materialistic society.

The demon Molech (see Leviticus 20:2-5; 2 Kings 23:10) is still seeking, and finding, those who will offer up the blood of innocent children for which he thirsts. He has just turned his temples into abortion clinics and his altars into surgical suites. The demon Ishtar is still seeking those who will worship her with every sexual perversion, but now she can find all the supplicants she desires through the "sex industry," or in the many places in every town where prostitution and public sex are taking place each day.

Yet we must keep in mind that many of those enslaved by the Kingdom of Sexual Perversion are former and future citizens of the Kingdom of God. For all their brazenness and fanaticism, this is a group of very confused, very lost, very damaged people who are suffering much inner pain. There is no true love in the culture of sexual indulgence. Lust reduces the person it desires to a piece of a three-dimensional pornography to be used and then discarded. Lust drives an endless cycle of using others to satisfy selfish desires or of being used by others and then being discarded when they grow tired of you.

Why do you think Jesus spent so much time with prostitutes and the other outcasts of his day? I believe it was because, of all the people He met, they were the most desperately needy and, thus, the most responsive to His love.

Let me ask the Christians who are reading this book: When is the last time you had lunch with a prostitute or a gay/lesbian/bisexual/transsexual?

Notes.

1. These facts come from Judith A. Reisman and Edward W. Eichel, *Kinsey, Sex and Fraud* (Lafayette, LA: Huntington House, 1990).

2. Such "sexual orientation sensitivity training" provided by the Gay, Lesbian, and Straight Education Network has already been done for counselors in the Dallas Public Schools and is scheduled to be completed for all staff by the fall of 1999. ("Sensitivity Training," *Dallas Voice*, 25 September 1998). A similar program has been temporarily halted in the suburb of Mesquite due to parental objections. ("Gay Youth Workshop Canceled," *Dallas Morning News*, 21 February 1999).

3. From "The P.E.R.S.O.N. Organizing Manual," Introduction, version 1.4, release date February 1996.

4. Ibid.

5. *Diagnostic and Statistical Manual IV* (Washington, D.C.: American Psychiatric Association Press, 1994).

6. Jeffrey Satinover, *Homosexuality and the Politics of Truth* (Grand Rapids: Baker Books, 1996). This excellent work documents in great depth how the mental health field has been infiltrated and subverted by the kingdom of sexual perversion. See also, "Pedophilia Not Always a Disorder?" *NARTH Bulletin*, April 1995, p. 1.

7. Bruce Rind, Philip Tromovitch, and Robert Bauserman. "A Meta-analytic Examination of Assumed Properties of Child Sexual Abuse Using College Samples," *Psychological Bulletin* 124 (July 1998): 22-53.

8. Much of the "data" in this study was nothing more than a series of interviews with college students about how they remembered incidents of being sexually abused and how they felt about the abuse. A thorough analysis of this study and the growing acceptance of pedophilia within the psychological community is contained in "The Problem of Pedophilia," published by the Encino, California-based National Association of Research and Therapy of Homosexuality (NARTH), December 1998. It is available at: www.narth.com.

9. *The Journal of Homosexuality* (Haworth Press)—a scholarly journal, found in most university libraries, that publishes psychological papers from a pro-gay perspective—has also published quite a number of articles that are pro-pedophilia, even to the point of describing the therapeutic benefits for a group of delinquent boys who had sex with a male social worker. Its editor, John De Cecco, was quoted in *Newsweek* (1 November 1993) as saying that pedophilia is "not intrinsically" wrong.

10. "Interview: John Money," *PAIDIKA: The Journal of Pedophilia* 2 (spring 1991): 5. Quoted in "The Problem of Pedophilia" (see note 8).

VIII

The Prevalence of Sexual
Problems among Christians

In the second part of this book I want to speak very plainly about the sexual problems that exist today in the lives of Christians and within our churches. To bring healing to a sickness, we must first diagnose it.

In the years I have worked as a Christian counselor, I have had abundant opportunities to learn what is really going on behind the scenes (and under the covers) across a broad spectrum of American churches. It is not a pretty picture! Because I specialize in counseling Christians with sexual problems, I am often called in to help when a church or ministry has been rocked by sexual scandal.

My heart has been broken many times as I have witnessed the destruction brought about by sexual sins upon ministries, families, and individual lives. The sexual scandals we see reported on the evening news, whether of fallen televangelists or local pastors, are just a very small part of a very pervasive problem that is undermining *the whole church*, not just its leadership.

It is no mystery that non-believers become involved in every variety of sexual sin. But the question we desperately need to answer is, "Why are so many Christians, with all the credentials we esteem most highly—born-again, fundamentalist, evangelical, conservative, Bible-believing, Spirit-filled—being ensnared and overcome by sexual sins and problems?" The average Christian sitting in a pew has no idea just how many in his church are secretly struggling with sexual sin—and this very atmosphere of secrecy (and shame) is what perpetuates a true epidemic of sexual sin within our churches.

The topic of "sexual sin" is still wrapped up in layers of shame for most Christians and church leaders. Because of this, many of us just want to stay as far away as we can from the whole subject. We would rather not think about it, not talk about it, and certainly not hear our pastor preach about it on Sunday morning. But this is being "ostrich-minded." We are maintaining our comfort level at the expense of allowing sexual sin to remain unexposed and undealt with.

THE TOPIC OF "SEXUAL SIN" IS STILL WRAPPED UP IN LAYERS OF SHAME FOR MOST CHRISTIANS AND CHURCH LEADERS.

I am afraid that the only cure for being ostrich-minded is a good, hard look at the truth. That is the purpose of this chapter. I have gathered the very latest and best statistics available on the extent of sexual sins and problems among American Christians today, so that there can be no more excuses for avoiding this issue. Every pastor, church leader, and church member needs to know just how pervasive these problems are today in our own churches.

Sexual Sin among Our Leaders

The average American remembers more about the sexual scandals of fallen Christian leaders than about the messages they preached. So, what are the actual statistics on the incidence of sexual sin among church leaders?

- The Presbyterian Church reported 10–23% of clergy have had "inappropriate sexual behavior or contact."

- A survey of Southern Baptist pastors in *The Journal of Pastoral Care* (Winter 1993) reported 14.1% of pastors admitted to inappropriate sexual behavior.
- A United Methodist report showed 38.6% of ministers admitted sexual contact with church members.
- The Survivors of Clergy Abuse Linkup, a support organization for survivors of clergy abuse, estimates that 6–16% of American Roman Catholic priests are active pedophiles.
- The Center for Domestic Violence reports that 12.6% of clergy admit they had illicit sex with church members.[1]
- In a survey by *Leadership* magazine, 23% of pastors who responded admitted to inappropriate sexual behavior and 12% to sexual intercourse with someone other than a spouse.[2]

These statistics are alarming enough, but the biggest issue we need to be concerned about is what is happening in the lives of everyday, pew-warming Christians. Let us examine the most common sexual sins and problems found in our churches. What are the facts?

Divorce

America currently has the highest divorce rate in the world: 25% of Americans who have been married have also been divorced,* 10% of adults are currently divorced, and 4% are separated.[3] Are the numbers any different for the Christian segment of the population?

---

* The much publicized "divorce rate" of around 50%, which is just the ratio of the number of new marriages to the number of divorces *in the current year*, is highly misleading. This is often misinterpreted to mean that every marriage has a 1 in 2 chance of failing. Not so! Only about 1 in 4 of those who have been married have also been divorced. The risk of divorce for any particular marriage is affected by a number of factors, such as cohabitation, length of marriage, and previous divorce. (This topic is explored more fully in *The Future of the American Family*, George Barna.)

Table 8.1		
Divorce/Separation Rate Compared to Church Attendance[4]		
Church Attendance[5]	Currently divorced or separated (%)	Ever divorced or separated (%)
Rarely	16.3	30.9
Occasionally	14.7	26.8
Regularly	9.7	19.3

As Table 8.1 shows, there *is* an inverse relationship between church attendance and divorce. Those who attend church more often show a lower rate of divorce than those who attend less often. But this does not necessarily prove what many would hope: the more you attend church, the less your risk of being divorced. Surveys by the Barna Research Group show that although Christians keep their same religious views after divorce, they become less involved in their church, attend less often, and are more likely to leave the church.[6] So these attendance-based numbers are likely to reflect somewhat of a "church dropout" effect among divorced Christians.

When faced with statistics like these, it is a common temptation to think, "Well, my church could not possibly have that bad of a problem because we are *XYZists*. Those high numbers must be coming from those *other* churches." So, let us look at statistics for different categories of Christians.

Table 8.2	
Divorce Rate Compared to Religious Identity[7]	
Religious Identity	Ever divorced (%)
Non-Christians	23
Born-again Christians	27
Fundamentalist Christians	30
Note: 87% of these divorced Christians had divorced *after* becoming Christians	

A survey by the Barna Research Group compared divorce rates for different types of Christians (Table 8.2). The surprising results revealed higher divorce rates among those who considered themselves "Fundamentalist" or "Born Again" than in the general population. This finding may (and should) be troubling to those churches that are proud of these labels.

Table 8.3 Divorce/Separation Rate among Conservative/Moderate/ Liberal Christians[8]		
	Currently divorced or separated (%)	Ever divorced or separated (%)
Fundamentalist	15.8	31.0
Moderate	11.9	22.2
Liberal	13.7	26.3

Another way to look at divorce rates for Christians is to see how they vary on the spectrum of identity from conservative to liberal, as shown in Table 8.3. Again, those who classify themselves as Fundamentalists seem to show rates of divorce/separation higher than other Christian groups and higher than the general population.

George Barna, who has directed extensive surveys of Christian attitudes and behaviors over the years, sums up the situation in this way: "A person's faith doesn't seem to have a lot of effect on whether they'll get divorced. Even among born-again Christians, most don't exhibit attitudes or behaviors any different than non-Christians."[9]

One other noteworthy difference in divorce rates shows up when comparing Protestants and Catholics. Data from the General Social Survey reveals that 28.3% of Protestants have been divorced/separated versus only 20% of Catholics.[10] This no doubt reflects the fact that Catholic churches are much stricter in their regulation of divorce and remarriage than are Protestant churches.

Adultery

Recent surveys (Table 8.4) indicate that about 10% of married people who attend church regularly (that is, one or more times per week) have committed adultery at some point during their marriage, and 2% have done so within the last twelve months. Marital faithfulness shows a definite connection to church attendance, but conservative labels seem to make little difference. Those who identify themselves as "fundamentalist" or "born-again" *and* attend church once a week or more show similar life-

Table 8.4 Adultery Rate Compared to Church Attendance[4]		
Church Attendance	Committed adultery in the last 12 months	Ever committed adultery
Rarely	3.8	20.9
Occasionally	4.3	16.4
Regularly	2.1	10.3
–And "Fundamentalist"		9.9
–And "Born Again"		8.3

time rates of adultery of around 10% and 8%, respectively.[11]

Those who attend church only occasionally or rarely show about twice the rate of adultery as those who attend every week. But again, we must be careful in speculating about the connection. Does being in church every week make you less likely to commit adultery or do those who have committed adultery find themselves reluctant to attend church as faithfully as they had in the past? Adultery occurs most often when there are existing problems in a marriage, problems that can lead to divorce, particularly when the adultery is discovered; and we have already seen evidence that divorced Christians tend to drop out of church.

Yet we must ask, "If church membership and weekly attendance do, indeed, serve to restrain the impulse toward adultery, is it *enough* of a restraint? Is the current adultery rate of around 8-10% among *the most faithful Christians* acceptable as a norm?"

Premarital Sex

For nearly a century now, American society has shown a trend of increasing rates of premarital sex. The average age of first marriage has been rising while the average age of first sexual intercourse has been dropping.[13] Because social and economic pressures are encouraging young adults to marry later (around 25–27 years of age), they must learn to restrain their sexual desires over ten to fifteen years of celibacy if they wish to remain virgins until marriage. This fact, combined with the attitude of sexual permissiveness that pervades modern society, means that young adults today face much more sexual temptation than their parents or grandparents ever did, who typically married at around 18–20 years of age.

As might be expected, most American youth are giving in to temptation, but it is still a shock to realize just how many. A national survey in 1992 found that for married couples aged 18–24 only *2% of the husbands and 5% of the wives were virgins on their wedding night.*[14]

What about the state of sexual purity among Christian singles? Table 8.5 shows the percentages of single adults, 18–24 years of age, who have had premarital sex since turning 18, compared with their church

Table 8.5 Premarital Sex Compared to Church Attendance[15]		
Church Attendance	Never-married adults (18-24) who have had sex since 18 (%)	
	Men	Women
Rarely	91.2	94.4
Occasionally	87.7	91.6
Regularly	68.3	66.1
–And "Fundamentalist"	54.8	59.3

attendance. Again, regular church attendance is associated with lower rates of premarital sex (68/66%) while the lowest rate is found among Fundamentalists who attend church regularly (55/60%).

Many studies have shown that American teens are starting to have sex earlier and are having more sexual partners; and as they grow older, more become sexually experienced.[16] Table 8.6 shows how the rate of sexual experience increases among American high school students as they grow older.

Statistics on sexual experience among Christian youth under the

Table 8.6 Sexual Experience among American High School Students[17]	
Grade	Sexual Intercourse (%)
9th	38.0
10th	42.5
11th	49.7
12th	60.9

age of 18 are much harder to find. However, a 1994 survey of Christian teens from thirteen evangelical denominations revealed that though the rates of premarital sex among conservative, church-going Christian teens are lower than that of their unchurched peers, they show the same trend of increasing sexual experience as they get older (Table 8.7). By 18, 27% had had premarital sex and 44% had participated in mutual genital fondling.

Just as troubling were their moral views on premarital sex. Only

Table 8.7 Sexual Experience among Evangelical Christian Teens (1994)[18]			
Age	Grade (Approx.)	Genital Fondling (%)	Sexual Intercourse (%)
13-14	8th - 9th	14	8
15-16	10th -11th	30	18
17-18	12th	44	27

45% thought genital fondling between unmarried people was always wrong and only 38% thought premarital intercourse was always wrong.[19]

On the positive side, these statistics show that being a committed Christian does reduce the incidence of premarital sex among young people. But since up to 45% are willing to excuse some premarital sexual activity under certain circumstances, it is evident that far too many of our youth lack a clear understanding of exactly *why* sexual purity is so important.

This perhaps explains why the commitment of Christian youth to biblical standards of sexual behavior wavers and weakens in the face of temptation that grows with each passing year. From the trend revealed in these numbers (5% more have intercourse with each additional year), it is easy to see how, eventually, *55–60% of the most conservative, church-going young adults aged 18–24 have had premarital sex*, compared with 90–95% of their nonreligious peers (Table 8.5).

The principle of "saving yourself for marriage" is the one clear message about sex taught most consistently to youth by all conservative churches. So these disappointing statistics should be a wake-up call to parents and church leaders. They are a sign that we must thoroughly reevaluate *what* and *how* we are teaching our children about sex. We need to have our eyes opened to see the "real world" in which our youth are living and our ears opened to hear what they are really thinking and believing.

Bible-based abstinence programs, such as "True Love Waits," are certainly a step in the right direction. Yet researchers caution that it is premature to credit these programs for the slight drop in rates of premarital intercourse among teens that occurred in the 1990s. Those numbers may be concealing the fact that some teens have substituted other sexual practices for vaginal intercourse and so remain "technically" virgins. One study found that 35% of ninth to twelfth graders who had never had vaginal sex nevertheless had experienced either mutual masturbation, oral sex, or anal sex.[20]

We must look not only at what we are teaching about the meaning of sexual purity, but also at such things as our acceptance of secular dating practices and the current social trend to delay marriage. Whatever we have been doing until now, it is clearly not enough, especially when we look at the statistics for the frequent consequence of premarital sex: abortion.

Abortion

After three decades of heated public controversy over abortion, and with all the campaigns waged by conservative Christian groups who oppose it, there is still one aspect of the issue that we do not often hear discussed: Christian women who have abortions—especially, *Christian women from churches whose doctrinal position is pro-life* who have abortions.

The statistics on this situation are truly shocking:

- 1 in 4 women who attend church regularly has had an abortion.[21]
- 70% of abortion clients say they have a church affiliation and 27% attend church weekly;[22] 37% are Protestant and 31% are Catholic.[23]
- Nearly 1 in 5 (18%) abortion clients describe themselves as "born-again" or Evangelical Christians (up from 16% in 1987).[24]
- 81% of women who have abortions are unmarried.[25]
- 30% have an abortion because they do not want others to know they are pregnant or have had sex.[26]

This last statistic is perhaps the most telling. Secular opinion leaders have worked strenuously over the past three decades to remove from the public conscience all vestiges of shame about premarital sex or illegitimate births—and they have achieved complete success. Never before has the world seen high-profile single women (such as Madonna or Rosie O'Donnell) become objects of mass adulation for choosing to have babies on their own, often fathered by anonymous "sperm donors."

So where do those 30% of abortion clients come from who still feel shame about being pregnant and unwed? The only possible place left is from conservative pro-life church backgrounds, *where there is still so much shame attached to having premarital sex and being an unwed mother that these young women choose infanticide over public humiliation and rejection by their church and families.*

Notice that Evangelical "born-again" Christians constitute 18% and Catholics 31% of all American women having abortions. Put these two numbers together and you will realize *49% of all the women having abortions in America are from pro-life churches.* Even if pro-life demonstrators never picketed another abortion clinic, the number of abortions in America *could be cut in half* if pro-life churches could only convince their own members not to have abortions!

Remember, every young, church-going Christian woman who gets pregnant outside of marriage did so with the help of a young man, most likely from her church group. That nearly doubles the number of young conservative, pro-life Christians who are involved in premarital sex and infanticide.

Yet, how many pro-life churches are truly taking the time, making the effort, and really *succeeding* at getting across to their young people a message like: "Honey, we all know premarital sex is wrong, but if you do get pregnant (or get a girl pregnant), we will forgive you and stand with you and help you have that child because there is no reason on earth to kill that precious baby."

Few churches seem to be really accomplishing this, and the statistics bear this out. The truth is, in these numbers we are seeing the fruit of decades of our own compromise, of accommodation, of taking the easy way out instead of dealing honestly with sexual problems. To radically change this situation, it is going to require radical changes in how our churches are confronting *all* the issues of human sexuality.

Pornography

The problem of pornography is exploding in Western society, perhaps in large part because society as a whole no longer considers it a problem (except for child pornography). The American porn industry takes in more than 8 billion dollars a year, making it the world's largest. The amount Americans spend on porn each year exceeds our combined spending on movie tickets, rock music, and country/western music.[27]

Porn's general availability has been greatly expanded through the medium of the Internet. For the millions of people who now spend hours a day working, studying, or shopping on the World Wide Web, the ability to view pornographic images has never been easier, and the temptation has never been greater. Even those who do not wish to view porn can scarcely avoid it, since many of the major portals and search engines used for navigating the Internet now flash unsolicited porn ads across their computer screens many times each day.[28] For those who are tempted, just pressing a single button is all that is necessary to view a series of free porn images before they are asked to pay for more.

However, the pornography industry is not the real problem facing the church. The real problem is Christian men who are addicted to pornography, some since childhood, who find no one in their church is even talking about the problem, much less extending a hand to help them get free.

One group that *is* addressing this problem among Christian men is Promise Keepers. Through their prayer groups and training materials, they confront Christian men with the negative effects of pornography addiction and provide help to overcome it.

Nevertheless, a three-year study of men who attended the 1994–1996 Promise Keepers conferences showed that 33% admitted they "enjoy looking at sexually oriented material" and 16–17% had "purchased pornographic material in the past year."[29] Men who attend these meetings are, for the most part, highly committed Christians from a broad spectrum of conservative churches, so it seems likely that these statistics present an accurate picture of the use of pornography in such churches.

Homosexuality

This former unmentionable has been capturing headlines for more than two decades now. Fighting political battles with "gay rights" groups has become the new great cause for Christian political activism. Yet there is still a dark secret that no one wants to talk about: Where are all these gays and lesbians coming from? (They are certainly not reproducing themselves the way true minority groups do.)

The answer is . . . from the church! Eighty-three percent of men and 92% of women who have had same-gender sex within the last year were raised in church.[30]

Is there any Christian family today that does not know of a family member or someone in their church who has suddenly "come out of the closet" to join the gay subculture? Yet how many churches, in addition to raising a battle cry against the encroachments of gay political groups, are proactively extending help and hope to their members who are secretly wrestling with same-sex attraction? The lack of just such a compassionate attitude is why so many of these people, who were raised in the church, become alienated, convinced that the church has no answer to their problem and really does not want them around. Meanwhile, the gay underworld is beckoning to them with open arms.

Though some do leave the church where they grew up to seek a new identity as "gay" or "lesbian," many do not. They choose to remain faithful church members but keep their problem deeply hidden.

The latest statistics on the incidence of homosexual behavior in the general population and in the church are shown for men in Table 8.8, and for women in Table 8.9.

The figures in these tables reveal some interesting things.

The rates of same-gender sex among men show no relationship to church attendance. They are virtually the same in the general population as among those men who attend church one or more times a week. This is not so for women. The rates of same-gender sex are more than doubled among women who attend church rarely (once a year or less). But no one would

Table 8.8
Sexually Active Men Having Same-Gender Sex (%)[31]

	In Last 12 Months	In Last 5 Years	Since Age 18
All men	3.0	3.9	5.9
By Church Attendance			
Rarely	2.7	4.1	5.9
Occasionally	2.5	3.5	5.6
Regularly	3.0	4.2	6.2
By Self-identification[32]			
Fundamentalist	2.3		
Born-Again	5.0		

Table 8.9
Sexually Active Women Having Same-Gender Sex (%)[33]

	In Last 12 Months	In Last 5 Years	Since Age 18
All women	2.0	2.9	4.6
By Church Attendance			
Rarely	3.4	4.7	6.6
Occasionally	1.3	2.2	4.3
Regularly	1.3	2.1	2.9
By Self-identification[34]			
Fundamentalist	1.3		
Born-Again	<1		

dare argue that this is evidence that churches are more successful in ministering to women than to men who experience same-sex attraction.[35] The truth is that very few conservative churches even realize that a significant number of their members have this problem, much less try to minister to them. They still view homosexuality as primarily a political issue of "us" versus "them," not realizing the problem is just as much "in here" as it is "out there."

When the figures for men and women are combined (based on the proportionate attendance of men and women), they show that roughly 2% of *faithful* church members (who attend one or more meetings per week) have had same-gender sex within the last year and 4% have done so since turning 18.[36] These are not gay political activists, but church members who are there every week—though they know their behavior contradicts accepted Christian teaching on sexual morality and are likely to be experiencing much inner turmoil over the conflict between their sexual desires and their beliefs.

I have found, in working with pastors, that the more conservative churches seem to have the greatest difficulty in accepting this fact: homosexuality is a problem that occurs among their members at about the same rate as in the rest of society. That is why I have included statistics for those who identify themselves as "Fundamentalist" or "born-again." The problem of same-gender attraction and same-gender sex is most likely to remain hidden in the very churches that condemn it the most fervently. They are also the least likely to offer practical help in overcoming it since their members "obviously" do not have such problems.

A disturbing trend among today's teenagers is the growing fascination with bisexuality. For several years now, public schools have been teaching acceptance of bisexuality and homosexuality. School counselors and guest speakers from the gay community repeatedly encourage teens to "come out" and be identified as gay or lesbian if they feel any degree of same-sex attraction. Hollywood and MTV have been consistently preaching the message that androgyny is "in," "bi" is now "cool." A record number of teen movie idols and rock stars now openly proclaim their bisexuality (for example, male rock stars Marilyn Manson and Michael Stipe, actress Drew Barrymore, singers Courtney Love and Ani Difranco). Thus, a common attitude among teens is, "Maybe I should try it (same-gender sex) to see if I am gay or bi." Unfortunately, no one has warned them that same-sex experimentation in the teenage years can lead to a lifelong struggle with abnormal sexual compulsions.

A 1998 study reveals that 2.5% of teens are now openly identifying themselves as homosexual. It also found that these teens engage in life-threatening behaviors—such as drug use, dangerous sexual practices, and suicide attempts—at twice the rates of heterosexual teens.[37] An earlier study showed that as many as 10% of all teens are unsure of their sexual orientation at some point during adolescence.[38] Since, as we have seen, rates of homosexuality are roughly the same within the church as in the general population, I believe these figures also apply to Christian teens: 10% experiencing some sexual confusion and 2.5% eventually accepting a gay identity (though they may be hiding it from their family and church).

How many churches are consistently reaching out to their members who are secretly struggling with same-sex attraction? How many are frankly discussing with their youth the problems of same-sex attraction, confusing sexual feelings, and the bisexual trend in youth culture? The great tragedy is that churches are so ignorant of this situation that many of our own children feel they must struggle alone with problems of sexual confusion. Few church youth leaders are able to talk about this issue openly and offer help to those who may be suffering in silence. All most teens hear from Christian leaders today is criticism of gay political groups with the implicit message that "Christians do not have this problem," and if they do, they have only themselves to blame. Meanwhile, gay activists are able to preach their message freely to our kids through the public schools, the Internet, and the media to try to convince them that if they feel any sexual confusion at all, their only recourse is to abandon the church and accept a new identity as gay or lesbian.

The Southern Baptists stand out as one of the few conservative denominations to begin to openly address this issue within their own churches. In January of 1999, they introduced some new Sunday school lessons on homosexuality, designed to offer hope for change to their members who are struggling with homosexuality and to educate everyone else on how to deal with the issue.[39]

Molested Children

For many years now, America has been suffering from a hidden epidemic: our children are being sexually molested. Solid statistics have been difficult to determine for several reasons. Surveys often classify borderline "noncontact" abuse—such as "flashing" or exposing a child to explicit pornography—in different ways. Also, it is believed that many incidents of sexual abuse go unreported until years later due to the overwhelming guilt and shame experienced by victims. Boys, in particular, seem to be very reluctant to report such incidents.

In any case, the most recent estimates by experts in this field are that *25–35% of girls and 10–20% of boys will be sexually abused.*[40] That is *1 in every 3 to 4 girls* and *1 in every 5 to 10 boys.* This seems almost unimaginable to the average person when he looks at a playground full of children and realizes the odds they are facing.

The evidence continues to mount that children who are sexually abused can suffer long-term emotional damage, resulting in many behavioral problems. But there is also evidence that the damage is greatly lessened or avoided when such children receive help in dealing with their feelings about the abuse. There is also evidence that children who receive proper training can avoid becoming victimized. There is an urgent need in our churches for those who work with children to be educated about pedophiles and learn how to prevent them from infiltrating child care programs.

Truly, the most tragic situations I have been asked to deal with involve Christian children who are molested in a church child care facility by a Christian worker. This is totally unnecessary and completely preventable. Yet it continues to happen because Christians would rather not think about such things. So their children are not forewarned and church workers are not trained to prevent abuse. No one wants to believe that a Christian could feel sexual attraction toward children, but some do, both *men and women.* The best time to help them and prevent them from ever acting on their desires is during the teenage years when these abnormal desires first appear. (In many cases, these desires may result from their own sexual abuse as children, for which they have never received help.)

In Summary

These statistics are the very best I could find on the incidence of sexual problems within American churches. My purpose is to emphasize one simple point: *even the most faithful Christians in the best of churches are subject to the same sexual problems that are rampant in our society— and at the same or nearly the same levels.* Because this fact has not yet "sunk in" for most Christian leaders, the response of churches to prevent and heal these sexual problems among their members has been inadequate at best.

> FAITHFUL CHRISTIANS IN THE BEST OF CHURCHES ARE SUBJECT TO THE SAME SEXUAL PROBLEMS.

Pastors and leaders, next Sunday when you stand on the platform and look out over the sea of faces staring back at you, I want you to keep in mind this profile of your most faithful members, the ones who are there week after week. The odds are:

• 1 in 4 has been or will eventually be divorced (1 in 3, if your church is Fundamentalist). 1 in 10 is currently divorced/separated.

• 1 in 10–12 has already committed or is headed for adultery. 1 in 50 did so in the last year.

• 1 in 50 had same-gender sex in the last year.

• 1 in 3 men enjoys pornography and 1 in 6 purchases pornography.

• 1 in 4 of the youth will have premarital sex by age 18.

• 1 in 10 of the youth is experiencing some degree of confusion about sexual orientation.

• One-half to two-thirds of the young adult singles

aged 18–24 have had premarital sex.

• 1 in 4 women has had an abortion.

When you look at the crowd of happy children in your Sunday school classes, remember that the odds are that 1 out of every 3–4 girls and 1 out of every 5–10 boys will be sexually abused before reaching adulthood. A similar number of adults in your church were sexually abused as children and are likely to still be suffering from unresolved emotional or sexual problems because of it.

Church members, when you look up at the church leaders on the platform, or the next time you meet with one for counseling or prayer, remember that 1 in 4–10 church leaders becomes involved in some form of improper sexual behavior with a church member.

I hope that seeing these startling figures all at once will provoke some sincere self-examination among our leaders:

> • Do you truly know the extent of these sexual problems in your own church or denomination?
> • Are the truths about these problems being taught and discussed freely in your congregation?
> • Has your church put safeguards in place to protect people from falling into these problems?
> • Are you offering restoration to those who have already fallen and counseling to help ensure that they will overcome their weakness in the future?
> • Or does your church prefer not to even think about such things, much less hear them discussed on Sunday morning?

Even after being confronted with these facts, perhaps some are still convinced that there is no need to take drastic action because the fine people in their church do not have these problems. (Or perhaps if they do, then they are no longer welcome there.)

Unfortunately, this last attitude is the one I see most commonly in churches today, particularly when I am called in to help after a sexual scandal has shaken a congregation. It is this very conspiracy of silence and a fearful ignorance, rooted in a deep shame about sexual matters, that creates a dark and fertile environment in which sexual problems can grow unhindered until they reach fruition. In far too many churches, those who do fall find only ostracism and unending shame instead of loving restoration.

Because God has called me to minister to those who are sexually broken, I have spent countless hours studying the spiritual, biological, and psychological roots of sexual problems. The more I have learned, the more convinced I have become that there is something deeply and fundamentally wrong with how most churches are handling the whole area of sexuality and its many problems. That is why these problems have continued to increase in our churches until they have reached the same record levels as in our society.

At the heart of this predicament is the fact that Christian leaders, for the most part, are still failing to first address sexual problems *within the church and among Christians* with frankness, accuracy, and compassion before venturing out to "fix" society. So many of the resources of the church are being focused outward to fight political battles against cultural enemies and against the manifestations of sin in our society. Many raise money and stage protests to voice their opposition to pornography, abortion, and gay political initiatives. Though such efforts have their place, I suspect a deeper reason they hold our attention is that they are *comforting diversions*. Keeping busy with all these external problems is so much easier than turning our attention inward to address the roots of these problems within ourselves, our own families, and our churches.

(That such political efforts are necessary at all is a sign that the American church has been losing ground in terms of evangelism. Political maneuvers directed at thwarting the will of the majority in a democratic society are ultimately just a holding pattern. They are not the actions of a victorious, advancing army, but a retreating one, fighting desperately to hold on to each bit of ground.)

Perhaps some truly believe that if we reduce the availability of the various temptations in the society surrounding us, then we have solved the problem. But the real problem is, and has always been, what is *within* the human heart, not what is outside of it (Matthew 15:11).

So many times when I hear leaders speak to their churches about sexual sins and problems, they are preaching only the Old Testament message instead of the New. "Thou shalt not" is the message of the Old Testament law, which cannot cure sin but only makes it weigh more heavily on the conscience (Romans 7:7-24). Christians involved in sexual sin already know what they are doing is wrong, though some may be trying to rationalize it or to just not think about it. What they are *not* hearing from the church is a message of hope and reconciliation—only condemnation, shame, and rejection. So, for many there seems to be no way of escape.

The only way to truly confront these sexual problems within the church and bring real change is to provide clear and detailed teaching on the specific sexual sins in which people can become trapped. However, this must be accompanied by a compassionate offer of help: "We still love you, no matter what you have become involved in, and we are ready to give you whatever practical help and support you need in your struggle to get out of it."

Many churches are just now coming to this realization concerning drug and alcohol addictions. We have learned that such addictions have deep roots in the bodies, souls, and spirits of those addicted. To become truly free often requires more than just responding to an altar call. It takes a long-term commitment from others to help these addicts tear down a lifetime built on deception and rebuild their lives on a foundation of truth (Galatians 6:1-2). It is now time for the church to apply these same principles to sexual addictions.

> "WE STILL LOVE YOU, NO MATTER WHAT YOU HAVE BECOME INVOLVED IN, AND WE ARE READY TO GIVE YOU WHATEVER PRACTICAL HELP AND SUPPORT YOU NEED IN YOUR STRUGGLE TO GET OUT OF IT."

Recall the warning Jesus gave His followers about the religious leaders of His day:

> The teachers of the law and the Pharisees sit in Moses' seat. So you must obey them and do everything they tell you. But do not do what they do, for they do not practice what they preach. They tie up heavy loads and put them on men's shoulders, but they themselves are not willing to lift a finger to move them. (Matthew 23:2-4 NIV)

This passage contains a vital message for those of us in leadership. God has given us *spiritual authority,* but with it comes a *responsibility to shepherd His people* ("Moses' seat"). Can you see how merely telling those caught in sexual sin, "Thou shalt not," without helping them find the way out of their mess is just what the Pharisees were doing? It is easy to condemn sinful behavior, to use the Word of God to put a heavy load on people's backs. But are we willing to "lift a finger" to help them in their struggle to escape? Are we ready to honestly face and overcome the sexual sin in our own lives?

In Galatians 6:1-2 the Apostle Paul gave us a commission:

> Brothers, if someone is caught in a sin, you who are spiritual should restore him gently. But watch yourself, or you also may be tempted. Carry each other's burdens, and in this way you will fulfill the law of Christ. (NIV)

What does Paul mean by "restore him gently" and "carry each other's burdens"? Is that just giving an altar call, leading in a quick prayer of repentance, and issuing a stern warning not to do it again? I believe much more is required.

Throughout the rest of this book, we will be addressing practical ways to fulfill the Galatians 6:2 commission. I have found the most powerful tool available for healing the sexual brokenness in our churches is simply the truth. We must begin by recognizing the prevalence of sexual problems in the Church, but we also need practical knowledge of how such problems originate, how to help people avoid them, and how to bring healing to those who are trapped in them.

Notes.

1. All of the preceding statistics were collected and published by the Survivors of Clergy Abuse Linkup, Inc. on their website at http://www.thelinkup.com/stats.html.

2. "How Common is Pastoral Indiscretion?" *Leadership* 11 (winter 1988): 12-13.

3. Current divorce and separation statistics obtained from the General Social Survey (GSS) data set through 1996 (Marital question), collected by the National Opinion Research Center, University of Chicago. These are full-probability, in-person surveys of adults living in the USA. The statistics were generated from the GSS data by the survey Documentation and Analysis Tool, which is made available to the public (at http://csa.berkeley.edu:7502) by the Computer-assisted Survey Methods Program, University of California, Berkeley.

4. From the General Social Survey data set through 1996 (see note 3). Cross-tabulations on (MARITAL, ATTEND) and (DIVORCE, ATTEND).

5. Many demographers report on church attendance instead of church affiliation because it has been shown to be a stronger predictor of other behaviors. Church attendance in this and the following tables was classified as follows: Rarely – once a year or less; Occasionally – less than once a week, but more than once a year; Regularly – once a week or more.

Additional statistics from the Barna Research Group ("Data & Trends: Answers to Frequently Asked Questions," available on the WWW at barna.org) help clarify the significance of denominational ties and religious self-identification of Americans:

• 43% of adults and 34% of teenagers are born again (that is, "they have made a personal commitment to Jesus Christ" that is still important to them today and believe "they will go to Heaven because they have confessed their sins and have accepted Jesus Christ as their Savior")

• 15% say they are "evangelical"

• 25% say they are "fundamentalist"

• 29% are Catholic

• 20% are Baptist

• 22% attend a mainline Protestant church

• 5% attend a nondenominational, Christian church

6. George Barna, *The Future of the American Family* (Chicago: Moody Press, 1993), 82-83.

7. Report entitled "Family In America," Barna Research Group, 1992. These findings are also confirmed by the General Social Survey data (see note 3) showing that 27% of those who claimed to be "born again" had been divorced versus only 25% of those

who were not. (Statistics generated for cross-tabulation on EVDIV, REBORN.)

8. From the General Social Survey data set through 1996 (see note 3). Cross-tabulations on (MARITAL, ATTEND) and (DIVORCE, ATTEND).

9. Jim Killam, "Don't Believe the Divorce Statistics," *Marriage Partnership Magazine* 14 (summer 1997): 46.

10. From the General Social Survey data set through 1996 (see note 3). Cross-tabulations on (MARITAL, ATTEND) and (DIVORCE, ATTEND).

11. From the General Social Survey data set through 1996 (see note 3). Cross-tabulations on (EVSTRAY, ATTEND, FUND) and (EVSTRAY, ATTEND, REBORN).

12. Tom W. Smith, *American Sexual Behavior: Trends, Socio-Demographic Differences, and Risk Behavior* (Chicago: National Opinion Research Center, University of Chicago, December 1998), 46. (Based on the General Social Survey conducted through 1998.)

13. Ibid., 3, 29. The median age for first marriage in 1960 was 22.8 for men and 20.3 for women. By 1997, this had become 26.8 for men and 25.0 for women. In 1970, 4.6% of 15-year-old girls had premarital intercourse. By 1988, 25.6% had done so.

14. Findings from the National Health and Social Life Survey performed by the National Opinion Research Council in 1992. (E. O. Laumann et al., *The Social Organization of Sexuality: Sexual Practices in the United States* (Chicago: University of Chicago Press, 1994), 329-330.

15. Tom W. Smith, 46 (see note 12).

16. Tom W. Smith, Table 1, "A Summary of Studies," 25-34 (see note 12).

17. Laura Kann, Steven A. Kinchen, Barbara I. Williams, James G. Ross, Richard Lowry, Carl V. Hill, Jo Anne Grumbaum, Pamela S. Blumson, Janet L. Collins, and Lloyd J. Kolbe, "Youth Risk Behavior Surveillance – United States, 1997," MMWR, 47 (14 August 1998): 1-89.

18. "1994 Churched Youth Survey," Barna Research Group, published in Josh McDowell, *Right From Wrong* (Dallas: Word Publishing, 1994), 269.

19. Ibid.

20. Mark A. Schuster, Robert M. Bell, and Davis E. Kanouse, "The Sexual Practices of Adolescent Virgins: Genital Sexual Activities of High School Students Who Have Never Had Vaginal Intercourse," *American Journal of Public Health* 86 (November 1996): 1570-1576.

21. Marcia Ford, "When Abortion Comes to Church," *Charisma* (July 1996).

22. "What They Didn't Tell Me about Abortion," *Today's Christian Woman* 18 (September /October 1996): 74.

23. Stanley K. Henshaw and Kathryn Kost, "Abortion Patients in 1994-1995: Characteristics and Contraceptive Use," *Family Planning Perspectives* 28(4):140-147, 158 (1996).

24. Ibid.

25. Ibid.

26. Akinrinola Bankole, Susheela Singh, and Taylor Haas, "Reasons Why Women Have Induced Abortions: Evidence from 27 Countries," *International Family Planning Perspectives* 24(3):117-127, 152 (1998).

27. "The Business of Pornography," *U.S. News & World Report*, 10 February 1997.

28. Some of the search engine companies, such as *Alta Vista* and *Excite*, are actually profiting from porn because they make money whenever a viewer clicks on a porn ad at their sites. Other search engines, such at *Goto* and *Infoseek*, are beginning to offer filtering options to exclude "adult material" from search results.

29. Statistics provided by Ken R. Canfield, President, National Center for Fathering. Quoted in "The XXXtent of the Problem," *New Man*, May 1997.

30. From the General Social Survey data through 1996 (see note 3). Cross-tabulation on (SEXSEX, RELIG16, SEX).

31. The statistics on same-gender sexual behavior in men by church attendance are from Tom W. Smith, 50-53 (see note 12). It is important to note that Smith provides many more breakdowns of these statistics according to other demographic differences (such as income, age, education, race, and location) that may be helpful in estimating the incidence of this problem for a particular church.

For example, there are definite differences in the geographic distribution of men who have had same-gender sex. Though only 2.4% of all American men have had same-gender sex in the last 12 months, 6% since turning 18, these numbers are 8.5% and 14.7% for men living in the 12 largest cities versus 1.5% and 4% for men living in rural areas. So it is likely that urban churches will see more men affected by this problem than will rural churches.

It is also interesting to note that the rates of same-gender sexual behavior in European nations are reported to be only about one-half of what they are in America. For example, a 1998 study showed that only 1.1% of British men had same-gender sex within the last 12 months and only 3.6% had ever done so. (Smith, Table 8.B, 50, see note 12).

32. Figures for those men who identified themselves as "born again" and "fundamentalist" are from the General Social Survey data through 1996 (see note 3). Cross-tabulation on (SEXSEX, ATTEND, REBORN) and (SEXSEX, ATTEND, FUND).

33. The statistics on same-gender behavior in women by church attendance are from Tom W. Smith, 50-53 (see note 12).

34. The statistics for self-identification by women were determined as described above for the men. But the reported rate of less than 1% for those women identified as "born again" is likely to be too low, because the samples used to calculate this also showed a much lower rate in the general population, implying a sampling error.

35. The most likely explanation of this statistical difference lies in a fundamental difference between male and female homosexual behavior—men choose primarily brief encounters, which are easy to hide, while women choose extended relationships, which are not. So, women who become involved in a same-gender relationship would have a greater incentive to leave a church that condemns such visible behavior. Male and female homosexuality are examined in greater depth in Chapter 10.

36. From the General Social Survey data through 1996 (see note 3). Based on combined attendance and same-gender sex figures for men and women. Cross-tabulation on (SEXSEX, ATTEND, SEX).

37. R. Garofalo, "The Association between Health Risk Behaviors and Sexual Orientation among a School-based Sample of Adolescents" *Pediatrics*, May 1998.

38. Gary Remafedi et al., "Demography of Sexual Orientation in Adolescents," *Pediatrics* 89 (1992): 714-721.

39. Yvette Cantu, *Culture Facts*, 3 February 1999, Family Research Council.

40. "Study—Boys' Sex Abuse Underreported," Associated Press, 2 December 1998.

IX

Freedom
from Shame

*And they were both naked, the man and his wife,
and were not ashamed.* (Genesis 2:25 KJV)

Modern society has become saturated with sexual images and information. Sexual issues that most people had never even heard of ten or twenty years ago are discussed daily on television, on the radio, and in print. The Internet has arrived in homes, schools, and offices across the country with the promise of making available to everyone the greatest wealth of knowledge ever assembled by humankind. But do you know the number one topic people search the net for information on? S-E-X! People are so hungry for information about sexuality because it is one of the most powerful and mysterious forces at work in our lives. Many are troubled by sexual problems or are just unsure if they are "normal."

But where is the Church in this information blitz? Do we really have answers for all the complex and troubling sexual issues with which people are now wrestling? Since the 1960s American society has been questioning traditional Christian sexual morality and rejecting it. However, instead of standing up to society's questions and really answering them, it seems like the church has been in retreat, hiding behind walls of tradition, dogma, or just an embarrassed silence.

Today, we still find many Christians caught in an inner conflict about sexual issues. Like everyone else, we have a natural curiosity about this powerful sexual force and often wonder about the normality of our own sexual experiences. Many of us are wrestling with various sexual problems. Yet, for most Christians, the whole subject of sexuality is surrounded by clouds of guilt, shame, and uncertainty. Society bombards us with sexual messages that seem to conflict with our upbringing and our understanding of the Bible. Yet the Church is not voicing a clear and complete answer to counter the secular viewpoint. It often seems as if the church has no answers. It is struck speechless in the face of its critics. So without clear guidance from our churches, each of us is left to deal with these issues on our own as best we can.

THE POWER OF SHAME

What has led us to this sorry predicament? I believe there is only one force responsible for disarming the Church on this issue and keeping so many in captivity: *the power of shame.* Not only does shame keep the Church silent and in a state of confusion on sexual issues, but I believe *association of sexuality with feelings of shame is the most important reason for the high incidence of sexual problems among Christians today.* I have come to this conclusion after hearing many life histories over the years from those who have come to me for help.

Shame can directly cause certain sexual problems, such as inhibiting normal marital relations. But its greatest destructive power comes through 1) *keeping us ignorant about sexual matters,* thus making it easy for us to fall into sexual problems we have never been warned about, and 2) *keeping us bound up in sexual problems for years* because we are too ashamed to seek help—and most churches are too ashamed to offer help.

Most of those who contact my office for help in overcoming a sexual problem were raised in a Christian home, have attended church regularly for most of their lives, and experienced the first symptoms of their sexual problem in childhood or adolescence. Unfortunately, many of these people are in their thirties or forties and are only now getting help. This means they have been suffering needlessly for two or three decades—sitting in church every Sunday—because they were bound for all those years under so much shame about their problem that they could not even talk about it. When they finally became desperate enough to break through their shame and ask a church leader for help, they were often met with fear, revulsion, ignorance—and more shame.

In how many churches today do pastors and teachers feel free to regularly offer clear and compassionate teaching about sexual issues? In my experience, very few indeed. The few who attempt to do so often suffer a barrage of criticism from those members who are so bound by shame that they cannot bear to hear even scriptural truths about sexuality. For many Christians, sex is something they feel they are not supposed to even think about, much less talk about. For Christian teens and singles, it often seems that the only consistent teaching on sexuality from the church is, "Don't do it! Don't even *think* about it!" For married couples, the corollary might be "Do it if you must, but *try not to think about it!*"

I received a call not long ago from an associate pastor of a very large, nationally-known church who wanted to refer one of their members to me for help in overcoming homosexuality. As we saw in the preceding chapter, this problem is as common in churches today as in our society as a whole. Around 4% of men and 2% of women who attend church weekly have had a same-sex encounter within the past five years.

Whenever I get a call like this, I see it as a golden opportunity, not only to help one Christian step out of homosexuality, but to help a whole church grow in its understanding of sexual problems and develop its own ministry to those who are struggling with such things.

So, I not only agreed to counsel this man, but also offered to train the church's entire pastoral staff in the fundamentals of how sexual problems develop, how to prevent them, and how to help Christians overcome them. I was stunned when the pastor replied, "To tell you the truth, that is just not a ministry God has called us to. We rarely have this sort of problem in our congregation, and if it does occur, our policy is to out-source."

I could not believe what I was hearing. I tried my best to convince him that in such a huge congregation there were sure to be many people struggling with a host of sexual problems, not just homosexuality. I was willing to make whatever sacrifices were necessary to spend the time training his staff, because the need—though currently hidden—was so great. (According to the statistics, a church of that size would have more than 200 men and women involved in homosexuality alone, not even counting all the other sexual problems. One counselor could not begin to handle that kind of case load.)

But my efforts were to no avail.

The subtext I was picking up from this pastor's words and tone of voice is one I have heard so often before: "This is a really embarrassing situation. I can't believe it happened in our church! I sure hope the media doesn't pick up on this. We need to get rid of this person as quickly and as quietly as possible. Will you help us?"

This situation demonstrates the tremendous hold that shame has over the Church today. We claim to be a house of healing, a refuge for the broken, a haven for the hurting. But those with sexual problems we find too embarrassing are hustled out the back door and on down the street.

Does this pastor even want to know how many in his church are wrestling with life-destroying sexual sins and problems? All it would take to find out is some frank teaching on the subject in the men's and ladies' meetings, followed by an invitation to come forward for prayer or to call the church office for counseling. When I work with a church to help them set up a ministry for sexual healing, pastors are always astounded by the number of people who ask for help.

But such healing cannot even begin as long as church leaders are bound by their own shame.

The price to maintain such shameful silence is very high. I know of no other issue for which Hosea's warning is more true today: "My people are destroyed for lack of knowledge" (Hosea 4:6 KJV). The tragic truth is that many Christians have troublesome sexual thoughts or compulsive sexual behaviors that are slowly destroying them, weighing them down under a tremendous burden of guilt. They long to get free but do not know where to turn. From seeing what has happened to others over the years, from hearing the jokes told in Sunday school about the sexually broken, they have learned they must keep their struggle a deep, dark secret or risk rejection and ostracism by their family and church. So they suffer on in silence, and many fall by the wayside.

Before the Church can even begin to deal with its multitude of sexual problems, the chains of false, unreasoning, misdirected shame about sexual issues must first be broken. This kind of shame is not just an emotional condition; it is a demonic stronghold. It is a great, sprouting weed of a lie with deep roots and powerful tendrils that choke sexual fulfillment out of our lives, and Satan is the one who plants it in us. Deception is really the only weapon he has that is effective against Christians. He and his minions have had centuries of practice in manipulating us with the falsehood of sexual shame.

One of my chief aims in writing this book is to expose this stronghold of sexual shame that has so subtly infiltrated our minds and our churches, to root it out so it will no longer have any power over us. To accomplish this we must come to understand just how sexual shame originates and how it operates to keep us in bondage.

What Is Shame?

It is essential that we understand what *shame* is and how it differs from *modesty* or *guilt,* with which it is often confused.

Modesty (or *decency*) in the way we dress or in how we discuss sexual matters stems from a concern for others. We choose to dress modestly so that our bodies will not inadvertently become a source of sexual temptation for someone else. We avoid telling dirty jokes or using indecent language so that we will not offend others.

179

Guilt has two different aspects: the *fact of guilt* and the *feeling of guilt.* When we transgress God's laws or man's laws, we are guilty in a legal, factual sense, no matter what we may feel. We may be totally unaware that we have broken a particular law until it is brought to our attention. But we *feel guilty* when our actions or thoughts violate our own conscience. When we realize that we have done something that hurts God, hurts another person, or even hurts ourselves, the pain of a guilty conscience urges us to right that wrong and seek forgiveness.

Shame is a feeling we experience when we lose the respect and approval of others or even of our own selves. *Embarrassment, humiliation,* and *mortification* are other words used to describe varying degrees of shame. Feeling ashamed is the opposite of feeling honored, esteemed, and respected.

WE LEARN EARLY IN LIFE TO FEAR SHAME, AND THE MORE WE FEAR IT, THE MORE POWER IT HAS OVER US.

But shame never operates alone; it draws its real power from fear, including fear of rejection and of being unloved. Being shamed by others, or just feeling ashamed of yourself, is an exceedingly painful experience. Being ridiculed or rejected by those whom you love and respect is not something anyone desires. And those who who matter the most to you can cause you to feel the most shame. So we learn early in life to fear shame, and the more we fear it, the more power it has over us.

Each of these three—modesty, guilt, and shame—can be powerful motivators of behavior, yet shame seems to be the most powerful. True, we all feel guilty for having done something wrong. But for many of us, guilt is just not strong enough in itself to keep us from repeating a wrong if we gained significant pleasure or benefit from it. However, if others shame us because our actions violate their standards, that is likely to be a much greater deterrent. This is undoubtedly why public humiliation has been used in both ancient and modern cultures as a powerful means of enforcing social order.

So, shame does have a proper role as an enforcer of necessary moral standards. In this role, it stands behind modesty and guilt, so that if an individual's own conscience or sense of modesty is not enough to restrain his behavior, then society will quickly put him to open shame for violating community standards.

The New Testament church used public shame in this way to confront those Christians who willfully violated biblical standards of behavior, such as refusing to work for a living (2 Thessalonians 3:10-15) or living openly in an improper sexual relationship (1 Corinthians 5). However, such shame was never a permanent condition. It was only to persuade people to repent so they could be welcomed back into fellowship. This is a healthy, helpful, lifesaving kind of shame.

However, what is giving us problems in the church today is *destructive* shame.

Destructive Shame and How It Operates

Let us look at one example of how shame can be unhealthy and destructive:

> A doctor greets a worried wife and her stone-faced husband. It seems he has been having stomach pain off and on for over a year, but she only found out about it last week when she discovered him sitting out in the car, doubled over in agony. A CT scan is quickly done and the results show an advanced malignancy. It is really too late for effective treatment, but the doctor recommends chemotherapy anyway to give him some chance. When they ask the man why he ignored his painful symptoms for so long, he is obviously embarrassed, but he really cannot give them a good answer.

181

This situation is not at all uncommon today. It presents a well-known anomaly in the field of public health. Many American men consistently avoid seeking medical attention for their symptoms until it is often too late for effective care. The underlying reason seems to be that many men feel it is *shameful* for a "real man" to show any kind of vulnerability or weakness or to ask someone else for help, even when faced with a life-threatening illness. The root of this attitude is *pride.*

Another factor working with destructive shame in this situation is *fear:* fear of the unknown, fear of hearing bad news, fear of unpleasant and embarrassing medical treatment, fear of becoming helpless and dependent on others and so losing their respect.

Shame and fear working together produce *denial.* This is a tendency to avoid even thinking about the problem, to focus on innocent explanations and forget about serious possibilities. Those in denial do not seek out more information about their symptoms, but instead try to think about the problem as little as possible, maintaining some degree of comfort in their *ignorance* of the warning signs of serious ailments, such as cancer or heart disease. They may take pain killers or use some other means of *concealment* to hide their symptoms and prevent others from noticing that anything is wrong. But the problem does not go away with this kind of treatment. It just gets worse and worse until there is major crisis, and then everyone finds out.

Destructive shame about sexual problems can work in much the same way. A man may realize that he has been having some troubling sexual thoughts. But he has learned the lesson early in life that it is *shameful* to have such thoughts, that only "bad" people have those desires. He grew up *ignorant* of how sexuality functions, of how his own actions may have allowed such thoughts to take root in his mind and grow stronger. He is *afraid* he will be shunned by family and friends if they ever find out what is going on inside his head. So, above all, he must keep it a secret. He avoids asking for help for a number of reasons: he does not know where to look for help; his church does not offer such help and never even discusses such subjects; he is afraid those in his social circle might find out; he is afraid of what treatment he might have to endure; and it hurts his *pride* to ask for help. He may ultimately *deny* that he even has a problem, since it is something he feels he can control. If he starts to act out his abnormal fantasies, then he is forced to start spinning a fabric of lies to *conceal* his behavior from family and friends.

This pattern continues to reinforce itself. Shame, driven by fear and pride, discourages people from seeking help and encourages denial of the problem. This maintains an atmosphere of ignorance and concealment, which allows the problem to grow worse. These factors are always found working together in destructive shame: *shame, fear, pride, denial, concealment,* and *ignorance.*

When a sexual problem is suppressed like this, it only grows worse and worse, until the day when there is a crisis of behavior that cannot be hidden. Then the whole church is stunned and wonders, "How could such a fine Christian man commit such a despicable act?" But they do not realize how great a role they all have played in his self-destruction and would be outraged if anyone suggested that they must shoulder some of the blame. To understand how this could be, we need to examine the way destructive shame operates in families. After all, isn't the church really supposed to be a family?

A well-studied example of how entire families can become caught up in destructive shame can be seen in those families where one member abuses drugs or alcohol, or has a sexual addiction. Addiction of any sort has long been publicly condemned, so families of addicts are placed in a very shame-filled situation. They are ashamed of and for the addict, who may be a father or mother or spouse. They often blame themselves for the addict's behavior, feeling both guilt and shame. And the whole family risks public humiliation if the addict's problem becomes known to the community.

The common dilemma faced by members of such families is whether to reduce their own feelings of shame by ignoring or minimizing the problem—even helping the addict conceal his behavior—or to risk even greater public humiliation by confronting the problem and trying to get help. It is quite common to see in these families a great avoidance of the truth—popularly termed "being in denial." This occurs, not because they are any more dishonest than average, but because facing the harsh reality of their situation is so painful. Denial can be a mental "escape hatch." Many people choose to live in their fantasies (delusions) when reality becomes too painful to bear.

Such a retreat from reality can produce what seems to be a tacit agreement among the family members to never speak about the "family secret" among themselves. They try to convince themselves that they are a "normal" family, just like all the other families. Above all, they must never let those outside the family know about the addict's problem behavior, even if they have to tell lies. Preserving the family's reputation seems even more important than preserving the addict's life. The net result of this unspoken conspiracy is that the addict continues in his addiction, aided by his whole family in their unspoken pact of deception. All of them are equally trapped by the addiction and the web of shame and deception surrounding it.

This family situation is called *co-dependency* or *co-addiction*. Those who claim to love the addict, yet by their attitudes and actions enable him to continue in his addiction, are just as disturbed as the addict himself. Therefore, it is appropriate to call them *co-addicts, co-dependents,* or *enablers*.

We saw in the preceding chapter the great numbers of church members who are living with serious sexual problems. But did you realize that our churches are filled with *even greater numbers* of enablers? These are the people who do not want to admit sexual problems even exist in their church because that would be too shameful. They are quick to complain if their pastor teaches on sexual issues because it is too embarrassing for them. They would rather just not know about such disgusting things. If they notice something "funny" about another member's behavior or overhear some whispered rumors, they either ignore it or just make a mental note to avoid that person in the future. If a member is caught in sexual sin, enablers are absolutely mortified. If the news spreads through the community, what will their friends think? So they do not want their church to become involved in the often messy and difficult job of offering healing and restoration. They would really prefer the offender leave the church as quickly as possible to save themselves any further embarrassment.

In situations where the sexual sinner is a popular leader, enablers may actually be too quick to offer him forgiveness and the restoration of his ministry—before he has received sufficient counseling and has truly overcome his weakness. This is motivated, not by a real concern for the fallen one, but by a desire to get the whole embarrassing mess over with as quickly as possible so everything can return to "normal."

Though they can usually come up with good, spiritual-sounding excuses for their actions, enablers are really not acting as spiritual, rational, or mature Christians. They are being driven to act compulsively by the same dark undercurrents of destructive sexual shame that also compel the sexual sinner. We see the same cofactors of destructive shame at work in their hearts: *shame, fear, pride, denial, concealment,* and *ignorance.*

At the root of such behavior is a fundamentally selfish motive to avoid *shame-by-association* and feelings of *embarrassment.* They *fear* harm to their reputations. They prefer that the whole church remain in *ignorance* about sexual matters rather than risk being embarrassed by hearing sexual truths discussed openly. They are *proud* of their church's great achievements, historic traditions, spirituality, reputation for holiness, and fine standing in the community, so they *deny* that such sexual problems could exist in their church. If such problems are uncovered, they make every effort to *conceal* them, often getting rid of the problem by getting rid of the person.

As long as these hidden motives remain in control of their hearts, enablers cannot deal honestly, rationally, or compassionately with sexual issues. So they become just as much a part of the epidemic of sexual sin in the church as those with sexual problems.

Any church that truly desires to clean out the closet of sexual sin (and keep it cleaned out) must first deal with these deep motives of the heart. In some way, we all are affected by these forces that tempt us to turn away from facing the truth.

The Development of Sexual Shame

Have you ever noticed that very young children have absolutely no shame about their bodies or their bodily functions? Like Adam and Eve before they sinned, toddlers can play in the front yard or run off to visit the neighbors "naked . . . and . . . not ashamed" (Genesis 2:25 NKJV). Yet in most families, as children grow up and learn lessons about modest behavior, they also learn a deep and abiding shame about their sexuality.

Children soak up attitudes from those around them as sponges soak up water. So our first lessons in sexual shame are often taught to us, even if unwittingly, by our parents. If parents avoid all discussion or explanation of sexual matters, if they harshly punish their children for innocent (and ignorant) sexual play without explanation, if they respond to questions about where babies come from with fables about storks and cabbage leaves, then the message they are communicating is quite clear to the child: sexuality is so shameful and evil that it should never even be mentioned.

Think about it. Is there any other subject to which parents respond to innocent childish questions with so much embarrassment, awkwardness, and avoidance? Although they do not mean to teach such an extreme message—they are just acting out of their own shame, awkwardness, ignorance, and embarrassment—nevertheless, the child is left with a deep and abiding sense of shame about sexuality.

Even if parents do attempt to convey a positive message about sexuality when they sit their child down to have "the talk" about the facts of life, they cannot undo in one hour the negative messages they have been sending for years. Despite their words, a child can easily read any feelings of unease or shame the parents experience during the discussion.

I believe Christian children are more at risk for developing sexual shame than are their unchurched peers. Christian parents and churches are often so intent on warning their youth away from premarital sex that they spend more time teaching the "Thou shalt nots" about sexual behavior than the "Thou shalts." This contributes to an unbalanced, negative view of sexuality. Sex comes across as mostly evil, something to be avoided at all costs. (And as the statistics show, this approach is not even doing a good job of preventing premarital sex!)

Such an environment of negativity, accompanied by ignorance about sexuality, provides fertile ground in which many different sexual problems can develop as a child journeys on through adolescence and young adulthood.

For some children who grow up in such a sex-negative environment, as they enter puberty and realize they are developing sexual feelings, shame can reach a new level: it becomes *internalized*. Not only do they feel shame about sexual subjects, they begin to view *themselves* as shameful persons because they have these shameful sexual feelings that they do not know how to manage and that cannot be discussed with anyone.

Some follow the path of fear and suppression, fighting every sexual thought or feeling as an evil thing to be overcome through the exercise of their will. Those who achieve some degree of success on this path often feel more righteous or holy than others who falter. Yet they often have problems later on in fully enjoying a marriage relationship. For them, sex remains too closely associated with sin and shame.

Others—after having always done everything that their parents or church ever expected of them—still find, to their horror, that behind the perfect facade they have made of their lives, some secret sexual addiction or fantasy life is eating away at them from the inside. But they can find no answer for this problem at church and have no friends within their religious circle with whom they can share such a monstrous secret. So they struggle on in shameful silence.

Some people eventually come to the following conclusions because their sexual feelings are so unmanageable: "I have no hope for change" and "I must be a really bad person." So they give in to their lower nature and pursue all of their desires. They become rebels, rejecting the burden of sexual shame along with all the other lessons their parents taught them, including their Christianity. Since all sexual thoughts, feelings, and behavior seem to be equally loaded down with shame and sinfulness, they just scrap the whole concept. They no longer respect any boundaries that distinguish right sexual behavior from wrong sexual behavior. Anything goes!

Yet the majority never really succeed at resolving the issues of sex and shame either way. So they grow up to be just like their parents. As young singles, they may play around with illicit sex or pornography like their friends do, but they soon feel guilty and repent, promising God they will absolutely never do it again—until the next time temptation proves too strong. Thus begins a secret life of continual struggle and defeat, which only reinforces their shame.

If they are fortunate enough to fall in love and begin a marriage, then in addition to furniture and dishes, each partner brings along his or her own secret closet, full of all the confused and shameful lessons he or she has learned so far about sex. This is often the source of much conflict

WE OF ALL PEOPLE SHOULD ENJOY THE GREATEST SEXUAL FULFILLMENT.

in a marriage—when unrealistic fantasies collide with shameful inhibitions. All this happens because they lacked a good sexual education. Oh, sure, the school system taught them about the basic plumbing in sex education class. But no one ever sat them down and instilled in them an appreciation for the holiness and beauty of God's design for sex, or taught them how their masculinity and femininity reflect God's very nature, or how to manage sometimes overwhelming sexual feelings, or how sexual union deeply affects the spirit, soul, and body.

Unless these couples get some help in changing their viewpoint, they will most likely pass along to their own children their own confusion and shame about sexuality. Thus, the pattern of sexual shame is imprinted on another generation.

The Cure for Sexual Shame

Isn't it ironic that, in the midst of a society that has thrown off all remnants of sexual shame (along with all guilt and modesty), the one group that is still so heavily bound by such shame is the Church? Because we have the revelation of God's purpose and plan for sexuality, we of all people should enjoy the greatest sexual fulfillment. We should have the greatest confidence in speaking about sexual issues. The world should be coming to us for help with their sexual problems.

Instead, Christians are turning to secular sources because their churches do not seem to have the answers to their sexual problems. The Church stands mute and confounded at the continual flood of sexual scandals that topple both leaders and followers. So the world calls us hypocrites, saying, "You do all the same things we do. We just don't feel any guilt or shame about it."

It is past time for us to realize that *the very concept that sex is something shameful is, itself, a sexual perversion.* God created our sexuality to express His nature and teach us about Himself. So, to denigrate it and demean it and make it into something dirty is to pervert it from its original purpose just as surely as any illicit sex act.

Yet just such a perverse concept has been taught by many church leaders over the centuries.* We saw in Chapter 7 how the Kingdom of Sexual Perversion has its origin in false religion. Well, the teaching of sexual shame in the church is just a "covert operation" of the Kingdom of Sexual Perversion, equally grounded in false religion.

In fact, the infiltration of sexual shame into the church is the very thing that has allowed all the other sexual perversions to creep in and remain hidden, because shame prevents the church from dealing honestly and openly with sexual sins and problems. All the while, so many remain in secret bondage to those very things.

For too long, shame has been a winning strategy for the Devil's kingdom. The winds of the doctrines of Gnosticism, legalism, asceticism, and Victorianism have swept through the Church over the years and have added to our burden of shame and confusion about sexual matters.

---

* Augustine and Origen were two early church theologians who devalued marriage and heaped shame on sexuality. (Origen eventually castrated himself.) The leaders of the Puritan colonies, in addition to such punishments as wearing "the scarlet letter," enforced the tradition of sexual shame by executing a number of their flock who were caught committing sexual sin.

Nevertheless, it is now time for the stronghold of sexual shame to be torn down. To do so requires a three-step attack:

First, it is absolutely essential that we have restored to us the vision of God's perfect purpose and plan for sex. We must come to understand that, at its very core, sexuality is holy and good. Once we have this vision of the beauty and holiness of sexuality firmly implanted in our hearts, then there will be no more room for a childish, unreasonable shame or embarrassment about sexual matters. We will be able to more clearly distinguish right from wrong with respect to sexual thoughts, feelings, and behaviors when we know the principles underlying God's design for sexuality.

Second, the issue of sexual shame in our hearts and in our churches needs to be addressed directly. The false doctrines based on shame and the subtle ways in which it keeps us in bondage must be exposed. Each person must take an inventory of his or her own heart to uncover the roots of sexual shame and begin to restore the damage it has done.

Third, we need some basic information about sexual issues. When we learn how sexual forces operate, they no longer seem so mysterious and overwhelming. Remaining ignorant of these natural forces means we cannot protect ourselves from their destructive potential. Christians need practical advice for managing their sexuality in accordance with biblical standards. Parents need guidance for raising children with a healthy sexuality. We also need some understanding of the common sexual problems people get caught in. This gives us more compassion for those who are trapped in sexual sin and builds confidence that they can be helped. Those with sexual problems need to learn that they are not alone; they are not exceptional. Others have dealt with the very same issues and have overcome them. This shrinks the problems from mountain-sized to dirt-pile-sized.

In every church where I have taught this three-part message, dramatic changes have taken place. First, the altars were filled with those who, for the first time in their lives, could confess the sexual sin in which they had been involved and ask for help. Others, who had been molested or had experienced other sexual trauma, told of being set free from a lifetime of incredible shame. Many women have testified that they had not been able to fully enjoy union with their husbands until these truths delivered them from their shame.

I once taught this message in a Mexican brothel and saw more than sixty prostitutes receive Christ. They left that lifestyle behind and joined the church across the street that had sponsored the outreach. So this is a powerful message for the unsaved as well as for the believer.

I promise you, proclaiming these truths will set many people free in your church. But church leaders must be bold enough to take the first steps to breach the stronghold of shame. Then, they must be prepared to deal with all the problems that are uncovered and maintain an atmosphere of openness. This means the Senior Pastor must make a solid commitment to deal with this issue *consistently* until the attitude of the whole church has changed.

It is a simple question, really. Which force is stronger: your compassion for those caught in sexual sin or your shame about being associated with them? As I recall, Jesus faced that very same dilemma.

Test Your Level of Sexual Shame

As I designed the cover for this book, I realized that the majority of Christians have unresolved feelings of sexual shame that could keep them from even picking up this book in a bookstore. So I put a great deal of effort into making the cover attractive and interesting, yet not too embarrassing to the average Christian bookstore browser. For the same reason, I pondered for quite some time over the exact wording of the title. Yet, I realized that many people would still be uncomfortable buying it.

Here is an exercise to help you see just how subtle and insidious sexual shame can be. Try the following quiz as a way of measuring your own level of sexual shame:

1. If you discovered this book while browsing
in a bookstore, what first caught your eye? Was it

Michelangelo's nude renderings of Adam and Eve or the word *Sex* written in bold letters across the cover?

2. Before you walked over to pick up the book, did you look around to see if anyone else was watching?

3. As you skimmed through the book, did you keep an eye peeled for other customers walking by?

4. Did you perhaps walk over to another aisle away from all the "sex books" so you could read in peace?

5. As you stood in line to buy the book, did you place another book on top so that others could not see the title?

6. Did the thought cross your mind that if other people saw you with this book, they might think you had some sort of sexual problem?

7. Are you being careful where you read the book? Are you at all concerned about who might see the title (friends, family members, children) and what they might think or the questions they might ask?

Scoring: Answering "Yes" to any of the questions 2–7 means you have some degree of sexual shame. The higher your score, the more you need to read this book!

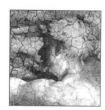

Uncovering the Roots
of Sexual Problems

The first part of this book focused on restoring the vision of God's incredibly beautiful plan and purpose for our sexuality. Yet if we truly wish to understand and to help those with sexual problems, we need to learn the basics of how such problems develop. Dealing with such issues may be unpleasant for some, but it is necessary if we are to understand the truth.

Nearly everyone at some point in his or her life has had struggles and difficulties with his or her sexuality. Perhaps we have had to battle to control our fantasies or behavior, or to deal with fear and guilt about sexual matters. We all know what it means to sin sexually, even if just in our thoughts. And we have all felt shame.

Nevertheless, what I find lacking among many Christians today is a real empathy for those with sexual problems *different from their own.* Through the efforts of ministries such as Promise Keepers, Christian men are becoming more willing to talk about their struggles with fantasy or pornography, and many are finding the help and support they need to overcome these things. This is true progress. But if a man confesses to his men's group that his fantasies are about naked men, not naked ladies, he had better watch out! All too often the attitude expressed is, "Hate the sin, *but let somebody else love that sinner!*" Those whose sexual problems are not on the "acceptable" list—if their secret gets out—often find that they are treated with prejudice, a certain coldness, or just avoidance. This can be very painful.

This less-than-Christlike attitude originates in our natural feelings of disgust toward sexual desires we cannot even imagine experiencing ourselves. Yet, this "natural" disgust can hinder us from fulfilling spiritual mandates, such as maintaining loving relationships in the church and helping others overcome their problems. It also reinforces the atmosphere of sexual shame that allows sexual problems to develop and flourish in secret.

These attitudes of shame, prejudice, and disgust are really birthed out of ignorance, mingled with a bit of fear. However, when we begin to understand what causes unusual sexual desires and compulsions to develop, we become much more at ease in dealing with the whole issue. What at first seemed incomprehensible begins to make sense. Any fears of "contamination" are dispersed. Sexual sins lose their menacing aura and shrink to the size of any other sin. We see that healing is available for all who want to change, if they receive the necessary help.

I believe the facts presented in this and the following chapter will not only give you a new understanding of sexual problems, but will also help you to break free of any remaining shame you feel in dealing with sexual issues. It will be necessary for me to speak plainly about sexual topics many perhaps have never heard of. But these are just the realities of God's creation, the details of His design. So there is really no cause for shame.

To help us gain perspective on how sexuality develops and changes throughout life, I like to use the following analogy:

The River of Sexuality

Human sexuality as it develops over a lifetime can be compared to the course of a river. In its infancy, a river begins as a spring of pure water trickling out of the ground, forming a small stream. Its flow is quite weak at this stage and can be easily diverted by rock slides or earthen dams. It may even flow back underground for a time. Yet, its course is always downhill. It will eventually find a path, no matter what is blocking the way.

This represents the sexuality of childhood, which is delicate, weak, and not very noticeable. Through subtle messages or traumatic experience, it can be easily repressed or diverted from the normal course of heterosexuality.

When the spring rains come, the stream swells into a raging river. If the river has not been tamed with dikes and levees, or if it has been dammed up in some way so that it lacks a sufficient channel for its power, it will overflow its banks at the weakest point and flood the surrounding lands. When the flood waters recede, much of the surrounding landscape will have been permanently altered, and the river will have cut a new channel for itself.

This represents adolescent sexuality from its emergence at puberty to the peak of its strength. Sexual confusion and experimentation are common as this phase begins. If teenagers have not been taught to understand and cope with their sexual feelings, they may find expression in destructive sexual behaviors and attitudes that have lifelong effects. This is also when any damage done to sexuality during childhood is exposed by the appearance of abnormal sexual desires.

As the river flows on over the plains, it broadens and deepens in its channel, though not flowing as swiftly as it did before. Now, only a cataclysmic event can change its course.

This represents the mature and established sexuality of middle and mature age—gradually broadening, though still flowing within the boundaries established during adolescence and young adulthood, and weakening somewhat in force over time. To change sexual feelings and behaviors at this point in life usually requires considerable effort.

Early Sexual Development

To really understand the components of our sexual nature and how problems can develop, it is necessary to begin our study at the moment of conception and trace the development of sexuality over the life span. A major theme illustrated throughout this chapter is that sexuality—sexual attributes, feelings, and behaviors—does not suddenly arrive at puberty, but begins in the womb and develops during the years of childhood.

Prenatal Sexual Development

We all have been taught that our biological sex is determined by our sex chromosomes. However, much more is being learned about how male and female physiological differences are actually shaped during critical periods of development in the womb, and how environmental factors can disturb that development. So it is important that we look at how sexual differences develop in the womb and some things that can go wrong with the process.

Biological sex begins with the sex chromosomes X and Y. Men receive an X chromosome from their mother and a Y from their father. Women receive an X chromosome from their mother and another X from their father. The Y chromosome is what makes a child a genetic male, and the lack of a Y produces a genetic female. A very small percentage of people have abnormal combinations of sex chromosomes, such as XXY, XYY, or X, but even in these cases, a single Y chromosome produces a male, and the lack of a Y produces a female.[1]

Up until about the sixth week of development, the embryo has no obvious male or female organs. It has only a pair of structures (called *gonads*) that can become either testes or ovaries. At about this time, if the fetus has a Y chromosome, a gene called the *Testis Determining Factor (TDF)* on the Y chromosome is activated and sends a chemical signal to the gonads, causing them to become testes and start producing testosterone. It also activates other genes necessary for male development, initiating a complex process that converts the embryo into a fully equipped boy. In the absence of the TDF gene, the gonad cells will develop as ovaries. Further development will produce a fully equipped girl.

An important principle to understand about fetal sexual development is that the default developmental pathway is female. All fetuses are programmed internally to develop in the feminine direction, which they will do unless they receive a multitude of hormonal signals initiated by the TDF gene and maintained by testosterone—all at the proper time to keep the embryo developing in the masculine direction. This process of masculinization is complex and may partially explain why men are at much greater risk than women for many types of birth defects, as well as sexual and mental disorders of all kinds. This masculinization process is also important in light of emerging evidence for differences in the way male and female brains function, since these differences begin in the womb.

Sex Differences in Brain Development

We all know that men and women tend to think differently in many ways. So it should come as no surprise that there is growing evidence for differences in brain function and organization for men and women. There has been much debate about whether these differences result from biological factors, such as differing hormone levels during gestation, or from the fact that girls and boys are treated differently, resulting in different learning experiences. A growing consensus is that biology and learning both have a role and interact to a great extent. But we will examine first those brain differences that seem to be most strongly linked to hormone exposure and thus would have their origins in prenatal brain development.

Many cells throughout the human brain have been found to contain receptors to the three types of sex hormones: androgens (testosterone and its derivatives), estrogens, and progesterone. These receptors are known to be especially concentrated in areas of the brain associated with sexual functioning, such as the hypothalamus. We tend to think of testosterone as the "male hormone" and estrogen and progesterone as "female hormones." Actually, both women and men have all three types of sex hormones circulating in their bloodstream, though at quite different levels.

We become aware of the effects of major changes in these hormone levels when they introduce a new stage in life, such as puberty or menopause. However, hormone concentrations also fluctuate dramatically in an individual from hour to hour and day to day. This fluctuation is believed to affect our thinking and behavior, though the details are not yet well understood. Women are perhaps most aware of these subtle hormonal effects on their emotional state as their levels of progesterone and estrogen vary during the monthly cycle. For both men and women, testosterone levels are the major influence on what we experience as our libido or "sex drive."

It is while in the womb that our brains become sensitized to hormones to respond in a typical male or female pattern later in life. The effects of prenatal exposure to testosterone (or the lack thereof) have been studied the most extensively. Testosterone is the primary determinant of physical sex differences and seems also to be the most powerful hormonal organizer of the human brain. A number of studies have linked prenatal testosterone exposure to the following characteristics:

> 1. *Male-typical brain specialization and organization.* The right hemisphere of a typical male brain tends to be more specialized for visual-spatial problem solving and certain types of mathematical reasoning.[2] Women who have a genetic flaw that makes them insensitive to the effects of testosterone have weaker visual-spatial skills than normal women, who are exposed to a small amount of testosterone produced by their ovaries.[3]
>
> 2. *Energetic "rough-and-tumble" play and aggression.* This is a typical characteristic of boys, but also occurs in girls exposed to high prenatal levels of testosterone.[4] A portion of the brain known as the *amygdala*, which is closely connected to the hypothalamus and has large numbers of androgen receptors, has been linked to this type of play and to aggressive behavior. Damage to the amygdala eliminates rough-and-tumble play and aggressive behavior.
>
> 3. *Erotic response to images.* This is a typically male sexual response evidenced by a greater incidence of visual erotic dreams in men and the high level of male interest in pornography. However, women who were exposed to high prenatal levels of testosterone share this typically masculine erotic response.[5]

A lack of prenatal exposure to high levels of testosterone, as is true for most women, has been linked to the following characteristics:

1. *Female-typical brain specialization and organization.* The left hemisphere of a typical female brain tends to have specific areas that are specialized for language skills, such as verbal fluency, spelling, and reading. The right hemisphere also contains additional areas specialized for processing verbal information and reading emotions from facial expressions.[6] Female brains seem to use both left and right hemispheres more equally in solving problems. The structures that connect the two hemispheres of the brain and allow nerve impulses to travel between them (the *corpus callosum* and *anterior commissure*) show greater development in women and may be responsible for their greater intuitive skills.[7] The unique power of "a woman's intuition" may come from a greater ability to assemble all types of sensory information from both sides of the brain when drawing conclusions.

2. *Maternal interest, beginning in childhood play.* Maternal behavior occurs in normal girls who are exposed only to the very low levels of testosterone produced by their ovaries. It is found to an extreme degree in girls with Turner's Syndrome (who have even less testosterone than normal females), but it is completely lacking in girls exposed to high prenatal levels of testosterone.[8]

3. *Erotic response to tactile stimuli.* Women tend to require stimulation of the sense of touch (or imagining such stimulation)—as in hugging, kissing, or cuddling—to become sexually aroused.[9]

Evidence for differences in brain specialization and organization between the sexes comes from studies of people whose brains have been damaged in specific areas, studies of people born with hormonal abnormalities, experiments where different regions of the brain were stimulated, and new scanning techniques (PET and FMRI) that can produce a three-dimensional map of the activity level in different regions of the brain while a person is performing mental tasks. Combining information from all these sources allows researchers to create a rough map of where and how male and female brains process information. There are definite differences.

Many measures of mental ability (such as general IQ) show no average difference between the sexes. However, even when solving problems with equal facility, male and female brains tend to show activity in different areas. It is almost as if they are running different "programs" that yield the same results. Even while the brain is idling (test subjects were told to just relax), there are noticeable differences. Male brains show activity in the regions associated with physical movement and aggression while female brains show activity in an area associated with emotions and communication.[10]

However, it is important to keep in mind that all such sex-based differences refer to the "average" male or female brain. Researchers often find individuals with brain functional and organizational patterns more typical of the opposite sex or that are a mixture of typical male and female patterns. On average, men seem to have more ability for solving certain visual-spatial problems, and women typically have greater social and verbal skills. Yet, there are still some women who have better visual-spatial skills than most men and some men who have better social and verbal skills than most women (politicians, for example).

Man, Woman, or Eunuch?

In both Old and New Testament societies, people could be divided into three categories: men, women, and eunuchs. At birth it was obvious which babies were boys and which were girls. Any baby who could not be put in either of the first two categories because of genital abnormalities was considered a eunuch, along with boys who had been castrated or whose testes had been damaged.

Because of our modern understanding of genes and how sex is determined through the X and Y chromosomes, most people today would think that if a child was born with a mixture of male and female genital structures (known as an *intersex* condition, occurring in 1.7 out of 1000 live births), the "true" sex could be determined by checking the child's genes for either the male or female pattern. The genital defects could then be repaired to make them match the genes. This approach does seem to work for most of these children. However, there are some extreme cases that defy conventional wisdom and give us more of an understanding of what it takes to make a man or a woman.

One of the more interesting situations involves children with *androgen insensitivity syndrome* (also known as *complete testicular feminization*). This occurs in chromosomal males (XY) whose body cells have a genetic inability to respond to testosterone. This insensitivity to testosterone during gestation causes fetal development to proceed completely along the female path, even though the developing child has internal testes. At birth, the external genitals have a normal female appearance, though the vagina is somewhat shorter than normal, and there are no internal female organs, such as a uterus or ovaries. This syndrome is usually not discovered until puberty, when there is a failure to menstruate and little or no pubic hair (because growth of pubic hair in men and women is initiated by testosterone). However, breasts develop normally because of the small amounts of estrogen secreted by the testes.

Studies of these "women" have shown them to be highly feminine in behavior and entirely heterosexual.[11] They are often tall, thin, and attractive—the very ideal of feminine beauty in popular culture. All desired marriage and children. One study compared them with chromosomal women (XX) who also had a congenital lack of internal female organs but had normal ovaries (*Rokitansky syndrome*). The two groups were found to be identical in every aspect of sexual and erotic development.[12] These cases demonstrate that a lack of prenatal exposure to testosterone, plus being reared as a woman, are all that is necessary to produce a "woman" who is outwardly indistinguishable from any other normal woman.

(An interesting note: the Olympic Committee reports that an average of one out of every 500 female athletes is disqualified for being a chromosomal male. It must be assumed that these women were ignorant of their genetic condition before being tested, since the genetic screening is such a well-known requirement, instituted to prevent men from competing in the women's divisions.)

In the few cases where this syndrome has been diagnosed in childhood, attempts to correct it have been less than successful. Some corrective genital surgery may be attempted, but there is no known way to create a functioning penis when one does not exist or to make a body with this metabolic defect respond to testosterone. If such a child is raised as a boy, developing some kind of masculine identity is sure to be a struggle because he is stuck in a body that will always look female.[13]

The counterpart to this example of genetic males who appear to be females is found with the *adrenogenital syndrome*, which can cause genetic females to appear to be males. This syndrome is one of the more common causes of a variety of genital deformities among women. It results from one of several metabolic defects that cause the adrenal glands to produce testosterone during gestation.

In the most extreme form of this condition, a chromosomal female infant appears to be a normal boy with undescended testes, though the internal organs are all female, including ovaries and a uterus. A number of cases have been recorded where this defect was not detected in childhood, and so these children were raised as boys. At puberty they experienced the normal process of masculine sexual development—though they lacked testes—because their adrenal glands continued to produce testosterone. Reports on these "men" indicate that they develop into fully heterosexual men with masculine behavior and identity. They function sexually as men, and even marry and adopt children. There is no evidence that they have ever felt any sexual attraction to men or have felt like a woman trapped in a man's body. All along, they thought they were normal men with undescended testes.

This demonstrates that prenatal exposure to sufficient testosterone, plus being raised as a boy, is all that is necessary to produce a "man" who is outwardly indistinguishable from other men. While it is possible for these children, if given early surgical and hormonal treatment, to become fertile women who could bear children, reports of actual cases show that, by puberty, "boys" left with this condition untreated are very masculine. They are interested in girls and will vigorously oppose any attempts to turn them into girls.[14]

These two extreme situations—a genetic male becoming an apparently normal woman and a genetic female becoming an apparently normal man—challenge our preconceptions. Until genes were discovered under a microscope, no one had an inkling that such people even existed. In biblical times or in any other society, they would have lived out their lives as normal, though sterile, men and women.

No one today would seriously consider telling such people in midlife that they need to leave their mates and undergo surgery to make their genitals match their genes. They are absolutely certain of their sexual identity and are quite successful and happy with it. These cases demonstrate that just the presence of sufficient male or female hormones during gestation, even by accident or defect, is enough to create what we call a man or woman, irrespective of genetic sex.

Since their genitals appeared normal, these children were raised as boys or girls with no uncertainty. But the most important factor in their success as men or women may be that their developing brains were bathed in hormones opposite of their genetic sex, thus giving them fully masculine or feminine brains to match their genitals.

The general rule seems to be that the more testosterone to which a fetus is exposed, the more masculine brain function will become. A study of girls who were exposed to high levels of testosterone prenatally demonstrates its powerful effects on brain development.[15] Even though their masculinized genitals and hormonal defects were corrected shortly after birth, these girls were predominately "tomboys," preferred aggressive outdoor games to dolls, and dreamed of future careers more than marriage and raising a family. Their interest in boys seemed to develop somewhat later than their peers, but they did *not* show any lesbian or transsexual tendencies. (Similar results have been reported for girls who were accidentally masculinized by hormones their mothers took during pregnancy.)

Clearly these girls had their brains masculinized to a considerable degree. But since they were comfortable being women and were attracted to boys, not girls, this essentially proves that women who are sexually attracted to women (lesbians) or women who wish to become men (female-to-male transsexuals) are not compelled to do so by a masculinized brain. Early childhood experiences and later social influences seem to play more of a role in both these sexual problems.

This point is further illuminated by a study of girls with similar defects who did not receive medical attention until adolescence, including some who never had their genital defects corrected.[16] These girls lived through childhood with somewhat masculine-looking genitals and experienced a virilizing puberty that made their bodies look even more masculine (the "bearded lady" effect). These girls showed the same "tomboyish" characteristics as the first set of girls. But they likely had more confused feelings in childhood about their gender because of their deformed genitals. They surely endured a great deal of social distress and peer rejection because of their unusual appearance. Yet, despite these hindrances, as adults, all of the women identified themselves as female, and 40% said they were exclusively heterosexual. The rest admitted some degree of sexual attraction to women. Comparing these two groups of girls suffering from the same disorder—one group treated early and one group treated late—provides strong evidence that social factors, not brain masculinization in the womb, are responsible for homosexuality in women.

Mild intersex birth defects are not much of a problem today because they can be easily repaired with surgery shortly after birth.

WOMEN WHO ARE SEXUALLY ATTRACTED TO WOMEN (LESBIANS) OR WOMEN WHO WISH TO BECOME MEN (FEMALE-TO-MALE TRANSSEXUALS) ARE NOT COMPELLED TO DO SO BY A MASCULINIZED BRAIN.

However, in more severe cases, there are no easy answers. The traditional medical approach has been to assign such children to one sex or the other based on their chances of being able to function sexually as that sex. This means that most genetic-boy babies with missing penises are reassigned as girls—since it is relatively easy to construct a normal-looking vagina, but impossible to create a working penis. Most of these children do accept the gender in which they are raised. It makes sense that if they were exposed to enough contradictory hormonal messages in the womb to give them mixed genital structures, then it is quite likely that their brains will have some mixture of male and female organization. This may enable them to easily adapt to whichever gender role is chosen by their parents.

THERE IS STRONG EVIDENCE THAT SOCIAL FACTORS, NOT BRAIN MASCULINIZATION IN THE WOMB, ARE RESPONSIBLE FOR HOMOSEXUALITY IN WOMEN.

However, problems have occurred when a child's "brain sex" is later found to be diametrically opposed to his or her reassigned "genital sex." The most notable of such cases involve boys who were completely normal at birth, but who later had their penises destroyed in a medical accident.[17] The doctors handling these cases advised the parents to have their boys surgically converted into girls and the parents agreed because they felt their children would at least be able to marry as women instead of having to live as eunuchs. Yet, despite the parents' best efforts to raise them as girls, these children exhibited very boyish behavior during childhood and expressed a desire to be boys. One such boy, who was studied until adulthood, eventually began living as a man, was sexually attracted to women, and decided to have reconstructive surgery to make his genitals look as masculine as possible. In truth, he had always been a normal boy on the inside, even without a penis. This illustrates the power "brain sex" can have—and perhaps teaches us a lesson about medical arrogance.

Because of these and other mistakes that have been made in gender reassignment of such children, many adults who were born with an intersex condition are now advocating that children with serious intersex conditions be left alone until they are old enough to reveal what their true "brain sex" is. Then they can have the appropriate surgery or choose to remain as they are. Some intersex adults also report that after years of artificial hormone therapy and expensive and painful reconstructive surgeries, they are now much happier living just as they were born—as eunuchs.

Reviewing all of these studies and unusual cases further illuminates what we learned in the previous section about the prenatal sexual development of the brain and "brain sex":

- The presence of testosterone in the fetal environment causes the brain to be "wired" in such a way that these characteristics are emphasized:
  - visual-spatial skills
  - a high level of physical activity/energy or aggression
  - sexual arousal primarily through images

- The lack of testosterone in the fetal environment causes the brain to be "wired" in such a way that these characteristics are emphasized:
  - verbal-intuitive skills
  - maternal interests
  - sexual arousal primarily through touch

- A very high level of testosterone during gestation produces the first set of characteristics to an extreme degree. A very low level of testosterone during gestation produces the second set of characteristics to an extreme degree. Intermediate levels of testosterone are likely to produce some combination of these characteristics without any extremes.

- Most men exhibit the first set of characteristics to a greater degree than most women. Most women exhibit the second set of characteristics to a greater

207

degree than most men. Yet, there also seem to be many men and women who exhibit a mixture of these characteristics. (Brain scans also show that a significant number of men and women have gender-atypical brain patterns.) Such "brain wiring" outside of the norm has been speculated to result from fluctuations in testosterone levels in the womb that were too small to affect genital development (or occurred at the wrong time), yet did leave an imprint on brain development.

It is important to note what these studies do *not* prove: that having brain "wiring" more typical of the opposite sex, or with some elements typical of both sexes, *directly* affects one's identity as a man or woman, or causes sexual attraction to the same sex. However, brain sex does have a powerful influence on our temperament, skills, and the activities we find most enjoyable. These all can have an *indirect* effect on sexual development by affecting how others behave toward us and influencing how we react to and interpret experiences during childhood. We will examine this in more detail in the following sections.

Sexual Development in Childhood

By birth, biological sex has been determined (for the fortunate majority). But there are many more aspects of sexuality yet to develop.

Early childhood learning seems to be critical to many types of future behavior because the brain is still developing during this time. The brain grows significantly throughout childhood, being only 25% of its adult weight at birth, but reaching 50% in the six months after birth and 95% by the age of 10. An important principle discovered through many studies is that early learning actually changes the size of brain structures. For example, the area of the brain that controls the fingers of the left hand is highly developed in string players, but it has been found to be largest in those who had begun playing the earliest in childhood.[18] Research has also revealed that there are windows of opportunity in early childhood when the brain is particularly adept at certain kinds of learning—such as learning a new language—that become more difficult after the time window has closed.

Throughout childhood there is evidence that boys and girls learn in different ways and at different rates because of the sex-based brain wiring that was begun in the womb. In boys, the right hemisphere of the brain is typically more mature than the left until about the age of puberty. This leads boys to develop right-brain visual-spatial skills earlier than left-brain verbal skills, and perhaps to use right-brain visual skills more actively in learning. The situation is reversed in girls, whose left-brain hemisphere tends to be more mature than the right. They seem to develop verbal skills earlier than visual-spatial skills and to use left brain verbal skills more actively in learning.[19] Thus, it is not at all surprising that experiences in early childhood have a significant and lasting impact on the development of sexuality, since the wiring of the brain is still being run during this time.

Two foundational elements of adult sexuality that develop during these early years are *gender identity* and *gender role*.

Gender Identity

Gender identity is at the core of an individual's personality. It is the answer to the fundamental question: "Am I a man, or a woman, or something in between?" This is a question most people do not remember asking because it was asked and answered at a very young age. If this question is not clearly answered in early childhood—"Who am I? What am I?"—it clouds a person's very identity and remains a source of sexual problems throughout life.

For most people, biological sex determines gender identity. But the bulk of the evidence shows that it does so indirectly through a learning process.[20] Adults treat children differently according to their biological sex from the moment of birth. Infant boys receive much more energetic physical stimulation. Infant girls receive more talking and gentle touching. Parents also dress the children in gender-appropriate clothing and encourage gender-appropriate types of play. With so much encouragement children soon learn how to act like little boys or little girls.

Researchers believe that a child's gender identity is normally set at one and a half to three years of age. They base this on the results of sex reassignment surgery performed on children born with an intersex condition. These children were found most likely to develop a consistent gender identity when corrective surgery to make them appear fully male or fully female was completed by the age of eighteen months. After that, the children showed various degrees of confusion in trying to adopt a new gender identity.[21]

After the age of three, gender identity becomes strongly fixed for most children. Yet even physically normal children can become confused about their gender identity when parents send mixed signals, such as dressing the child in clothes of the opposite sex, or saying things like, "You would have made a beautiful girl" to their little boy, or, "You are such a tomboy" to their daughter. A child may also mistakenly identify with the parent of the opposite sex—for example, a boy who spends most of his early years in close contact with his mother and fails to develop an emotional bond with his father.

Even though gender identity may be fixed, there is still room for insecurity. Some children become unhappy with their gender. Many more develop some fears of "losing" their gender identity. Even men who have no question about their basic gender identity still may feel insecure at some point in their lives and wonder, "Am I manly enough?" or "Am I a real man yet?" This may lead them to engage in risk-taking behavior that society considers especially masculine—such as getting drunk or fighting—in an attempt to prove their manhood. Women seem to have greater security with their feminine identity, unless it is threatened by a crisis, such as infertility or a mastectomy.

Gender Role

Each society has a set of typical behaviors that distinguish men from women. These may include style of clothing, gestures, use of language, occupation, leisure activities, behavior toward the opposite sex, and so forth. Taken together, these established patterns of masculine or feminine behavior create a masculine or feminine *role* for each person to play in the society.

The original basis for these roles is rooted in the obvious biological differences between men and women. Particularly where people must struggle with a harsh environment to survive, it makes sense that men and women divide the work between them so that each can do the tasks they are best suited for physiologically. Men are more muscular and so are better adapted for activities such as hunting, heavy labor, and defending the family, while women have greater finger dexterity and can do a better job with tasks like weaving and sewing clothing. Their children will need to learn the appropriate role behaviors for their gender at an early age, because they will soon need to be exceptionally good at those skills to survive. They do not have the luxury of trying many different things and developing only those skills they enjoy the most.

When a young man and woman marry in this type of society, they can be confident they will survive as a team because each has become an expert in a complementary set of essential skills. This keeps them highly dependent on each other throughout their marriage. So we see that complementary and well-defined gender roles help strengthen families and societies wherever living conditions are difficult. We see gender roles becoming more flexible only in relatively prosperous societies, where food is plentiful and life is easy.

Three major areas of childhood experience seem to be the most critical to development of gender identity and gender role and thus can have a lifelong effect on sexuality:

- Parent-child relationships
- Social relationships
- Childhood sexual experience

Parent-Child Relationships

There is nearly universal agreement among counselors and psychologists that the mother-child and father-child relationships are two of the most critical influences on lifelong mental health. These relationships are also believed to be the foundation for the development of gender identity and gender role because they exert the first influences on how one perceives and relates to the sexes.

The following phases of the parent-child relationship occur sequentially in the early years of life: bonding, modeling, and identification.

1. Bonding

Within the first six months of life, an infant has formed an attachment to his or her primary caregivers, usually mother and father. Failure to achieve this attachment, such as has occurred in some orphanages, has been shown to result in severe and permanent retardation of physical, mental, emotional, and social development, and a greatly increased mortality rate. It is not until the age of 12–18 months that an infant is able to form significant relationships beyond the primary caregivers, such as with babysitters or grandparents.

Extensive study[22] of the initial mother-child relationship has revealed three basic types:

> (a) *Securely attached* – These infants eagerly sought contact with their mothers, were only moderately distressed by separation, and sought reassurance from their mothers in strange situations. Of all the infants studied, these were the most responsive,

obedient, and content, and cried the least. The mothers of these infants had been the most affectionate, sensitive, and responsive to their needs—for example, feeding them when they were hungry and giving them extra cuddling.

(b) *Ambivalently attached* – These infants approached but then avoided their mothers after a brief separation. These mothers had a habit of responding to their infants' cries only when they were in the mood.

(c) *Avoidantly attached* – These infants were severely distressed by a brief separation from their mothers, yet avoided contact with their mothers when reunited, and seemed angry or hostile. They were more hesitant to leave their mothers to explore. These mothers tended to avoid physical contact and had rarely shown affection or responses to their infants' cries, even ignoring them when they were hungry.

The securely attached infants were more friendly, outgoing, competent, curious, persistent, and showed better relationships with peers. There is no doubt they had been given a significant boost toward future emotional well-being, while the insecurely attached infants had already been emotionally handicapped. The folk wisdom that a crying child should be ignored lest it be spoiled was clearly shown to be wrong. The most securely attached infants had received the most attention. The mother's behavior proved to be the crucial factor in determining the quality of the mother-infant bond.

The father-infant relationship has not been as extensively studied, but what has been observed of it shows great similarity to the mother-infant relationship. Most fathers bond to their children shortly after birth.

An infant develops an attachment to his father at about the same time as he does to his mother (usually by six months) even though most fathers spend less time with their infants than do the mothers. The initial bond is established more through touch and holding than feeding, so fathers can bond with their infants equally as well as mothers. As with mothers, the father's behavior is believed to be the crucial factor in determining the quality of the father-infant bond.[23]

Many fathers seem to be reluctant to get involved with their children until they are a little older, perhaps because they are uncomfortable handling an infant or just think that a child that young cannot really bond to them. However, in one study of babies just over a year old, almost half were as strongly attached, *or even more so*, to their fathers as to their mothers.[24] This should be a strong encouragement to dads that they need to make the effort to be involved with their children from birth.

The mother-infant bond is believed by many to be the foundation for all other emotional bonds that are formed over the lifetime, particularly romantic relationships. We can only speculate at this time on the long-term effects of the father-infant bond. However, failure in the subsequent father-child relationship is now emerging as a crucial factor in creating the tremendous social problems afflicting our society today. Over the past few decades the lack of a father (or father-figure) has been identified by a growing number of psychological and sociological studies as *the primary cause of all adolescent delinquency for both boys and girls.*[25] Yet, how many fathers today realize just how crucial they are to their children's emotional development?

Another critical influence in early child development that continues to be studied is the effect of day care. One pivotal study showed that more than 20 hours of nonmaternal care each week puts a child at risk for an insecure attachment to his mother.[26] Full-time nonmaternal care has also been shown to put a child at risk for an insecure attachment to his father. Though this subject is still hotly debated, I believe the evidence so far indicates that institutionalized day care is emotionally unhealthy for very small children. For the first 12-18 months infants are simply unable to form social attachments other than the parental bonds. Even worse, institutional facilities can never provide the same level of adult-child interaction that full-time mothers do, and that is so critical to mental and emotional development.

As Christians, we should be cognizant, not only of the mental and emotional aspects of the parent-child bond, but also of the spiritual. We know that children are spiritual beings. The bond they seek with their parents and other caregivers has a spiritual component, and this is as God intended. The parent stands in the place of God in caring for the child. It is evidently God's plan for each of us to first learn of His love and care from the way our parents care for us. We have all experienced an infant or toddler clinging to us, nestling in our arms. Those who are spiritually aware may have sensed at those times the intimacy the child's spirit is seeking, desiring to draw love and strength from us. An infant is, as we all are, in essence an immortal spiritual being who *senses* and *knows* at a deep spiritual level, even though his brain is still developing in many ways. It is revealing to note in the studies of maternal attachment summarized above that some infants expressed anger and hostility toward their mothers. Though their brains may be undeveloped, children's *spirits* know if they are being loved or rejected. Their *spirits* know if they were unwanted, even in the womb.[27]

> THOUGH THEIR BRAINS MAY BE UNDEVELOPED, CHILDREN'S SPIRITS KNOW IF THEY ARE BEING LOVED OR REJECTED. THEIR SPIRITS KNOW IF THEY WERE UNWANTED, EVEN IN THE WOMB.

Infants have been shown to have different temperaments at birth, some being easily upset and others more sanguine. Yet, it is still clearly the responsibility of the parents to develop and maintain a close bond with their children from birth and throughout childhood. Based on the success of this initial bond, *modeling* and *identification* are the next phases of learning that take place.

2. Modeling and Identification

New research shows that infants are veritable learning machines. Every sight, every sound, every smell, every touch causes new connections to form among the cells of the brain. There is now evidence that children who are *not* exposed to certain stimuli at this early age—such as the basic sounds of a given language—will never develop the brain circuitry to process them. (This is believed to be the explanation for the difficulty most Japanese have in distinguishing and saying the "l" and "r" sounds of English. Since the Japanese language does not contain those sounds, Japanese infants are not exposed to them during the critical period.)[28]

Modeling, or learning through imitation, is the way in which infants first learn behaviors. One study has shown that even newborns, 7–72 hours old, try to imitate the facial expressions of their caregivers.[29] There is a similar modeling mechanism for speech development. Beginning at about eight months, the cooing and babbling of an infant as it responds to its mother's voice changes to imitate the sounds she has been using to speak her native tongue.

The theory of childhood development advanced by Piaget says that by age two, children are using categories to organize everything they learn. However, more recent evidence shows that categorization (at least gender-based categorization) may begin slightly before two. By 15–26 months of age, most children show a preference for gender-appropriate toys. By two, they show a preference for same-gender playmates. By two and a half they know the stereotypes of gender-appropriate behavior.[30] Seeing that the parent-child bond is the primary relationship for at least the first year of life, it should be obvious where 15–18-month-olds learn their own gender identity and appropriate gender role behavior: from Mom and Dad.

Studies of infant and adult interactions show that parents treat children differently based on their sex from the moment of birth.[31] Mothers show less gender-specific interaction, but fathers are quite active in reinforcing gender-appropriate behavior for both sons and daughters. Fathers encourage sons to compete, to be independent, to be assertive, and to engage in active play and sports. Fathers encourage girls to be affectionate, obedient, and nurturing. Boys raised by single mothers show less typically masculine play and behaviors, particularly under the age of five. However, in adolescence they may show more exaggerated and aggressive masculine behavior, perhaps in an attempt to compensate for insecurity about their masculinity. Girls raised without fathers exhibit less feminine behavior and tend to be more promiscuous in adolescence.

From the evidence to date, it appears that the bond with the father throughout childhood is critical in developing a secure gender identity and appropriate gender role behavior. Both father and mother provide a daily demonstration of the behaviors appropriate for their respective genders. However, fathers seem to be most important in *reinforcing* the modeling of gender-appropriate behavior. Boys raised without fathers, or boys with poor father-son relationships, often seem to model feminine behavior from their mothers, since there is no negative reinforcement from Dad to prevent it. This can cause significant problems when they begin to interact with their peer group. Learning gender-appropriate behavior is usually easier for girls, since the mother is most often the primary caregiver. Modeling continues to be a major force in learning gender role behavior for boys and girls throughout childhood through fantasy play, such as playing house or "cops and robbers."

Becoming intertwined with bonding and modeling influences at some point is the force of *identification*. A child who is secure in his or her gender identity and has good parental bonds will begin to identify with the parent of the same sex. This is an important step because the child is no longer being molded only by indiscriminate modeling and parental reinforcement, but is actively seeking to emulate the same-sex parent out of love and admiration.

"I want to be just like Dad when I grow up" is a healthy expression of this attitude by a small boy. Boys without fathers, or boys who have poor relationships with their fathers, are motivated to seek a male "father figure" with whom to identify. This is the basis for the "hero worship" common to boys of a certain age—which may indicate that their own fathers are not fulfilling the role of "hero" very well. Identification with their mothers is just as important for girls, but this may, again, be easier for them to accomplish since mothers tend to be more available and involved as primary caregivers.

A crisis in the child's relationship with the same-sex parent at any point can lead to a break in the relationship and motivate the child to *dis-identify* (reject the identification) with the parent. Elizabeth Moberly, a Christian psychologist, has termed this reaction by the child "defensive detachment." She believes this is an underlying factor in many cases of male and female homosexuality.[32] Such a crisis can stem from many events: divorce, abandonment, a severe conflict or disappointment—or even the death of the parent, which the child *interprets* as abandonment. The determining factor is the child's *reaction* to the crisis. Such an event may lead the child to identify instead with the opposite-sex parent and become "Daddy's little girl" or "Momma's little boy." This may lead them to unconsciously model opposite-gender behaviors and mannerisms that can cause them to suffer ridicule and rejection by their peers.

Many therapists believe that, over the long term, the rejection such children feel from a same-sex parent and same-sex peers causes them to develop a *same-sex love deficit.* They feel deeply hurt and rejected by members of their sex, yet they have an overwhelming desire to seek the love they have been denied. This seems to be a primary motivation for many (though not all) who suffer from homosexual feelings. Somehow, the desire for same-sex love becomes entangled with sexual needs and is expressed as an erotic attraction to others of the same sex.

It is essential to understand a child's view of gender and gender roles at this point. A significant study showed that, though children are aware of their own gender at age two, they do not realize that it is an unchangeable trait until around age seven.[33] Children below this age tend to think that gender is defined by outward appearance, such as hair, clothing style, or behavior, and that changing the outward appearance can cause a change in gender. Children who are happy with their gender are then motivated to strictly follow the stereotypes of gender role behavior for fear of losing their gender identity. Children who are unhappy with their gender identity, because of parental wishes for a child of the opposite sex ("You would have made a lovely girl"), or because a break in the relationship with the same-sex parent causes them to dis-identify with that parent, may then try to change their gender by deliberately adopting gender role behaviors of the opposite sex. They are conscious of their genital sex, but they also seem subject to the magical belief that penises might suddenly drop off little boys or appear on little girls overnight, if they only wish hard enough. It is perhaps more appropriate to call this a case of *gender rejection* rather than *gender confusion*.

This fragility of early childhood gender identity, which is so dependent on gender role behavior, seems to be the reason that some aberrant parenting practices have been so strongly linked to adult disorders of gender identity and abnormal erotic feelings. Case histories of male transsexuals frequently describe a mother who dresses her boy as a little girl "because he looks so cute, and I always wanted a little girl." Likewise, small children who see their cross-dressing father "dressed," or who have a transsexual father reintroduced to them after his sex change as their new "auntie," can become very confused and fearful of losing their own gender identity.

A case history of a heterosexual male *transvestite* (someone who dresses in clothes of the opposite sex to fulfill erotic desires) revealed that his mother had frequently dressed him as a little girl to punish him. As an adult, although he is sexually attracted to women, he can function sexually only when dressed as a woman.

Social Relationships

The influences of relatives, teachers, babysitters, and other children start to become noticeable by the age of 12–18 months. By this age, children can form social attachments, and anxiety over separation from their parents begins to ease. The most important influences by far are peer relationships. These are second in influence only to parental relationships, and typically supercede even those by adolescence.

It is after the age of two that children first begin to seek out same-sex playgroups. This is evidence of their growing awareness of gender and its importance. Some experts believe they do this in an attempt to reinforce their own sense of gender identity. Children at this age are categorizing to a great extent, and making up their own rules about what belongs in each category, though many of the rules do not make sense by adult standards, such as "all four-legged animals are 'dog.'" One of the rules for categories is that of polar opposites. If boys are one thing, then girls must be the opposite: "Boys are good at ball; girls are not."

In Western societies, within the artificial environment of age-segregated public schools, boy and girl groups continue to develop along divergent lines, until they form their own separate subcultures, further segregating the sexes. Boy culture focuses on competition and establishing a dominance hierarchy. Girl culture is more egalitarian, but becomes increasingly centered on appearance and popularity with other girls. Boy culture is quite rigid about what is considered proper masculine role behavior and becomes even more so throughout the school years. The standards for masculine behavior are enforced through ridicule and physical punishment. Girl culture is more flexible with respect to appropriate gender role behavior for girls, perhaps because our society is more accepting of women dressing like men and doing everything men do. Yet, girl culture has its own unwritten rules of social interaction and physical appearance that may be violated only on pain of social death.

Some friendships between boys and girls do occur during this time, but it seems that only the boys at the top of the dominance hierarchy are allowed to get away with them. One of the worst epithets a boy of pre-pubescent age can hurl at another is "You love Cindy!" "No, I don't!" is the typical reply.

The major drawback of these separate boy and girl cultures occurs for the children who don't make the team, or who don't get invited to the sleepovers. Fat boys, small boys, handicapped boys, boys who throw like a sissy, intellectual boys, boys with mixed up gender role behaviors, big girls, plain girls, girls who can't afford nice clothes, late bloomers—all these children become social outcasts, and being an outcast for fifteen or more years of childhood can take a tremendous psychological toll. One researcher asked a group of ten-year-old boys to define the derogatives ("queer," "faggot") they were using toward one of their peers. They said, "It means he can't play ball."[34]

Many children are given homosexual labels such as these, years before they even understand the concept. Sadly, many eventually accept this as their destiny. For the child who did not get a secure grounding in his or her gender identity, or who has unconsciously modeled the behaviors of the opposite-sex parent, such flaws are a social death blow. Their age-mates shut them out of the power hierarchy, the social whirl, and the dating games.

These boy and girl cultures spawned by our public school system have serious flaws. Children are really searching for adult role models, but our culture feeds them only caricatures and fantasy figures. From these they construct their childish standards for masculine and feminine behavior. Boys seem drawn to emulate fictional male characters who are extremely violent, are emotionally inhibited, and exploit women. Girls often seek to emulate the physical appearance of fashion models through an obsession with clothes and unhealthy dieting, or the behavior of female movie characters who manipulate men with their sexuality.

American men and women seem to maintain these childish attitudes about appropriate gender behavior through the teen years and young adulthood. Feminists marvel at how little impact three decades of feminism seems to have had on the attitudes of young women, who still seem unnaturally obsessed with their bodies and their appearance. The irony, now, is that these young ladies are not starving themselves and spending a fortune on clothes to attract young men as much as they are to win the approval of other young ladies.

American men cannot play a musical instrument, cook, or grow flowers without having their masculinity called into question, though most European cultures consider these to be quite masculine pursuits. The nature of American male culture is that those who do not measure up to the most rigid standards—originally developed by preteen boys—are stripped of their gender and their right to heterosexuality.

Tomboys and "Sissy" Boys

Tomboys and "sissy" boys are well-known concepts in American culture. These are the boys and girls who exhibit gender role behaviors more appropriate for the opposite sex than for their own. We have already seen how, through the natural learning mechanisms of modeling and identification, a young boy or girl can end up emulating the gender behaviors and attitudes of the opposite-sex parent instead of the same-sex parent.

A question well worth asking is why American culture is so accepting of girls being tomboys but abhors boys being "sissies." Girls may dress like boys anytime they wish and do anything boys do. With the help of "equal opportunity" laws, that can now mean joining the boys' football team or wrestling squad. But consider the reaction if a boy were to come to school dressed like a girl and ask to be in the school beauty pageant or fashion show. He would be considered seriously disturbed by most people, and his parents would be encouraged to get him some counseling. (However, nondiscrimination laws are now beginning to be used to force schools to support even this sort of behavior.)

What is most troubling to us about such behaviors is also a part of folk wisdom: children with gender-inappropriate behaviors are likely to grow up to become homosexuals. Sadly, this suspicion has been confirmed by research. In fact, gender-inappropriate behavior in childhood—for both boys and girls—has been shown to be *the strongest predictor of homosexuality developing later in life.*[35] In extreme cases it also may indicate a problem with gender identity, where children reject their own sex and desire to become a member of the opposite sex.

Just how gender-inappropriate behavior is connected to the development of homosexuality is hotly debated. Not all children with gender-inappropriate behavior become homosexuals, but the majority of adults who identify themselves as homosexuals report gender-inappropriate behavior in childhood.

As we saw in the earlier section on brain development, from earliest childhood some people seem to exhibit some basic behavioral characteristics more typical of the opposite sex, apparently due to fundamental differences in the way their brains work. For example, a girl may have lit-tle interest in dolls and prefer more active pursuits, perhaps a rough-and-tumble sport. A boy may have poor visual-spatial skills and a naturally low energy level that hinders him from enjoying or excelling in sports, so he may prefer quieter activities, such as reading or insect collecting. If such natural temperaments and behaviors cause the same-sex parent to be dis-appointed and withdraw from the child, while the opposite-sex parent is encouraged to spend more time with the child, then the child is likely to come to identify more with the opposite-sex parent and model gender-inappropriate behavior.

This is where the reaction of the parents becomes so critical. A father may be overjoyed to have a daughter who follows him everywhere, watches all the games with him, and imitates everything he does. A moth-er may be ecstatic to have a son who shares all of her interests. This can come about because of a child's natural temperament. Yet if a girl becomes close to her father but feels estranged from her mother, if a son grows emo-tionally closer to his mother while growing distant from his father, this sets the stage for future trouble.

First, cross-gender behavior sets these children up for rejection and ridicule by their peer group, further reinforcing their self-image as "differ-ent." But even deeper problems of gender identity can develop if a tomboy-ish girl begins to reject her mother and her own femininity to actively pur-sue a masculine identity, or if a "sissy" boy rejects his father, all male role models, and even his own masculinity to pursue a feminine identity.

However, when a mother accepts her daughter's naturally energetic or outgoing temperament, yet finds ways to help her develop and appreci-ate her feminine identity, or when a father accepts his son's quieter tem-perament, yet affirms his masculinity and finds other masculine pursuits they can enjoy together, then gender-inappropriate behavior becomes less of a problem. Same-sex parents can also be of great help to their children in learning how to relate to same-sex peers. With this type of parenting, the likelihood that such children will develop gender or sexual problems is greatly reduced.

Childhood Sexual Experience

It is a common misconception that children have no sexual feelings or interest. Actually, children do have a very low level of sexual feelings and response from birth, though it is not often noticeable, and parents often ignore any evidence of it out of embarrassment.

Sexual arousal for both males and females begins in the womb. There is ultrasound evidence for erections in male fetuses and similar arousal is presumed to occur in females. Spontaneous, periodic penile erection and vaginal arousal continues through infancy and childhood—for example, during breast feeding, or in response to touch, as when a diaper is changed. Infant boys have nocturnal erections during sleep, which occur throughout life in all healthy males.[36] The purpose of these is still unknown, but they are suspected to help the penis stay in good working order. The sexual arousal of childhood is mildly pleasurable, but it does not yet have the strong emotional connotations that it will after puberty begins.

> **SEXUAL AROUSAL FOR BOTH MALES AND FEMALES BEGINS IN THE WOMB.**

Children begin to touch their genitals as soon as they discover it feels good. There is no known harm in this, but there is definitely harm in parents creating an association of shame, fear, and guilt toward body parts, body functions, and sexuality. Children need to learn modest behavior without learning to be ashamed of their sexuality. Most children just need to be told that they should only touch or examine their genitals in private.

There are rare reports of children who begin to masturbate compulsively and even seem to experience an orgasm. Many of these children have other developmental problems or a history of sexual or physical abuse. However, such problem behavior can be eliminated through distraction with other activities and rewards for good behavior.

The most well-known expression of childhood sexuality is "playing doctor and nurse." Similar games (called *sexual rehearsal play*) are found in all cultures. As we have seen, gender awareness develops early, and children have a natural curiosity about the differences between the sexes. They are also intent on modeling adult behaviors, so if they are being raised in a healthy family, this would naturally include the affectionate and romantic behavior they see expressed between their parents. Even though most children are just "playing house" as "mommies" and "daddies" at this age, a definite attraction has been noted between boys and girls as young as three. Cases have been reported of children who formed such a strong bond throughout childhood that they eventually married when they became adults.

It is interesting to compare these early experiences of Western children with those in societies we would call more "primitive" (such as the Aborigines of Arnhem Land, Australia,[37] or the Cotabato Manobo of the Philippines[38]). In these primitive societies there is much less modesty about nudity and sexuality. Because of close quarters, children are unavoidably exposed to adult sexual relationships. Thus, the sexual rehearsal play these children dream up is typically "pretend intercourse." They are imitating what they see adults doing, and such games are just laughed at by the rest of the community.

The surprising result of all of this apparently immodest behavior is that these "primitive" societies show no evidence or even awareness of the many and varied sexual perversions and disorders (including homosexuality) that afflict our more "advanced" Western cultures. Because of this amazing quality, sociologists and sexologists who have studied these societies conclude that heterosexuality is, indeed, natural. Everyone achieves it when there are no obstacles placed in the way. Along with our many social and technological advancements, we Westerners seem to have inflicted a great host of sexual problems on ourselves and on our children.

Now, I am not advocating any radical changes in dress codes, but when parents catch their child "playing doctor" with the neighborhood children, they should use this opportunity to teach some basic lessons about sexuality at an age-appropriate level (along with reasons for modest behavior) without making this a lesson in sexual shame. It is truly sad to realize that when children call such sexual games "playing doctor," they are revealing that they have absolutely no knowledge of the connection between love and sex. Such intimate contact has only an unemotional association with what happens to them at the doctor's office. Christians, especially, tend to raise their children in an atmosphere of ignorance about sexuality—not just ignorance of the mechanics, but of all the mental, emotional, and spiritual issues that accompany it. I am convinced this is one big reason why "good Christian families" keep raising "good Christian kids" who get into serious sexual sin. Learning to manage our sexuality is a life-long learning process that must begin in childhood, before sexual feelings become so strong that they feel out of control. Most parents spend more time teaching their teens how to drive a car than they do teaching them how to control their sexual urges or how to choose a good mate.

If this book accomplishes little else, I would be more than satisfied if the parents who read it would decide to take charge of their children's sexual education. Christians have fought to keep secularized, value-free sex education without moral values out of the schools. But many of us are still abdicating our God-given responsibility to teach the children He gave us the full truth of His purpose and plan for sex. When children begin to become curious about their sexuality, they should never be misled or kept in a state of confusion. That can lead to potentially damaging misconceptions. Children need to have their questions about sex answered promptly with as much factual information as they can handle at the time. The information in this book is a place to start, and I certainly recommend it for teens. For additional guidance in teaching younger children age-appropriate lessons about sexuality, I heartily recommend *How & When to Tell Your Kids About Sex*[39] by Stanton and Brenna Jones.

Sexual Abuse of Children

The risk of a child being sexually abused in our society is incredibly high: *1 in every 3 to 4 girls and 1 in every 5 to 10 boys.* Though incidents of children being kidnapped, raped, and murdered get the most attention from the media, the overwhelming majority of sexually abused children are molested by people with whom they are acquainted and see on a regular basis—family members, child care workers, neighbors, friends of the family, and people from church.

Because of the great ignorance and shame about sexual matters that we inflict on our children, many of those who are abused do not talk about it with anyone until many years later, if ever. So these estimates are probably too low.

There is now an abundance of evidence that childhood sexual abuse can be quite harmful, causing lifelong disturbances to sexuality. Because children can experience sexual pleasure and respond sexually while being molested, their thoughts and emotions can become very confused. They feel a mixture of fear, pain, and shame, but at the same time enjoy the sexual pleasure and affection. If these children have been kept in ignorance about sexuality, they can become very confused about the meaning of what happened to them. A boy may learn the lesson that, since an older man found him sexually attractive, it must be his fault for being somehow "female." A young girl in the same situation may develop a deep hatred for men and of her own sexuality because of what one man did to her. She may learn the lesson that to make yourself look beautiful or to behave in a feminine way is to put yourself in danger of rape.

BECAUSE CHILDREN CAN EXPERIENCE SEXUAL PLEASURE AND RESPOND SEXUALLY WHILE BEING MOLESTED, THEIR THOUGHTS AND EMOTIONS CAN BECOME VERY CONFUSED.

The process of sexual *imprinting* can also occur during molestation, causing the child to develop a pattern of arousal to abnormal stimuli. Remember, the child is a virgin and this sexual experience is his "first time," so the powerful mechanisms of sexual bonding can be set in motion, particularly if the child experiences an orgasm. The majority of pedophiles (those with a sexual attraction to children) were themselves molested as children. For many of them, the lesson they seemed to learn from the incident was that sexual feelings are supposed to be expressed in sexual acts between adults and children.

My counseling office has been filled over the years with people whose lifelong sexual problems began with incidents such as these, and who learned wrong lessons that were never corrected. The good news is that molested children can recover from the incident, without lifelong effects, *if they receive counseling and the loving support of their parents.* But this means they have to be free enough from sexual shame so they can report what happened to them. Even better, children can be "molestation-proofed" by receiving early education about their sexuality, learning what areas of their bodies are off-limits to others, and practicing how to resist an improper advance by an older child or adult. But parents must first overcome their own sexual shame and ignorance if they are going to provide their children with this protection.

Sexual Development in Adolescence

Most parents would agree that puberty arrives far too early. Actually, studies have shown that it has been arriving earlier with each generation. Over a century ago, girls did not begin menstruating until around 16 or 17. Today the median age for the beginning of menstruation is 12 or 13, and many girls begin at 9.[40]

Since for many mammals the onset of puberty occurs after reaching a certain body weight, many experts believe that children today are entering puberty earlier because they weigh more at younger ages, perhaps because of a high-fat diet and sedentary lifestyle.

Whenever it arrives, puberty brings with it the gradual unveiling of the remaining components of adult sexuality: *sexual object choice, sexual desire,* and *sexual behavior.*

Sexual Object Choice

Sexual object choice is the set of visual or other sensory stimuli that stir up erotic interest and sexual arousal in an individual. Calling it a "choice" is somewhat misleading because for most people it seems as if they have no choice in what attracts their sexual interest; the origin of our sexual interests often seems hidden from us. The concept of the *lovemap*, mentioned in Chapter 4, is broader in scope. It includes not only the attributes that stir up sexual object choice, but also those attributes that lead to feelings of romantic love—all the ideal qualities that people look for in a mate.

Some of the greatest differences between men and women are manifested in the area of sexual object choice. Research has shown that men respond erotically mostly to visual stimuli, while women respond more to touch and verbal cues, and even to the sound of a man's voice. When choosing to indulge in sexual fantasy, men prefer pornography while women prefer romance novels and soap operas. Men can, and often do, seek sex without a relationship because they are sexually attracted to "body parts," while this is rare for women. Women are erotically attracted to whole persons, including their personalities. Sexual involvement for them almost always requires emotional involvement.

Men are also much more prone to abnormalities in sexual object choice than are women. This may be because male sexuality, being oriented more toward images and objects, can be more easily misprogrammed or misdirected by life events. These observations substantiate the fact that the sexual area of the brain functions quite differently in men and women.

Erotic dreams may provide a particularly clear, uncensored window into the true state of a person's sexual object choice, since we have little conscious control over their contents. These dreams are frequently accompanied by sexual arousal and even orgasm in both men and women. However, we must bear in mind that people often have erotic dreams about sexual activities in which they have never engaged and would never choose to do in real life.

Sexual object choice can be determined in a laboratory with a device called a *plethysmograph,* which measures sexual arousal. This equipment is similar to a polygraph in its function and reliability. It is frequently used to evaluate sex offenders as to their degree of arousal to abnormal stimuli, such as scenarios of rape or molestation.

The brain mechanism that governs the development of sexual object choice is still somewhat of a mystery, but we do have some strong clues and emerging theories as to its functioning; these clues and theories have often come from studying those who have developed an abnormal sexual object choice.

Sexual Desire

Sexual desire (libido) is the level of interest in sexual activity experienced by an individual at a particular time. For both men and women, the level of sexual desire and "arousability" they feel at any particular time is influenced by many internal and external factors: age, general health, nutrition, physical fatigue, stress, mood, current frequency of sexual relations, the quality of the emotional relationship with his or her partner, and so forth.

Although there is still much debate about the details, the most fundamental influence on the level of sexual desire for both men and women is unquestionably the level of the hormone testosterone in their blood. (Women produce testosterone in their adrenal glands, though at much lower levels than men produce in their testes.) As blood levels of testosterone rise toward the high end of "normal," there is an increase in sexual desire. When blood levels of testosterone are reduced to zero, sexual desire eventually fades, though this may take some time.

Exactly how the other internal and external factors interact with testosterone levels to determine sexual desire is still being studied. In many cases, it seems that external factors, even purely psychological ones, can somehow raise or lower blood testosterone levels. One study showed that, for men, experiencing success—such as receiving a promotion at work—causes a rise in testosterone level, while experiencing failure causes the level to drop.[42] For many men, this is true even vicariously. Watching their favorite team win a game has been found to cause testosterone levels to rise in male sports fans, while seeing their team lose causes their levels to drop.

This may indicate that emotional states, such as elation or depression, can affect the level of sexual desire by changing the levels of blood testosterone. A low level of sexual desire is the primary complaint of 15% of men and 30–40% of women who seek counseling for sexual problems.[43] Low sexual desire may have physical causes, but it is more commonly associated with psychological causes, such as feelings of stress, depression, and conflicts in a relationship.

Contrary to earlier reports that sexual desire in men peaks in the late teens and early twenties while sexual desire in women peaks in the mid-thirties, more recent studies have shown comparable levels of sexual desire in both young women and young men,[44] though how that desire is experienced, interpreted, and expressed differs between the sexes. Some experts believe women need to "grow into" their sexuality as a learning process. With greater maturity, they become more comfortable with their sexuality and more aware of their sexual needs.

Sexual desire gradually decreases with age for both sexes.

Sexual Behavior

Sexual behavior includes the entire history of a person's sexual activities. The sexual activities in which we choose to participate (including sexual fantasies) are primarily the outcome of our lovemap, sexual object choice, level of sexual desire, and beliefs about what is or is not proper sexual behavior. Of all the components of human sexuality, sexual behavior is the one over which we have the most direct control. As we will examine later, sexual behavior is *self-reinforcing*.

The Beginnings of Sexual Attraction

The beginnings of sexual attraction is still one of the most mysterious areas of human sexuality. Why, exactly, do 12- or 13-year-old boys and girls suddenly begin looking at each other in a new light? We know that surging hormones in their bodies are causing them to feel sexual urges and sensations that they have never before experienced. Yet, what channels those sexual feelings toward the opposite sex? And why are some members of the opposite sex preferred over others? Also, why do some unfortunate teens feel aroused by members of the same sex, or an assortment of other weird things?

To begin to understand this complex process, we need to consider all the influences that come into play. So let us look at an example of a typical teenage boy just entering puberty. We'll call him "Johnny."

Johnny is just about to turn thirteen, and everyone can tell that he is turning into a man because his voice is starting to crack, he is shooting up like a weed, and he has a new layer of peach fuzz sprouting across his upper lip. Johnny is excited about these changes because he knows becoming taller and more muscular will help him excel at his favorite sport: baseball. In addition, he looks forward to spending more time hunting and fishing with his dad. Johnny also has noticed some changes and new feelings in his genital area. He is not really concerned about this because he had one sex education class that explained how these changes were just a normal part of becoming a man. But there is still a lot of joking that goes on in the locker room about such things.

Johnny does not yet have a girlfriend, but some of his friends do. Some of them even say they have had sex. Johnny's older cousin, Jeff, dropped by the other day with his new girl hanging on his arm. Johnny had always enjoyed hanging out with Jeff and talking about cars and sports, but he does not see him as much now that Jeff is dating. Jeff and his dad (Johnny's uncle) sometimes tease Johnny about why he has not yet found a girlfriend. Johnny has not really spent much time with girls over the past few years because he has been too busy playing baseball and racing model planes with his friends. But he knows he needs to start dating because that is part of becoming a man, even though the thought makes him a little nervous. There are some girls at school that he sort of likes, but they are really popular with the older guys and probably would not want to go out with him.

Johnny finds himself looking at girls more, especially the ones with "curves." One of his friends found some pictures of naked women and passed them around at school so Johnny and his other friends could see them. Looking at those pictures made Johnny feel excited in a way he had not felt before. They looked much different from the girls at school. He often lies awake at night thinking about the women in the pictures and finds himself becoming sexually aroused. But he also gets aroused when riding in the car or riding his bicycle, or sometimes just sitting in math class doing word problems, which has the potential for being really embarrassing. Sometimes he just wishes it would all go away.

This example reveals a lot about the forces that work to shape the emerging sexuality of a boy just entering puberty. First, Johnny has had only a little sex education, but it is enough to keep him from becoming worried about the sexual changes in his body. (Some boys have been kept so ignorant of what to expect that they become quite anxious at these changes and, for example, may think their first nocturnal emission, or "wet dream," is a sign they have a dreadful disease.) Johnny is happy with his masculinity and is looking forward to developing a big, muscular male body.

Second, Johnny learned at least the mechanical details of how sex is supposed to work between men and women before he actually began to have sexual feelings. So he knows where those feelings are supposed to lead, eventually. Being around girls still makes him nervous, but he knows he is supposed to feel sexual feelings toward women—that it is a good thing.

Third, there is social pressure for Johnny to date girls and talk sexually about girls. His older friends and role models, like his cousin Jeff, are already dating, and he wants to emulate them. They tease him about not having a girlfriend, so he wants to get a girlfriend just to win their approval. He also learns to join in when his friends are joking about sex and bragging about their sexual adventures because he does not want to feel left out of the group.

Obviously, there are a lot of forces at work pushing Johnny toward sexual involvement with girls. But why, exactly, does he find pictures of naked women arousing, but not naked men?

A new theory that attempts to answer this question has been advanced by Daryl Bem, a psychology professor at Cornell University. He calls his theory "Exotic Becomes Erotic" (EBE).[45] According to this theory, since Johnny has spent most of his childhood hanging out with his male friends and avoiding girls, he feels relaxed around boys, but nervous around girls. Whenever we feel nervous or anxious, our sympathetic nervous system stimulates the body for "fight or flight" by releasing adrenaline, raising the heart rate and blood pressure, and stimulating the sweat glands. This is called *autonomic arousal*. But this very same autonomic arousal also occurs when we become sexually aroused. There is evidence that autonomic arousal can trigger or strengthen sexual arousal.

Johnny had felt autonomic arousal (nervousness) around girls for years (except for his sisters and mother, of course). At some point, Johnny started having general feelings of sexual arousal, even though he had not yet started thinking sexual thoughts about girls. It is common for adolescent boys to become sexually aroused many times a day for no apparent reason and often in the most inappropriate places. So the opportunity is likely to occur that Johnny will be talking to a girl or looking at a girl and feeling that same old autonomic arousal, but suddenly it will gain a new significance brought on by sexual arousal. So the two types of arousal become joined, and Johnny realizes, "Wow! I have never felt like this before." He has felt sexual arousal just riding in the car and autonomic arousal around girls, but now he is feeling a powerful combination of both in the presence of a girl. At this point, Johnny realizes he is sexually interested in girls. He is heterosexual.*

This theory explains quite a lot. First, Johnny would never be sexually aroused by his sisters or his mother and would actually be quite disgusted at the thought, because he has lived with them all his life and is quite comfortable around them. They do not make him nervous, so he is unlikely to associate his sexual feelings with them. Many studies confirm that boys and girls raised in close quarters, such as in an orphanage or on an Israeli kibbutz, may remain close friends for life, but *never* develop romantic feelings toward each other.

Johnny is also unlikely to feel sexual feelings toward his buddies on the baseball team for the same reason. He knows them quite well. They have a lot in common. He is quite comfortable just hanging out with them, and he has often seen them naked in the locker room. So they have nothing interesting or "exotic" to offer. Instead of making him feel excited, they make him feel relaxed.

Let us review now all the factors that are helping Johnny to develop a healthy heterosexuality:

> 1. He is happy with his male gender. He is accepted by his peers and is doing well in boyhood activities such as sports, hunting, and fishing. This

---

* It is also possible that Johnny associates the two types of arousal because they are so similar. He feels excited and nervous when he is with a girl, and it reminds him of the way he feels when he is sexually aroused, so he begins to interpret the excitement as sexual arousal.

makes him a "successful" boy. (He can thank his father for much of this: for teaching him masculine skills that make him acceptable to his peers, and for helping him to be proud of his maleness.)

2. When he first notices sexual changes and feelings in his body, he does not become anxious because he has been taught about them.

3. He has been taught basic information about sex and knows where sexual feelings are supposed to lead. So he does not have to deal with confusion and misconceptions. He knows that sexual feelings for girls are "good."

4. He gets a lot of encouragement to interact with girls and to discuss sexual feelings for girls with his friends. Doing these things gives him the respect and admiration of his friends, and pleases the men who are his role models.

5. According to the EBE theory, his close friendships with other boys and relative distance from girls throughout childhood ensure that his sexual feelings will be directed toward girls.

However, there are some negatives in Johnny's situation. Pressure from his friends and a desire for their admiration could encourage Johnny to become sexually involved with a girl. He has seen some pornographic pictures of women that he finds more exciting to think about than the girls at school. The women in these pictures are likely to be highly exaggerated caricatures of what real women look like without their clothes. So if Johnny continues to focus on these images, he may ultimately find himself somewhat disappointed by real women and start looking for a "dream woman" who does not really exist.

The EBE theory also explains how some boys with a different childhood experience can later develop homosexual feelings:

Andy is also about to turn thirteen, but his life is not going so well. He makes good grades, but that is about the only bright spot. He has always been small and thin for his age and not particularly coordinated, so he has never been good at sports. His older brothers do well in sports, and the family is always going to their games. His father tried to teach him to throw a football, but eventually gave up. His mom tried to get him involved in soccer, but he was not very good at it and soon dropped out.

He hates gym class because he is always the last boy to be picked for any team. The other guys tease him unmercifully, calling him "sissy" and "queer." He avoids them between classes because they just hit him or make fun of him. His only real friends are a few of the girls in the Literature Society. At home, he spends most of his time reading adventure novels, watching movies, and listening to music. His older brothers and cousins keep asking him if he has a girlfriend yet, but he just makes up some excuse. He knows none of the girls at school would want to go out with a "geek" like him. They all want to date "jocks."

Andy is also experiencing the changes of puberty, but he finds them just a little scary, and he really does not have male friends with whom he can discuss the subject. He is a lot closer to his mom than his dad, but he is too embarrassed to ask her any questions about it.

He feels sexually aroused several times a day, for no particular reason that he can tell, but he just tries to ignore it. The only fantasies he has are not sexual. They involve fighting battles across the galaxy alongside his favorite fictional heroes.

According to the EBE theory, Andy is in the ideal situation to develop a sexual attraction to men. His natural temperament runs counter to most men in that he prefers to be quiet instead of active, is more passive than aggressive, and has better verbal skills than visual-spatial skills. These all hinder him from enjoying or succeeding at team sports. These things are perhaps what caused his father to lose interest in him and his mother to take more interest in him over the years. Since he has spent more time with his mom than with his dad or brothers, he may have picked up some effeminate mannerisms from her. When he entered school, his somewhat effeminate behavior plus his poor skills in sports caused the other boys to ridicule and reject him. He has always gotten along better with girls because they seem to share many of his interests. So, girls have become his best friends and playmates over the years.

The net result is that, by puberty, Andy feels nervous around boys and comfortable around girls. Older boys and men often seem like alien creatures to him. He does not understand them very well and even finds them somewhat scary. The boys at school make him very nervous because when they are around, he never knows when he is going to get punched. At this point, he does not fantasize about having sex with men or even know what that would involve. He does not consider himself to be gay. But he does spend a lot of time fantasizing about his favorite heroes, the "supermen" with whom he wishes he could spend time and from whom he would like to receive approval. This is because he never completed the identification phase in childhood, where he identified with his father or other male role model and said, "I want to be a man like him," and was never affirmed with, "You can become a man like me." He is still seeking a man with whom to identify and who will affirm him. Though he knows he is male, he is really not comfortable with the fact. His peers often tell him he is not a man according to their standards. Andy gets some pressure from his family to date girls, but this just reinforces his feelings of failure as a man because he knows he does not measure up to what girls want to see in a guy.

At this point, Andy is experiencing undirected sexual arousal and feels autonomic arousal whenever he is around men. All he needs for the "exotic" to become "erotic" is an event that joins the two feelings into one. Perhaps an older boy at school makes a crude pass at him, or perhaps he comes across a novel in the library about "gay love" or finds some gay pornography. Then his hero fantasies can quickly become eroticized, and he will be set on the path toward homosexuality.

The EBE theory explains the development of heterosexual feelings in girls in a similar fashion. It also can explain the development of homosexual feelings for those girls who are tomboys and have difficulty with their peers. However, allowances must be made for the different characteristics of female sexuality, such as not being as focused on sexual images or as aware of sexual arousal.

Programming the Sexual Brain

While the initial sexual object choice is developed in early adolescence, another force begins to exert a powerful influence over it: sexual behavior. An essential fact to understand about sexual behavior is that *it is self-reinforcing* in a very powerful way. *Your sexual past affects your sexual future.*

YOUR SEXUAL PAST AFFECTS YOUR SEXUAL FUTURE.

We all know how a taste or distaste for certain foods can develop. If you become violently ill after eating a particular food, it may be a long time before you eat that food again, if ever. But with a new food, the more you try it and enjoy it, the more likely you will be to eat it in the future. It begins to grow on you. Eventually, your diet changes as you eat more of the new food and less of older foods, which now seem less pleasurable.

A similar process can occur with our sexual appetites. If you have a novel, yet pleasurable sexual experience, you are more likely to want to repeat it in the future. Any sexual experience culminating in an orgasm is certain to involve some pleasure, even if some initial disgust, shame, discomfort, or even pain was also experienced. With time and repetition, the power of emotions such as disgust or shame tends to diminish—you become desensitized to them—yet the sexual pleasure remains. (However, an extremely traumatic and painful sexual experience, such as being raped, can act in the opposite way to inhibit enjoyment of any sexual activity reminiscent of the painful event.)

This process may be helpful to young brides who begin their marriage uneducated about the realities of sexual intercourse and often experience initial physical discomfort, as well as some shame or disgust. However, on the negative side, it is through just such a process of *desensitization* that many sexually normal adults can become involved in sexual practices they once considered abnormal or sinful. They lose their inhibitions. All it takes is a little experimentation with something that seems quite pleasurable. Feelings of shame, guilt, or disgust gradually fade, as what was previously "weird" becomes comfortable and familiar, while what was once "normal" becomes uninteresting. This process works in many common sexual temptations, such as adultery, which can begin with just a little flirting and "innocent" physical contact. As the adulterous behavior continues, feelings of guilt or shame grow weaker.

Our sexual object choice can also be changed through *association*. A notorious experiment that demonstrates this effect was done on male college students in the 1960s. These men were repeatedly shown a picture of a pair of women's boots followed by slides of female nudes. Eventually, these men experienced arousal when shown only a photograph of the boots.[46] Their brains had learned to associate the boots with sex.

A similar process can occur in men who view pornography. Pornography often includes bizarre elements such as instruments of torture and bondage, or it may depict scenarios such as rape. Men who become addicted to pornography often find that their sexual interests become more and more abnormal; they begin to respond to unusual images and scenarios, such as bondage or rape, that they did not previously find erotic.

There is another more direct way in which the sexual part of the brain can be programmed through sexual behavior. We are all aware of certain sexual images or fantasies that we find arousing. But the question we may not be able to answer is just *how* those particular fantasies *became* arousing. Research on this issue has come up with a very simple answer: *whatever fantasies or images your brain is focused on at the point of orgasm become programmed into your memory with great erotic power.* The next time you think those thoughts or see those images, they will have an even greater erotic attraction to you.[47]

In a marriage relationship, focusing your attention on your spouse during sexual union serves to bond you even more strongly to your spouse. For a husband, the sight of his wife, her touch, and the sound of her voice will become even more strongly associated in his mind with sexual excitement and fulfillment. However, if he allows his mind to entertain fantasies of other women while making love to his wife, those fantasies will become associated in his mind with sexual excitement and fulfillment instead of his wife, and his wife will lose the attraction she once had.

This same process can occur when someone is indulging in sexual fantasies and masturbating. Whether you are looking at pornography or thinking about a woman you saw earlier in the day, you are programming your brain to respond erotically to that image or fantasy in the future.

> **WHATEVER FANTASIES OR IMAGES YOUR BRAIN IS FOCUSED ON AT THE POINT OF ORGASM BECOME PROGRAMMED INTO YOUR MEMORY WITH GREAT EROTIC POWER.**

Jesus really put his finger on this fundamental process that is at the heart of most sexual sin when he said, "Whoever looks at a woman to lust for her has already committed adultery with her in his heart" (Matthew 5:28 NKJV). This statement is quite literally true. The deepest part of your brain cannot really tell if you actually had sex with a particular woman or just fantasized about having sex with her. In either case, the brain circuits form a powerful erotic memory of the event based on the images in your mind when you had an orgasm. In your mind you had sex with her, and in some ways the mental results are the same as if you had done so physically. The next time you see the woman or picture her in your mind, you will become even more aroused.

Nearly every sexual perversion or addiction known has been found to be based on a pattern of masturbation to a deviant fantasy culminating in orgasm. Most therapists consider this pattern of fantasy-masturbation-orgasm to be the cornerstone of sexual perversion and regard breaking this pattern as essential to helping a person recover from the perversion.

The repetition of this cycle of fantasy-masturbation-orgasm is also believed to help break down any inhibitions to carrying out the fantasy in real life. So the more you fantasize about a sexual act in this way, the more likely you are to actually carry it out if given the opportunity.

In recognition of just how powerful this effect is now believed to be, some parole programs now require child molesters to come in regularly for evaluation, and, while connected to a polygraph, they are asked if they have recently masturbated to fantasies about children. If they have, they are considered to have violated their program and can be punished in various ways, up to and including revocation of parole.[48]

To summarize, our sexual object choice can be influenced by sexual behavior in at least four ways:

1. *Reinforcement* – The pleasure of a sexual act makes you more likely to do it again in the future.

2. *Desensitization* – Any inhibitions or guilt about a sexual act tend to lessen each time that behavior is repeated and you experience pleasure.

3. *Association* – Bizarre images and scenarios can become erotic when paired with images you already find erotic.

4. *Orgasmic conditioning* – The images in your mind just before the point of orgasm acquire even greater erotic significance.

Sexual Addiction

The problem of addiction to drugs or alcohol has been with us since nearly the beginning of history. However, the past few decades have brought a much greater understanding of the forces behind addiction and new ways to treat it. With this increase in knowledge has a come a realization that people can become addicted not just to chemicals, but also to behaviors. Addictions to eating and to sex are notable examples of this.

Many people consume alcohol in small amounts for a lifetime without becoming alcoholics. Yet a few seem to become addicted after having their first drink. We see the same scenario with an addiction to eating or sex. Many people have trouble believing that someone could become addicted to something so common and necessary as eating or sex. However, the cause of the addiction lies not with alcohol, eating, or sex, but deep within the person who becomes addicted.*

An addiction develops when a person misuses something in an attempt to meet an emotional need it was not designed to meet.

For example, food was designed by God to sustain the physical life of our bodies, and He was kind enough to make eating a pleasurable experience. But some people have found that the pleasure of eating can distract them from their problems and temporarily soothe emotional pain or anxiety. Yet, eating can only *cure* the problem of needing nourishment; it cannot cure the causes of people's emotional problems and was never intended to be used to ease emotional pain. When the pleasure of eating is misused consistently in this manner, it sets up the trap of addiction.[49]

Pain is a signal that a part of us is injured and needs to be healed. But a food addict ignores the real cause of his or her pain and tries to make

---

* This is not true of "hard" drugs like heroin, cocaine, or methamphetamine. These immediately interfere with the normal chemistry of the brain and can cause anyone, even laboratory rats, to become quickly addicted. It is now known that such drugs cause permanent damage to the area of the brain responsible for self-control, thus initiating a lifelong struggle with impulse control that makes breaking the addiction even more difficult. There is also evidence that some people who become addicted to alcohol, sex, or food may have some difference in their brains that allows them to become addicted more readily than others.

the pain go away by smothering it with the pleasure of eating. Yet, the pain keeps getting stronger since its cause is being ignored.

The same principle applies to sexual addiction. In addition to producing children, sex was designed by God to meet a fundamental need for spiritual, mental, emotional, and physical union with a mate. It is perhaps the most highly pleasurable experience most people will ever know in this life. So it is not surprising that some people have sought to use the pleasure of sex to ease their emotional pain. Sex addicts typically have experienced terrible traumas in childhood, such as being abused or abandoned by parents, or being victims of rape or violence. They often discover in adolescence, or even in childhood, that giving themselves sexual pleasure eases their emotional pain, at least temporarily.

The sex addict comes to view sex as a "wonder drug." It can be used to soothe any emotional pain or meet any psychological or even spiritual need. If he is lonely or afraid, if he is stressed out at work, if he feels an emptiness in his life or is just bored, that means it is time to "act out." Trying to meet so many needs with sex quickly exhausts its pleasurable power, particularly since the true satisfaction of body/soul/spirit union with a spouse is missing.* So the sex addict must continually look for ways to get an even stronger "fix" of sexual pleasure and excitement. This can lead him to try every kind of sexual practice imaginable and eventually violate all the moral principles he has ever had. As with alcoholics, it is often not until his secret life is discovered by others and he is forcibly confronted that he will seek help.

These are some of the primary characteristics of a sex addict:

- The addict has had a troubled childhood and has many current sources of stress and emotional pain that are not being addressed in healthy ways.
- The addict spends a lot of time fantasizing about

---

* Even if he is married, the sex addict is often fantasizing about his addiction while making love to his spouse, so he misses out on the satisfaction of true emotional and spiritual union.

the addictive behavior, accompanied by masturbation.

• The addict spends a lot of time "acting out"—seeking to act out the sexual fantasies.

• The addictive sexual behaviors are done compulsively. To stop them seems beyond the addict's control.

• There is no emotional connection with sex partners, even a spouse. Large numbers of anonymous sex partners are preferred.

• The addictive sexual behaviors are often very self-destructive: endangering personal safety; putting career, reputation, and family relationships at risk; and consuming precious time and much money.

• Over time, the addict must graduate to even more extreme and risky sexual behaviors to maintain the same "high."

One more "coming-of-age" story can help us see how all of the preceding principles (the EBE theory, programming the sexual brain, and sexual addiction) can work together to cause a sexual problem. This story can also help us understand how some people develop very unusual sexual obsessions. This summary is from an actual case history. It concerns a young male college student who asked for help in overcoming *autoasphyxiophilia* (an erotic obsession with self-strangulation).[50]

> During childhood this patient experienced a lot of stress due to an undiagnosed hearing loss that hurt his academic performance and his peer relationships. He also had a strained relationship with his stepfather, who seemed to show favoritism to his own children. He recalls being first attracted to girls at age six, but his parents discouraged him from having friendships with them.

A traumatic incident occurred when he was eight that seems to have formed the core of his autoasphyxiophilia. He developed a crush on a girl his age who soon drowned while swimming in the ocean. As a result, he began to have dreams and fantasies about girls who were drowning. It was shortly after this that he first began to masturbate to these same fantasies. He continued to be attracted to girls throughout his school years but was repeatedly rejected. He feels this was because he was ugly and had to wear glasses, braces, and a hearing aid.

He did not begin acting out his fantasies of self-strangulation until his first year in college, when some setbacks put him under severe stress. He developed a preference for strangling himself with a woman's leotard (required to be white or light blue stretch nylon) in front of the mirror while fantasizing that he was being strangled by a strange man. He was also sexually aroused by scenes from television and movies showing women drowning or being strangled. He sometimes pretended to drown himself in the bathtub. All of these activities provided him with fantasies for use during masturbation, which he performed, on average, six times per day, while often strangling himself to near unconsciousness.

This soon became a compulsion that he could not control. He sought help because he feared for his life after seeing a television program about those who had died from this practice (500–1000 people, mostly men, die accidentally each year in the U.S. from autoerotic asphyxiation).

This case clearly illustrates how traumatic events that happen around puberty can derail the development of normal heterosexuality. As a young boy, this patient was deeply affected by the death of a young play-mate. He was troubled by obsessive thoughts of drowning girls that filled his dreams and waking fantasies. This was sure to have caused a great deal of autonomic arousal. Feelings of sexual arousal that began at puberty could easily have become confused and entangled with the feelings of auto-nomic arousal brought on by his obsession, so that he eventually became sexually aroused by his fantasies of girls drowning. By masturbating to these abnormal fantasies, he strengthened his erotic response to them. He was definitely attracted to girls but was repeatedly rejected by them. This meant that he did not have the opportunity to develop a more normal sex-ual interest in girls and healthy relationships with them. In college he began to use masturbation with these fantasies to relieve stress, which ultimately resulted in sexual addiction. His cycle of deviant fantasy-masturbation-orgasm had desensitized him and removed inhibitions so that he started acting out his fantasies by self-strangulation. He continued to feed these fantasies with movie images of drowning and strangulation. His abnormal sexual activities eventually became a life-threatening addiction he could not control.

Similar stories are told by those who suffer from all kinds of abnormal sexual compulsions. In childhood or early adolescence, some dis-turbing or alarming event occurred that they continued to think about obsessively. Then a link was established between the emotional arousal of the disturbing event and growing feelings of sexual arousal, which were not yet strongly focused on the opposite sex.

We all remember how obsessive sexual thoughts and feelings can seem during adolescence. Try to imagine what it would be like to have to struggle with sexual feelings plus an additional set of equally powerful and obsessive thoughts, all at the same time—for example, memories of being molested, of being constantly beaten, or of your mother humiliating you by forcing you to wear opposite-sex clothing.

Often, such a child discovers that masturbation can temporarily relieve the emotional pain of his or her terrible memories or obsessive thoughts. However, this practice also causes such thoughts to gain a new erotic power. Even if a boy in this situation eventually begins to explore relationships with girls (since there are many social forces that encourage this), his "habit" is always lurking in the background as something to which he can resort. If he repeatedly chooses to indulge his deviant fantasies to compensate for the failure of a relationship or to relieve stress, then the power of sexual addiction can take hold.

Misusing Sex to Meet Emotional and Relational Needs

As was discussed earlier, God designed us to be part of a fabric of emotional relationships that center around the family. The primary emotional need for children is a secure, loving relationship with each parent. After that is accomplished, they can develop a variety of social relationships with other relatives and friends that satisfy a variety of emotional and relational needs—such as for companionship, learning social skills, perfecting gender skills, mentoring, or recreation. These relationships all involve different types of love and other positive emotions, such as feeling accepted, approved, and needed by others.

Emotionally healthy adolescents will have enjoyed a decade or so of constructive relationships and will have had all their childhood emotional needs met through them. So, as sexuality emerges, they are ready for a new kind of love. They begin to seek a mate, a lifetime companion. Then all the powerful bonding forces of a mature sexual relationship begin to take hold to create the nucleus of a new family.

But emotional development is not yet finished. New parents often describe how profoundly they were affected by the birth of their first child. This event seems to develop the capacity for a new level of "sacrificial love" that can produce incredible acts of self-sacrifice. Finally, the sum of a lifetime of these loving relationships helps us to better understand and relate to God, as we find our ultimate fulfillment in Him.

We seem to have not only a capacity for all these different types of relationships, but a real need for them as well. In reviewing this situation, some have pictured the human heart as a house containing many rooms, each room designed for a specific type of relationship. The biggest rooms are reserved for God, parents, a spouse, and children—who are all at home there—but there are many guest rooms for all the other people who pass through our lives and stay just for a while.

As you develop relationships with others, it is almost as if they move into the empty rooms in your heart and begin to furnish them. The furnishings are the things they say to you, the things they do for you, the things you learn from them, and all the memories of your time together. Even if they eventually move out of your life, you can still visit their rooms in your heart, furnished with all the things, both good and bad, that they have left you as remembrances.

But having too many empty rooms in the house, particularly in the family area, causes us to sense the echoing emptiness in our hearts and can make us very unhappy. So, we try to find people who are willing to move into these empty rooms. A lack of fulfilling relationships with God, parents, spouse, or children can become particularly compelling, leading us to make great efforts to fill those empty rooms any way we can.[51]

This analogy illustrates very well how emotional pain can often be traced directly to a feeling of relational emptiness—a deficit or a loss in one or more emotionally essential relationships. It also illustrates how problems can arise in current relationships when we ask others to meet emotional needs that they are really not able to fulfill. We are asking them to move into rooms in our hearts for which they are unsuited. The pressure our unspoken need is placing upon them often makes them uncomfortable and unhappy.

Counselors see many examples every week of how such relational deficits continue to cause problems. For example, people with troubled childhoods and from broken families often find they have difficulty building strong and healthy friendships because they have so many unfilled rooms in their hearts. They often find themselves unconsciously pressuring casual acquaintances to fill much deeper emotional needs. For that reason they can often seem neurotic, "clingy," and unstable to potential friends.

Because sexual union creates such a fulfilling emotional bond, some are tempted to misuse a sexual relationship in an attempt to satisfy their other unmet relational needs. It is not unusual to see marriages in trouble because the husband or wife did not get enough love from the opposite-sex parent. One spouse keeps trying, often in unconscious ways, to maneuver the other into a parental role so that the half-furnished "parent room" can be finished out. (One sign of this is that they stop calling each other "Honey" or "Sweetheart" and start substituting "Dad" or "Mom" when talking to each other.)

Understanding this principle is essential to uncovering the deep emotional and relational needs that often compel people to seek out deviant sexual relationships. Often the sex is not as important as the emotional needs that seemingly are met through the relationship. Yet, a sex partner is only a poor substitute for God, a parent, or a child. The illusion eventually wears thin, which explains the great conflict and instability found in such illicit relationships.

For example, making up for deficits in parent-child relationships seems to be the driving force in some homosexual pairings, particularly where there is a large age difference. It is quite common to see personal ads where a younger man is looking for "an older daddy-type." Some of these relationships even depend on the older man being very authoritarian and using physical punishment, such as spanking the younger. The older men in such relationships are often looking for a "cub" or a "daddy's boy." They seem to be seeking the emotional fulfillment of fatherhood through a sexual relationship with a young man.

In ancient Greece this same perversion of the father-son emotional bond was the basis for the practice of *pederasty*—where a married man mentored an adolescent boy from another family, teaching him to become a well-rounded citizen, but also having sex with him. Bizarrely, many Greek writers and philosophers considered this type of relationship between a man and a youth to exemplify the highest form of love, though they condemned sex with prepubescent boys.

A very different example of trying to meet an emotional need through sex is found in a particular type of pedophile. This type of pedophile is attracted only to children of a specific age range and tries to gain their approval and acceptance *as an equal*. Sexual involvement is only in terms of what children of that age normally do, such as "playing doctor." This type of person seems desperately driven to attain success in peer relationships that was never achieved in childhood. Needless to say, they never truly achieve the emotional fulfillment they are seeking, though they can become so obsessed with the pursuit that it becomes the center of their lives.

Spiritual Causes of Sexual Problems

Thus far, we have considered the root causes of sexual problems that come from the physical world around us or from our own thoughts and emotions. However, as Christians, we are aware that humans also have spirits, that we live simultaneously in this physical world and in a spiritual dimension. In Chapter 5 we considered several spiritual causes of sexual sins and problems, such as demonic influence, spiritual adultery, and spiritual defilement. It is important to keep in mind that any of these spiritual influences may be present in addition to all of the physical, mental, and emotional factors we have considered above.

Fundamental Points about Our Sexual Nature

Here are some fundamental points to keep in mind that will help us to maintain a proper perspective about our sexual nature, its potential problems, and the hope for change:

1. *Our sexual nature integrates body, soul, and spirit.*

It is a mistake to think of sexuality as just an isolated (perhaps darkened) corner of our minds. As we have seen, our sexuality is a product of our biology, our temperament, our beliefs and attitudes, our social and sexual experiences, our emotional needs and responses, our spiritual condition, and all the decisions we have made in our lives. Sexual problems can have roots in any or all of these areas.

2. *Our sexual nature is dynamic, not static.*

It is a mistake to think that our sexuality is fixed and unchangeable. It grows, develops, and changes throughout life, with the childhood and adolescent years being the most formative. This means that sexual problems *can* be corrected. It also means that new sexual problems can develop if we are not careful to maintain a healthy sexuality. For example, men who do not have a good sexual relationship with their wives are at risk for sexual problems such as adultery or addiction to pornography.

3. *Human sexual behavior is mostly learned behavior and can be unlearned.*

Nearly all human behavior is learned. Only a few reflex actions, such as sneezing, yawning, swallowing, and sleeping, seem to be purely instinctual. (This is in contrast to animals, who show more instinctual behaviors as they move down the scale of complexity.) Except for the reflex actions of arousal and orgasm, human sexual behavior and gender role behavior are complex behaviors that must be learned—which means they can be unlearned or relearned. Even the triggers of arousal and orgasm can be modified through a learning process. Gender identity and sexual object choice, which seem to be the most mysterious aspects of our sexuality, can also be traced back to early learning experiences. Genes do not *cause* sexual problems, such as sexual addiction or homosexuality, but only exert an indirect influence through factors such as temperament or brain organization. Learning, social influences, and an individual's own actions still determine the ultimate outcome.

The influences on sexuality we have already examined, such as temperament, brain organization, hormone levels, and social interaction, clearly influence the outcome of the sexual "lessons" learned in childhood. We know that small children are particularly impressionable and most vulnerable to being shaped by these forces. As we have seen, gender identity is formed before the age of two, and gender-appropriate behaviors are learned throughout childhood. Any experiences that produce sexual feelings during childhood and adolescence are powerfully reinforced by those feelings, whether it is the pleasure of your first kiss or the shame and pain of being molested.

However, we must remember that no matter how deeply ingrained or compulsive a behavior pattern has become, a person can change his sexual behavior if he is given the proper help and is willing to work at it. Even problems with gender identity and sexual object choice have been shown to be correctable. Those with abnormal development in these areas often experience spontaneous, though gradual, changes in their sexuality throughout their lifetimes. Nevertheless, making consistent and deliberate changes on the road back to normality may require considerable effort.

EVEN PROBLEMS WITH GENDER IDENTITY AND SEXUAL OBJECT CHOICE HAVE BEEN SHOWN TO BE CORRECTABLE.

4. *Our freedom to choose is the most important factor in developing and overcoming sexual problems.*

A common error is to view sexual problems as merely the product of forces beyond individual control—things such as hormone levels, brain wiring, or bad childhood experiences. Those schooled in the biosciences are particularly prone to fall into this error due to their characteristic bias, which leads them to see all human behavior and personality as mere byproducts of biochemical reactions occurring in the brain. However, Christians understand that humans are immortal spirits that inhabit a mortal body and express themselves through it. This enables us to more readily appreciate how the choices we make, even in childhood, can affect the course of our lives.

The truth is that much of the development of our sexual nature is governed by the choices we make, even those choices made in childhood.

As we have seen, even infants choose whether or not to bond to their parents, and children can choose to identify or dis-identify with a same-sex parent. Clearly, the parents bear primary responsibility for the quality of the parent-child relationship in the early years. However, as many counselors have discovered, people must often choose to change the negative attitudes they developed toward their parents in childhood before they can receive complete healing as adults.

A primary reason we all make wrong choices is a lack of good information. Children frequently misinterpret sexual events and may develop confused notions about gender and sexuality when their parents and their culture provide little information and guidance for them in that area. As in so many other aspects of life, ignorance makes us vulnerable.

Notes.

1. John Money and Anke Ehrhardt, *Man & Woman, Boy & Girl* (Baltimore: The Johns Hopkins University Press, 1972), 29.

2. Eleanor Maccoby and Carol N. Jacklin, *The Psychology of Sex Differences* (Stanford, CA: Stanford University Press, 1974).

3. J. Imperato-McGinley, M. Pichardo, T. Gautier, D. Voyer, and M. P. Bryden, "Cognitive Abilities in Androgen-insensitive Subjects: Comparison with Control Males and Females from the Same Kindred," *Clinical Endocrinology* 34 (1991): 341–347.

4. This is due to a genetic defect called adrenogenital syndrome. Money and Ehrhardt, 98-100 (see note 1).

5. Money and Ehrhardt, 10–11 (see note 1).

6. Jerre Levy and Wendy Heller, "Gender Differences in Human Neuropsychological Function," in *Handbook of Behavioral Neurobiology,* vol. 11, eds. Gerall, Moltz, and Ward (New York: Plenum Press, 1992).

7. De Lacoste-Utamsing and Holloway, "Sexual Dimorphism in the Human Corpus Callosum" *Science* 216 (1982): 1431–1432.

8. Money and Ehrhardt (see note 1).

9. John Money, *Gay, Straight and In-Between* (New York: Oxford University Press, 1988), 66.

10. Ruben C. Gur, Lyn Harper Mozley, P. David Mozley, Susan M. Resnick, Joel S. Karp, Abass Alavi, Steven Arnold, and Raquel E. Gur, "Sex Differences in Regional Cerebral Glucose Metabolism during a Resting State," *Science* 267 (27 January 1995), 528–531.

11. Money and Ehrhardt, 108–114 (see note 1).

12. Money, *Gay, Straight, and In-Between*, 38–40 (see note 9).

13. Money and Ehrhardt, 112–113 (see note 1).

14. Money, *Gay, Straight and In-Between* 34–37 (see note 9).

15. Money and Ehrhardt, 98–103 (see note 1), and Money, *Gay, Straight and In-Between*, 36 (see note 9).

16. Money and Ehrhardt, 103–105 (see note 1).

17. Milton Diamond, "Bisexuality: A Biological Perspective," in *Bisexualities: The Ideology and Practice of Sexual Contact with Both Men and Women*, eds. Erwin Haeberle, and Rolf Gindorf (New York: Continuum, 1998), 67.

18. Sharon Begley, "Your Child's Brain" *Newsweek*, 19 February 1996, 57.

19. Jerre Levy and Wendy Heller (see note 6).

20. Susan Golombok and Robyn Fivush, *Gender Development* (New York: Cambridge University Press, 1994), 78–79.

21. Money and Ehrhardt, 12–13 (see note 1).

22. Samuel E. Wood, Ellen Green-Wood, and Mark Garrison, *The World of Psychology* (Needham Heights, MA: Allyn and Bacon, 1996), 274.

23. Robert L. Crooks, Richard H. Ettinger, and Jean Stein, *Psychology: Science, Behavior and Life* (New York: Holt, 1997), 356.

24. N. A. Fox, N. L. Kimmerly, and W. D. Schafer, "Attachment to Mother/Attachment to Father: A Meta-Analysis," *Child Development* 62 (1991): 210–225.

25. For a good summary of this subject read *Life Without Father: Compelling New Evidence that Fatherhood and Marriage Are Indispensable for the Good of Children and Society* by David Popenoe (New York: The Free Press, 1996).

26. J. Belsky, "Infant Day Care and Socioemotional Development," *Journal of Child Psychology and Psychiatry* 29 (1988): 397–406.

27. John and Paula Sandford have written extensively on the factors affecting spiritual development in childhood, particularly in *Restoring the Christian Family, The Transformation of the Inner Man,* and *Healing the Wounded Spirit.*

28. Begley, "Your Child's Brain" (see note 18).

29. A. Meltzoff and M. Moore, "Newborn Infants Imitate Adult Facial Gestures," *Child Development* 54 (1983): 702–709.

30. Wood, Green-Wood, and Garrison, 370 (see note 22).

31. Wood, Green-Wood, and Garrison, 371 (see note 22).

32. Elizabeth R. Moberly, *Homosexuality: A New Christian Ethic* (Cambridge: James Clarke & Co, Ltd., 1988).

33. R. G. Slaby and K. S. Frey, "Development of Gender Constancy and Selective Attention to Same-sex Models," *Child Development* 46 (1975): 849–856.

34. S. Luria and E.W. Herzog, "Gender Segregation in Play Groups: A Matter of Where and When." A paper presented at the Society for Research in Child Development, Detroit, April, 1983. Quoted in Serbin and Sprafkin. "A Developmental Approach: Sexuality from Infancy through Adolescence," in *Theories of Human Sexuality*, eds. James H. Geer and W. T. O'Donohue (New York: Plenum Press, 1987), 191.

35. Bell, Weinberg and Hammersmith, *Sexual Preference: Its Development in Men and Women* (Bloomington, IN: Indiana University Press, 1981).

36. Lisa A. Serbin and C. H. Sprafkin, 168–169 (see note 34).

37. John Money, J. E. Cawte, G. N. Bianchi, and B. Nurcombe, "Sex Training and Traditions in Arnhem Land" *British Journal of Medical Psychology* 43 (1970): 383–399.

38. According to community development specialist Doug Fraiser, the Manobo have no knowledge of any sexual practices except premarital heterosexual intercourse, heterosexual marriage, adultery, and polygamy. The concept of sexual perversions such as homosexuality

can only be explained to them with great difficulty. (From the author's files.)

39. Stanton L. and Brenna B. Jones, *How & When to Tell Your Kids About Sex* (Colorado Springs: NavPress, 1994).

40. P. B. Eveleth, "Timing of Menarche: Secular Trend and Population Differences," *School Age Pregnancy and Parenthood Biosocial Dimensions*, eds. J. B. Lancaster and B. A. Hamburg (New York: Aldine de Gruyter, 1986).

41. John Money, *Lovemaps: Clinical Concepts of Sexual/Erotic Health and Pathology, Paraphilia, and Gender Transposition in Childhood, Adolescence and Maturity* (New York: Irvington, 1986), xv-xvi.

42. Theodore A. Mazur, Allen, and Lamb, "Testosterone, Status and Mood in Human Males," *Hormones and Behavior* 14 (1980): 236–246.

43. Raymond C. Rosen, S. R. Lieblum, eds. *Case Studies in Sex Therapy* (New York: The Guilford Press, 1995), 4–5.

44. Richard A. Maier, *Human Sexuality in Perspective* (Chicago: Nelson-Hall, 1984), 116–117.

45. Daryl J. Bem, "Exotic Becomes Erotic: A Developmental Theory of Sexual Orientation," *Psychological Review* 103 (2): 320–335 (1996).

46. S. Rachman, "Sexual Fetishism: An Experimental Analogue," *Psychological Record* 16: 293-296.

47. H. H. Schaefer and A. H. Colgan, "The Effect of Pornography on Penile Tumescence as a Function of Reinforcement and Novelty," *Behavior Therapy* 8 (1977): 938–946.

48. "Managing Adult Sex Offenders in the Community," Series: NIJ Research in Brief, U.S. Department of Justice, Office of Justice Programs, National Institute of Justice, National Institute of Justice Research in Brief, Jeremy Travis, Director, January 1997.

49. The tremendous success of the "Weigh Down Workshop," a program for helping people lose weight, is based on this very principle. Participants are taught to recognize when they are using food to meet emotional or spiritual needs and how to turn to God for help instead.

50. John Money, *Lovemaps*, 227–348.

51. I am indebted to Clay McLean for this illustration.

XI

Learning the Facts
about Sexual Problems

The purpose of this chapter is to broaden our perspective on the many different kinds of sexual problems in which people, even Christian people, can become involved. Some of these problems are quite common, while others are quite rare. However, I have found that learning the facts about a variety of sexual problems can be very helpful because it removes a lot of uncertainty, or even fear, in discussing and dealing with sexual issues. The society around us is discussing and dealing with these issues every day from a secular viewpoint. Christians need to lose their fear, shame, and confusion about sexual problems and be able to provide some knowledgeable, reasonable, compassionate, and biblical answers.

I have found that there are many significant facts about these sexual problems that are just not being presented to the Christian public. So in discussing the following topics, I have chosen not to rehash what is considered common knowledge or conventional wisdom. Instead, I have focused on what I believe are the most essential and significant facts that every Christian should know, and I have endeavored to clear up common misunderstandings. Since a single chapter cannot be considered a comprehensive reference on these subjects, I have included some recommended resources for further study.

Adultery, Spiritual Adultery, and Spiritual Defilement

Because the concept and implications of adultery are familiar to most of us, earlier chapters made extensive use of it as an example to help us understand some of the many facets of sexuality and how they can become corrupted through sexual sin. However, there is a unique aspect of adultery of which most people are entirely ignorant: its spiritual dimension. This aspect is especially relevant for Christians because of the spiritual nature of our daily lives. I believe it is essential for every Christian to come to understand and be aware of these two powerful spiritual principles that can draw even mature Christians into sexual sin: *spiritual adultery* and *spiritual defilement*. (These topics were introduced in Chapter 5, but this section provides more specific information about them.)

Spiritual Adultery

Spiritual adultery occurs when either a husband or wife achieves a depth of spiritual (and subsequent emotional) intimacy with someone outside of the marriage that is proper only for a spouse. *Spiritual adultery often leads to physical adultery.* This is how the Law of Sexual Union can operate in reverse: a close spiritual relationship between a man and woman can create a deepening emotional bond that eventually leads to a sexual relationship unless something or someone intervenes. Many mature Christian people with fruitful ministries have become ensnared through this very process.

Spiritual adultery is wrong because it is a betrayal of the husband-wife relationship. Each spouse should be the other's best friend, prayer partner, and confidant. They rightfully feel betrayed if they find another competing for that special position.

But there is a spiritual dimension to spiritual adultery that goes beyond the merely emotional or physical relationship. With spiritual adultery there is a *spiritual link* established between one spouse and another person outside the marriage.

Women tend to be more sensitive about spiritual matters than men. So, it is often the case that a wife will sense such a spiritual link between her husband and another woman and be troubled by it, though she may not be able to put what she feels into words. If she tries to tell her husband what she is sensing, he may respond with disbelief because he has had no impure thoughts or motives in dealing with the lady. She may be a colleague in ministry, a member of their home prayer group, or a new believer who needs teaching and encouragement. Yet, the husband is unaware that through their times of prayer and sharing, her spirit has latched onto his and formed a deep attachment. This spiritual link is beyond any merely emotional or physical attraction that may or may not exist between them, and it represents a very real threat to his marriage.

Spiritual adultery seems to be particularly dangerous for Christians since we have so many opportunities for developing a spiritual and emotional closeness with others through praying together, counseling, or sharing. In fact, we cannot disciple or counsel others effectively without a relationship of mutual love and trust. Joining in prayers of faith requires that our spirits touch and unite us in the Holy Spirit. We need good friends who know our hearts and can agree with us in prayer. We cannot truly fulfill God's purpose for our lives without developing these spiritually intimate relationships with others in the church. But we can and must exercise wisdom and due caution in any relationships where there is some danger of spiritual adultery.

The situation requiring the greatest caution is where a man and a woman work closely together or spend significant time alone with each other. We have already examined the many ways in which the Law of Sexual Union can begin to unite minds and bodies, even before we are fully aware of what is happening. Even those who have not been spiritually reborn can fall into adultery in such a situation. But when you add the spiritual relationship required of two Christians working in ministry together—joining their spirits in intercessory prayer, or ministering to the spiritual needs of others—this situation becomes even more precarious.

Even two single Christians in such an intimate setting could certainly "fall in love." But, as we have seen, that feeling is really just a hormonal "high," based very much on sexual attraction plus times of emotional/spiritual intimacy and physical contact. Despite our modern mythology, "falling in love" is no indication two people are truly suited for a life-long marriage. It is certainly possible that two single Christians in ministry together could "fall in love" in this way and actually miss, or hinder, God's plan for their lives.

In my years of pastoring and counseling, I have talked and prayed with many women concerning matters of the most intimate nature. To fend off potential problems with spiritual adultery, I have learned to take some necessary precautions:

1. First of all, depend on your spouse's assistance. I have learned that my wife, Phyllis, is my God-given partner in ministry. I depend on her spiritual sensitivity to watch my back. (If you are in full-time or even part-time ministry and have not yet acknowledged that your spouse was ordained by God to be your ministry partner, then you have not even begun to accomplish what God has planned for your ministry together as a team.) I share everything

with Phyllis. I keep her informed of the counseling sessions I have with women, and she holds me up in prayer. If I feel the slightest attraction or attachment to any of these women, I immediately tell Phyllis and ask her to pray for me. Sin cannot live and grow in the light of transparency.

2. Do not spend so much time in ministry that you exhaust yourself. You need to balance your times of giving with times of emotional and spiritual refreshment. Your spouse is appointed by God to be the center of your emotional life and provide you with renewal and refreshment. If you are seeking that refreshment from someone other than your spouse, then you are already in spiritual adultery.

3. Do not spend time alone with someone of the opposite sex who is not your spouse. (This is so simple and obvious, but many Christians think they are so spiritually mature they can ignore this advice. Believe me, only Jesus is that spiritually mature.) My counseling sessions are conducted in an office with a glass door and plenty of traffic on the other side. This provides the necessary confidentiality but allows for no secrecy or feelings of intimacy.

4. If at all possible, the person receiving prayer, teaching, counseling, or discipling should involve his or her spouse in the process. They both need to understand that God has ordained them to be partners in life. If one has a problem, then both must be involved in its solution. I realize that there may be times when past sins or deeply buried emotional wounds are first confessed to a counselor or prayer partner. But these issues should be shared with a

spouse as soon as he or she is prepared to listen in love and help "bear the burden."

If you are helping a single person of the opposite sex, then involve your spouse at some point in the process. Your spouse can provide valuable insights as a member of the same sex, and the counselee will benefit by seeing a couple with a healthy marriage ministering as a team.

Any Christian who is active in any kind of ministry should consider adopting these guidelines in all applicable situations.

I would also advise Christian singles to take a similarly cautious approach in relating to the opposite sex in a church or ministry setting, just to avoid being overwhelmed by the powerful forces at work in all male-female relationships. A spiritual relationship of counseling, discipling, or ministering together can suddenly and unexpectedly become romantic, and marrying that person may or may not be God's best plan for your lives.

Two Christian friends of the same sex can also develop a spiritually adulterous relationship. This is typically just a case of giving priority to a friend instead of your spouse in praying together and sharing intimate matters of the heart. It indicates a lack of necessary emotional and spiritual intimacy in the marriage. This type of relationship seems to occur most frequently between women who have husbands who are unbelieving, emotionally distant, or spiritually inert. This is a difficult situation for a Christian wife, and her Christian lady friends can provide a spiritual lifeline. However, her vision must remain fixed on bringing her husband into a fully developed relationship with God and with her. If her husband begins to feel that she has shut him out so she can spend time with her church friends, he is certain to distance himself even further from her, God, and the Church.

Even worse, spiritually adulterous friendships can turn into *emotional dependency*[1]—a very unhealthy, obsessive, and even idolatrous relationship where one person looks to another to meet a multitude of emotional needs that the other cannot truly fulfill. To understand the risk for this situation, we must first look at a person's life experiences.

For example, an emotionally fulfilled woman has had her need for parental love completed during childhood through close bonds with her father and mother. She has learned social skills through relationships with her friends and siblings. As an adult, she has developed a mature relationship with God, has found completion in her relationships with her husband and her children, and enjoys a variety of social relationships with colleagues and friends.

An emotionally needy woman is lacking in one or more of these areas, but she has a choice in how she seeks to fulfill these unmet emotional needs. The best approach is to deepen her relationship with God, seek counsel on how to mend the broken relationships in her life, and develop a circle of friends for mutual support. But instead, if she finds one other woman to be her best friend and begins to draw on her more and more for all of her unmet needs—for a mother, for a counselor, for a spouse, and for direction from God—the stage is then set for emotional dependency.

In general, the more unmet emotional needs there are in your life, the greater your risk for developing an emotionally dependent relationship. The most precarious situation is one in which two people with complementary emotional needs develop an exclusive friendship. For example, a woman grown distant from her husband, with few friends and no children, befriends a younger single woman from church with many problems and emotional needs.

Sadly, an unhealthy relationship between two Christian friends of the same sex that begins with spiritual adultery, then leads to emotional dependency, can conclude with sexual involvement. Over the years, I have counseled many Christians (mostly women) who have fallen into this sinful situation. *These relationships always began with a noble spiritual purpose.* One friend was discipling or counseling the other, or they became prayer partners in an effort to save one friend's troubled marriage. But as they found more and more of their needs being met in the other, they abandoned other relationships and became involved in spiritual adultery, then emotional dependency, until only one need remained unfulfilled, the sexual need. It was then only a matter of time before they sought sexual completion in each other.

There is a definite difference between men and women in these matters. While both sexes can develop unhealthy same-sex relationships, my experience and that of other counselors is that women are generally at much greater risk.

I see two reasons for this.

First of all, the unwritten rules of North American culture encourage women to develop close, heart-to-heart friendships, but discourage men from doing so. Men have been trained by our culture to see other men as competitors, so they keep their "game face" on and resist exposing their innermost feelings. Most Christian men actually have an unmet need for *greater* emotional involvement with other men in friendships where they can truly know and be known. Promise Keepers, a well-known men's discipling ministry, has become so popular among Christian men of all denominations because it directly addresses this issue. This ministry teaches men that they have an unmet need for soul-baring friendships and then provides the small-group environments where these friendships can develop.

The second reason lies in a very basic difference between male and female sexuality that has its roots in the wiring of the brain. Male sexual arousal is centered on visual images, while female sexual arousal stems more from emotional relationships and physical affection.

This is illustrated by the typical lesbian "coming out" story we hear so often today. A woman in her mid-forties has been married for twenty years with never a thought of sex with another woman. But she and her husband have grown emotionally distant and she has compensated by becoming more involved with her best friend. She is utterly surprised when the comfort she has been receiving in the arms of her lady friend suddenly deepens into a desire for an even more intimate, sexual touch. The messages beamed to her by the popular media convince her that this must be her "true self" that has lain dormant for forty years. So she leaves her husband, moves in with her friend, and joins NOW (National Organization for Women).

I have heard many Christian women relate a similar scenario of their fall into a lesbian relationship. But I have never heard of even one case where two solidly heterosexual Christian men became best buddies and one day just decided to begin having sex with each other. The typical heterosexual male's visual fixation on the female body just does not allow this to occur. In the cases I have seen where two Christian men become sexually involved, one or both have been struggling with homosexual feelings since adolescence. In a few of these situations, a homosexual man has persuaded his heterosexual friend to experiment sexually, but for the heterosexual man it remains a guilty pleasure. He retains his heterosexual feelings and identity.

Can two unmarried Christians commit spiritual adultery? Yes, but in a different sense. The Apostle Paul explains in his first letter to the Corinthian church (1 Corinthians 7:32–34) that a married Christian's primary commitment in time and effort should be to his or her spouse, but an unmarried Christian's primary commitment should be to God. Remember, adultery involves the betrayal of a committed relationship. In that sense, any relationship a Christian single becomes involved in that detracts from his relationship with God is adulterous. Christian singles can also be caught up in emotional dependency and improper sexual involvement.

The message here is *not* to stop ministering to needy people or to avoid all close friendships. We just need to become more mindful of what is going on in our own hearts by getting feedback from God and from others.

As the book of Jeremiah says, "The heart is deceitful above all things, and desperately wicked; who can know it? I, the LORD, search the heart, I test the mind" (Jeremiah 17:9–10 NKJV). The Bible also says, "In the multitude of counselors there is safety" (Proverbs 11:14 NKJV).

Spiritual Defilement

Spiritual defilement occurs when we are affected by another person's sinful condition through spiritual contact with them. We all have experienced how another's thoughts and feelings can affect us, through spoken words and facial expressions, so as to cause us to change our minds or our moods. Since the human spirit is just as real as the body or mind, it is no surprise that our spirits can also be influenced by contact with another's spirit.

Christians are often in situations where they can be affected by another's spirit. Even in casual conversations with others, there may be some degree of spiritual contact. Have you ever met someone for the first time and felt uneasy about him in a way you could not quite put into words? He may have been well-dressed, well-spoken, and good-looking, but you just could not trust him. You even may have felt so disgusted that you wanted to take a shower after he left, just to get the "gunk" off that he seemed to have transferred to you. I have met people like this and only later learned that they were scoundrels, liars, con artists, or enthusiastic practitioners of gross immorality. Nothing they did or said gave them away. They could not have been so "successfully" wicked had they not developed exceptional skills in deception. Yet, a Christian's awakened spirit can perceive the evil that is within them.

But a disgusting feeling, which goes beyond the gift of spiritual discernment, is not given by God's Holy Spirit. He and His gifts are pure and holy. We feel dirty and defiled by these people because our spirits have contacted theirs in some way—perhaps this is because we are too inexperienced in spiritual matters to know how to avoid doing so, or because their attempts to deceive and manipulate us involve a spiritual component. Afterwards, we are in need of a spiritual cleansing by the Holy Spirit to get rid of the spiritual defilement they have left with us.

The greater our spiritual contact with another person, the greater our risk of spiritual defilement by them. Whenever we are ministering to another in some way—encouraging, comforting, teaching, counseling, or praying with them—not only are feelings expressed and thoughts exchanged, but there is a spiritual interchange taking place as well. God's Holy Spirit is certainly present, but so are our own human spirits.

In my years of counseling, there have been many occasions in which I have been affected by a client's spiritual condition. Sometimes a person struggling with depression has imparted to me a feeling of heaviness that I have had to struggle to throw off—though I had felt just fine before the counseling session began. In other sessions, I have felt peculiar emotions and desires—similar to what my client was struggling with at the time —that I had never felt before. I was certain they did not come from within me. Sometimes these strange feelings would persist and I would have to get my wife to pray with me until they were gone.

Counselors and pastors who consistently work with those caught up in sexual sins often report experiencing this type of defilement. It may manifest as perverse sexual thoughts or dreams unlike anything they have known before. It may also be experienced as an uncomfortable feeling of being spiritually dirty and weighed down after a counseling session. This defilement can even proceed to the point where the counselor becomes confused and begins to accept these bizarre feelings as his own, ending up in the same sexual sin as his client. (Or perhaps even *with* his client!) I am convinced this is an example of what Paul was warning about in Galatians 6:1: "Brethren, if a man is overtaken in any trespass, you who are spiritual restore such a one in a spirit of gentleness, *considering yourself lest you also be tempted*" (NKJV).

During our years of ministering to male and female prostitutes in New York City, my ministry team members and I unfortunately witnessed several volunteer workers fall into sexual sin through spiritual defilement. Most had been happily married and did not have a history of struggling with temptation in that area. We warned them to stay on guard against this phenomenon. Yet, some who seemed overconfident were swept into sexual affairs with those we were trying to help. Others just lost their zeal and love for the Lord as they were overcome by the indifference and slothfulness of spirit that was being projected by the "street people."

It seems that several conditions can make us more susceptible to spiritual defilement through ministry. When we are worn down in spirit, soul, or body, then we are just not as well protected. Our energy level is low, we let our guard down, and we can be more easily deceived or confused.

In some situations, our own natural feelings of compassion overwhelm our training and better judgment. We may become so caught up in sympathy for a person and a desire to help that we are no longer listening to the voice of the Holy Spirit. Our spirit senses the person's deep need, and we respond to meet his need from within our own being, no longer directing him to God, but drawing him closer to ourselves. This is also a form of defilement, which not only is very draining, but also can turn into idolatry as the counselor begins to take on a role that properly belongs only to God. This situation can easily progress to emotional dependency, as well as spiritual and physical adultery.

There also seems to be a greater risk of defilement when the counselee is not truly repentant of his sin. He may be enjoying the attention and sympathy he is receiving, but in his heart, he has decided to hang on to his sinful habits a while longer. If you are not able to perceive by the Holy Spirit the true state of his heart, continuing to encourage and sympathize with him will only deepen your risk of being defiled and weakened by his sinful state.

As with spiritual adultery, the risk of spiritual defilement is no reason to avoid ministering to others. We simply need to become better informed of spiritual matters, develop our sensitivity to what is happening spiritually in a given situation, and exercise due caution. According to John

Sandford, as a counselor learns through experience to detect and ward off spiritual defilement, he can actually be provided with helpful clues in uncovering a counselee's hidden problems.[2]

Defilement through spiritual ministry can also flow in the other direction, from the minister to the recipient. Whenever we receive from a minister at church, whether he is preaching, teaching, or leading us in worship, not only are we hearing his words, but there is also a spiritual impartation occurring. We trust that the Holy Spirit is present in the man and ministering through him, but we know that does not make him inerrant. (Believe me, all teachers and preachers can look back and remember many things they wish they had never said.) Nor does the fact that he has been truly called of God and is ministering through the gifts of the Holy Spirit guarantee that his own spirit is always pure. (Recall that Judas was chosen by Jesus and participated in the same ministry as the other apostles.)

I have, on occasion, been called in to provide spiritual "first aid" for a church that has been hit by a mysterious epidemic of affairs and adulteries in the congregation. Invariably, these were traced back to someone who had recently ministered there who was flirting with a sexual temptation or had fallen into overt sexual sin. No one in the congregation had been aware of his sin. But through receiving his ministry, many seemed to have been defiled by the sexual impurity in his spirit and had begun to manifest the same sin.

Recall the case of the woman called "Jezebel," a leader at the church in Thyatira who was openly teaching the members that it was permissible to engage in sexual sins (Revelation 2:18-24). Equally brazen deceivers have invaded a few American churches in recent years. But in our experience, even the *secret* sexual sin of a leader is enough to produce a similar effect in the congregation through the power of spiritual defilement.

Another situation in which spiritual defilement can occur is within a marriage relationship. Because of the strong spiritual bond between a husband and wife, it is impossible for one to be secretly involved in gross sin without affecting the spouse in some way. This seems particularly true of sexual sins. I have heard many Christian ladies describe how they began to feel a sense of spiritual defilement and betrayal after times of intimacy with their husbands. It was only later that they discovered their husbands had become involved in some form of sexual sin.

As we saw in the section on spiritual adultery, a wife can often sense when her husband is in a spiritually adulterous relationship with another woman because her own spirit is being defiled by it. Even a husband who only indulges in sexual fantasies about other women is committing adultery in his heart (as Jesus explained in Matthew 5:27–28), and this can cause his wife to sense defilement in her spirit.

The effects of spiritual defilement are greatly intensified if there is some form of demonic involvement. It is logical to assume that since demons are spirit beings, they are aware of these principles of spiritual adultery and all the forms of spiritual defilement and can use them to their advantage.

Demons also seem to be able to exert an evil influence through any type of spiritual link that is established with an infested person. There have been many times in our ministry when, through our efforts to witness and minister to those living in bondage to sin, we have come under focused attack from demons that were inhabiting those individuals or somehow responsible for keeping them in bondage.

I recall one incident where my wife, Phyllis, was praying in church with a "drag queen" (a male transvestite prostitute) when she felt a demonic spirit wrap itself around her like a giant snake. She was overcome by feelings of filth and the shame of perverse lust. She immediately came to me for prayer. Together, we broke the hold of this thing and drove it away. Still, it took several weeks of rest and prayer together to restore her spiritual strength, rebuild our "oneness," and shake off the last effects of this attack.

Quite a few demonically infested people come through our counseling office and residential program. On occasion, we find that one of the "drop outs" has left one of his demons behind. Not too long after, a sensitive person will sense an evil presence, or a new resident assigned to the drop out's old room will experience bad feelings and troubling dreams there. A few of us will then hold an impromptu prayer meeting, using the authority of Jesus Christ to bind and drive out any dark forces that are present, and asking the Holy Spirit to fill the place with His holiness and peace. The situation is much like having a stray dog hanging around your back porch for a few days. As you would chase away the dog, you just have to chase away the demon and avoid leaving anything around (like pornography) on which it likes to feed.

Recommended Reading

Adultery and Spiritual Adultery
John Sandford, *Why Some Christians Commit Adultery* (Tulsa: Victory House, 1989).

Lori Thorkelson-Rentzel, *Emotional Dependency: A Threat to Close Friendships* (Downers Grove, IL: InterVarsity Press, 1991).

Spiritual Defilement and Spiritual Warfare
Rebecca Brown, *He Came to Set the Captives Free* (New Kensington, PA: Whitaker House, 1992).

———, *Prepare for War* (New Kensington, PA: Whitaker House, 1987).

———, *Becoming a Vessel of Honor* (New Kensington, PA: Whitaker House, 1990).

———, *Unbroken Curses* (New Kensington, PA: Whitaker House, 1995).

John and Mark Sandford, *Deliverance and Inner Healing* (Grand Rapids: Revell, 1992).

Dating, Premarital Sex, and Youth Culture

There is no question that premarital sexual activity (fornication) is a major problem among Christian youth today. We reviewed the statistics on the incidence of this in Chapter 8. In Chapters 3, 4, and 5, we also examined how the forces of sexual attraction tend to pull dating couples of any age toward greater levels of union.

However, premarital sex is just one among many terrible and destructive forces that are ripping apart America's children, even those from Christian homes. Drug and alcohol abuse, gangs, violence, sexual perversions, occult practices, demonically inspired music and movies—any child who attends our public schools is exposed to these things on a regular basis, even in the smallest towns and wealthiest suburbs.

We are the wealthiest and most powerful nation on earth, with the greatest freedoms, with the greatest centers of learning drawing the best minds from all over the world, and with a public education system that is the envy of many other nations. Is it not incredible that our children—raised in the midst of this great "utopia"—seem to be trying to destroy themselves in every way possible?

It is time we faced the fact that American society is very sick, and we are seeing the greatest symptoms among the weakest members—our own children. The recent number of young boys who have become mass murderers, slaughtering as many children as they possibly could, is just the latest symptom of a steady downward spiral that shows no signs of hitting bottom. We cannot consider premarital sex apart from all of these other things, since they all have the same root cause: the abnormal, pathological youth culture *we* have created and forced upon our children.

The fact that few are willing to face is that we have created a totally artificial world in which to raise our children, centered around the public school system. What Americans do not seem to realize is that many of the very things we found so monstrous about the Soviet Union in the 1950s, we have now freely chosen to impose upon ourselves. Many of our children are separated from their mothers within six months of birth and cared for in nurseries so the mothers can return to their jobs. From that point on, they are raised by massive, impersonal state institutions. (Forty-two percent of children today are being raised in single-parent homes, while the state and its institutions substitute for the missing parent.)

Throughout childhood our children are brainwashed with the secular "party" doctrines—whether developed by the educational elite or the lead singer of a "thrash metal" band—through school curriculum, or through television programs, movies, and music aimed at their "market segment." Most children still spend a few hours a week with a parent, but the state is always standing at the back door, ready to intervene if the parent is deemed unsuitable.[3] The state will also furnish children with abortions and birth-control devices, without the parents' knowledge and even against their wishes, because children have a right to "sexual freedom." In accordance with the doctrine of "diversity," schoolchildren are encouraged to experiment sexually to decide if they are gay, straight, or bisexual. Teenage girls who choose to have a baby on their own are given the status of a new "family" and are supported by the state, which serves as the "father" for this family.

The demon Molech, who convinced ancient Israelite parents to sacrifice their children to him in return for material gain (see, for example, Jeremiah 32:35), has renamed himself "Convenience," "Personal Fulfillment," and "Career Development." He seems satisfied today to get American parents to sacrifice their unwanted children to him in the womb through abortion. Then he convinces them to sacrifice their *wanted* children to him through the public school system in return for material goods or personal fulfillment in their careers. These are just a few of the things he has accomplished:

- 25% of high school students consider suicide each year.
- More than 25% of high school seniors have used drugs in the past 30 days.

• 90% of twelfth-graders say it is easy to get marijuana if they want it.[4]

• 10% of all teens are unsure of their sexual orientation at some point during adolescence.[5]

The price of this artificial child-rearing system, which has developed for the convenience of adults and serves to isolate children from adults, is that the children create their own childish subculture under the noses of the system administrators. This youth culture bears a not-too-surprising resemblance to the culture found among prisoners in state penitentiaries, because, when you really think about it, the state prison system resembles the state school system in so many ways.

THE PRISON SYSTEM AND TODAY'S PUBLIC SCHOOL SYSTEM HAVE A SIMILAR SET OF PROBLEMS: DRUG ABUSE, GANGS, VIOLENCE, AND ILLICIT SEX.

Both systems confine certain people against their will, requiring them to do things they do not desire to do, under the watchful eyes of a small number of guards (or teachers). Discipline is not very effective because neither system can easily get rid of troublemakers. Both of these systems exist, not to serve individual captives (or students), but to achieve the larger goals of society as a whole. Some of the individuals within these systems are outcasts from the rest of society. So it is not surprising that when placed in such an environment, they will develop a variety of hidden subcultures—cliques or gangs—both to resist the authority imposed upon them in whatever way possible and to meet their emotional and social needs. The result is that *both the prison system and today's public school system have a similar set of problems: drug abuse, gangs, violence, and illicit sex.*

An article in *Newsweek*—printed in the wake of the massacre of high school students in Littleton, Colorado, by two of their peers—struggled to explain why these tragedies are happening so frequently in our schools today. A journalist interviewed Los Angeles school psychologist Richard Lieberman about why so many kids see warning signs of violence, such as other kids carrying handguns or making death threats, yet do not report them. According to Lieberman, "They're afraid of being called a snitch. They're also afraid that if they report someone carrying a gun, that gun may be used against them." He explained that both fears are quite reasonable, but that schools must "assure students that they are doing the right thing by informing, and that their identities will be protected."[6]

The irony that both this school psychologist and the *Newsweek* reporter failed to notice is that the very same statement could equally describe the attitude of the inmates at any penitentiary in the country.

We need to look in more detail at how this abnormal and unhealthy youth culture originated.

How Did Our Abnormal Youth Culture Originate?

Throughout the Western world, society and the Church have come to accept the "generation gap" as normal. Each generation of our children, starting in the 1950s or even earlier, have developed their own language, their own musical style, their own moral code, their own native dress— essentially, their own culture. Many Christian parents accept as unavoidable the notion that they will "lose" their children for about a decade—say from age 14 to 24—and can only hope and pray that they will eventually return to the family's beliefs and values.

However, from the standpoint of all the nations of the world, viewed over the entire span of human history, our "generation gap" is *highly abnormal*. Just think of the many nations in the Far East and Middle East that have preserved their way of life unchanged for thousands of years, handing their cultural values down from parent to child over many generations. Consider also that these are not Christian nations. So, how did our basically Christian nation begin to lose each new generation of its children?

Let us first examine how these historic societies—often considered to be nations of the Third World—raise their children in ways that are different from our own. First of all, their children are raised in extended families, in small communities, where they are continuously exposed to, learn from, and are cared for by family members and friends of all ages. All these societies consider puberty to be the sign that a child is ready to enter the adult world, and they mark that passage with special coming-of-age ceremonies. These ceremonies celebrate the boy's entrance into manhood and being welcomed by the men of the community into their company, and the girl's entrance into womanhood and being received by the other women. After the celebrations end, these new young men and women are given new responsibilities, as well as new privileges. They begin as "junior apprentices" to learn the skills of the adult world that will carry them throughout their lives.

OUR YOUTH ARE LEFT TO BUILD THEIR OWN SOCIETY FROM THE SCRAPS THAT FALL TO THEM FROM AN ADULT WORLD AT WHICH THEY CAN ONLY GAZE.

This description of child-rearing also applied to America for much of its early history. However, forces were at work to change this favorable situation. In the 1950s two major shifts in American society occurred:

1. The extended family was replaced by the "nuclear" family, because, as a nation, we chose material prosperity over maintaining extended family relationships. People left the old homestead to find better jobs and then went wherever their new jobs took them.

2. The days and hours that children were required to spend in public school classrooms increased dramatically. This meant that our children were being physically segregated throughout most of their formative years with other children of the same age.

What is the net effect of these forces on our children? Instead of developing a variety of relationships with adults and children of many different ages, as in the past, they end up socializing only with other children of exactly the same age for most of the day. When they arrive home from school, Dad is still at work, Mom is still at work or in the kitchen, and there are no longer any other adult members of the extended family present for them to socialize with. So the children end up spending their afternoons with other children. Instead of gradually being introduced to adult society as participants, instead of learning to model adult behaviors and values when they most desire to, our youth are left to build their own society from the scraps that fall to them from an adult world at which they can only gaze, but not yet participate in. This is why "peer pressure" wields the power that it does: our youth are forced to socialize only with those in their age group. They, in turn, become *socialized* by their age group (that is, they are taught the accepted standards of social behavior by that group).

Most parents recall that at a certain point their teens entered a stage where they began to slavishly imitate their peers in an effort to fit in with the group. It is almost as if young people, at some point, feel an "identity vacuum"—"Who am I? What shall I become?" They grasp at everything around them to try to build a sense of self that fills this empty place. This is the time when lifelong values, habits, and preferences are set in stone. This further illustrates what is so abnormal about the way we raise our children. In a "normal," non-Western society, when teens enter this phase, they have already been officially accepted into the adult community, so the peers they will so slavishly emulate are *the adults* of their community. This ensures that they will absorb the same values that have been handed down through the generations. By segregating our children by age for so many years, we have created an abnormal, age-based peer group that does not even exist in these more ancient societies. One expert after another has come to the same conclusion: *American teens are starved for adults' time and attention*. But since they cannot get that, no matter how much they act up, they make do with whatever else they can find to fill the emptiness they feel inside.

AMERICAN TEENS ARE STARVED FOR ADULTS' TIME AND ATTENTION.

How many of us have known young men, remarkably mature for their age, who were considered to be responsible by adult standards, but somewhat "square" by their peers? Invariably, I have found that these young men had a special advantage over their peers. Perhaps they worked with their father in his business, or perhaps they joined a volunteer organization. But the result was that, at some point, they had an opportunity to be welcomed into a group of older men who treated them as equals and shared responsibilities with them. Do you have any idea what it means to a 12-year-old boy to be accepted into a community of men as an equal, though junior, member? It is a life-changing experience.

The "Generation Gap" in the Church

There is no evidence that the New Testament church had a youth group and a youth pastor. The evidence is to the contrary because their society did not have that gray area between childhood and adulthood that we call adolescence. By roughly the age of puberty, Jewish boys and girls had completed their basic spiritual education and, after their *bar mitzvah* or *bat mitzvah*, were received as full-fledged adult members of the synagogue, with all rights, privileges, and responsibilities. They were then expected to minister alongside the adults in the religious services. This is still true in Jewish communities today, and I believe it is the primary reason that observant Jews have been able to resist assimilation over the centuries and maintain such a strong religious tradition, no matter in what society they happen to be living.

I believe a passage from a prophecy in the book of Isaiah speaks to this issue of the generations:

> Those from among you shall build the old waste places; you shall raise up **the foundations of many generations;** and you shall be called the Repairer of the Breach, the Restorer of Streets to Dwell In. (Isaiah 58:12 NKJV)

In this passage God is speaking primarily to the Jewish culture of that day, but I believe that what He is saying also applies to the Church culture of today. The Church is also built on a foundation of many generations.

So if there is a separation between the generations, then there is a crack in the very foundation of the Church. The repairing of walls and streets indicates that the Church is to be more than a place to visit once a week; it is to be a place in which to dwell, a community in which people can live and raise their families. The fact that it has walls means that it is a place of safety and protection, strong enough to withstand the social forces that rage beyond those walls.

We can see just how much the American church suffers from breaches in its walls by observing how many Christian youth in our churches have been swept away by the same social forces that rule others of their generation. I believe this happens when we in the church merely reflect and emulate the society around us regarding how we raise our young people. Almost universally, our young adults (aged 13 and above) have been segregated into youth groups—with a few youth leaders to ride herd on them—while they are entertained by "Christian artists" and wait for the day to finally come when they can leave home. The only requirement placed on them by the church during this time is, "Don't cause us any grief." They need to be shown that they have a valuable place in the Body of Christ where they can serve alongside their parents and other adults. They must have a chance to work together with the Body—"joined and knit together by what every joint supplies, according to the effective working by which every part does its share" (Ephesians 4:16 NKJV)—so that they are not swept away.

I believe it is high time for the Church to start bridging the generation gap within its walls to prevent it from continuing into future generations. The question is, What can we do that will counteract the overwhelming social forces around us?

I believe the crux of the solution lies in creating a church community that can substitute for the extended family and the small town community of several generations back. Then, we must receive our youth into the church community as equal participants, at around the age of puberty, with valuable roles and responsibilities.

Home schooling can certainly play an important part. Studies of home-schooled children consistently report that they not only outperform their public-schooled peers, but also demonstrate more social maturity for their age because of their greater interaction with adults. Small Christian schools can also be a part of the solution, *but only if* they provide greater opportunities to interact with adults and do not recreate the age segregation found in the public schools.

I believe a better vision for the future of the Church is for young men (say, over 13 years old) to be accepted into men's groups and activities and for young women to be accepted into women's groups and activities. They need to be given positions of real service according to their abilities. We need to teach them to develop the spiritual gifts God has given them, and learn, ourselves, to receive from God through them.

I believe that if churches and parents will work together to start doing these things, we can go a long way toward overcoming and reversing the negative influences our society has had on our children.

Dating or Courting?

"Dating" is very much an invention of the abnormal youth culture we have created. It is something very different from what our grandparents and many of our parents practiced. They "courted" instead of "dated," because the whole point was to find a suitable partner for a lifetime marriage. We have somehow accepted the bizarre notion that Christian youth, beginning at around age 14 or 15, are supposed to start dating as a means of entertainment. Along with this, the frequently accepted idea is that they should have no plans for marrying until they finish college and are established in a good career, somewhere in their mid-20s. With this attitude, we are expecting young Christian adults (they are no longer children once they pass the age of puberty, according to biblical standards) to remain virgins for ten years or so during the lifetime peak of their sex drives, while engaging in highly intimate couple relationships. This contradicts every fact we have been learning about sexual forces. So, it is really not surprising that

55–60% of the most conservative, churchgoing young adults 18–24 years of age have had premarital sex (compared to 90–95% of their nonreligious peers).[7]

Premarital Sex

Let us look at the facts about premarital sex in the United States. Most young people today are involved in a series of casual dating relationships that often lead to sexual activity. Some continue in a pattern of short-lived affairs with little emotional involvement. Still, most eventually find someone with whom they want to have a "serious," long-term relationship.

A one-time act of intercourse is enough to establish a "one flesh" union to some degree. It is mostly physical at this point, but there are also emotional and spiritual attachments. However, if the "couple" have little or no prior emotional involvement and no intention of having a further relationship (such as occurs with a "one-night stand" or a prostitute), this is clearly in the category of what the Bible calls fornication. The effect of these loveless, casual, even anonymous sexual unions is to deaden the emotional sensitivity of those involved and weaken their ability to form a fully committed relationship with a future spouse. One who lives a promiscuous lifestyle is repeatedly being joined with another, then having that brief union ripped apart.

Some persist in this condition for the rest of their lives, remaining single and promiscuous (16.9% of men and 9% of women have had two or more sex partners within the last 12 months[8]). They never seem to make the connection between sex and love. Perhaps they were emotionally traumatized in childhood. In any case, extensive promiscuity by itself is enough to cause emotional hardening and scarring. But most people eventually realize that sex without a loving, committed relationship is ultimately unsatisfying.

As we have seen, repeated sexual intercourse between two people deepens their union at all levels. For example, a couple may have started out in a casual sexual relationship that could be classified as fornication, but over time, the Law of Sexual Union does its work. They begin to develop a deeper, romantic attachment to each other and spend more and more time together. Eventually, they move in together if their circumstances will allow it. (Around 45% of adults aged 25–34 have cohabited at some point in their lives.[9])

These cohabiting couples have become "one flesh" to a much greater degree than a single act of fornication could produce. Separation would cause them some degree of emotional pain in proportion to the strength of their bond. The practical reality here is that the *Law of Sexual Union has married them*. Many governments recognize this cohabitation as a "common law" marriage if it exceeds a certain length of time, even if most churches do not. I believe God considers such couples married because His Law of Sexual Union has joined them together, whether or not they have dignified it by a license and ceremony. (These cohabiting relationships last 1.3 years on average, and 60% ultimately result in a formal marriage.[10])

However, if the cohabiting couple have not made vows of lifelong commitment to each other, there is likely to be some level of anxiety and mistrust that can only weaken their relationship. If they have begun this relationship after a period of promiscuity, then this can further weaken their ability or desire to make a lifelong commitment. There is abundant evidence that marriages formed from cohabitation are less stable and are nearly twice as likely to result in divorce.[11]

If these cohabiting couples encounter difficulties in their relationship and decide to move on to other partners, then, in reality, they are committing adultery—even though they were never legally married—because they are ripping apart their God-created one-flesh union to be united with another.

Sadly, this scenario is the norm for young adults in Western societies today. Some sociologists call it "serial monogamy," but it would be more accurate to call it "serial adultery." Perhaps it is just ignorance of how the Law of Sexual Union works that explains why this tragic situation has become so common, even for some Christians.

Must a Single Christian Who Has Sexual Intercourse with Someone Marry That Person?

The Old Testament laws governing Israelites caught in a sexual relationship outside of marriage prescribed either death by stoning or a forced marriage, depending on the circumstances. Obviously, these civil and criminal laws of the ancient Jewish theocratic state are not directly applicable to Christians today, although the moral principles behind them are still valid.

There is nothing in the New Testament to indicate that, for Christians, a single act of fornication should be grounds for a forced marriage (or a stoning!). The Apostle Paul, speaking to Christians, warns us to "flee fornication" (1 Corinthians 6:18 KJV); furthermore, the Bible says, "Fornicators and adulterers God will judge" (Hebrews 13:4 NKJV). Repentance for the sin and prayer for restoration are needed. But, as we have seen above, a more involved relationship is a more complicated matter that often requires some counseling with both parties to properly resolve.

The Apostle Paul had a simple prescription for preventing fornication: *get married!*

> To avoid fornication, let every man have his own
> wife, and let every woman have her own husband.
> (1 Corinthians 7:2 KJV)

This wise counsel is being ignored by many Christians in Western societies who are following prevailing cultural trends of prolonged and intimate dating relationships, while postponing marriage until the mid- to late-twenties. Consequently, many of these Christian couples are also following another cultural trend: premarital sex.

As we have seen from our examination of the practical effects of the Law of Sexual Union, a dating couple who spend a lot of private time together sharing their intimate thoughts and being affectionate are inevitably drawn into deeper levels of communion, leading ultimately toward sexual intercourse. This is just the way God designed our sexuality to work. When people ignore or try to circumvent this process, they always get into trouble. Young couples who try to maintain an emotionally, physically, and spiritually intimate relationship for years without having sex *are fighting a battle God never intended them to fight.* Many eventually break up or succumb to premarital sex due to the pressures of this highly unnatural situation.

Studies have shown that Christian couples who have premarital sex create more problems for themselves when they marry. They carry a burden of guilt for violating their moral convictions that can cause continuing marital strife. The guilt may also impair their ability to fully enjoy marital sex. Even couples who were able to restrain themselves from premarital intercourse may have trouble in their sexual adjustment after marriage, because of the ways they have learned to suppress their natural sexual feelings over the years in a highly unnatural dating situation.

Parents and pastors who want to help their youth avoid sexual sin and its problems need to stop creating an environment where so many of their young people *are destined to fail.* If churches and families are going to encourage the type of teenage dating practiced in America today, then they should be prepared to encourage early marriages.

The present situation—where Christian teens are expected to start having serious, affectionate, romantic dating relationships at 15 or 16, but not marry until they have established a career in their mid-twenties—may make sense economically, but it just flies in the face of biological reality. These teens are sexually mature (the male sex drive reaches its peak at around age 18), and modern dating practices allow them to become deeply bonded—emotionally, mentally, and biologically—even without experiencing full intercourse. But they are expected to refrain from sex (and avoid all impure thoughts) for another five to ten years! Can no one see that this current "standard" of acceptable behavior does not fit God's plan for sexuality?

Certainly, Christian dating practices need to change. But the Apostle Paul offered another option when he said, "It is better to marry than to

burn" (1 Corinthians 7:9 KJV). There is no reason why Christian teens—
if they have been raised in a healthy family, have learned to handle responsibility, and have some degree of emotional maturity and a solid spiritual
foundation for their lives—cannot begin a successful marriage at 18 or 19
with the support of their families and their church. I have seen many successful examples of these early marriages. I believe these couples can actually have a better chance for success than those who have waited until their
mid-twenties but have been involved in a series of broken relationships.
Some older singles who have been sexually involved in a series of relationships could be considered to be in an adulterous state. They have experienced the emotional and sexual equivalent of being married and divorced
several times already.

If you are a single person who is currently involved in any kind of
improper sexual relationship, the wisest thing you can do is to talk it over
with a pastor or counselor at your church. What is best for both people
involved in the situation can best be determined through prayer and the
wise counsel of a more experienced person. At the very least, the goal
should be to immediately put a stop to the sinful elements of the relationship, bring mutual repentance and reconciliation, and establish a new
ground for the relationship based on true Christian love.

*How Far Can Christians Go in Expressing Physical Affection in a Dating
Relationship without Committing a Sexual Sin?*

Too many Christian singles get hung up on this issue. I hope, after
reading this far, you can see that this is simply a foolish question. The Law
of Sexual Union begins to operate when you first glimpse "across a crowd-
ed room" someone who matches your lovemap. The more you touch each
other, the more you are bonded together by the release of oxytocin. When
you first kiss each other on the lips, you both have made a life-altering decision to take on any orally-transmitted viral diseases that the other may be
carrying. As you share your deepest thoughts and pray together, a spiritual bond is being established. As the two of you spend more time alone

together, your bodies begin responding and adapting to pheromones emitted by the other. Every time you are sexually aroused by seeing and touching your "date," the pleasure bond between you is being strengthened. Giving each other an orgasm through "heavy petting" establishes a deep sexual imprint of each other in your minds. It is the emotional equivalent of intercourse, even if you are technically still virgins. Sexual intercourse is just the final phase in this continuing process of union, mingling your bloodstreams and perhaps creating a new life.

The key concept that Christian singles need to grasp is that romantic relationships involve a continuous, almost automatic, process of deepening attachment at many levels. The more deeply you have become attached, the more emotional pain you will suffer if you separate. If your relationship is at the stage where you are both struggling to avoid "going all the way," then you need to make a decision: either get married or break off the relationship completely. It is very difficult at this point to return to a previous level of less intimate involvement. Christian singles need to decide much earlier in a relationship whether "This is someone I would be willing to spend the rest of my life with," before any extensive romantic bonding has taken place.

The American dating culture tends to set this "one flesh" bonding process into motion long before basic issues of friendship and compatibility have been resolved. We are bombarded by images from soap operas, romance novels, movies, ads, and television shows that have created a "script" for dating couples to follow. Even Christian singles tend to follow this script blindly, though they may choose to make it an "R-rated" version instead of the "NC-17" their unsaved friends are following. Here is a typical situation:

A nice Christian boy meets a nice Christian girl at a church social. He invites her to go see a movie and have dinner. He makes sure to pick a good "date" movie, not the latest action thriller he would really like to see.

Meanwhile, she is thinking nonstop about what she should wear. She wants to show off her best features, but not seem "too sexy," at least not on the first date.

All during the movie, he is thinking, "Is it too soon to put my arm around her?" She is thinking, "Is he going to try to put his arm around me?"

They go to a nice restaurant afterwards and have a pleasant conversation. But are they discussing their deepest beliefs and highest ideals? It is more likely that they are each saying what they hope will make the most favorable impression. He may want to let her know that he has a great career and plenty of money. Meanwhile, she is making sure she laughs at all his jokes and keeps a tight reign on her own sharp wit so he will not feel intimidated.

On the ride home, they are both wondering if he is going to try to kiss her on the cheek or just give her a quick hug at the door.

So what is wrong with this scenario? First, the relationship begins with hypocrisy. Each party is so focused on making a good impression that, in trying to cover up their flaws and enhance their strengths, they end up concealing their true selves. So each gets to know a false image instead of a real person.

Second, there is a primary focus on "romance," on physical attraction and involvement, such as when to touch, kiss, hold hands, and embrace. Each is waiting to feel that "special feeling" to know whether this person is "the one for me," not realizing that warm, fuzzy glow is just the first stage of the sexual bonding process, which is almost inevitable if they follow the script toward ever more intimate physical contact. If this couple continues to follow the "script," then each date will have a little more touch, a little more intimacy. As they fall deeper under the spell of the sexual bonding process, they will focus much more on what they are "feeling" for each other. Instead of honestly discussing and settling their differences on such fundamental issues as their values and life goals, they are much more likely to avoid and gloss over any perceived incompatibilities so as not to disturb the pleasurable feelings they are giving each other. This is why so many couples have problems and divorce after just a few years of marriage. The natural high called "being in love" wears off about then, and they realize they have many basic incompatibilities that were never resolved. As Amos 3:3 says, "Can two walk together, unless they are agreed?" (NKJV).

In Summary

This whole issue of the infiltration of American youth culture into the Church is certain to be highly controversial, and even explosive, because nearly every church in America today falls under this condemnation: *through our complacency we have put our children at risk.* Is there any church that has not lost some of its youth to the seductions of drugs, gangs, and premarital sex? Read *Right from Wrong* by Josh McDowell if you want to see just how seriously our Christian youth have been seduced and subverted by the American youth culture.

The American church must begin to examine what it has done to its children and what it has allowed others to do. Parents and churches must consider whether now is the time for drastic measures, such as withdrawing our children from the public school system, as some Christian leaders are now urging us to do.[12] As we saw in Chapter 7, public schools across America are now firmly committed to teaching our children to honor and respect every form of sexual sin and perversion, but to dishonor God and reject their parents' beliefs.

It is now time to consider radical changes to our church cultures that will enable us and our children to break free from the influence of the American culture around us. Parents and pastors need to examine whether what they are teaching their youth about dating is really scriptural, or even practical in light of the truth about the Law of Sexual Union. Joshua Harris, a Christian youth leader, has written an excellent book about the problems with American dating practices called *I Kissed Dating Goodbye*. He explores in great detail why "dating," as we know it today, is a bad way to find a good mate. Perhaps we should look more closely at replacing "dating" with "courting."

Even such bold ideas as holding coming-of-age ceremonies for our teens and receiving them into the adult community of the church as full partners in ministry, are beginning to be developed by more adventurous churches.[13] (This was the original purpose of traditional "confirmation" ceremonies.)

These issues certainly need to be explored more fully. I am not claiming to have all the answers. But we must wake up to the reality that *we have put our own children in harm's way and God will hold us responsible.*

Recommended Reading

Elisabeth Elliot, *Passion and Purity* (Grand Rapids: Baker Book House, 1984).
————, *Quest for Love* (Grand Rapids: Baker Book House, 1996).
Joshua Harris, *I Kissed Dating Goodbye* (Sisters, OR: Multnomah Books, 1997).
Josh McDowell and Bob Hostetler, *Right from Wrong: What You Need to Know to Help Youth Make Right Choices* (Dallas: Word Publishing, 1994).

Divorce

As we all know, divorce has been a highly controversial subject within the Church for centuries.* Each denomination has developed its own doctrines and rules concerning divorce. Often, these have developed from a mixture of religious theories interacting with the current social or political climate. My purpose in this book is to refocus our attention on the actual consequences of divorce.

No matter how good your reasons are for divorcing your spouse, no matter what the circumstances under which your church doctrines or state laws permit it, anyone who seeks to tear apart the "one flesh" union established through God's Law of Sexual Union will suffer the inevitable consequences.

The best analogy I can think of for understanding this comes from a tragic story with which we are all familiar. From time to time, we hear of a man working alone, deep in the wilderness, who gets his foot crushed and trapped under a falling rock or log. He works with all his might to free himself, but to no avail. As night comes, the snow begins to fall, and he feels himself growing weaker as his wound continues to bleed. He knows he cannot survive the night in that condition, so he grasps the only option remaining that can save his life. To free himself, he takes his knife and saws off his foot at the ankle, then drags himself to safety. He has escaped with his life, but he has paid a high price to do so.

Many people have divorced to escape severe mental and physical abuse. Some have even felt their very lives were at stake. Yet even with the best of reasons, there is no escape from the deep wounding that occurs in severing a "one flesh" union. Psychologists have concluded that the emotional pain and physiological stress incurred in divorcing a spouse *nearly equals* that incurred from the death of a spouse.[14]

If young children are involved, then they are also wounded. Evidence continues to mount that children suffer severe emotional harm from

---

* The Church of England was split off from the Roman Catholic Church by the king of England so he could grant himself a divorce that the Pope had refused him.

their parents' divorce. If the divorce is very bitter and the children become pawns in a continuing battle, the resulting emotional damage is far worse than would have occurred if one parent had simply died.

Let us look at some of the harm divorce has been shown to cause:

- Divorced adults, especially men, have significantly more health problems than married people of the same age. Divorced men have double the death rate for married men from heart disease and stroke. Their suicide rate is four times higher.[15]
- Children of divorce show signs of severe and lasting emotional trauma. They are 70% more likely to be expelled or suspended from school,[16] twice as likely to drop out of school,[17] and show higher rates of delinquency.[18] They have higher rates of suicide than their peers.[19]
- Children from divorced families are more likely to divorce (60% more likely for women, 35% more likely for men) and have children outside of marriage.[20]
- Children from divorced or blended families are at much greater risk for being molested, especially boys living with a single mother and girls living with a stepfather or their mother's boyfriend in the home. These boys may be looking for a father figure, which makes them more susceptible to pedophiles. The girls seem to face more risk from being molested by nonrelated males: her mother's new husband or boyfriend, or his friends and family members.[21]

As we saw in Chapter 8, the divorce rate among American Christians is slightly higher than among non-Christians. Why has this happened? The most obvious answer is that American Christians are not understanding or practicing marriage any differently from their non-Christian neighbors. Churches have yet to address this problem effectively. The annual

"Marriage Enrichment Seminar" is just not doing the job. Nor are our young people being taught—by the schools or the churches—the skills they need to have successful marriages.

(By the way, if you think your church is better than the rest, why not ask your pastor to calculate the actual divorce rate in your church? Be sure to include those people who have left the church because they were ostracized after their divorce or were so emotionally torn apart that they could no longer put on a "happy face" at church functions. Do not hesitate to print the results in next Sunday's bulletin, along with the national divorce rates for non-Christians and for your particular style of church. This could either be a pat on the back or a stimulus for change.)

This book was not intended to be a manual for fixing troubled marriages, yet the principles we have explored so far are foundational for truly understanding what marriage is and why divorce is always so destructive.

I have seen a few divorces over the years that seemed necessary for the wife's physical safety. But the vast majority of divorces I have witnessed between Christian couples have resulted from strongholds of demonic delusion. There is no doubt that Satan wants to destroy as many Christian marriages as possible. In each marital shipwreck I have observed, there were unquestionably demonic forces at work: stirring up hatred, blinding minds to reality, promising an idyllic future with a new spouse, and twisting Scriptures to justify the action. I often see Christians couples who choose to disregard the Bible, the Holy Spirit, the advice of their pastors and counselors, the emotional damage they are suffering, and even the harm they are doing to their own children, so that they can engage in a self-righteous contest of wills. Typically, the Scriptures forbidding divorce become so twisted in their minds that they each hope the other will be the first to remarry. They think this will put all the guilt for the divorce on the other for having been the first to commit adultery, thus freeing themselves to remarry without sin. They repeatedly block out the pain and suffering they and their children are experiencing to focus on who is going to win their little battle.

On the other hand, I have known many Christian couples over the years who admit that they married for all the wrong reasons and were highly incompatible with each other. Sometimes, one had even attacked the other in a violent rage or had committed adultery. Yet, as they grew in spiritual maturity, sought counsel, and asked for God's help, He brought understanding and resolution for their conflicts and gave them a wonderful marriage.

If a husband and wife both have truly committed their lives to God, then there is no problem in their marriage, or anywhere else in their lives, that cannot be resolved with the help of the Holy Spirit, an *experienced* counselor, and the support of a loving church family.

I do not feel truly qualified to tell other Christians when they should consider divorce. I always refer them to the Apostle Paul for his advice:

> I instruct married couples to stay together, and this is exactly what the Lord himself taught. A wife who leaves her husband should either stay single or go back to her husband. And a husband should not leave his wife.
>
> I don't know of anything else the Lord said about marriage. All I can do is to give you my own advice. If your wife isn't a follower of the Lord, but is willing to stay with you, don't divorce her. If your husband isn't a follower, but is willing to stay with you, don't divorce him. Your husband or wife who isn't a follower is made holy by having you as a mate. This also makes your children holy and keeps them from being unclean in God's sight.
>
> If your husband or wife isn't a follower of the Lord and decides to divorce you, then you should agree to it. You are no longer bound to that person. After all, God chose you and wants you to live at

peace. And besides, how do you know if you will be able to save your husband or wife who isn't a follower? (1 Corinthians 7:10–16 CEV)

Recommended Reading

There are many good Christian books on strengthening troubled marriages. I particularly recommend the following:

Jimmy Evans, *Marriage on the Rock: God's Design for Your Dream Marriage* (Amarillo, TX: Majestic Media, 1994).

Gary Smalley, *Hidden Keys of a Loving, Lasting Marriage* (Grand Rapids: Zondervan, 1988).

These are some excellent books that document the terrible consequences of divorce. I recommend them for any Christians who are considering divorce:

Barbara Dafoe Whitehead, *The Divorce Culture* (New York: Alfred A. Knopf, 1997).

Maggie Gallagher, *The Abolition of Marriage: How We Destroy Lasting Love* (Washington, D.C.: Regnery Publishing, 1996).

David B. Larson, James P. Swyers, and Susan S. Larson, *The Costly Consequences of Divorce: Assessing the Clinical, Economic, and Public Health Impact of Marital Disruption in the United States* (Rockville, MD: National Institute for Healthcare Research, 1995).

Gender Disturbance, Transsexualism, and Transvestism

Gender disturbance is a topic that is quite confusing to many. There is widespread misunderstanding and misinformation about this subject, particularly concerning the terms *transsexual* and *transvestite*. Those who have these problems are often paraded around on talk shows as a source of entertainment, but no one is really providing factual information about these conditions.

Gender disturbance is a very broad category that includes all persons who feel some degree of uncertainty, confusion, or unhappiness about their gender identity or exhibit gender role behaviors more appropriate for the opposite sex.

Therapists often view gender disturbance as a spectrum of gender-related problems, ranging from mild to severe. In its mildest form it could describe people who have no doubt or unhappiness about their gender or heterosexuality, yet have some speech patterns and mannerisms that seem more appropriate for someone of the opposite sex—a somewhat masculine woman or a somewhat effeminate man. Such individuals may be completely unaware of their incongruous behavior. Typically, as children, they were raised in an environment that caused them to model the mannerisms of the opposite-sex parent instead of the same-sex parent. Yet, at some point they still managed to identify as a person of the proper gender and develop normal heterosexual feelings at puberty.

However, for some children, gender disturbance in childhood goes far beyond modeling the behaviors of the opposite-sex parent. The following signs of gender disturbance in children have been strongly linked to later development of homosexuality.

The prehomosexual child:

1. Has a strong dislike for sex-typical pursuits, such as sports, for boys, or playing with dolls, for girls.

2. Prefers toys and play activities more typical of the opposite sex.

3. Is rejected by same-sex peers and called names such as "sissy."

4. Chooses mostly playmates of the opposite sex.

5. Exhibits behavior/mannerisms/dress more appropriate for the opposite sex.

6. Has a much closer bond with the opposite-sex parent than with the same-sex parent.

These symptoms of gender disturbance often disappear spontaneously around puberty. It is believed that such children in their teen years become more willing and able to camouflage any behavior that attracts persecution from their peers. Yet the damage to their developing sexuality has already been done, since they often find homosexual desires beginning to emerge at this time.

Androgyny

Another type of gender disturbance now common in the teenage years, and being actively promoted by the manipulators of youth culture, is *androgyny*. This is a deliberate attempt to incorporate the behavior and dress of both sexes. It often includes bisexual practices. A child with a history of gender disturbance may feel particularly attracted to the androgynous role models provided by the entertainment industry. The genre of music and youth culture known as "gothic" or "goth" is particularly malicious, since it glorifies occult practices and everything evil or perverse, in addition to gender-bending dress and behavior. The androgynous (male) rock singer Marilyn Manson is perhaps the most notorious leader of this movement today.

Transsexualism

An even more severe form of gender disturbance can afflict children who express genuine confusion about their true gender or who become unhappy with their gender and actively reject it (termed *gender identity disorder* or *gender dysphoria*). These children will often speak of their desire to become a person of the opposite sex and may spend a great deal of time fantasizing about how such a change could occur. They often receive support, or at least complicity, from one or both parents, which enables the problem to continue and grow worse. Unless someone intervenes, they may eventually become fully *transsexual.*

Transsexuals have convinced themselves that somehow they were born with a body of the wrong sex and their only hope for happiness lies in assuming the identity of someone of the opposite sex. They usually begin by assuming the dress and mannerisms of the opposite sex and attempting to "pass" as the opposite sex in public. Many begin taking artificial hormones to give their bodies the secondary sexual characteristics of the opposite sex, such as breast development or facial hair. Transsexuals, whether male or female, who show early gender dysphoria are invariably homosexual.

With the progress in surgical techniques over the past few decades, many transsexuals have convinced surgeons to reshape their genitals to look like those of the opposite sex. The medical establishment has gone along with this aberrant practice for two reasons: (1) it is highly profitable, and (2) it is often much easier to perform cosmetic surgery on transsexuals than to convince them they actually have a gender disturbance that can only be corrected through lengthy counseling.

Transsexuals are truly obsessed individuals who often have other psychological problems in addition to their desire to change their sex. Some therapists have noted that transsexuals behave more like caricatures than true members of the opposite sex. For example, real women show a tremendous interest in children—having children and caring for children—that is not seen in male transsexuals, who seem to care only about making their bodies look as feminine as possible and fooling as many people as they can.

Medical professionals consider transsexuals quite unstable and difficult to work with. Some doctors have tried to distinguish "genuine" transsexuals, who truly deserve sex-change surgery, from those who are in some way "faking" the signs of transsexualism because they are just obsessed with having sex-change surgery. This effort has not proven very fruitful, the most obvious explanation being that *all* transsexuals are suffering equally from a delusion. Only individuals who were born with genital defects truly need corrective surgery. And, as we saw in Chapter 10, it should not be used to arbitrarily assign a child to one sex or the other at the whim of the surgeon.

Knowing that someone is a transsexual does not necessarily tell you about their sexual object choice. This underscores an important point: gender identity and sexual object choice are only indirectly related. Depending on how their problem originated and developed, some male transsexuals are sexually attracted to men, some are attracted to women, and some are bisexual. The majority of female transsexuals are attracted to women, but some are attracted to effeminate or gay men.

Transvestism

The medical definition of *transvestite* is "someone who dresses in clothing of the opposite sex for purposes of sexual stimulation." It is important to distinguish those with this condition from "drag queens"— homosexual men who dress as women to entertain others or because they have some transsexual inclinations. Drag queens do not have erotic feelings about dressing as women because they are sexually attracted to men. The entertainer known as "Ru Paul" is a notable example of a drag queen.

Transvestism typically begins around adolescence when a boy finds an article of women's clothing, such as stockings or underwear, that he uses to stimulate sexual fantasies about women. He begins a habit of fantasizing and masturbating with his focus on this article of clothing, perhaps trying it on and looking at himself in the mirror. He may even get an erotic thrill from fantasizing about being transformed into a woman. Over time, his sexual object choice becomes more and more fixed on the article of clothing until he ultimately finds it to be more arousing than a real woman. At this point he has developed a *fetish*—a condition of *being sexually aroused by an object instead of a person*. Depending on his social development, he may become preoccupied with this fetish or indulge only occasionally in his secret "hobby."

Transvestites are nearly always heterosexual men, most of whom successfully date and marry women. However, at some point, they find that their habit of cross-dressing begins to take up more and more of their time. It really becomes a form of sexual addiction, because it is often used to resolve emotional problems, such as loneliness, stress, or anxiety. Psychologists have also noted that many transvestites have a masochistic bent; that is, they like to fantasize that women are dominating, punishing, and humiliating them. This often seems to stem from childhood experiences of being dominated, punished, and humiliated by their mother or other adult women.

Most transvestites find that wearing female clothing eventually loses its erotic power yet still gives them a sense of security or comfort and relieves stress. So they begin to wear women's clothing for longer periods of time, just because it makes them feel "comfortable." Because of this comfortable feeling, a few of these men eventually convince themselves that they must actually *be* a woman trapped in a male body. It just feels so "right" when they are dressed as women. At this point they have become transsexuals, though by a completely different route than that described above for those whose gender disturbance began in early childhood.

This type of transsexual man fits the comedic stereotype of cross-dressers so often seen on television. They are often middle-aged husbands and fathers with very masculine bodies who look totally ridiculous when dressed as women. They still love their wives and are sexually attracted to women (though they now may fantasize about having sex with women only *as* a woman). Yet, many eventually convince themselves that they will only find ultimate fulfillment when their bodies have been transformed by hormones and surgery into the semblance of a woman. Of course, such surgery does nothing to change their lifelong sexual attraction to women, so any postsurgical sex partners will have to be lesbians.

Transvestism is extremely rare in women and most reported cases of it have involved women who were lesbians.[22]

Gender disturbance is a serious matter that can require years of effort to fully correct. Children with gender disturbance show clear warning signs. Yet, tragically, parents so often ignore these signs, thinking the child will "grow out of it." In most cases, the parents are a part of the problem because they allow the child to persist with gender-inappropriate behavior or even encourage it. In families where a child is showing signs of gender disturbance, both the parents and the child should receive counseling to uncover the roots of the unhealthy family situation that is producing these symptoms in the child.

The good news is that gender disturbance can be corrected. Correction is certainly easier in children. (George Rekers, a highly respected Christian child psychiatrist, has done much work in developing therapies for these children.) However, I have counseled a number of people who had been living as transsexuals all their adult lives, yet have now had their God-given manhood or womanhood restored. Some of the men had even undergone surgery to make their genitals look female, yet are happy to be living again as the men God destined them to be, even though they are now eunuchs.

THE GOOD NEWS IS THAT GENDER DISTURBANCE CAN BE CORRECTED.

Because the problems of gender disturbance, transsexualism, and transvestism have been so sensationalized in the media, and because those with these problems have been made into heroes and role models by gay political groups, many Christians seem to be somewhat coldhearted toward gender-disturbed people. I often see a real lack of compassion. (To be frank, many American churches today still have a problem fully accepting someone of a different race or culture, much less someone with gender disturbance or other sexual problems.)

Gender-disturbed people truly need a loving church family that will stand by them and faithfully love them as they learn to reclaim their God-given gender, a process that can take several years. In my work with transsexual male prostitutes, I have learned that Jesus loves these men and saves them just the way they are—with fully-developed female breasts from taking hormones, wearing seductive women's clothing, addicted to various drugs, infected with HIV and other diseases, with bad attitudes, and often in dire need of a bath. Because their lives are so miserable, many of these men are quite ready to receive the Gospel. They are truly the outcasts and lepers of modern society, and Jesus wants to go to them and spend time with them as He did with society's outcasts when He was living here on earth. But now He does this through people like you. Do you love Him enough to let Him move through you to reach these men? Is your church ready to welcome them with open arms as part of the family, even though it may take them some time before they stop wearing dresses to church?

Or is your church the kind of place where crude jokes are made about homosexuals and transsexuals, where such people are presented only as political enemies and not potential believers, where a somewhat effeminate man or masculine woman is whispered about behind their backs and quietly ostracized because they might be "one of them"?

Remember the words of Jesus: "I tell you the truth, whatever you did for one of the least of these brothers of mine, you did for me" (Matthew 25:40 NIV).

Recommended Reading

George Rekers, *Gender Identity Disorder*, available on the World Wide Web at www.leaderu.com.

———, *Shaping Your Child's Sexual Identity* (Grand Rapids: Baker Books, 1982).

Homosexuality

The problem of homosexuality is currently the subject of much debate in American society and has received considerable attention in the media over the past few years. It is a problem for which I have had a special concern since the day fifteen years ago when God first moved on my wife and me with His compassion for the young men whom we saw selling their bodies on the streets of New York City.

We began working with these young men in a very practical way, by giving them food and clothing, but more importantly, by accepting them, loving them, and showing them how much God loved them—just as they were.

As we spent time together, we learned as much from them as they did from us. Since neither my wife nor I had ever been tempted with same-sex desires, we had to learn from these young men what combination of circumstances and choices had reduced them to this miserable lifestyle. Some had even become transsexuals. At the same time, they learned from us that an entirely new way of life was opening to them. We had the great joy of seeing God deliver many of them from hell-on-earth as they received Jesus, had their broken sexuality restored, and were welcomed into a loving family at our church home, Brooklyn Tabernacle.

That experience taught us a great deal about homosexuality. Over the years, we have counseled a large number of Christian men and women who are struggling with the problem of same-sex desires, and I have learned something new from every one of them. Seeing the pervasiveness of this problem in America today (and in the American church) has compelled me to study countless case histories, research reports, and theories in my efforts to understand this problem and help those who want to change.

However, despite all the media attention that has been focused on this issue in recent years, I have come to see that very few people have a true grasp of homosexuality, because so few of the actual facts are being proclaimed. The growing flood of news articles, television programs, and movies dealing with this issue are painting a carefully drawn yet illusory picture, designed more to shape public opinion than reveal the full truth of the matter.

Even though parachurch ministries for Christians dealing with homosexuality have been in existence for more than twenty years, conservative Christian churches have only just begun to address this issue—though their focus is primarily political—in reaction to the political victories of gay activist groups. Such a political focus tends to frame this issue in terms of "us versus them," distracting us from the fact that a certain percentage in every church are afflicted with this problem. Sadly, many Christian families remain blissfully unaware that they are raising children who will become homosexual unless someone intervenes. Even among those parachurch ministries that seek to help Christians overcome their homosexual past, it seems to me that there is often a tendency to oversimplify a complex issue.

Underlying all these problems is a lack of perspective. All of us have a tendency to focus on the things with which we have had the most experience—things that are right in front of our noses—and ignore those things with which we have had little experience. The only solution is for more information to be laid out on the table so we can all start focusing on these concerns. My purpose here is to broaden our perspective on what homosexuality is, why it occurs, why it is a problem, and what can be done about it. There is not enough space available here to go into great detail on any of this. However, more detailed information is available from the sources listed at the end of this section.

What Is Homosexuality?

The first step in understanding *homosexuality* is defining what we mean by that term. The word *homosexual* has held different meanings and associations over the years. Many labels are often used to describe people with this condition, such as *gay, lesbian, bisexual, queer,* and so forth. Because of this, there is often confusion when discussing the subject, so that there is a need to be very specific in defining just what we are talking about.

The word *homosexual* was made up from Greek root words that literally mean "same sex." So, *homosexual desire* is sexual desire for the same sex, and *homosexual behavior* (or a *homosexual act*) is a sex act performed with a member of the same sex—more specifically, *genital contact for sexual pleasure between members of the same sex*.

My approach to understanding the problem of homosexuality, whether in general or in one individual's life, is to begin with examining the homosexual behavior (what did a person do, with whom and in what circumstances) and then move back to examine all the *motivations* that led up to that behavior. In my experience, what people choose to call themselves —whether "gay," "straight," or "bi"—may tell you how they like to think of themselves, but it does not necessarily give you an accurate picture of their sexual behavior or their motivations for engaging in that behavior. So, I have found it necessary to be quite specific in dealing with this issue.

Homosexual Behavior

Homosexual behavior is the most directly observable and easily understood aspect of homosexuality. When dealing with this issue, social scientists try to make it clear when they are addressing only the behavior, but not the motivations or the self-identification of the people involved, by using the terms *Men Who Have Sex with Men* and *Women Who Have Sex with Women*, instead of labels like *gay, lesbian,* or *homosexual.* This underscores the fact that, although there are often many different reasons that people choose to engage in these behaviors or to label themselves, there can be little confusion about whether a person has or has not participated in a specific same-gender sex act. Using this approach, a researcher can do a survey to determine, for example, what percentage of a specific population has had same-gender sex and how often within a given period. (The statistics on same-gender sexual behavior presented in Chapter 8 are based on such an approach.)

Such things are important to study because same-gender sex acts have real consequences, such as the transmission of diseases. From this perspective, people's motivations are irrelevant to the inevitable consequences of their actions.

It is interesting to see that the Old Testament law takes a similar approach with the issue of homosexual behavior:

> Do not lie with a man as one lies with a woman; that is detestable. (Leviticus 18:22 NIV)

This is a very matter-of-fact statement, part of a list of twenty other prohibited types of sexual couplings, including adultery, incest, and bestiality. (Lest some think that homosexual acts are being singled out by God as particularly bad, note that in verses 26, 29, and 30 of this passage, He uses the same Hebrew word—translated as "detestable"—to describe the entire list of forbidden couplings.) In this passage, and throughout the books of the Old Testament law, God does not address people's motives or what they might choose to label themselves. He focuses only on right and wrong behavior. As with contemporary medical research, He seems primarily concerned with the negative *consequences* of these forbidden acts, not why people choose to do them. As He explains in verses 24–30, doing these acts "defiles" (or pollutes) those involved and also their nation, and He promises to punish those who do these things.

Motivations for Homosexual Behavior

Since we have established what homosexual behavior is, the next logical question is, Why do people do it? Today's socially acceptable myth is that some people are just born gay or lesbian, while others are born "straight." The truth is actually much more complex and harder to grapple with. There are many different and quite varied reasons that people choose to engage in homosexual behavior. In most of these people's minds, there are also some definite reasons for *not* doing so. Therefore, for anyone, it is always a question of the choice made in a given situation, and the lasting effects of a *series of choices* made over many years.

I have a problem with the statement "homosexuality is a choice" because it often hides a lack of understanding of the problem. Certainly, people choose whether or not to engage in a particular sex act. Yet, they often feel driven and compelled by forces and feelings that they do not understand and do not know how to control. My experience in counseling many who have become involved in homosexual behavior has helped me to see that the development of this problem is best understood as a process of *adaptation*. No one is born with this problem or develops it overnight. Neither is it one problem with one solution.

In general, each of us is born with a particular set of abilities and temperaments, yet we learn to adjust as our lives are shaped each day by a variety of influences. We make decisions, accept beliefs, and take actions that, in ways we may not realize, determine our future course of development. Thus, we adapt and are changed by what we experience and how we choose to respond to those experiences. Anyone who engages in homosexual behavior, or has come to identify himself as homosexual, has taken many steps (experiences, reactions, and adaptations) along a lengthy path leading to that final choice.

It is as if life has posed the question to us all: "What are you going to do to meet your needs for love, affection, companionship, and sexual fulfillment?" So we get busy trying out different ways to meet those needs, often not really even thinking about what we are doing, but acting impulsively or intuitively. If we do not have good guidance about where to start looking and what pitfalls to avoid, then it is quite easy to travel down many blind alleys and come up with a great many wrong answers to this question. At the end of one large cluster of blind alleys is a really big pit of a wrong answer called "homosexual behavior." People can arrive there after taking many different paths and making many wrong turns. But once they fall into the pit, it is difficult to get out without some help. Once they are helped out of the pit of homosexual behavior, each must then retrace his steps to the place where he first got on the wrong path. Then he must start again from that place to find a healthy and legitimate solution to life's question.

Researchers have been stymied in their quest for a biological cause of homosexuality by the sets of identical twins they encountered where one twin identified as homosexual, but the other identified as heterosexual. These twins had identical genes and were raised in the same home environment, yet a statistical analysis of many identical twins showed there was only a 50% chance that if one was homosexual the other would be also. The only thing such studies have clearly proven is that, although genetic or environmental factors may influence sexual behavior, they cannot predetermine it. Individual choice (really, a series of individual choices) is still the ultimate deciding factor.

Experiences in Childhood and Adolescence

The most commonly recognized reason people choose to engage in homosexual behavior is that they feel some degree of same-sex arousal. In Chapter 10 we looked at one theory ("Exotic Becomes Erotic") that explains how same-sex arousal might be produced early in adolescence as the outcome of childhood social experiences. Cross-gender behavior and gender disturbance in childhood have been proven to be linked quite strongly with later development of homosexual desires. Certainly some people can trace the origin of their same-sex desires back to their first sexual feelings of puberty.

Others trace the origin of their homosexual feelings back to a time when they were molested. A boy who is molested by an older boy or man, even before puberty, may come to associate sexual feelings with men since that was his first and only sexual experience. When sexual feelings grow stronger during puberty, he may fantasize about his first sexual experience and seek more such sexual contacts with other boys or men. He may also interpret a man's sexual interest in him as signifying that he is somehow "feminine," which can cause confusion about his gender identity.

It is common knowledge among pedophiles that boys without fathers make the best "targets" because they are hungry for attention and affection from an older man and are less likely to report the molestation, since their emotional need for a father is being met through the relationship.

However, so much depends on how the molestation experience is interpreted and resolved by the child. Not all boys who are molested by men enjoy it or pursue further homosexual contacts. Many of them turn their hurt and shame from the experience into anger against gay men. Some may eventually express their anger in violent acts.

Some women can trace the origin of their same-sex attraction to being molested in childhood by a male. Because the experience was so painful and traumatic for them, they turned away from any further emotional or sexual involvement with men. This left them with only the option of seeking sexual fulfillment with other women.

We also reviewed in Chapter 10 some ways that "the sexual brain is programmed"—how the objects that produce sexual arousal can be modified through experience. The four factors mentioned, *reinforcement*, *desensitization*, *association*, and *orgasmic conditioning*, all seem to play a role when same-sex desires develop in people who had normal opposite-sex desires at puberty. Such people have a history of romantic interest in and experience with the opposite sex, yet at some point, they also had a same-sex experience. They may have been seduced by someone older or were just curious and "messed around" with a friend. Still, they found it pleasurable enough to repeat, until it was an established habit. They gradually became desensitized to what was at first disgusting.

Some men report that their same-sex desires began in adolescence with an exposure to homosexual pornography. They often fantasized about the images while masturbating. Some teenage boys have been known to view heterosexual pornography together and then masturbate as a group. They may end up masturbating each other, which is a homosexual act. In such ways, their inhibitions or disgust about homosexual acts is broken down, and they learn to receive sexual pleasure from other males.

Any of these teens who had a normal interest in the opposite sex at puberty and had enjoyable opposite-sex relationships are likely to continue to develop and identify as heterosexuals. However, their early exposure to homosexuality remains with them so that they may be more likely as adults to engage in homosexual behavior under certain circumstances. Some may even continue a secret habit of sporadic homosexual behavior throughout their lives. For example, when a man with this background gets divorced or just becomes emotionally estranged from his wife, he may find himself drawn to easy and convenient homosexual outlets at a local park, health club, or porn shop. He still prefers to have a sexual and romantic relationship with a woman, but he has lost any inhibitions to receiving some momentary sexual pleasure from men who may offer it.

Sexual Addiction

Many people engaged in homosexual behavior today, whether they think of themselves as gay or straight, still show all the characteristics of homosexual sex addicts:

- They had a troubled childhood and have many current sources of stress and emotional pain that are not being addressed in healthy ways.
- They spend a lot of time fantasizing about homosexual behavior and masturbating.
- They spend a lot of time "acting out"—seeking the specific environments and types of partners needed to act out the sexual fantasies.
- Homosexual behaviors are done compulsively. To stop them seems beyond the addict's control.
- There is no emotional connection with sex partners; large numbers of anonymous encounters are preferred.
- The addictive homosexual behaviors are often very self-destructive: endangering personal health and

safety; putting career, reputation, and family relationships at risk; and consuming precious time and much money.

• Over time, the addict must graduate to even more extreme and risky sexual behaviors to maintain the same "high."

Some of these sex addicts may have had childhood experiences that primed them for an addiction to homosexual behavior. However, some start out entirely heterosexual, but eventually add homosexual behavior to their repertoire because it provides a sexual outlet that is so readily available—and free. Every city has places where men gather for public, anonymous sex, such as wooded parks, public restrooms, or porn shops.

Most porn shops actually encourage sex acts between men in their "video arcades," as long as they pay the booth "rent." Many heterosexual men with a pornography addiction first get involved in homosexual behavior when they visit these shops to watch heterosexual videos. They are often propositioned by other men, who can always be found loitering around the booths, because *their* form of sexual addiction drives them to seek to perform oral sex on as many "straight" men as possible. Since this sexual outlet is free and easily available, it can quickly become a routine. Similar activities occur in parks and public restrooms.

Married men can become heavily involved in these types of homosexual acts, yet without arousing their wives' suspicions, since the men can stop off at a park or porn shop for a few minutes during lunch or on their way home from work.

Meeting Emotional Needs

For those who seek a continuing relationship with another person based on homosexual behavior, a major factor in establishing such a relationship is seeking to fulfill unmet emotional needs. What is so interesting is the incredible variety of normal emotional needs that people seek to fulfill *abnormally* through a homosexual relationship. Browsing through the personal ads of any counterculture newspaper will give you a glimpse of this. There are "daughters" seeking "mamas," "dads" seeking "sons," men seeking "husbands," men seeking male "wives," women seeking "wives" or female "husbands," men seeking their "twin," and men and women just seeking a "best buddy" of the same sex.

Such unusual combinations of sexual/emotional relationships may begin accidentally when someone who has been having a series of casual sex partners suddenly realizes that he has found greater emotional fulfillment with one particular partner, who perhaps treats him like a "father" or a "son." For some married and previously heterosexual women, it is often the case that an emotionally dependent friendship with another woman can later take on a sexual dimension (as we examined in the preceding section on *Adultery, Spiritual Adultery, and Spiritual Defilement*).

In any case, a continuing sexual relationship creates its own set of "spousal" emotional bonds—and accompanying problems—because the Law of Sexual Union sets in motion deep emotional and spiritual mechanisms that were designed to join a man and woman into "one flesh"—not two individuals of the same sex.

In male couples, conflict often develops over who will be dominant ("the husband") in the relationship. In female couples, a deepening obsession with each other brings with it a great deal of jealousy that often erupts in violence. Combining such a malformed spousal bond, created through sex, with the original emotional dynamic of "father/son," "buddy/buddy," or "mother/daughter" is somewhat the emotional equivalent of Dr. Frankenstein's notorious experiments. Trying to become a "father/husband" to a "son/wife" can only result in much emotional confusion, pain, and damage.

Such emotional pain often leads to physical pain in the form of domestic abuse. Whereas only 5% of heterosexual marriages report an incident of domestic abuse each year, many studies show that around 50% of lesbian couples and 30–40% of gay male couples report domestic abuse annually. Several writers have noted that more gays and lesbians are injured each year by their "significant others" than by all the incidents of "gay-bashing" put together.

It is no surprise then that few such relationships can endure. The typical monogamous gay male relationship lasts only about a year, and the typical monogamous lesbian relationship lasts only from one to three years. It has also been observed that, for those very rare relationships that endure beyond four or five years, the sexual component ends completely.[23] Male partners begin to seek sexual outlets with others. Female partners may become celibate. So the only thing that holds these couples together is whatever remains of the original emotional dynamic that drew them together in the first place.

Restriction of Heterosexual Behavior

Many societies report incidents of homosexual behavior wherever adults are kept in same-sex groups with no access to the opposite sex. Common examples include prisons, men's work camps in the mining or logging industries, military organizations, and groups of young female factory workers living far from home. Some cultures even condone such behavior as reasonable under the circumstances. For example, men working away from their families in African mines often "adopt" young local boys to cook, clean up, and share their bed.

Sometimes, there is great violence involved, as in American prisons where it is common for the stronger prisoners to force smaller and weaker prisoners into the role of sex slaves. Recently, it has been reported that desertion among Russian army troops is at record levels. One reason being given is the passive homosexual role often forced upon young recruits.

For hundreds of years, in many countries, same-sex boarding schools have been notorious training grounds for homosexual behavior. Though it is certainly true that the majority of students from these schools eventually marry, there can be no question that many have lost their inhibitions to homosexual behavior and have learned to enjoy it. Countless memoirs detail the lasting effects of such early exposure on later sexual feelings and behavior. The situation is not helped any by the fact that pedophiles often seek staff positions in such institutions with the goal of seducing as many students as they can.

Most people would not consider those who engage in homosexual behavior under such conditions to be "true" homosexuals. Yet we cannot consider this to be normal or healthy behavior. Certainly, not all of those who are put in these situations choose to meet their sexual needs in this way. However, there are still negative consequences to homosexual behavior no matter what the motivation. While most return to heterosexual relations when they leave these segregated situations, there is still no doubt they have been changed by their homosexual experience, if only by developing a greater capacity and desire to indulge in it in the future.

Political Reasons

This is an odd one, but for a surprising number of feminists, it seems that wearing a "lesbian" label demonstrates a higher form of feminism, and to have a sexual relationship with another woman is to make a political statement, since they are refusing to "consort with the enemy." Recently, a number of leaders of lesbian political causes have drawn criticism for maintaining their leadership roles in the lesbian community even though they are living in long-term emotional/sexual relationships with men. These lesbian leaders, however, fail to see any irony or inherent conflict in their conduct. They insist they are not heterosexual or bisexual, because they are still lesbians in their beliefs, though they have learned to love a man.

> A NUMBER OF LEADERS OF LESBIAN POLITICAL CAUSES HAVE DRAWN CRITICISM FOR MAINTAINING THEIR LEADERSHIP ROLES IN THE LESBIAN COMMUNITY EVEN THOUGH THEY ARE LIVING IN LONG-TERM EMOTIONAL/SEXUAL RELATIONSHIPS WITH MEN.

What Is the Cure?

I hope that just reviewing some of the many reasons that people become involved in homosexual behavior has brought a new perspective on the question, What is the cure? It should now be obvious that each person entrapped in this predicament has followed a unique path. Each has sought to meet an individual set of needs through homosexual behavior. Each has particular temptations or compulsions, and each has suffered a specific pattern of spiritual, emotional, and sexual damage along the way.

Any concept of a cure certainly must begin with stopping the homosexual behavior, since it is so destructive. But that is just the first step. An often lengthy process of retracing the many wrong turns along the path that led the person into homosexual behavior must follow.

For those whose homosexual involvement originated in childhood, to seek to uncover and rebuild all the layers of mental, emotional, and spiritual damage done through years of homosexual thoughts and behavior often seems a monumental task. Yet, it must be done if they are to achieve the fullness of their humanity and fulfill the plan God has for their lives. Others who have had only a limited involvement with homosexual behavior require less restoration because they have suffered less damage, perhaps limited to learned sexual responses and habitual behaviors.

The incredible variety in the causes of homosexual behavior is the reason that a great variety of therapies are also needed, even with one individual, to fully address all the roots of the problem. A counselor who seeks to work in this arena must learn how to deal with the continuing effects of deeply buried childhood experiences, such as a failure to model or identify with a parent or peers of the same sex. The wounds from any incidents of molestation must be brought to light and healed. While some may have extensive experience and success in relating romantically to the opposite sex, others may never have learned even the rudiments of romance. Some may have deep-seated resentments toward the opposite sex and hidden emotional barriers to interacting with them.

In the area of sexuality, the sexual brain must be "reprogrammed," using techniques to stop old homosexual responses and introduce new heterosexual ones. Depending on their initial strength, it may take years to fully extinguish homosexual response patterns, but they gradually grow weaker when they are not indulged and as heterosexual feelings take their place. Sexual addiction is often a factor that must be overcome. Spiritual growth must begin again after being stunted through years of sin.

Christian ministries focused on helping those who wish to overcome a homosexual past have only been around for about twenty years, paralleling the creation and growth of the gay subculture in America. However, the fields of psychology and psychiatry have a much older tradition of helping people overcome abnormal sexual feelings and desires, including homosexuality. Research still continues in this area, focusing on how to change pathological sexual feelings and behaviors our society still considers abnormal, such as rape and pedophilia. While such therapies fail to address spiritual issues, some have been found to be quite effective in changing problem behaviors.

The very fact that effective therapies for changing sexual object choice and behavior exist—and are being used daily by secular therapists across the country to treat rapists, pedophiles, exhibitionists, voyeurs, and other paraphiles—uncovers the gaping hole in the reasoning of those who claim that homosexuality is normal, healthy, and unchangeable. The fact is, there is no scientific basis on which to distinguish any inherent differences between the desires of men who are sexually attracted to 8-year-old boys, 14-year-old boys, or 18-year-old boys. To say that the first two desires are sick but the third is inborn, normal, and healthy is merely a political statement with no scientific support at all.

When looking at the many different histories and needs that must be addressed in those seeking to overcome homosexuality, it seems to me that too many Christian ministries emphasize only a few favorite approaches. Often, there is a priority placed on spiritual exercises, with the thought that if the homosexual struggler just does enough prayer and Bible study, all his problems will be miraculously resolved. Certainly, there is a need for spiritual growth. I have seen God do many miracles of restoration in the lives of the sexually broken. Yet there is also a need for personal growth. I believe there are many things God requires us to do before He will do for us the things we cannot do. Typically, much work must be done by those recovering from homosexuality to undo the many harmful things that others have done to them and that they have done to themselves in ignorance over the years, as well as to complete any remaining phases of emotional development necessary to reach full maturity.

Many Christians seem wary of the therapies developed by psychologists or psychiatrists because those professions often seem to be fundamentally antireligious. However, at the first sign of a pain or sniffle, most of these same Christian people will run to their doctor for some pills. Therefore, I really cannot see why any Christian would have a problem with using medically and scientifically based therapies for sexual problems, if such therapies *do not conflict with scriptural principles and have proven to be effective.*

I have found a "multimodal" approach, which combines selected spiritual and psychological therapies chosen to address each person's specific needs, to be the most effective means of bringing rapid improvement at many levels simultaneously. I believe that such an approach is fast becoming the forefront of "reparative therapy" for homosexuality, and for all other types of abnormal sexual desires, because it has shown the greatest success.

For those interested in learning more about the multimodal approach from a Christian perspective, I recommend a treatment manual by Christian psychologist and therapist Christopher J. Austin, entitled *Cleaning Out the Closet: A Step by Step Approach for Christian Men Exiting from the Homosexual Lifestyle.*[24] This manual is in the form of a workbook with many different sections, each addressing a different aspect of the problem.

How Can Homosexual Behavior Be Prevented?

There are certainly many paths by which people can end up involved in homosexual behavior, yet all these paths begin and are sustained through ignorance. The most significant action any parent or church can take to prevent young people from ever becoming trapped in homosexuality is to *provide a full and complete sexual education.* Every Christian who has been given a full understanding of God's purpose and plan for sexuality is protected from so many potential pitfalls. Learning to manage sexual feelings in a godly way, as well as learning the many terrible consequences of sexual sin—including homosexual sin—provides a hedge of protection that can keep our young people from taking the wrong path. Western society is now sending such overwhelmingly false messages to our children about sexuality, and homosexuality in particular, that it is imperative our children be given such a strong foundation of sexual truth that they cannot be shaken.

It is also essential that parents become informed about certain problems that can occur in the emotional and social development of children that push them down the path toward homosexuality. One of the greatest tragedies unfolding today in churches all across America is the tremendous number of faithful Christian families—who are in Sunday school and church every week—whose children are destined to become homosexual unless the parents wake up and take some drastic action to prevent it.

As we have seen above, there are many causes for homosexual feelings and behavior, yet those causes with roots in early childhood produce the types of homosexuality that are the most resistant to change. The warning signs for children who are on the path to homosexuality are no longer a mystery. They have been well documented in a number of studies. (In Chapter 10 we looked at one example of how these factors can lead to homosexual attraction.)

As we saw in the last section, the prehomosexual child shows signs of gender disturbance, such as:

1. Having a strong dislike for sex-typical pursuits, such as sports, for boys, or playing with dolls, for girls.

2. Preferring toys and play activities more typical of the opposite sex.

3. Being rejected by same-sex peers and called names such as "sissy."

CHARACTERISTICS OF PREHOMOSEXUAL CHILDREN

4. Choosing playmates of the opposite sex almost exclusively.

5. Exhibiting be havior/mannerisms/dress more appropriate for the opposite sex.

6. Having a much closer bond with the opposite-sex parent than with the same-sex parent.

Even though the natural temperament of such children may play a role in their choosing these opposite-gender behaviors (such as a very quiet and timid boy or a very aggressive and energetic girl), they need help in learning gender-appropriate behavior, gender-appropriate skills, and social skills for being accepted by same-gender peers. The person most critical in this process is the same-sex parent or caregiver. A strong father-son or mother-daughter bond is essential for such children to learn to accept and appreciate being the sex they were born. Studies of gender-disturbed boys have shown that, in the majority of cases, the father was absent from the home during the earliest years of the child's life, or, if present, the father was remote and emotionally detached from the child.

The same-sex parent must become involved in helping a child with an atypical temperament learn gender-appropriate skills. Some researchers suspect that same-sex parents may react negatively to a child's opposite-gender behavior and withdraw from the child. This is exactly the opposite of what the child needs. Remember, children need a same-sex role model or "hero"—whom they identify with and want to emulate—to help them learn gender-appropriate behavior and develop a positive self-image as successful members of their sex.

A nonaggressive boy may never make a good football player. However, instead of making him feel like a failure and giving up on him, the boy's father can help him to learn other sports, like tennis or volleyball, so he can feel some success at "manly" things and be accepted by his peers. A girl who plays sports nonstop with the neighborhood boys can take a day off to go shopping with her mother and perhaps have a "makeover" to bring out her feminine side.

Persecution of children with opposite-gender characteristics can be quite severe (particularly of "sissy" boys, since tomboys are more accepted), and the effects are long-lasting. Children who endure this persecution for years may eventually learn to minimize their atypical behaviors on their own to avoid further persecution. Yet, significant damage has been done to their self-image as successful members of their gender, and continued alienation from their peers can still lead to homosexual tendencies emerging at puberty.

A parent should determine if a child is being persecuted by peers in this way and do whatever is necessary to put a stop to it. A method that has been proven to work is to teach the child specific social skills that enable him or her to make friends and resolve conflicts with peers. The problem can be brought to the attention of teachers and counselors for their assistance in stopping such persecution. Unfortunately, because of the times in which we live, it is now necessary for parents to make certain that public school employees will not try to encourage a child in this situation to identify as a homosexual or bisexual.

More help in raising sexually healthy children can be found in the works by George Rekers, a noted Christian child psychiatrist, listed under "Recommended Reading" at the end of this section.

All children should be given age-appropriate sex education by their parents so that they have no confusion at any time about what is or is not moral sexual behavior, and so that they understand the reasons why. Children also should be "molestation-proofed." A number of programs today teach children about inappropriate touch, escaping from bad situations, and reporting suspicious incidents.

Children who have been molested should definitely receive counseling from a Christian therapist experienced in dealing with this issue. The good news is that with proper help they can recover fully with no ill effects.

Recommended Reading

Christopher J. Austin, *Cleaning Out the Closet* (Nashville: Power Source Productions, 1998). For further information, contact: P.O. Box 40304, Nashville, TN 37204, 800-331-5991.

Andrew Comiskey, *Pursuing Sexual Wholeness* (Lake Mary, FL: Creation House, 1989).

Joe Dallas, *Desires in Conflict* (Eugene, OR: Harvest House Publishers, 1991).

B. Davies and L. Rentzel, *Coming Out of Homosexuality: New Freedom for Men and Women* (Downers Grove, IL: InterVarsity Press, 1993).

George Rekers, *Growing Up Straight*, available on the World Wide Web at www.leaderu.com.

———, *Gender Identity Disorder*, available on the World Wide Web at www.leaderu.com.

———, *Shaping Your Child's Sexual Identity* (Grand Rapids: Baker Books, 1982).

Paula Sandford, *Healing Victims of Sexual Abuse* (Tulsa, OK: Victory House, 1988).

Jeffrey Satinover, *Homosexuality and the Politics of Truth* (Grand Rapids: Baker Books, 1996).

Marital Sex: Problems and Issues

Even people with a happy childhood and a healthy sexuality can have problems adjusting to a sexual relationship in marriage. Because a husband and wife may have different attitudes toward sex and may bring with them differing expectations for the marital relationship, there is always some potential for misunderstanding and initial incompatibility. However, problems with marital sexuality can be resolved if both husband and wife are willing to investigate the source of the problems and work together in a loving way to overcome them. Since so much has been written on these problems from both a secular and a Christian viewpoint, they are only summarized here to provide perspective. I have included Christian sources for further information and self-help at the end of this section. These materials are also helpful for couples who wish to enrich their relationship.

A major issue for many couples is what sexual practices should be included in their marriage relationship. Two practices that Christians often have questions about are oral sex and anal sex. I will present my views on these topics at the end of this section.

Problems with the Sexual Relationship

Below is a brief summary of the most commonly occurring sexual problems that can cause difficulty in the marital sexual relationship. Much has been learned in the last thirty years about these problems, their origins, and successful treatment for them. Perhaps the greatest advance is in understanding that there are often underlying medical conditions that cause or contribute to many of these problems—they are not necessarily "all in your head." There is also a greater understanding of how negative emotions, thought patterns, and past experience can contribute to or perpetuate some of these problems. Marriage counselors are now better equipped with practical and effective therapies.

I would strongly encourage couples who are experiencing any of these problems to overcome your fear, shame, and embarrassment and get some help. God has given us sexual union as the foundation of a marriage relationship. When there are problems in that union, it threatens the marriage. Couples who are not enjoying a mutually satisfying sexual relationship are opening themselves up to the temptations of alienation, adultery, and eventual divorce. Men, in particular, are much more likely to become involved in various forms of sexual sin and to excuse their behavior when their sexual relationship with their wives is not satisfying.

It is always a great tragedy when Christian couples suffer with sexual problems for many years out of shame and ignorance, if only for the reason that they are missing out on years of pleasure and fulfillment. For husbands, sexual fulfillment is right at the top of the list of what they need from marriage. Wives often place less emphasis on sex, but I wonder how much of this is because they have not found their husbands to be unselfish lovers who put their wives' fulfillment ahead of their own.

If you are having sexual problems in your marriage, the least you can do is find a good Christian book on the subject. If that does not provide enough information for you to help yourselves, then, by all means, make an appointment with a Christian marriage counselor. But make sure the counselor has had specific training, experience, and success in dealing with marital sexual problems.

Sexual Desire Disorders

1. *Hypophilia* - an abnormally low level of sexual desire
2. *Hyperphilia* - an abnormally high level of sexual desire
3. *Sexual aversion* - aversion to sex or avoidance of sexual contact

A variety of underlying causes can lead to the symptoms of too much or too little sexual desire. Both physiological and psychological factors may be involved, but medical treatment should certainly be pursued first to rule out any medical causes. A number of medications are known to have a side effect on sexual desire.

Sexual aversion can have many causes, such as feelings of shame about sexuality, basic misconceptions about sex, bad sexual experiences, negative feelings about the opposite sex, or negative feelings about a spouse. It usually requires some help from a counselor to uncover its origins and fully overcome it.

Sexual Arousal Disorders

> 1. *Female sexual arousal disorder (frigidity)*
> 2. *Male erectile disorder (impotence)*

These disorders are signified by an inability to achieve or maintain sexual arousal when appropriate. The symptoms of these disorders are different for men and women. The causes can be both physiological and psychological, though recent medical research has demonstrated that physiological problems have played a much greater role than they were previously given credit for.

Impotence in men seems to attract the most attention, but women also can experience times when their sex organs fail to undergo the normal changes necessary to prepare for intercourse.

Orgasm Disorders

> 1. *Delayed ejaculation* - in men, an inability to ejaculate during intercourse
> 2. *Premature ejaculation* - in men, an inability to control timing of ejaculation
> 3. *Anorgasmia* - in men and women, an inability to experience orgasm

These disorders relate to a delayed, premature, or absent orgasm. The cause may be a lack of training in good sexual technique or some bad sexual experiences, though sometimes biological factors are present. Many prescription drugs can produce these symptoms as side effects, so it is wise to first consult with your doctor. The Christian self-help books listed under this section's "Recommended Reading" address the problem of poor sexual technique.

Sexual Pain Disorders

1. *Dyspareunia* - in men and women, experiencing pain during or after sexual activity
2. *Vaginismus* - in women, an involuntary contraction of the vaginal muscles that hinders or prevents intercourse

Both men and women may experience pain during or after sexual activity. There are frequently medical reasons for this that should be ruled out before looking for psychological factors.

Relational Sexual Problems

1. *Adultery* - physical, mental, emotional, *or spiritual* unfaithfulness to one's spouse (see the sections on *Adultery* and *Spiritual Adultery*)
2. *Misuse of sexual relations* - sexual activity being misused as a weapon or a bargaining chip
3. *Sexual desire mismatch* - a disagreement between husband and wife as to the desired type and frequency of sexual relations

These relational problems are frequently encountered in couples with other marital problems. Both partners usually bear some responsibility for these problems, and both must be involved in their resolution.

Oral Sex

The issue of whether Christian couples should engage in oral sexual acts with each other is still being debated today in some circles. This is certainly one of those areas that is open to interpretation, since there is no direct mention of this practice in the Bible. In such situations, we always need to use wisdom and make certain we are not acting out of selfish motives. We should certainly never do anything harmful to ourselves or our spouses.

I have heard some Christian teachers claim that oral sex between a husband and wife is sinful. I have even heard of some churches giving altar calls for couples who wished to repent of the practice. However, I must confess I have never been able to follow the logic of their arguments, scriptural or otherwise, purporting to prove the sinfulness of oral sex. These people also seem to preach a message of sexual shame, and I suspect this is really the source of the problem for them. It is always a serious thing to claim to speak for God when His Word is silent on a matter.

As far as I can tell, God allows a husband and wife to kiss each other wherever they wish. The most widely-respected Christian teachers in the area of marital sexuality, such as Tim LaHaye, Ed Wheat, the Sandfords, and the Penners, all agree that this practice is not essentially sinful.

However, there is certainly a potential for problems when one spouse wants to experiment with this but the other is uncomfortable with it. Certainly, husbands and wives should practice unselfish love in this matter as in any other.

It seems that many teenagers engage in this practice today because they think it is not really sex, so they can have their fun but "technically" remain virgins. However, from what we have studied of sexual forces, any sexual act that culminates in an orgasm creates a powerful sexual bond between the people involved, joining them emotionally and spiritually.

Unless they are married, it is still fornication. The only essential difference I see between oral sex and vaginal intercourse is that the woman cannot become pregnant.

There are only two medical cautions given today about oral sex in a monogamous marriage. First, it has been shown that men who do not practice good dental hygiene—such as brushing, flossing, and using mouthwash—can increase the risk of passing a yeast infection on to their wives through performing oral sex on them. This is because yeast normally lives in the mouth.

MEN WHO DO NOT PRACTICE GOOD DENTAL HYGIENE INCREASE THE RISK OF PASSING A YEAST INFECTION TO THEIR WIVES THROUGH ORAL SEX.

Second, in addition to sperm, a man's seminal fluid contains many compounds that are designed to assist in fertilization. How all these compounds function is not yet completely understood. The internal female sex organs are designed to receive seminal fluid and are affected by its various components in complex ways. However, seminal fluid has been shown to cause depression of the immune system when body cells other than those in the vaginal area are exposed to it. Some researchers believe that human sperm also has the potential to cause normal body cells to turn cancerous. Based on this information, it seems advisable that a wife who is performing oral sex on her husband not swallow or retain seminal fluid in the mouth.

Anal Sex

The issue of whether Christian couples should engage in anal intercourse with each other is much less debatable. While this is not something the Bible explicitly forbids between a husband and wife, there is evidence that it is quite harmful to the health of those involved.

Many modern sex manuals elaborate in great detail about this practice, as if it were some wonderful new discovery without which no one can be sexually fulfilled. Actually, it is very difficult for the woman to avoid experiencing pain without elaborate techniques, aids, and conditioning exercises. What all these manuals fail to mention is that, no matter how careful you are, *there is no way to avoid inflicting damage on the woman.*

The anal opening and rectum are lined with an extremely thin layer of tissue. It is impossible for them to withstand the stress of intercourse without tearing and bleeding, suffering many small abrasions called *microtears*. These openings allow intestinal bacteria into the bloodstream, which can result in serious and even life-threatening infections. Additionally, the muscles around the rectal opening are quite fragile and can be easily torn. *This can cause permanent fecal incontinence.* Even more than with oral sex, the introduction of seminal fluid into the rectal area is believed to cause immune system suppression and has been linked to rectal cancer. (Anal sex was known to be a major cause of health problems in gay men long before AIDS arrived.)

It is troubling that anal intercourse is used by many heterosexual couples around the world as a means of birth control, since it is so strongly associated with the spread of disease. This practice is believed to be one of the primary reasons that AIDS has become so widespread in Africa as a primarily heterosexual disease.

GOD DID NOT DESIGN THE RECTUM FOR SEXUAL INTERCOURSE.

It should be obvious from even this brief synopsis that God did not design the rectum for sexual intercourse. Therefore, people who attempt this must suffer the consequences.

Recommended Reading

Ed Wheat, *Intended for Pleasure* (Tappan, NJ: Fleming H. Revell, 1980).
——, *Love Life for Every Married Couple* (Grand Rapids: Zondervan, 1980).
Tim and Beverly LaHaye, *The Act of Marriage* (Grand Rapids: Zondervan, 1976).
Joyce and Clifford Penner, *The Gift of Sex* (Waco, TX: Word Books, 1981).
——, *Restoring the Pleasure* (Dallas: Word Publishing, 1993).
James Robison, *Love, Sex and Communication* (video and audio tape set), 1997, LIFE Outreach International, P.O. Box 982000, Fort Worth, Texas 76182-8000, web site: lifeoutreach.org.

Masturbation

This topic is quite controversial among Christians today. I have found that it is also a source of much guilt and shame. Indeed, many researchers have remarked that among the general public, this issue seems to invoke more embarrassment and shame than any other sexual topic.

I have heard several different teachings on this subject, with Bible verses used to "prove" various points. However, no one has ever been able to show me any verse that explicitly forbids this practice. In fact, there is only one Scripture passage I am aware of that seems to refer to masturbation in men:

> 16 When a man has an emission of semen, he must bathe his whole body with water, and he will be unclean till evening. 17 Any clothing or leather that has semen on it must be washed with water, and it will be unclean till evening. 18 When a man lies with a woman and there is an emission of semen, both must bathe with water, and they will be unclean till evening. (Leviticus 15:16–18 NIV)

In this passage, verse 18 is clearly referring to a seminal emission occurring during sexual intercourse. But verse 16 is speaking of a seminal emission that does not occur as a result of intercourse. The editors of the *International Standard Bible Encyclopedia* suggest that verse 16 may be referring to masturbation, since there is no mention of this emission occurring during sleep, as in Deuteronomy 23:10.[25] That certainly seems reasonable to me.

If this is indeed a reference to masturbation, the matter-of-fact way in which God deals with this matter certainly indicates that no feelings of shame should be attached to it. The same instruction is given following seminal emission with a wife or without a wife: go take a bath!

It seems to me that if God were really bothered by such a practice, then He missed a teachable moment here in this passage. Since He clearly condemns sexual intercourse between men in Leviticus 18:22 and says "that is detestable" (NIV), I think that if He had really wanted us to avoid this particular practice, He would at least have said something like "That is disgusting!" instead of "Go take a bath!"

As with other things that are not explicitly mentioned in the Bible, we need to use wisdom. There is certainly room for differences of interpretation and individual choices. We also need to be certain that we are aware of all the facts.

During the nineteenth century, popular opinion held that masturbation was physically harmful and led to all sorts of terrible maladies. However, modern research has found this is just not true. There are no known harmful biological effects. Other research indicates that most male mammals masturbate, even when receptive females are available. It has been found that this practice flushes out aging sperm and increases their fertility.

Among humans, masturbation certainly serves to release sexual tension when a spouse is not available. However, researchers have wondered why some married men and women often continue to masturbate even though they have a satisfying sexual relationship. Results so far indicate that this seems to occur for the same reason as it does in other mammals: because it enhances fertility. It has also been found that when men get set on a regular schedule for sex, their bodies produce sperm and seminal fluid at a fairly constant rate. If they are prevented from having sexual release at the normal interval, then these fluids can back up, causing increased sexual tension and physical discomfort, and increasing the risk of prostate inflammation. Urologists now routinely prescribe regular masturbation for men who suffer from chronic prostatitis as the fastest way to return them to health.

Since there are proven medical benefits to masturbation and since it is a prevalent human and animal behavior, it is becoming rather difficult to make a case that this is essentially and always a sinful practice. However, as we have seen in earlier chapters, research into human sexuality has also uncovered some potential psychological harm that can occur through masturbation, and there are some people for whom it has caused serious problems.

As we examined in Chapter 10, Jesus identified the process at the heart of most sexual sin when He said, "Whoever looks at a woman to lust for her has already committed adultery with her in his heart" (Matthew 5:28 NKJV). Researchers have confirmed that when masturbation is coupled with sexual thoughts and images, they become powerfully charged with erotic meaning at the point of orgasm. This means they will seem even more erotic in the future. It is through this means that an individual's sexual desires can gradually change. We also saw in Chapter 10 how every sexual perversion or addiction known has been found to be based on a pattern of masturbation to a deviant fantasy, culminating in orgasm. It is through this process that addictions such as pornography can suddenly grab hold of men before they are aware of what has happened to them.

Compulsive Masturbation

Most people who are classified as "sex addicts" are driven by a habit of compulsive masturbation. Masturbation is considered compulsive only when it is the result of an uncontrollable, irresistible urge that produces irrational behavior, such as masturbating at inappropriate times and places. As with all compulsive behaviors, resisting the behavior produces mounting anxiety that can only be relieved by eventually completing the behavior.

Compulsive masturbation is also characterized by a frequency much greater than normal masturbation. A compulsive masturbator may masturbate 10 or more times a day, scheduling his day around the activity. He may even risk discovery by doing it at work. For example, a businessman may have his secretary delay his clients in the waiting room while he masturbates in his office between each appointment.

Compulsive masturbation is a key component of all paraphilias (unnatural obsessive sexual practices). The paraphilia may not in itself involve any sexual activity. But some type of related fantasy is replayed over and over in the addict's mind while he masturbates, thus creating a powerful sexual association. Typically, such an addiction began as a person tried to use the pleasure of sexual release to relieve some type of emotional distress. (An example of this type of case was given at the end of Chapter 10.)

In Summary

In my opinion there is no cause to conclude that masturbation is sinful in itself, though it certainly can be used in sexual sins. A husband and wife may properly masturbate and fantasize about each other when they cannot be together. Yet they should not fantasize about other sexual partners because—in addition to Jesus' prohibition of such fantasy—the effect of masturbation to orgasm with such thoughts causes those fantasies to become even more erotic, and so detracts from the sexual bond they have with each other.

COMPULSIVE MASTURBATION IS A KEY COMPONENT OF ALL PARAPHILIAS, WHICH ARE UNNATURAL OBSESSIVE SEXUAL PRACTICES.

For single people who feel it is necessary, masturbation does relieve sexual tension. But it should not be used in conjunction with sexual fantasies about other people because it causes an erotic bond to be established with that person in the mind of the one who is fantasizing. Other respected Christian teachers who have addressed this subject, such as John and Paula Sandford, have come to basically the same conclusion: masturbation is not essentially sinful unless it is practiced in conjunction with sinful sexual fantasies.

However, a warning should certainly be given, primarily to men, that masturbating to pornographic images quickly produces a powerful addiction to those images, even after doing it only once. I have counseled so many Christian men who have been enslaved by this problem that I have lost count.

So often I hear the same story: a Christian man is surfing the World Wide Web and accidentally stumbles across a porn site. He clicks on an image just to take a quick peek. But once he masturbates with that image in his mind, his life will never be the same again. For many men, it takes a tremendous effort to break free. To get free, they need to make a commitment that they will never again masturbate with those images in their mind. Each time they do so, it only increases the power of the compulsion.

However, I have heard a pastor teach this, and I agree: Men, if you are on a business trip and you are tempted to go to a strip bar or a porn shop, you will be much better off if you just masturbate and think about your wife. That reduces the biological force of sexual temptation. It is much better to do this than to get involved in some sexual sin that can lead to a sexual addiction or an STD. I have worked with too many men who wish they had taken that alternative years ago instead of becoming ensnared in compulsive sexual sin.

Pedophilia and Child Molestation

Do you want to know the greatest sexual tragedy American churches are facing (or refusing to face) today? It is *Christian pedophiles molesting Christian children at church.* I am talking about the possibility of pedophiles taking care of *your* children in *your* born-again, fundamentalist, evangelical, conservative, Bible-believing, gospel-preaching, Spirit-filled church, not just in the liberal church across town. This is another issue that many churches are just not dealing with, primarily because of sexual shame and the ignorance maintained thereby. Also, most churches are desperate for children's workers, so the director of Christian education is often reluctant to ask dear "Sister Edna" if she was molested as a child or has ever had any sexual feelings toward children.

The price for such laxity is staggering. In America *1 in every 3–4 girls and 1 in every 5–10 boys is molested before reaching adulthood.* I have every reason to believe these statistics are the same or even worse for Christian children, simply because the church's preparedness in this area is lagging so far behind the secular world.

There is no excuse for any church with children not to require pedophile-awareness training and some form of background check for all those who work with their children and youth. All major youth organizations, such as the Boy Scouts and Boys and Girls Clubs of America, have been forced to put such programs in place because of the large numbers of pedophiles who try to infiltrate those organizations and molest children. Church nurseries and Sunday schools are also prime targets.

I often have churches call me to come and help them *after* a child has been molested by a children's worker. I am glad to help them put a prevention program in place, but for at least one child, it is always too late. As a consequence, I have heard more than my share of horror stories.

One case I had to deal with involved a member of a church that was experiencing tremendous growth and therefore had instituted extended times of worship. Their youth pastor, responsible for over 1500 children, had developed a cutting-edge children's program. He had devised a seven-step approach for teaching the children "deliverance ministry." The only problem was, the seventh step involved having sex with the youth pastor. He had molested at least 20 children before he was discovered and arrested. This pastor fit the profile of a narcissistic pedophile with high pedophilic interest and normal social skills. (I will discuss these attributes later in this chapter.)

This was another church that had been too embarrassed to talk about the issue. When I was engaged to help, the people were still in shock, because this pastor was the last person anyone would have suspected. By all accounts, he was the most well-liked member of the staff and had successfully counseled many in the congregation. The youth workers were accountable to him, but there was no one keeping tabs on when and where he was spending time alone with children.

On the other hand, here is what can happen when a church does the "right" thing and begins to train its staff to deal with sexual problems. In one particular church, I was asked to conduct a thorough training program for the church staff on dealing with all kinds of sexual issues. As always, I focus first on helping the leadership confront and get healing for their own sexual problems. Then I train them how to help others.

Now, this was a very large church with quite a large pastoral staff. When I delved into the issue of child molestation, *a significant portion of the youth ministry staff, men and women, admitted they had been molested* and asked for counseling to finally resolve the matter. As I worked with them individually, I found that several had already taken the first steps down the path toward pedophilia, without even being aware of what they were doing. They had each begun to cultivate a romantic relationship with a particular child in their care, though none of them had yet touched a child sexually. (This fits the profile of an exploitative pedophile with low pedophilic interest and normal social skills.) This was a side effect of their molestation experience having remained undealt with for so many years. *A portion of the staff ultimately had to step down from their positions* and receive counseling for budding pedophilia.

These are just two representative cases out of many. If every senior pastor could see what I have seen and hear what I have heard, believe me, there would be no more shame-induced apathy in the Church concerning this issue.

It is essential that all church workers, particularly children's workers, learn the characteristics of pedophiles. Church administrators must put procedures in place to ensure adequate supervision so that molestation cannot occur in their children's department. (Some churches have found that an effective method of prevention is to have at least two adults with the children at all times.) The pedophiles most commonly found in churches are not the ones who kidnap children, but the ones who like to spend a lot of time with children. Many have excellent social skills and are hard workers, so they are often quite popular with both children and adults. Yet, they are driven by a secret compulsion to act out sexually with children.

Churches must take the lead in informing their members about pedophilia, not only to encourage parents to molestation-proof their children, but because there are some Christians who have a deep, dark secret: they feel sexually attracted to children. These Christians need to be encouraged to get help before they act out and harm a child.

This is truly "the last frontier" in Christian ministry. I have worked with a number of Christians who have struggled with pedophilia. Many of these people truly love God and are horrified to find they have sexual feelings for children. These feelings were most likely introduced into their minds when they themselves were molested, told no one, and received no counseling to help them overcome the trauma of that event. But now they do not know where to turn for help. Once they have touched a child sexually, then they may become the property of the legal system and be marked for life.

When you consider that the number of girls being molested today is 25-33% and the number of boys being molested is 10-20%, then whatever percentage of these children later develop pedophilia as adults, it is sure to be too high.

Facts about Pedophilia

Pedophilia is an erotic interest in children who have not yet reached puberty, from age 1 to around age 12. Pedophilia is distinguished from *nepiophilia* (erotic interest in infants) and *hebephilia* (erotic preference for adolescents). A *child molester* is someone who has touched a child in a sexual way or has used them in any way for sexual pleasure. Some argue that this definition should also include anyone who has deliberately exposed children to pornographic materials.

Someone struggling with pedophilia who has not acted on his desires is not a child molester, but there is some debate about whether all child molesters should be considered pedophiles. A certain percentage of first-time molesters seem to have acted on impulse under the influence of drugs or alcohol and deny any continuing erotic interest in children. If such individuals are placed in a treatment program for sex offenders, it is likely that they will be tested to see if they show any evidence of arousal to images of children.

Due to our society's extreme horror and fear of pedophilia, there is a great deal of denial, deception, and self-deception on the part of those who have pedophilic feelings and behaviors. The law tends to treat convicted child molesters as pedophiles who are likely to reoffend, unless and until they are proven otherwise through extensive psychological testing. Even so, there are too many documented cases of molesters, released by the legal system and considered by experts to be "cured," who molested again. Some states, such as Arizona, are instituting the idea of "lifetime parole" for molesters to ensure that they are prevented from ever molesting again. Once released, their movements are monitored, and they are regularly tested to see if they have even been fantasizing about children, since this is the first step in reoffending.

There is some dispute about the actual number of pedophiles and child molesters in America today. Psychiatrist Dr. Gene Abel, Director of the Behavioral Medicine Institute of Atlanta and an expert on sex offenders, estimates that *pedophiles make up 1 percent of the population.*[26] However, a nationwide randomized survey in 1988 uncovered an incredible number—an average of *10% of American men admitted to having molested a child*.[27] A 1989 survey of male undergraduates found that 21% reported having experienced sexual attraction to children and 7% would consider having sex with a child if they could be sure to avoid punishment.[28] In any case, the number must be fairly high because of the high numbers of children who have been sexually abused.

Public awareness of the problem is greater now than it has ever been. But our society, and in particular the Christian church, has yet to come to terms with the pedophile. They have not learned how to prevent children from growing up to be pedophiles, how to prevent pedophiles from molesting, and how to offer healing and restoration to pedophiles. There is quite a broad spectrum of people suffering from various forms of this condition, ranging from those who have never molested a child to those who are serial lust murderers.

We must bear in mind that, as with other paraphilias, a pedophile may be only partially and indirectly responsible for his abnormal sexual feelings. For example, some experts estimate that as many as 90% of pedophiles were themselves molested as children. This is believed to be a primary factor that causes pedophilia.[29] Yet, a person who molests a child is entirely responsible for his actions, even though he may have been under the influence of a strong compulsion. He is also responsible for his choice not to seek help, but instead to spend years indulging in sexual fantasies about children, which only strengthens the compulsion to be sexual with a child.

Most Americans would be shocked to find out that some revered historical figures of the last century, whose works still shape our culture, were pedophiles. It was a simpler time, and society was not concerned with some of their peculiar behaviors that today would get them arrested. Robert Baden-Powell, founder of the Boy Scouts, left extensive writings that describe his aversion to women and his fondness for looking at naked boys and friends' photographs of them. A number of authorities who have reviewed his writings, including Dr. Fred Berlin, founder of the Sexual

Disorders Clinic at Johns Hopkins University Hospital in Baltimore and an expert on pedophilia, have declared him to be a homosexual pedophile—though there is no evidence to indicate that he ever molested.[30] The Reverend Charles Dodgson, who wrote the *Alice in Wonderland* children's books under the pseudonym of Lewis Carroll, had a peculiar hobby of taking nude photographs of young girls. He made a habit of befriending their parents and then gaining their permission to photograph the children. He became quite attached to some of these girls, and it was for them that he created his stories. Sir James Barrie, creator of the Peter Pan tales, wrote them for some young boys he adopted and toward whom he expressed definitely romantic feelings. Both of these men are considered today to have been pedophiles, though there is no evidence that they ever molested.[31] Their writings and contemporary records of their lives illustrate their desire to have an emotional relationship with a child as an equal, characteristic of the *interpersonal* type of pedophile.[32]

Pedophilia is a fairly broad category, but it can be broken down into several distinct groups of people based on shared characteristics. There are several criteria used to classify pedophiles (see Table 11.1). The most obvious grouping is by sex. Male pedophiles are the majority (around 90%) and tend to receive the most publicity, but there is growing evidence—based on surveys of adults about their childhood sexual experiences—for the existence of a much smaller, but significant number of female pedophiles (around 10%).

For male pedophiles, the most discriminating factor has been found to be the relative strength of pedophilic attraction: whether they have a high or low fixation on children in their sexual fantasies (often referred to as either *regressed or fixated*[33]). Regressed pedophiles have a history of normal adult sexual relations, but at some point, for some reason, have had a sexual encounter with a child. Their sexual interest in children is relatively recent and situational. They do not have continuing sexual fantasies about children.

In contrast, for pedophiles with a high level of fixation on children, the majority of their sexual fantasies center around children. They typically

Table 11.1 Major Characteristics Used to Classify Pedophiles	
Characteristic	**Value**
Sex	Male or Female
Level of sexual interest in children	High level (Fixated) Low level (Regressed)
Sex of victims	Male, Female, or Both
Social development	Normal social skills Poor social skills
Seeks high level of contact with children	Yes/No
Seeks to form an emotional relationship with child victim	Yes/No
Degree of physical injury or pain to child victim	High level/Low level
Any organic factors involved	Mental illness, brain damage, alcohol or drug use

have an extensive history of sexual involvement with children, often beginning in puberty. They may establish enduring relationships with particular children. A further distinction is whether the pedophile is attracted to boys, girls, or both. Some pedophiles may be attracted only to children of a specific age.

Most pedophiles have not developed the normal social skills that would enable them to marry, hold a long-term job, participate in community activities, or develop a network of adult friends. They have difficulty relating to other adults, so they remain isolated or attempt to relate primarily with children. However, perhaps 25% or more appear to function socially in a relatively normal manner.

Some pedophiles seek positions where they can spend large amounts of time with children. Most who do so are primarily seeking sexual encounters, but some seem to be seeking an emotional relationship with a child. The most notorious pedophiles are those who cause physical pain and injury to children. Expressing aggression and "being in control" are important issues for many of these. Some may have a secondary diagnosis of sadism. Finally, organic factors such as drug and alcohol abuse, brain damage, mental retardation, or schizophrenia may be involved in some incidents of molestation.

Several researchers have developed classification schemes in an effort to better understand pedophilia. Most of these classifications have

Table 11.2 Types of Male Pedophiles and Estimated Percentage of Each Type[35]				
		High contact with children (41%)		Low contact with children (56%)	
		Relationship Emphasis	No Relationship Emphasis	Low Injury	High Injury
Types		Interpersonal (11%)	Narcissistic (30%)	Exploitative (35%)	Aggressive/ Sadistic (21%)
High pedophilic interest (Fixated) (84%)	Poor social skills	6	21	24	13
	Normal social skills	5	9	6	
Low pedophilic interest (Regressed) (13%)	Poor social skills			2	8
	Normal social skills			3	

been developed for males because they make up the vast majority of offenders. Table 11.2 illustrates a classification system for male child molesters developed by the Massachusetts Treatment Center for Sexually Dangerous Persons (MTC), which has done a great deal of research to validate its findings.[34] The table also shows representative percentages for the types of convicted offenders they have treated. The table is designed to show how the discriminating factors are used to assign pedophiles/molesters into four major categories: Interpersonal, Narcissistic, Exploitative, and Aggressive/Sadistic. Keep in mind that these categories represent major clusters of pedophiles. There are always a few individuals who fit somewhere in between. The descriptions of the categories that follow are based on Raymond A. Knight's work at MTC, with additional insights from other researchers.

Interpersonal Pedophiles

The most distinguishing feature of this type of pedophile is the need to develop an emotional, even romantic, relationship with a child, in addition to any sexual activity. Because of their own emotional immaturity, they relate to children as their peers. They prefer them to adults because they believe that children will not hurt them as adults are prone to do. Because they are primarily seeking friendship with a child, they may not think of themselves as pedophiles. They seek a high degree of access to children to the extent of organizing much of their lives around activities that give them such access. *Many seek a position, such as a volunteer in a youth organization, that allows them to spend a great deal of time with children.*

Their sexual activity with children is focused mostly on seeing and fondling the child, not so much on performing a sex act. They may seek to engage in mutual, "consenting" sex play with a child that resembles the "show and tell" sexual games children engage in with their peers. This enables the interpersonal pedophile to rationalize his behavior as something "natural" and not harmful to the child. He may also see his behavior as normal in situations that allow him to see children naked or touch them surreptitiously. For example, if he helps children use the bathroom or change clothes, he may be able to fondle them briefly while performing his duties. He justifies his behavior to himself as merely being affectionate.

Because interpersonal pedophiles are seeking an emotional relationship, they often focus their attention on one "special" child who appeals to them. They proceed to win the child's affection by showering him or her with special attention, favors, and gifts. They usually look for a child who matches a set of characteristics that their "ideal" child friend should have, such as a blond, blue-eyed boy, 11–12 years of age, who has an outgoing personality and likes to play sports. They particularly target children who are emotionally needy: those whose parents are divorced or who do not have a good relationship with their father. Typically, a single mom is grateful for the attention she and her father-hungry child are receiving from the pedophile, so she encourages the relationship.

This group seems to be split equally between those who have normal social skills and those who do not. Those lacking normal social skills have few adult friends and are basically loners. *Their volunteer activities with youth organizations may be their only social outlets*. This primary characteristic should be a major warning flag to those responsible for screening volunteers.

However, interpersonal pedophiles with normal social skills are often able to gain positions as teachers or youth leaders without arousing any suspicion. They may even be active in warning others about the dangers of pedophiles, because they do not see themselves as belonging in that category. This type of pedophile lives with a great degree of denial and self-deception.

Though they are the least aggressive of all the pedophiles, this type of pedophile seems to be the most difficult to treat and the most likely to reoffend after completing a course of therapy. (MTC reports 78% recidivism for this type over a ten-year period.[36]) This may be due to the fact that they have so little capacity to form adult romantic relationships, as well as to their extensive history of denial. It is interesting to note that, out of all the groups, these were exposed to the highest degree of sexual abuse and perversion in their homes during childhood.

Narcissistic Pedophiles

These pedophiles are referred to as narcissistic because their primary focus is their own sexual pleasure. Children just serve as sexual objects for them to use. Like the interpersonal pedophiles, they also organize their lives to maximize contact with children, but their primary goal is to have as many sexual encounters with children as possible. They do not feel an emotional attachment to their victims. They molest children they know and children they do not know. Any special attention, gifts, or favors they bestow on a child are purely manipulative, aimed at getting the child to cooperate with their sexual wishes. They become very skilled at manipulating children to fulfill their desires and at keeping them silent through threats or bribes. Their sexual activity with children often involves genital contact, such as intercourse or oral sex, but is not usually aggressive or involving force. The pedophiles in this category often report having had sexual encounters with several hundred children before they were finally caught.

Aggressive/Sadistic Pedophiles

These are the most notorious type of pedophile, because they are distinguished by the high degree of physical injury they inflict on their victims. They are typically very aggressive and impulsive, and some may also be sadistic. Their sexual activity with the child usually involves forced anal, oral, or vaginal penetration with subsequent tissue damage. Some seem to disregard the pain they are inflicting. The sadistic ones may actually relish it. Sadistic pedophiles may carry out sexual fantasies of bondage and torture, or perform bizarre rituals on their victims.

Aggressive/sadistic pedophiles do not typically have a lot of nonsexual contact with children. They have the highest rates of alcohol abuse of all the categories and typically molest while under the influence of alcohol. They have an extensive history of aggressive and violent behavior. For those with a low degree of pedophilic interest, it may only have been a chance encounter that led them to vent their aggressive or sadistic fantasies on a child instead of some other victim. Those with a high degree of pedophilic interest tend to brood on their fantasies over a long period of time until they eventually decide to go out and find a child to victimize. Pedophiles in this category usually fit the profile of someone with poor social skills. They are often loners with a marginal work history. They are likely to have a criminal record of nonsexual assaults as well. They are also more likely to have psychotic symptoms. Those with a sadistic orientation are likely to have had a severely disrupted childhood with placement in multiple foster homes. They also have the greatest degree of overall mental illness.

Exploitative Pedophiles

This is the largest and most diverse category of pedophiles, including some with high and some with low fixation on children. It is somewhat of a catchall category for those who do not fit in the other three. Exploitative pedophiles are distinguished by these characteristics: they rarely seek out contact with children other than for sexual purposes; they do not cause physical harm in sexual encounters with children; and aggression is limited to holding or threatening the child. Some may have sadistic fantasies, but they avoid doing physical harm to the child. Roughly two-thirds fit the poor social skills profile and have the most psychological problems. The remaining third function relatively well socially.

There are four subtypes in this category. Those with *high pedophilic interest/poor social skills* seem to have the most learning disorders in childhood, significant psychological problems, and a history of impulsive behavior throughout their lives. They have great difficulty in supporting themselves and tend to be employed in low skill jobs, if at all.

They also report a high level of other paraphilias and are more likely than those in the other groups to be arrested for a subsequent sexual assault. Roughly one-third of this group also has sadistic fantasies involving children. They tend to have significant problems with impulsive behavior and nonsexual aggression, and typically have a criminal record.

Those with *high pedophilic interest/normal social skills* have the fewest reported learning disabilities or psychological problems in childhood and throughout life. They seem to have few problems with impulse control. Their offenses are planned, and they may be the least likely to get caught because of their skill at manipulating others.

Those with *low pedophilic interest/normal social skills* seemed to be the most nearly normal psychologically, the lowest in impulsivity, and have the lowest rates of recidivism or other paraphilias. The following is a typical profile of such a man and how he might begin to molest.

> He is usually married. His primary sexual orientation is toward adult women. He has a leadership or volunteer position that provides a lot of contact with children. He may be a teacher, scoutmaster, or youth leader. He may be a "macho" man above suspicion, such as a coach or a policeman. He has had no prior homosexual activity as an adult. He showed no sexual interest in children until the first incident of molestation. He may develop a strong attachment to a particularly needy boy and be surprised by sudden erotic feelings. Sexual activity usually begins with horseplay that progresses to mutual masturbation, and may go no further than this.

Some youth organizations now warn volunteer workers that they may have unexpected erotic feelings for a child and discuss how to deal with those feelings. Some of these men seek help, but others continue to develop their habit. There is some evidence that these men had sexual experiences with other boys their age during adolescence, and that the memory resurfaces unexpectedly when they are exposed to boys of the same age. Or they may have been molested by older men when they were that age.

Pedophiles with *low pedophilic interest/poor social skills* would seem to be primarily heterosexual men who are impulsive. (They typically have a history of rash behavior and minor criminal acts.) They had their inhibitions lowered at the time through alcohol or drug use, were in a distressed mental state (angry or depressed), and were unexpectedly placed in a situation (such as being asked to babysit) that allowed them to behave sexually with a child. Also included in this category could be some teenage offenders considered "juvenile delinquents." They are typically antisocial (showing no concern for other's rights and feelings) and may see molestation as just an occasional and convenient sexual outlet, without having a sexual fixation on children.

Some incestuous fathers or stepfathers would seem to fit in either of the two categories above, but others could be in any of the other categories that possess normal social skills.[37] Some pedophiles and hebephiles have been known to court and marry single mothers just to gain access to their children.

Female Pedophiles

It is estimated that 10% of child molesters are female. Yet, not as much attention has been given to the existence of female pedophiles for several reasons. Women are primary caregivers for children, so there is less suspicion of female-child interaction. There has not been as much publicity about female pedophiles. Also, older boys may not report abuse by a woman because American male culture tends to view them as "lucky," not abused. Female pedophiles have almost always been extensively abused themselves as children.[38]

Pornography and Fantasy

The term *pornography* is usually defined as any material that violates prevailing standards of decency and was produced for no other purpose than to arouse. However, the issue that should concern us is much broader than this rather narrow legal definition. Modern society has become saturated with sexual images and messages of all kinds. From bikinis at the pool to suggestive billboards to R-rated movies on television, we accept things as commonplace today that would have been indecent fifty years ago. What is legally regulated today as "obscene" are only the most explicit depictions ("hard-core" pornography) and, of course, sexual images of children, since that is still so abhorrent to the overwhelming majority of average citizens (if not psychologists).

DO YOU HAVE A FANTASY LOVER?

The consumers of pornography are almost exclusively men, and the porn industry brings in eight billion dollars per year by creating and feeding their porn addiction. However, there are also sizeable industries dedicated to creating and sustaining in women an addiction to what I call "emotional pornography": romance novels and daytime dramas ("soap operas"). Some people are shocked to hear these compared with pornography. Yet, I believe they produce some of the same effects in women that pornography produces in men.

From what we have learned of the differences in male and female sexuality, it is not too surprising that there should also be differences in what men and women find erotically enticing. Male sexuality is very visually oriented, so pornographic pictures take direct advantage of that fact. Female sexuality is oriented more toward affectionate and romantic relationships, so romance novels and soap operas are designed to appeal to those needs. However, for both men and women, the end result is the same: through these means they are enticed into erotic relationships with fantasy lovers.

Fantasy Lovers

Do you have a fantasy lover? Fantasy lovers are so much easier to manage than real lovers. They are always beautiful and ready to love you when you need it. They have no needs of their own, so they make no demands on you. When your desires have been satisfied, they do not complain when you lay them aside for another day. They will always welcome you back with that same smile whenever you desire them again. And they never point out your flaws.

As Christian men and women, we need to ask ourselves a hard question: What role does fantasy play in my sexual and social life? God's plan is clearly for us to have fulfilling relationships with real people (including Himself), not to waste our lives chasing illusions of happiness in a dream world. Yet, I find that for too many Christians, their sexual, social, and *even spiritual lives* are all based on fantasy.

Let us take, for an example, a typical young, single Christian man. He has dated many girls over the past ten years and has even had sex a few times, but he has just not yet found the perfect woman to be his wife. Meanwhile, he feels justified in meeting his sexual needs with fantasy lovers. Like most men, he has been exposed to hard-core pornography, but even if he has not made that a habit, he is surrounded by more than enough images of beautiful women from television, movies, and advertisements to populate his dream world. In his mind he regularly has sex with these ideal women. Obviously, the girls he dates from church never quite compare with the world's most beautiful starlets and supermodels. So, it is not surprising that he has not yet married. Part of him is still holding out for that tall, thin, blue-eyed blond of his dreams, and there are just not that many of them available in the real world.

Finally, he does meet a girl from church who comes close to his ideal. She is not very tall, but she is thin and blond. However, he does not realize that her blond hair comes out of a bottle and that she must diet obsessively to maintain her slim figure. For years she has been seeing the same idealized media images of women that he has, but the lesson she has learned is that she must emulate them in every way possible if she wants to attract a man. Like our young man, she has also been dating for nearly a decade. A few times she thought she had found a man who wanted to marry her, so she gave him the sex for which he was so eager, but after that turning point, each relationship quickly floundered. She has almost given up hope but has been surviving on her romance novels and afternoon soaps. In her fantasies, the strong yet sensitive, sophisticated yet humble, passionate yet considerate, wealthy and artistic man of her dreams is always waiting to sweep her off her feet and carry her away to a tropical paradise where he fulfills her every desire.

Both of these typical Christian singles are imprisoned by their sexual fantasies. Not only have they created dream lovers to satisfy their emotional and sexual needs, but no real lover could ever hope to fulfill such an expectation of perfection. If these two marry each other, then they are destined for much disappointment and conflict, until and unless they learn to leave such self-centered fantasies behind for the genuine pleasure (and sometimes, heartache) of laying one's life down for another. As long as these strongholds of fantasy remain in their minds, it will always be a temptation for them to withdraw from each other and to retreat there when they experience difficulties in their relationship. If they choose to fantasize about their dream lovers during sexual union, *then they will be essentially committing adultery each time they have sex.* Not only will such emotional withdrawal and betrayal be very destructive to their marriage, but they will never know the true satisfaction of spiritual oneness between a husband and wife that should be the ultimate product of sexual union.

The Real World versus the Virtual World

I have counseled many Christian men seeking freedom from a pornography habit and from many other types of compulsive sexual behavior. Yet, I have often found that those who come to me for help in escaping from a life of sexual fantasy tend to be captives of fantasy in other areas of their lives as well. It is one thing to have a dream and a hope for the future, goals toward which you are steadily working and bringing into reality. It is quite another to live in a dream world instead of the real world, while your life and any chance of fulfilling your dreams and goals are slowly ebbing away.

One of the great flaws of our modern society is that, for many people, the "virtual world" is rapidly replacing the real world. We are surrounded by some of the most compelling and ubiquitous artistic media ever devised: movies, television, radio, recorded music, the Internet. Yet for many of us, these are becoming a means to escape from reality for longer and longer periods of time. For some, it is no longer even a question of life imitating art; for them, art is *replacing* life.

For many people, television viewing has replaced socializing to some degree. Television has become an artificial means of meeting social and relational needs. It is so much easier to lay back on the sofa, turn on the television, and enjoy your always-beautiful, always-entertaining *Friends*, than it is to find real friends and expend the effort needed to create and maintain lasting, rewarding relationships.

A mother may prefer her daily visits with *All My Children* to thinking about the heartache her own children have caused her over the years. But soap fans develop genuine emotional attachments to the characters. Wouldn't all that emotional energy be better invested in real relationships with real people? Couldn't the time be better spent in praying for those you love, for the healing of broken relationships, instead of merely anesthetizing your emotional pain with an escape into fantasy?

Because children are allowed so little time with real adults—most are spending more time with "interactive media" than with interactive parents—they must find their heroes and role models in the virtual world. But in that world they are given nothing but caricatures of real human beings: stone-cold, incredibly violent "action heroes"; surgically- and digitally-enhanced supermodels; sports figures whose only claim to fame is that they are really good at playing a particular type of game, while they make absurd amounts of money and bed vast numbers of women; or entertainers who model equally self-indulgent and self-destructive lifestyles. There is not a real hero in the lot. Is it really all that surprising, then, that some girls end up starving themselves to death in an attempt to look like a fantasy woman? Should we wonder when some boys begin slaughtering people indiscriminately or try to blow up their schools—things such as they have seen their "action heroes" do thousands of times?

When we step back and view a society that is so captivated by fantasy, that spends so much of its time living in a dream world, we can see that pornography is just a small part of a very pervasive problem: *choosing fantasy over reality*. The children fantasize about their movie heroes, rock stars, and teen idols; Mom lives for her soaps; and Dad has a porn habit.

It seems only natural that people raised in such a fantasy-based society would seek sexual fulfillment with fantasy lovers. Pornography, romance novels, and "steamy soaps" serve as aids to help us create in our minds truly seductive dream lovers, since few of us have great imaginations.

Certainly, pornography teaches wrong concepts of sex. But the same deceptions are taught far more widely and effectively through people's exposure to thousands of hours of sitcoms, soap operas, novels, movies, and top-40 song lyrics. False messages are taught, such as:

- Sex is just a pleasurable pastime in which two (or more) people may engage, involving no enduring connection or commitment, much like a game of racquetball.
- Sexual relationships (including marriage) are supposed to be temporary. They are meaningful only while they are meeting both people's needs. Eventually, one or both will outgrow the relationship, and

it will be time to move on.

- We can easily drift from one sexual relationship to another without any emotional harm.
- Other people, particularly women, are sexual objects to be used for our personal pleasure.
- Young, beautiful people do not contract STDs.
- You are completely protected from STDs if the man wears a condom.
- Relational conflicts are best handled with deception or with highly emotional confrontations that inevitably lead to violence.
- True happiness and fulfillment in life can only be found through immediate gratification of every desire.
- The only unpardonable sin is to criticize another person's sexual practices.

The problem with the majority of these beautifully crafted entertainments and artistic expressions is that, instead of helping us to understand the deep truths and the hidden mysteries of life—which is the true purpose of all art—they are drawing us into a dream world built on enticing lies. With respect to sexuality, such works fail to show us the great destruction and suffering caused by promiscuity, adultery, divorce, and STDs. They fail to link causes and effects. They deny the existence of the Law of Sexual Union and the inevitable operation of the moral laws of the universe, such as, "Whatever a man sows, that he will also reap" (Galatians 6:7 NKJV). Fictional characters can fornicate with great gusto and live happily ever after; real people never can.

It is no wonder that many Americans now live lives molded by and modeled after such false images. Increasing numbers of people worldwide are falling under their spell wherever Hollywood peddles its wares. Yet, the prophet Isaiah describes the fate of those who worship and serve false images: "He feeds on ashes, a deluded heart misleads him; he cannot save himself, or say, 'Is not this thing in my right hand a lie?'" (Isaiah 44:20 NIV).

As we share the joys and sorrows of fictional friends and develop emotional bonds with them; as we learn how to have fictional relationships from observing their fictional lives; as a song on the radio stirs up the pain of old wounds, yet soothes them with a promise of revenge or spite; as we find ourselves falling in love with an entertainer who does not care that we even exist except to buy his "product"; as we allow a film to take us on an emotional roller coaster and drop us back to earth a few hours later, having experienced for a brief time the excitement, fulfillment, meaning, success, and love that is missing from our own lives—in all these ways we are truly feeding our hearts a diet of dust and ashes.

Yet, we feel momentarily satisfied by such a meal. Our emotional needs have been met, for a time, by fantasy instead of reality. We can then return to the harried and unsatisfying lives we have built with our own hands, no longer compelled by the urgency of our unmet needs and unfulfilled dreams to seek genuine solutions to our problems, to save ourselves from such a life before it is too late.

Without realizing it, our attitudes, opinions, and morals have been reshaped by our time in fantasy land. Our fantasy friends have fed us sugar-coated lies about life and sexuality, and we eventually swallow them whole. Sin no longer seems so abhorrent, for our hearts have been deceived and deluded. We are left holding onto lies with both hands because they seem to offer the fulfillment for which we have been longing. The only thing left would be for us to actually put into practice the immorality we have been taught over thousands of viewing hours. In this way, a lifetime of seeking emotional fulfillment through fantasy also prepares us to seek sexual fulfillment through fantasy.

The Effects of Pornography

Of all the sources of seductive sexual fantasies, pornography is just the most immediately stimulating and addicting, especially for men. Researchers have been cataloging its harmful effects over the years:

- Use of pornography has been strongly linked to rape and sexual violence. Numerous studies indicate that exposure to pornography reduces men's inhibitions about rape, makes violence toward women sexually arousing, and teaches the myth that women want to be raped. One study found that, after viewing pornography, 35% of male college students said they were willing to rape a woman if they could be assured they would not be punished for it.[39]
- Use of pornography is one of the most common traits of serial murderers and rapists. FBI statistics indicate that pornography is found at 80% of the scenes of violent sex crimes or in the homes of the perpetrators. In an FBI survey of convicted serial sex murderers, 81% said pornography was their primary sexual interest.[40] Nearly all pedophiles seek pornographic images of children to feed their fantasies until they can get their hands on a child.
- Through normal learning processes (association and desensitization, as described in Chapter 10), pornographic materials can change a user's sexual object choice. Eventually, he becomes aroused by pictures of acts he once thought were bizarre or disgusting.
- Viewing pornography reduces a husband and wife's sexual satisfaction with each other, and men report less attraction to their spouse.[41]

- For most men, viewing pornography quickly becomes a sexual addiction. Pedophiles become so addicted to child porn that they willingly risk exposure and arrest just to obtain it. Users of other types of porn become just as addicted, but their porn happens to be legal.

- Being exposed to pornography can have such devastating and lifelong effects on young children that many experts consider it a form of child molestation. Indeed, many molesters use pornography to prepare children for sexual involvement by breaking down their inhibitions. Depending on what images they were exposed to and when, children can pick up terrible misconceptions about sexuality. They often begin to compulsively act out the images with other children. Some children have even had their sexual development derailed into some form of paraphilia as a result of such exposure.

- From a spiritual standpoint, pornographic materials are "cursed objects." They are produced and distributed under the guidance of demons, who desire to enslave humanity in every way possible. Demons hang around in the vicinity of pornographic materials looking for the chance to invade any human who opens a doorway for them by using such images for lustful fantasy.

The problem with porn is that the images are real enough to fool part of your brain so that you become aroused, yet another part of you realizes you can never have a real sexual relationship with just an image. Right there you have started a war between the different parts of your being. Part of you is fooled, but part is not. Part of you can be satisfied, but many more parts cannot.

By choosing to fantasize a sexual relationship with this image and choosing to masturbate to the point of orgasm with this fantasy in mind, you are setting the sexual bonding mechanism in motion—the mechanism God designed to create a lifelong union with a spouse. This mechanism can forge a bond so powerful that some have gladly sacrificed their own lives to save the lives of their spouse and children. But when this mechanism tries to bond sexually with a mere image of a person instead of a real person, that is so unnatural, so far outside of what God intended, that all kinds of things are bound to go haywire. The levels of hormones and neurotransmitters associated with arousal soar in the brain, yet there are no pheromones present, no affectionate touch from a spouse to release oxytocin. We may not yet understand exactly how the sexual bonding process goes awry in this scenario, but we should not be surprised that it so often results in bizarre and self-destructive compulsions.

Even during this fantasy sexual encounter, your spirit reaches out for spiritual union with your partner. But there is no human spirit there to respond, only dots on paper, glowing phosphors on a screen. If you have any spiritual sensitivity at all, at that point you will sense utter aloneness and emptiness. At worst, a demon may be hanging around in the vicinity, waiting for its chance to invade you. If that occurs, you will experience a most unholy and disgusting union with an unclean spirit; your soul and body will become the host for a spiritual parasite.

For a married man, such a fantasy encounter is an act of adultery because his sexual union with his wife has been breached, even though the other woman exists only in his mind. He is no longer fully devoted to his wife. His sexual energy is no longer focused only on her. If they are having an argument, it will become easier for him to withdraw from her and get his sexual needs met with his fantasy lovers.

Psychologist Victor Cline has studied pornography users and has found that they go through four levels of deepening sexual disturbance. First, they become *addicted* to viewing the pornography and masturbating to it. Then they undergo a period of *escalation*, where they get bored with material they had been viewing and seek out more bizarre and deviant material to give them the same erotic high. Third, they become *desensitized* to any scenes they once found disgusting or disturbing and become accepting of such behavior. Finally, they begin to *act out* the deviant scenes they have been viewing—things such as exhibitionism, voyeurism, group sex, inflicting pain on themselves or a sex partner, patronizing prostitutes, and much more.[42]

There is much anecdotal evidence that Christian men may struggle more than others with secret sexual addictions. Hotels report that their greatest use of in-room pornographic movies occurs when Christian conventions come to town. Prostitutes report such conventions provide their best business.[43] I believe this is generally true for several reasons. Certainly, the environment of shame, fear, and ignorance about sexuality in which many Christian children are raised sets them up to fall prey to sexual fantasy and addiction. Christians are also subjected to more intense demonic temptation. However, I am convinced there is a much deeper reason for this great weakness that has to do with the place of fantasy in the average Christian's life, particularly *spiritual fantasy*.

Spiritual Fantasy

We have seen how easy it is, aided by the products of the entertainment industry, for us to find our emotional and social fulfillment in a fantasy world. A more difficult question we as Christians need to ask ourselves is, What role does fantasy play in my spiritual life?

CHRISTIAN PORN?

The central theme of this book is that God designed sex to be holy, ultimately teaching us about the relationship He desires with us. So, if we can be drawn away from a real relationship with our spouse and be enticed into a fantasy relationship with a fantasy lover, is there a spiritual parallel to this? Is there something that can distract us from a genuine spiritual relationship with God and draw us away into a fantasy relationship with a fantasy god?

This is certain to be an explosive subject, far more disturbing to most Christians than the issue of pornography. Yet, I fear that some of us—no, *many of us*—are spending much of our spiritual lives in a Christian fantasy land and are using what I call "Christian pornography" to enrich the illusion and make it seem more satisfying.

The shocking truth few Christians realize is that the largest producers and distributors of Christian media today are *secular* companies. The Christian pop music market is now larger than the combined markets for classical, jazz, and New Age music. The handful of giant corporations that dominate the global music industry, smelling money, bought out much of the Christian music industry some time ago. The same process is occurring in Christian publishing.

Yet, it all makes some sort of perverse sense when we realize that these companies are in the business of creating and selling prepackaged fantasies. They are the gatekeepers of virtual reality. It really matters little to them to which of their virtual worlds you purchase admission. The same company that sells you Christian music and videos in one store, will gladly sell you sexually explicit music and videos a few doors down. It is all equally profitable "product," produced in the very same factories.

What about the Christian "ministries" that could not survive except by their use of every manipulative marketing technique ever developed by Madison Avenue psychologists? You know the ones I mean. Those mass mailings filled with holy cloths, holy oil, holy money, and holy rocks as "your point of contact to touch God." Maybe they issue weekly notices of "threats to our nation's freedom," or use phony telephone "polls"—just to pressure you for a donation.

Please hear what I am saying. All of the beautifully crafted Christian music, all of the glossily packaged and polished Christian inspirational books, all of the stirring motivational messages—all of these can *become* nothing but "Christian porn," aids to maintaining a fantasy relationship with a fantasy god.

Does your god speak to you only through the carefully polished phrases of Christian motivational speakers or the lyrics of the top-40 Christian pop songs? When you are feeling lonely and depressed, do you turn to your favorite Christian recording artist to lift your spirits? Is your hope and joy sustained only through a steady diet of "devotional" or "inspirational" books? When you have an urgent need, do you contact a "name" ministry for a "word" or "special prayer" in return for your "love gift"?

The most gifted, entertaining, and "anointed" preacher, with the most helpful and practical message, can never compare to the voice of God's Spirit whispering in your ear in the stillness when the two of you are alone together. If you do not regularly hear His voice in the silence, if you do not often feel His touch, if you do not run first to Him when you are hurting, if you do not seek your fulfillment and pleasure in Him, then although you may acknowledge Him as your King and your God, *He is not your Lover* (see Isaiah 54:5; Hosea 2:19-20). If you do not know Him as your Lover and allow Him to truly know you personally and deeply, then you are loving only a false image of Him. You are committing spiritual adultery with a fantasy god, a god you have created—or that others have created, packaged, and sold to you—designed only to meet your needs, to grant your wishes, to be pulled out and manipulated at will: an inflatable god-in-a-box.

Perhaps you once had a genuine relationship with God. You were truly "married" to Him. Yet, your relationship has grown cold over the years. You now have your differences. There are topics you can no longer discuss. You have just "grown apart." Now you are meeting your spiritual needs, resolving your guilt, and assuaging your anxieties and fears with your fantasy god, an illusion that can only be maintained through a continuous supply of "spiritual aids" and "Christian porn."

I believe many of our churches are perpetuating this climate of spiritual fantasy. The Sunday service has become a professionally staged, multimedia performance, with beautiful people and beautiful music, all taking place on a beautiful set, and designed to appeal to as wide an audience as possible. The senior pastor has become a "Leno," "Letterman," or "Conan," depending on the church's demographics—the always affable and entertaining master of ceremonies. The sermon has become his monologue, and woe to the supporting cast and stage hands if there is a glitch in the proceedings!

Where is God in all of this? He has become a bit player, a "regular," expected to appear on cue and perform a few tricks, give us a few thrills, take a few special requests, and then vanish behind the curtain until next week, when we want to see Him again. (How many churches today assemble, prepared to wait before the Great King in an attitude of worship until He gives them direction as to how they may best honor and serve Him that day? *That* is spiritual reality!)

Such churches never address the hard realities of Christian life, such as sexual problems, because that would make their audience uncomfortable and reduce the box office receipts. Instead, they focus on entertaining oratory, elaborate expositions of eschatology, or "12 Steps to Getting What You Want Out of God"—anything but reality. They are teaching their people to have a fantasy relationship with a fantasy god. He is either remote and harsh, to be feared and appeased, or a "sugar-daddy" who will give you anything you want and wink at your misdeeds as long as you know how to "work him."

Each Sunday, they must pump up their audience with the same emotional thrills offered by any good movie or Broadway musical. They keep them busy the rest of the week, running from one activity to another, because if they stop, even for just one moment, they might begin to sense the spiritual emptiness in their lives.

An addiction to pornography is bad, but this type of spiritual delusion is much worse. In my experience, and that of many other counselors, *Christians who lead such a fantasy-based existence are the very ones most likely to fall prey to every form of sexual sin and addiction.* I promise you, if your church is not openly confronting sexual problems, then your church is *full* of sexual problems.

Many recovered sex addicts will tell you that, though they were raised in a Christian home and were always very religious, they did not truly meet God or know His love until He met them and embraced them while they were still in the depths of depravity. Then He lifted them up in His arms and carried them out. Yet, they remain broken people. Many have lost marriages and ministries. But they now experience His love in a way that few of us do.

Jesus directly addressed these two issues of having a fantasy relationship with God and living a life based on fantasy instead of reality. We need to carefully examine what He has to say:

> Not everyone who says to Me, "Lord, Lord," shall enter the kingdom of heaven, but he who does the will of My Father in heaven. Many will say to Me in that day, "Lord, Lord, have we not prophesied in Your name, cast out demons in Your name, and done many wonders in Your name?" And then I will declare to them, "**I never knew you**; depart from Me, you who practice lawlessness!" (Matthew 7:21-23 NKJV)

Taking this passage at face value may threaten some people's favorite eternal security doctrines, but let me tell you, if your hope of eternal security is based on a doctrinal position instead of the reality of an intimate, daily communion with God, then you are already living in a spiritual fantasy world.

Here Jesus makes it plain that some who call Him "Lord" and even do supernatural works in His name do not know Him. More precisely, He has never known *them*. He has never had a spiritually intimate relationship with them. They are not His bride. They are rebels who practice "lawlessness" and violate His commands. Yet, they show utter surprise when He casts them out of His presence. You see, for all those years *they had a fantasy relationship with a fantasy god.*

Jesus continues:

> Therefore whoever hears these sayings of Mine, and does them, I will liken him to a wise man who built his house on the rock: and the rain descended, the floods came, and the winds blew and beat on that house; and it did not fall, for it was founded on the rock. But everyone who hears these sayings of Mine, and does not do them, will be like **a foolish man who built his house on the sand**: and the rain descended, the floods came, and the winds blew and beat on that house; and it fell. And great was its fall. (Matthew 7:24-27 NKJV)

We see from the word "therefore" that Jesus is speaking here of these same deluded people in contrast to those who truly know Him. These dreamers have heard His teachings and are busy building a life and apparently doing His works—but it is all an illusion. They do not truly know Him, so they misunderstand or misinterpret or explain away His teachings. The result is that their entire lives are wasted living in a fantasy world. They think they are building their dream house, but all they end up with is a sand castle. This is the price of a life based on fantasy.

The Apostle Paul uses a similar illustration in 1 Corinthians 3:11-15, where he explains that even someone who has the foundation of a true relationship with Christ can still build on it a "house" of wood and hay that burns to the ground, making his life on earth a total loss.

Ultimately, there are only two paths you can take with sexual expression:

You can follow the path that fully satiates lust, leading to many sexual encounters with many different people. You can indulge every whim of your sexual appetite to the fullest, whether in fantasy or reality. But this path is a dead end that will eventually destroy your humanity as well as your body. For many, pornography is the first step down this path.

Or, you can follow the path that leads to an ever deepening union of spirit, soul, and body with one spouse over the course of a lifetime, providing a secure foundation of love for creating a family and, finally, leading you closer to God Himself.

Recommended Reading

"The War Within: An Anatomy of Lust," *Leadership* 3 (fall 1982): 30. Also available on the Internet at http://www.christianity.net/leadership/classics/lewar1.html.

"Battle Strategy: Some Practical Advice," *Leadership* 3 (fall 1982): 46. Also available on the Internet at http://www.christianity.net/leadership/classics/lewar2.html.

"The War Within Continues," *Leadership* 9 (winter 1988): 24. Also available on the Internet at http://www.christianity.net/leadership/classics/ lewar3.html.

These three articles are a pastor's frank confession of his fall into sexual addiction through pornography. They tell how God met him in the depth of his addiction and brought him out.

Mark R. Laaser, *Faithful and True: Sexual Integrity in a Fallen World* (Grand Rapids: Zondervan, 1992).

Another pastor, once a sex addict and now a sexual addiction counselor, who looks at sexual addiction and the role played by pornography from both a psychological and spiritual standpoint.

Unusual Sexual Problems (Paraphilias)

There are a variety of unusual and bizarre sexual problems that afflict a small percentage of people. The average person is often disgusted and alarmed when he hears about such things. We have already discussed homosexuality and pedophilia, which are perhaps the most common of these conditions, though most people are aware of the existence of exhibitionists, voyeurs, and those who make obscene phone calls.

I believe every Christian needs to have some basic understanding of even the most unusual of these conditions and their causes. If such things are not becoming more common these days, they are certainly being more publicized.

Once we understand how people can get caught up in these things, we can have a little more compassion for them and can better relate to them with Christian love. If a church is doing its job of evangelizing, then eventually it will have some new converts who are trapped in some of these conditions. The last thing they need is for us to recoil from them in shock and horror. Sadly, even those raised in Christian homes can develop such problems, most often due to traumatic childhood experiences.

This chapter provides a brief overview of the many unusual sexual deviations that have occurred at least frequently enough to have been named, though counselors sometimes see cases that are not in any of the books.

Paraphilia is a word used to describe the condition of being dependent on or preferring an abnormal stimulus for sexual arousal and functioning. (An "abnormal stimulus" is anything that is not a part of what are considered normal heterosexual foreplay and intercourse in a society.) The word *paraphilia* comes from the Greek words for "outside of love," meaning sexuality that is outside the bonds of love. This is a good definition because it illustrates the truth that a paraphilia is a one-dimensional erotic obsession that cannot even begin to provide the many layers of fulfillment found in a loving marital relationship between a husband and wife.

In reference to the dimensions of sexuality discussed in earlier chapters, paraphilias involve primarily a disturbance of sexual object choice and subsequent sexual behavior, though a few (such as homosexuality or transsexualism) may also involve disturbances in gender identity/gender role. Each paraphilia has its own special characteristics and course of development. However, all involve at least some type of paraphilic fantasy, often accompanied by compulsive masturbation. There is usually some type of paraphilic act that feeds the fantasy. In its most extreme form, the paraphilic act either replaces heterosexual intercourse entirely or must be fantasized to enable heterosexual intercourse to occur.

Due to the current political climate in the academic world, psychiatrists no longer define homosexuality as a paraphilia.[44] However, it is still included in studies of the other paraphilias, though it is often categorized with a more euphemistic term such as "sexual anomaly." This is because it is implicitly understood to be as much a product of abnormal development as any other paraphilia and deserves further study, even if some of its victims object to such a categorization.

A distinction is made in the following brief definitions between "an erotic preference for" and "an erotic interest in." There are some paraphilic activities, such as necrophilia (sexual activity with a corpse), in which anyone showing any erotic interest is considered abnormal. There are other paraphilic activities, such as voyeurism, in which most men show some erotic interest. Though such activities are considered immoral, only a preference for those activities over normal heterosexual interaction is considered abnormal.

Root Causes of Paraphilias

As we have seen, human sexual development is the result of a complex interplay of biological, psychological, and social forces and, ultimately, the choices an individual makes along the way. It seems best to view the process of acquiring gender role behaviors and sexual object choice as a process of *adaptation* by a unique individual to the forces, relationships, and circumstances that surround him, particularly in the formative years of childhood and adolescence.

There is common agreement that the causes of paraphilias are to be found in a mixture of biological and social influences, as well as unique individual experiences and choices. The roots of paraphilias are found primarily in experiences of childhood and adolescence, though some people develop them through sexual experiences as adults. The following are some factors that are commonly found in the backgrounds of paraphiles and seem to be directly involved in the development of a paraphilia. Many, but not necessarily all, of these are found in every paraphile's background, though a few may have occurred in the background of a person with normal sexuality. However, the more of these that do occur, the more likely it seems that a paraphilia will develop.

1. *A blockage of normal heterosexual learning and development in early childhood.*

This may result from a traumatic experience, such as being severely punished for childhood sexual play. Or it may be a message from parents (spoken or unspoken) that sexuality is dirty, shameful, and sinful. Parents can send this message just by never discussing sexuality with their children and acting embarrassed whenever the subject is raised. Ignorance of normal sexuality can allow harmful misconceptions to take root in the child's imagination.

2. *A traumatic childhood experience that becomes sexualized at puberty.*

Many paraphiles report traumatic childhood experiences that dominated their dreams and fantasies, such as the death of a friend, or any type of severe punishment or abuse. At puberty, such obsessive fantasies can become associated with sexual feelings, perhaps because the autonomic arousal they produce is similar to the feeling of sexual arousal.

3. *Sexual molestation or abnormal sexual stimulation in childhood.*

This may result in some type of sexual disorder if the child does not receive counseling, because few children can understand and properly resolve what has happened to them without the help of an adult. There may also be some occurrences of abnormal sexual stimulation (not classified as deliberate molestation) that lead to the development of a paraphilia. For example, adults with *klismaphilia* (an erotic interest in receiving enemas) often report being given frequent enemas as children and receiving inadvertent sexual pleasure from them. Exposure to hard-core pornography is another example of abnormal sexual stimulation that can cause lasting harm.

4. *Traumatic failure in attempting normal heterosexual relationships during adolescence.*

Paraphiles often report humiliating incidents during their teenage years that destroyed their confidence in relating to the opposite sex and turned them inward toward fantasy instead.

5. *Abnormal initial sexual experience during adolescence.*

Some paraphiles report that their first sexual experience was bizarre in some way, but they felt compelled to repeat it. For example, some male exhibitionists report being powerfully affected during early adolescence by an incident where a woman accidentally saw them nude. Some psychologists believe a person's initial sexual experiences have an imprinting effect that may not be completely erasable.

6. *Abnormal sexual learning experiences.*

In Chapter 10 we reviewed a variety of learning processes that can change erotic interests: reinforcement, desensitization, association, and orgasmic conditioning. Whatever the origin of an abnormal fantasy, all of these learning mechanisms operating during sexual experimentation can reprogram sexual object choice. Adolescent sexuality seems particularly impressionable, but even some adults who experiment with bizarre sex practices evidently become addicted to them through such means.

7. *Failure to model gender-appropriate behavior.*

Paraphiles who have disturbances in their gender identity/gender role uniformly showed a lack of gender-appropriate behavior in childhood. They were "sissies" or "tomboys." This can be traced to a lack of same-sex role models or a disturbance in the relationships with same-sex role models (such as physical or emotional abuse) that led the child to reject the same-sex role model and instead identify with an opposite-sex role model.

Types of Paraphilias

Fetishes

Fetishes are perhaps the most notorious of the paraphilias because they seem so bizarre and incomprehensible to the average person. They always involve a foreign element—usually unrelated to sexuality for a normal person—that has been introduced into the fetishist's lovemap. When we see how sexual learning processes work to create fetishes, we can understand why there are many more possible variations than are listed here.

These are just the ones that have occurred frequently enough to be given a name.

> 1. *Coprophilia (coprolagnia, scat)* - erotic interest in feces.
>
> 2. *Hyphephilia* - erotic interest in the feel of fabrics, leather, hair, etc.
>
> 3. *Klismaphilia* - erotic interest in receiving an enema.
>
> 4. *Mysophilia* - erotic interest in articles soiled by bodily secretions such as sweat or menstrual flow.
>
> 5. *Olfactophilia (osmolagnia)* - erotic interest in body odors.
>
> 6. *Partialism (morphophilia)* - exclusive erotic preference for a specific body part or a body characteristic, such as feet, hair, or extreme obesity.
>
> 7. *Stigmatophilia* - Erotic interest in having oneself tattooed, scarred, or pierced. (The same word is also used for erotic preference for a partner who is tattooed, scarred, or pierced.)
>
> 8. *Transvestism (transvestophilia)* - erotic interest in wearing clothing of the opposite sex.
>
> 9. *Urophilia (golden shower, watersports, undinism)* - erotic interest in being urinated on or swallowing urine.
>
> 10. *Zoophilia* - erotic interest in sexual activity with an animal.

Displacement Paraphilias

This category is called displacement paraphilias because each one represents an element of a normal courtship or sexual relationship that has been displaced out of sequence or in some way distorted. For example, courtship usually involves touching at some point, but *toucheurism* is the desire to touch strangers. *Exhibitionism* may be seen as a displacement toward strangers of the natural desire to be seen and appreciated by a lover. Some people put rape in this category, but I consider paraphilic rape to be more of an act of violence. Some variations of displacement paraphilias are:

1. *Autagonistophilia* - sexual functioning dependent on being observed during intercourse by someone other than the partner.

2. *Exhibitionism (peodeiktophilia)* - erotic interest in evoking shocked reactions from strangers by exhibiting genitals.

3. *Frotteurism (frottage)* - erotic interest in rubbing up against the bodies of strangers in public places.

4. *Narratophilia* - sexual functioning dependent on using pornographic language with a partner ("talking dirty") or hearing/reading pornographic stories.

5. *Pictophilia* - sexual functioning dependent on viewing pornographic pictures or the act of showing them to the partner.

6. *Scoptophilia (mixoscopia)* - sexual functioning dependent on seeing others also engaged in sexual activity.

7. *Somnophilia* - erotic interest in awakening a sleeping stranger with sexual contact.

8. *Telephone scatophilia (telephonicophilia, telephone scatalogia)* - erotic interest in persuading a stranger to engage in sexually explicit conversations over the telephone.

9. *Toucheurism* - erotic interest in surreptitiously touching strangers with the hands.

10. *Voyeurism* - erotic preference for secretly watching a stranger undress or engage in sexual activity.

Distortions of Sexual Identity

These disorders stem from a distortion of the individual's own sexual identity: an inability to accept his or her own biological sexuality, gender identity, or adult sexual role.

1. Developmental stage regression - the individual rejects an adult sexual role and finds sexual release in imagining and acting out a return to an earlier stage of development.

a. *Infantilism (autonepiophilia)* - sexual functioning dependent on impersonating an infant.

b. *Juvenilism* - sexual functioning dependent on impersonating a preadolescent child.

c. *Adolescentilism* - sexual functioning dependent on impersonating an adolescent.

2. Disorders of gender identity/gender role - these disorders show a confusion and rejection of a normal gender identity/gender role.

a. *Androgyny* - a desire to be a combination of both man and woman.

b. *Transsexualism (gender transposition, gender dysphoria)* - unhappiness with one's biological sex and a desire to become a member of the opposite sex.

Distortions in the Choice of Sexual Partner

These disorders show a fetish-like obsession with a particular characteristic that defines who will be a desirable sexual partner.

1. Age-related distortions (chronophilias)

a. *Nepiophilia* - erotic interest in infants.

b. *Pedophilia* - erotic interest in preadolescent juveniles.

c. *Ephebophilia (hebephilia)* - erotic preference for adolescent partners.

d. *Gerontophilia* - erotic preference for partners the age of one's parents or grandparents.

2. Gender-related distortions

a. *Bisexuality* - having some degree of erotic interest in partners of either sex.

b. *Homosexuality (homophilia)* - erotic interest in a partner of the same sex.

3. Other distorted partner qualifications

a. *Acrotomophilia* - erotic preference for a partner who is an amputee.

b. *Clerambault-Kandinsky syndrome* - being romantically/erotically obsessed with someone who is far off and unobtainable, linked to stalking.

c. *Chrematistophilia* - sexual functioning dependent on the partner being a prostitute (or pretending to be), then paying for sexual services or being robbed.

d. *Necrophilia* - erotic interest in a human corpse.

e. *Nymphomania* - a woman with an erotic preference for intercourse with a series of strangers, "one-night stands."

f. *Satyriasis* - a man with an erotic preference for intercourse with a series of strangers, "one-night stands."

g. *Stigmatophilia* - erotic preference for partners who are tattooed, scarred, or pierced. (Also, erotic interest in having oneself tattooed, scarred, or pierced.)

h. *Troilism* - sexual functioning dependent on observing partner have sex with another person.

Paraphilias Involving Violence

These disorders link erotic interest to some form of violent behavior, either against the self or against others.

1. Violence against the self

a. *Apotemnophilia* - erotic interest in amputating a part of one's own body.

b. *Asphyxiophilia* - *(autoasphyxiation, autoerotic asphyxia, scarfing)* erotic interest in self-strangulation.

c. *Autassassinophilia* - sexual functioning dependent on an individual fantasizing, or actually plotting, his own murder.

d. *Autoelectrocution* - erotic interest in passing electric current through the body.

e. *Masochism* - erotic interest in being abused, subjugated, and humiliated by another.

2. Violence against others

a. *Hybristophilia* - sexual functioning dependent on a partner who has committed a violent crime, such as rape, robbery, or murder. May incite partner to commit crimes.

b. *Kleptophilia (kleptolagnia)* - erotic interest in burglarizing a home and stealing objects with erotic significance, such as undergarments.

c. *Lust murder (erotophonophilia)* - sexual functioning dependent on murdering an unsuspecting partner.

d. *Raptophilia (biastophilia, serial rape)* - sexual functioning dependent on violently assaulting and raping a resisting stranger.

e. *Sadism* - erotic interest in abusing, subjugating, and torturing another.

f. *Symphorophilia* - erotic interest in causing disasters, such as fires or traffic accidents, and viewing the results.

g. *Vampirism* - erotic interest in cutting or biting another person and drinking his blood.

Notes:

1. Lori Thorkelson-Rentzel has written an excellent and widely recommended booklet on identifying and recovering from unhealthy dependent relationships. It is titled *Emotional Dependency: A Threat to Close Friendships* (Downers Grove, IL: InterVarsity Press, 1991).

2. John Sandford provides a much more thorough exposition of how defilement and other forces, such as transference and attachment, operate in a typical counseling situation in *Why Some Christians Commit Adultery* (Tulsa: Victory House, 1989).

3. A new governmental program named "Parents as Teachers," adopted by 40 states so far, offers parents of small children a "free in-home health screening" that is really more of a smoke screen to allow state employees to secretly evaluate, report on, and make public (through open records laws) the "suitability" of the parents. If they are overweight, tired,

depressed, overindulgent of the child, or spank the child, parents are considered to be putting their children "at risk." The social worker then makes "recommendations" for caring for the child, but if the parent does not follow the "recommendations" or tries to withdraw from the program, Child Protective Services is notified to determine if the child should be removed from the home. Realize, this program is aimed at the *average* family, not those with a history of problems or abuse. There are already reported cases where parents who entered this program voluntarily were eventually forced to give their children Ritalin or lose them to a foster home because the state's doctors decided the children were hyperactive and should be drugged.

On a related issue, over the past few years, a number of Christian parents have been arrested and fined just for spanking their children. Many were placed under restraining orders forbidding them to ever spank their children again. Typically, the children were removed from their homes for several months and only brought back under a program of regular state inspections. Several of these cases have been investigated by the news media, and no evidence of child abuse was found, just an occasional spanking by a loving parent.

4. The first three statistics were taken from "How Well Do You Know Your Kids?" *Newsweek*, 19 May 1999.

5. Gary Remafedi et al., "Demography of Sexual Orientation in Adolescents," *Pediatrics* 89 (1992): 714–721.

6. Jerry Adler and Karen Springen, "How to Fight Back," *Newsweek*, 3 May 1999, 37.

7. See Chapter 8 (Table 8.5; endnote 15) for the sources of these statistics.

8. Statistics from the 1994 General Social Survey. See Tom W. Smith, GSS Topical Report No. 25: *American Sexual Behavior: Trends, Socio-Demographic Differences, and Risk Behavior* (Chicago: National Opinion Research Center, University of Chicago Press, 1994), Table 14.

9. Ibid., Table 3.

10. Larry L. Bumpass and James Sweet, "National Estimates of Cohabitation," *Demography* 26 (November 1989): 615–626.

11. E. O. Laumann et al., *The Social Organization of Sexuality: Sexual Practices in the United States* (Chicago: University of Chicago Press, 1994), 501.

12. D. James Kennedy; Tim LaHaye of Family Life Ministries and Beverly LaHaye of Concerned Women for America; John Ankerberg; R.C. Sproul, Jr.; E. Ray Moore, Jr., of Exodus 2000; Robert Simonds of The National Association of Christian Educators, Citizens for Excellence in Education, and Rescue 2010; and Brannon Howse of the Exodus Project are just some of the Christian leaders now advocating that Christian parents take their children out of public schools.

13. The Potter's House of Dallas, Texas, pastored by T. D. Jakes, has implemented a coming-of-age ceremony for their youth. Afterwards, teens begin to attend the men's and ladies' meetings. If they do not have a same-sex parent at home, a volunteer from the church is asked to stand in for that parent and bring them to the meetings.

14. T. H. Holmes and R. H. Rahe, "The Social Readjustment Scale," *Journal of Psychosomatic Research* 11 (1967): 213–218.

15. J. J. Lynch, *The Broken Heart: The Medical Consequences of Loneliness* (New York: Basic Books, 1977).

16. Judith Wallerstein, "The Long-Term Effects of Divorce on Children: A Review," *Journal of the American Academy of Child and Adolescent Psychiatry*, May 1991, 350.

17. Nicholas Zill, Donna Morrison, and Mary Jo Coiro, "Long-term Effects of Parental Divorce on Parent-Child Relationships, Adjustment, and Achievement in Young Adulthood," *Journal of Family Psychology* 7 (1): 91, 100 (1993).

18. Edward L. Wells and Joseph H. Rankin, "Families and Delinquency: A Meta-analysis of the Impact of Broken Homes," *Social Problems* 38 (1): 87 (1991).

19. Susan Larson and David Larson, "Divorce: A Hazard to Your Health?" *Physician,* May/June 1990, 16.

20. Sara McLanahan and Larry L. Bumpass, "Intergenerational Consequences of Family Disruption," *American Journal of Sociology* 94 (1988): 130. Also, N. D. Glenn and K. B. Kramer, "The Marriages and Divorces of the Children of Divorce," *Journal of Marriage and the Family* 49: 811–825.

21. Many of these studies are summarized in Maggie Gallagher's *The Abolition of Marriage: How We Destroy Lasting Love* (Washington, DC: Regnery Publishing, 1996), 31–38. These studies include: Martin Caly and Margo Wilson, "Child Abuse and Other Risks of Not Living with Both Parents," *Journal of Ethology and Sociobiology* 6 (1985): 197. Leslie Margolin and John L. Craft, "Child Sexual Abuse by Caretakers," *Family Relations* 38 (1989): 450. Leslie Margolin, "Child Abuse by Mother's Boyfriends: Why the Overrepresentation?" *Child Abuse and Neglect* 16 (1992): 541–552.

22. Robert J. Stoller, "Transvestism in Women," *Archives of Sexual Behavior* 11 (1982): 99-115.

23. D. McWhirter and A. Mattison, *The Male Couple: How Relationships Develop* (Englewood Cliffs, NJ: Prentice-Hall, 1984).

24. *Cleaning Out the Closet* by Christopher J. Austin is available from Power Source Productions, P.O. Box 40304, Nashville, TN 37204, 800-331-5991.

25. *The International Standard Bible Encyclopedia*, "Sex," III. Canonical Literature, A. Torah, no. 5.

26. Patrick Boyle, *Scout's Honor: Sexual Abuse in America's Most Trusted Institution* (Rocklin, CA: Prima Publishing, 1994), 32.

27. D. Finkelhor and I. A. Lewis, "An Epidemiologic Approach to the Study of Child Molestation," *Annals of the New York Academy of Sciences* 528 (1988): 64–78.

28. J. Briere and M. Runtz, "University Males' Sexual Interest in Children: Predicting Potential Indices of 'Pedophilia' in a Nonforensic Sample," *Child Abuse & Neglect* 13 (1989): 65–75.

29. William E. Prendergast, *The Merry-Go-Round of Sexual Abuse: Identifying and Treating Survivors* (New York: The Hayworth Press, 1993).

30. Boyle, 18 (see note 26).

31. John Money, *Lovemaps: Clinical Concepts of Sexual/Erotic Health and Pathology, Paraphilia, and Gender Transposition in Childhood, Adolescence, and Maturity* (New York: Irvington, 1986), 69-70.

32. Ibid.

33. These terms were originally developed by Groth to describe what he saw as two basic types of pedophiles. Groth is referenced in William Arndt, *Gender Disorders and the Paraphilias* (Madison, CT: International Universities Press, 1991), 220. Although these terms are still frequently used, most researchers now recognize that there are many other criteria that can be used to classify pedophiles.

34. Raymond A. Knight, "The Generation and Corroboration of a Taxonomic Model for Child Molesters," in *The Sexual Abuse of Children: Clinical Issues,* vol. 2 (Hillsdale, NJ: Lawrence Erlbaum Associates, 1992).

35. This table is a simplification of the Massachusetts Treatment Center Child Molester Typology, Version 3 [MTC:CM3] based on Knight's recommendations, such as combining the Exploitative and Muted Sadistic categories, and the Aggressive and Sadistic categories in "The

Generation and Corroboration of a Taxonomic Model for Child Molesters." The statistics are based on 177 convicted offenders he studied at MTC, so they are likely to be skewed by a relatively high representation of the most dangerous offenders and a lack of incest offenders. Empty boxes represent categories that had only a few (0-3) members.

36. Knight, 47 (see note 34).

37. Knight notes that this classification system has not yet been validated against a group of incestuous fathers, though he presents much evidence from other researchers that indicates incestuous fathers are similar to other pedophiles. MTC rarely deals with incestuous fathers because they are less likely to be convicted and imprisoned.

38. Jacqui Saradjian and Helga Hanks, *Women Who Sexually Abuse Children* (New York: Wiley & Sons, 1996).

39. N. M. Malamuth, "Rape Proclivity among Males," *Journal of Social Issues* 37 (1981): 138–157.

40. See these sources: Deborah Baker, "Pornography Isn't Free Speech," *Dallas Morning News*, 17 March 1989, Op-Ed page; "The Men Who Murdered," *FBI Law Enforcement Bulletin*, August 1985; Attorney General's Commission on Pornography, *Final Report of the Attorney General's Commission on Pornography* (Nashville: Rutledge Hill Press, 1986).

41. Dolf Zillman and Jennings Bryant, "Pornography, Sexual Callousness, and the Trivialization of Rape," *Journal of Communications* 32 (1982): 15. Also, "Pinups and Letdowns," *Psychology Today*, September 1983.

42. Victor Cline, *Pornography's Effects on Adults and Children* (New York: Morality in Media, 1999 reprint).

43. Mark R. Laaser, *Faithful and True: Sexual Integrity in a Fallen World* (Grand Rapids: Zondervan, 1992), 110.

44. For an interesting account of how homosexuality was declared to no longer be an illness by majority vote of the American Psychiatric Association, read Jeffrey Satinover's *Homosexuality and the Politics of Truth* (Grand Rapids: Baker Books, 1996).

XII

What You and
Your Church Can Do

The message of this book is that God has a plan and purpose for our sexuality just as He does for every other area of our lives. Christians, of all people, should have a healthy and fulfilling sexual life. Yet so many of us do not because we have been lied to and deceived. On the one hand are the forces that perpetuate fear, shame, and ignorance about sexuality; on the other, the forces that encourage total sexual indulgence and perversion. We must finally understand that both deceptions come from the same devilish source. In fact, for many people, fear, shame, and ignorance about sexuality is what opens the doorway to eventual sexual perversion and indulgence.

However, the good news is that both conditions are completely unnecessary. God has a plan to deliver His people from fear, shame, and ignorance just as surely as He has a plan to deliver them from sexual sins and perversions.

There are some fundamental steps that people can take to protect themselves and their families from sexual sins and problems. There are also some ways in which churches can become involved to help their members stay out of sexual sins and to help free those who have already become entangled.

What You Can Do

1. *Educate yourself about the facts of sexuality.* This is the central purpose of this book, so you have already done a lot to protect yourself from future problems just by reading it. God is our Father, and there is no reason to be afraid or ashamed to learn the facts about His creation. He blesses us with wisdom and knowledge so that we can be protected from foolish mistakes and deception (see Proverbs 2).

Every Christian must know:

> a. *Basic sexual information* - the fundamentals of how sex works: the physical, mental, emotional, *and spiritual* consequences.
> b. *Christian sexual morality* - what is sinful, what is not, and why. Remember, sin is anything that harms another person, yourself, or God.

2. *Learn to manage your own sexuality to keep yourself holy and healthy.* Each person is unique and has a different experience of sexuality. So all of us need to learn to understand and manage our own sexual feelings according to God's plan if we are to stay happy, holy, and healthy. The basic principles for doing so are outlined in this book. Our sexuality can be a source of tremendous joy and fulfillment, or it can be the source of life-long suffering and pain. Sexual sin can even kill you or shorten your life through disease. The choice is up to you.

3. *Get help in overcoming your own sexual problems.* We all have areas of weakness, whether it is lustful thoughts or just so much shame

about sexuality that we cannot even discuss it with others. If you have any kind of sexual problem, then educate yourself about it, pray about it, and *talk to someone about it.* Do not just leave things the way they have always been, because you will never get free that way. Envision it like this: your problem is like a big black wall that is keeping you penned up in a miserable place. God is standing on the other side of that wall, encouraging you to climb over it into a beautiful place where you can enjoy the freedom and fulfillment He has always planned for you.

4. *Work on having a wonderful marriage.* It is a great tragedy that so many Christian couples have put up with so much misery in their marriages for so many years. Not only have they missed out on years of happiness and fulfillment, but they have made themselves vulnerable to sexual temptations by not keeping their marital bond strong. There are an abundance of books and seminars today that provide help with every kind of marital problem, including sexual problems. Do not let another week go by with these problems unresolved.

What Parents Can Do

1. *Educate your children about God's purpose and plan for sex.* Parents, you have the responsibility to educate your children about their sexuality throughout their childhood and adolescence. This book is a good place to start, but there are many other good books at your Christian bookstore. Nearly all of the secular sex education materials available today advocate the philosophy of total sexual indulgence. So our children need to be firmly grounded in the biblical truths of sexuality before they are exposed to such things.

They also need to be made "molestation-proof."[1] The rates of sexual molestation today are incredibly high. Some statistics seem to indicate they are rapidly increasing. Do not let your children become victims!

2. *Learn how to raise sexually healthy kids.* Children pick up their first attitudes about sexuality from their parents by the process of osmosis,

even if nothing is ever said about it. This means that if parents have unhealthy and unholy attitudes about sexuality, this will affect their children. Children's happiness and security with their gender are based primarily on how their parents treat them in their first few years of life. So a parent's first priority in raising sexually healthy children is to *get healthy yourself!* If Mom hates sex and Dad has a pornography habit, this *will* affect your children. I have counseled many Christians who developed sexual problems from being raised in such "fine Christian homes."

Also, learn the signs of developing sexual problems in children. Chapter 10 and the sections on *Homosexuality* and *Gender Disturbance* in Chapter 11 list many of these. The earlier such problems are spotted and the earlier children get help, the greater their likelihood of having no ill effects later in life. Believe me, taking a child to a counselor to get help in overcoming a sexual problem that is just beginning is much more important than taking a child to the orthodontist to get his teeth straightened.

3. *Save your children from becoming casualties of the American youth culture.* This is the greatest catastrophe ever to strike our nation and the cause of incredible destruction in our children's lives. Whole generations are being chewed up and spit out by this monster we have created. Do not let the entertainment industry, the advertising industry, or the public school system raise your child. If you would have to admit, "My kids are strangers to me; we just live under the same roof," then you have already lost this battle. You will have to seek God and work hard to regain this lost territory. May God have mercy on you and your children.

Certainly, home schooling and small Christian schools are the best line of defense in raising your children in a Christian culture. But even if you cannot provide those things, you can still make an entrance for them into the world of Christian adults as they enter puberty. I know this seems like a radical concept, *but do not let your children become "teenagers."* They really do not want to be teenagers; they want to be adults. So give them responsibilities and help them learn adult skills. Children often rebel because their parents will not let them grow up.

What Churches Can Do

1. *Educate your staff.* If you want to shepherd sheep, then you need an understanding of all the problems sheep can get themselves into and how to get them out. Every church should ensure that their pastoral staff understands God's purpose and plan for sex. They should also have a good grasp of the many causes of sexual problems and how they can be resolved. Then the staff must educate the people.

2. *Educate your people.* As described in the sections above, there is a lot that Christians can and must do to keep themselves and their families free from sexual sins and problems. But the church has a responsibility to provide them with information, because God's plan and purpose for sex—the very foundation of holy sexuality—are laid out in the Bible. Church leaders have just shied away from talking about this subject for a century or two, and it shows.

One of the best places to begin addressing this topic is in existing men's and women's groups, such as prayer breakfasts and Bible studies. Men and women often feel more comfortable asking questions or asking for help when they are not in mixed groups. Frequent marriage seminars are another important means of helping those with sexual and other marital problems. Extensive premarital classes and counseling are becoming requirements in many churches. Churches must do more to lower the divorce rate in their own congregations.

Nearly every church has access to Christian counselors or medical professionals, such as doctors and nurses. These people can be a valuable resource in several ways to those who preach and teach. They are accustomed to dealing with sexual matters professionally. They have already overcome a great deal of learned shame about sexual issues. They can help in creating a curriculum for educating Christians about sexual matters from a Christian perspective. They can train parents how to educate their children about sex and how to molestation-proof their children. They can research books and outside speakers as resources for help with marriage, family, and sexual problems.

3. *Begin to address sexual problems among your members.* Once you start talking about holy sexuality and the causes of and cures for sexual problems, people will start coming forward for help. Leaders must have a plan in place to address these needs.

Surely, one of the greatest deceptions at work in the church today is when we preach only the Old Testament message, "Thou shalt not," without also preaching the New Testament "good news." Hearing the law is not a cure for sin; it just makes sin more sinful (Romans 5:20). Christians involved in sexual sin know they are wrong; they just do not know how to stop compulsive behavior, how to get out of their predicament, or how to repair the damage they have caused to themselves and others. Biblical instructions for us to "restore such a one in a spirit of gentleness" (Galatians 6:1 NKJV) and "[pull] them out of the fire" (Jude 23 NKJV) imply a very active intervention, not just saying, "Shame on you. You should not have done that."

Many churches today have gotten out of the "official" counseling ministry because of liability issues. However, lay leaders can still be trained to provide basic information about sexual problems. Just knowing the facts and having a spiritually mature friend to pray with can help many people overcome sexual sin and temptation. Larger churches may even wish to start a recovery group for sexual addiction or homosexuality. There are several national Christian organizations that furnish plans and programs for such groups.

However, there are some sexual problems that are more difficult to deal with and require the assistance of a counselor trained in that area. For this reason churches that do not wish to train their pastoral staff to provide such help should develop a working relationship with a local Christian counselor so they can refer individuals who need additional help.

However, such a referral relationship should not be used as an excuse for church leaders to remain silent on sexual issues and keep sweeping problem people under the rug or out the door. This is why our churches are so filled today with Christians who are secretly suffering from every kind of sexual problem.

4. *Save your children from becoming casualties of the American youth culture.* American youth culture is destroying our children before our very eyes, and most church youth programs are designed to blend right in with it. However, the way our youth dress and the music they listen to is not the real problem. It just reflects the fact that they feel excluded from adult society and so have set about to create their own society. But churches need to review their attitudes toward their youth. We need to examine the "programs" we have created for them to see if we are inflicting more harm than good.

Do we tell them to keep themselves pure, but encourage ten or more years of dating before marriage? That is putting them in a very precarious situation. We should know better than that. There is no scriptural evidence that this is God's plan for managing young adult sexuality.

Have we actually created a separate "youth church" so that the youth have their own worship, their own preacher, and their own activities? There is no scriptural basis for that. If you want to follow the Bible, then your 12- and 13-year-old boys need to be spending time with the men of the church learning how to be Christian men, not spending even more time with each other learning how to be "teenagers." Like all the other 12-year-old boys of His day, Jesus spent much of His time discussing the Bible in the temple or synagogue with the other men. The result was that Jewish society had no generation gap. The same principle goes for the girls. They need to learn how to be Christian women *from the Christian women* (Titus 2:3-4).

I realize this is a radical idea and is going to take some time to digest. Yet, there must come some fundamental changes in the American church, or things will just keep getting worse. The first-century churches were a tight-knit group that formed their own culture in contrast to the culture surrounding them. The result was that the Gospel eventually caused the world to change its culture to match the church culture. Today, it is the other way around. We must get back to our roots.

Notes.

1. The following is a good Christian source for educating your children about sex and making them "molestation-proof": Stanton L. Jones and Brenna B. Jones, *How & When to Tell Your Kids About Sex* (Colorado Springs: NavPress, 1994).

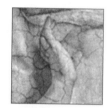

Appendix A

Being Spiritually Reborn

This is how Jesus explained the concept of being spiritually reborn to a religious leader of his day:

> Now there was a man of the Pharisees named Nicodemus, a member of the Jewish ruling council. He came to Jesus at night and said, "Rabbi, we know you are a teacher who has come from God. For no one could perform the miraculous signs you are doing if God were not with him." In reply Jesus declared, "I tell you the truth, no one can see the kingdom of God unless he is born again." "How can a man be born when he is old?" Nicodemus asked. "Surely he cannot enter a second time into his mother's womb to be born!" Jesus answered, "I tell you the truth, no one can enter the kingdom of God unless he is born of water and the Spirit. Flesh gives

birth to flesh, but the Spirit gives birth to spirit. You should not be surprised at my saying, 'You must be born again.' The wind blows wherever it pleases. You hear its sound, but you cannot tell where it comes from or where it is going. So it is with everyone born of the Spirit." (John 3:1-8 NIV)

This spiritual rebirth can only occur when the Spirit of God enters your being and infuses your human spirit with His life. This begins your new life as a child of God and enables you to have a new relationship with Him—as your Father. Once we become His children, He promises that He will never leave us. We will be with Him forever. But until and unless you are reborn, you will remain spiritually dead on the inside, and you cannot truly know God.

If you have not yet established such a relationship with God, then you need to realize that *that is the very reason you were given a lifetime on this earth*. Everyone must ask himself this question at some point in his life: "Do I want to know God?" If so, then he must ask, "How can I come to know Him?"

This is the very reason that God came to earth, becoming a man in the person of Jesus Christ. As a man, He lived life like we do, with all of its pains and problems, "yet was without sin" (Hebrews 4:15 NIV). He taught us His perspective on life, which was much different than people had ever imagined. He showed us how much He loves us, and how much He wants us to know and love Him. Then, in the ultimate sacrifice a man can make, He gave His life for us in a way that allowed Him, as the God-man, to take the punishment for all the sins and crimes we humans have ever committed, whether against others, against ourselves, or against God Himself. (This enabled God, who is also the Judge of the Universe, to offer us forgiveness for our wrongs instead of punishment, because He has already taken the punishment we deserve upon Himself.) After this, Jesus rose from the dead, guaranteeing that He will someday come back to raise up the bodies of believers who have died. In addition, believers who are still alive on the earth will then "meet the Lord in the air" (1 Thessalonians 4:17 NKJV). How wonderful that all believers will go to live with God forever!

Whether you have sexual problems or not, we want you to know this: *Jesus has great love for you!* He is the answer to all the questions you have been asking about your life. He is that missing piece to the puzzle of your heart. He is the key that will unlock whatever chains hold you captive. He never intended that you should have to live the life of pain, loneliness, emptiness, and sorrow that you have endured until now. We would like you to meet Him.

If you want Him to forgive you of your sins, cause your spirit to be reborn, and send His Spirit to live inside of you, then just ask Him! The only requirement is that you believe He truly was who He said He was, and that you ask Him to be your Lord (your "boss"), which means you are willing to do whatever He asks you to do from now on.

You can do this right now while reading this book or anytime. Wherever you are, He will hear you, and I promise you that your life will never be the same again.

B

Appendix B

Facts You Have Never Been Told about Sexually Transmitted Diseases

1. The prevalence of sexually transmitted diseases (STDs):

> • In addition to 25 well-known STDs, there are literally hundreds more that few doctors are even aware of. Researchers are finding that these little known STDs are actually quite common and that they cause serious chronic and deadly diseases, such as cancer.
> • Not including AIDS, there are 333 million new cases of STDs each year worldwide.[1]
> • The United States has the highest rate of STDs in the industrialized world—50 to 100 times greater than other industrialized countries. It is estimated that the U.S. spends 17 billion dollars each year treating these STDs and their aftereffects.[2]
> • Twelve million new cases of STDs are reported to the U.S. Centers for Disease Control (CDC) each year. Many more go unreported because two-thirds cannot be detected without a specific

test.[3] Eighty-five percent of the infectious diseases reported to the CDC are STDs.[4]

• Three million of these STD cases (25%) occur in teenagers, 13–19 years old.[5] That means 1 in 6 teens aged 13–19 contracts an STD every year. Eighty-six percent of all cases occur in young people 15–29.[6]

• One respected survey showed that, of those surveyed, 1 in 5 Americans aged 25–49 admitted having had an STD.[7] However, another study found that while only 2% of Americans *admit* to having genital herpes, testing of blood samples has shown that 22% of Americans *actually have* genital herpes.[8] That is more than a 1 in 5 infection rate, just for genital herpes, not to mention the 2 out of 5 Americans that have oral herpes.

2. All STDs (not just HIV) are serious diseases that eventually lead to many chronic and even fatal illnesses.

Many people think of STDs as inconvenient, but harmless, like having the flu. When you feel sick, you go to the doctor to get some medicine. Then you get over it and go on with your life.

Nothing could be further from the truth. Most STDs cause serious, permanent, lifelong damage to your body, and many lead to an early death. The popular media (and even STD education programs) tend to perpetuate the attitude, "Go ahead and sleep with whomever you want, but use a condom and go to a free clinic if you get sick." Well, besides the fact that condoms can leak and break, have a 30% failure rate in preventing HIV, and are only about 85% effective in preventing pregnancies, they *cannot and do not* protect you from many of the viral STDs.

Common long-term consequences of STDs include:

• sterility
• cervical cancer
• liver cancer
• leukemia
• anal cancer
• cirrhosis of the liver (a gradual scarring and destruction of the liver leading to total liver failure)
• arthritis
• blindness, neurological defects, bone deformity,

mental retardation, and death for infants whose mothers were infected during pregnancy

Recent discoveries have caused researchers to suspect that many of our most troubling and crippling diseases, such as atherosclerosis (hardening of the arteries) and various autoimmune disorders, such as multiple sclerosis, are caused by hidden bacterial and viral infections. All these may be transmittable through an exchange of bodily fluids.

The following are the most common STDs in America today.

Viral STDs

The STDs caused by viruses are incurable. Once you contract a viral STD, you will have it for the rest of your life. Most viral STDs will shorten your life while giving you chronic pain and illness.

WARNING: CONDOMS DO NOT PROTECT YOU FROM SOME VIRAL STDs. Skin contact is all that is necessary to transmit genital herpes, HPV (human papilloma virus), and some forms of hepatitis. Some viral STDs can be transmitted through kissing where there is an exchange of saliva.

Herpes

There are two variants of the herpes virus:

- Herpes Type 1 (herpes simplex virus 1 or HSV1), which is the usual cause of "cold sores" in and around the mouth
- Herpes Type 2 (herpes simplex virus 2 or HSV2), which typically causes painful sores in the genital area

However, *either of these viruses can infect both the mouth and genital areas and can be spread from one place to the other through oral sex.* The two types can only be distinguished by a laboratory test.

Herpes is the most common STD in the United States. As many as 500,000 new genital herpes infections are believed to occur each year.[9] It has been estimated that 55 million Americans (22%) have genital herpes (*that is more than 1 in 5*).[10] Around 40% of Americans aged 29 or below (*that is 2 out of 5*) are infected with Herpes Type 1.[11]

There is no cure for herpes. Once infected, a person will experience periodic outbreaks of painful sores throughout his life. When the virus finds an opening in sensitive skin, it invades the nerves and travels to your spinal column where it lives for the rest of your life. During times of stress or other illness, the virus then travels back out through the nerves causing sores at the original site of infection. It may also spread through the nerves to other places on the body. Herpes virus has been found in brain lesions, so it may play a role in some diseases of the brain and nervous system.

The herpes virus is spread through contact with infected skin. CONDOMS DO NOT PREVENT THE SPREAD OF GENITAL HERPES, since they do not cover all the skin surfaces that may be infected. The virus is most contagious when sores are present, but the virus is present and can be passed on *even when there are no visible sores*. The virus can also infect any other skin area where there is a cut or opening, such as the hands, eyes, back, abdomen, buttocks, or anus.

In the U.S., HSV is the most frequent cause of blindness due to corneal damage. It is the most common cause of encephalitis (infection of the brain) and frequently causes meningitis (infection of the membranes surrounding the brain and spine). It can also infect and damage other organs in the body.

Genital herpes is particularly dangerous to babies born to infected mothers. Most infected mothers are not even aware that they have herpes. It usually infects the infant's brain and nervous system, causing blindness, neurological defects, mental retardation, and often death. Without proper treatment, it is estimated that 65% of infected newborns will die. Even with the proper treatment, 25% die anyway. Less than 10% of infected infants will ever be normal, even with the best care.[12]

Human Papilloma Virus (HPV)

It is estimated that 25 million Americans (10%) are now infected with HPV.[13] One million new cases of HPV are reported in the U.S. each year, but many more go unreported because the initial symptoms may be so mild as to go unnoticed. This group of viruses is now believed to be responsible for 95% of all cases of cervical cancer and many cases of anal cancer.

More than seventy different strains of this virus have been discovered in humans.[14] Some of these strains will produce visible warts anywhere on the body, including the genital area, but other varieties produce abnormal growths so small that they are virtually invisible. Visible warts can be removed, though with some difficulty if they are located inside the mouth, anus, or genital openings. However, the strains that do not produce visible warts are believed to be the most likely to cause cancer.

There is no cure for HPV. Once infected, you will have it for the rest of your life. You will have repeated occurrences of genital warts, and you can infect all future sex partners. CONDOMS DO NOT PROVIDE PROTECTION AGAINST HPV. It can be transmitted just by contact with infected skin. As with herpes, skin infected with HPV remains infectious, shedding virus particles that can infect others, even when there are no warts visible.

Even worse, many people eventually contract cancer in whatever part of their body was infected. Women whose reproductive tracts have been infected with HPV have many abnormal growths. Doctors recommend that they have a pap smear every six months for the rest of their lives to detect these abnormal growths so they can be removed before they develop into cancer.[15]

Researchers have found that Southern Asian societies have some of the highest rates of cervical cancer in the world, and HPV is believed to be responsible. Like many societies, they have a double standard: girls are closely supervised to make sure they remain virgins, while young men are allowed to have sex with prostitutes. Sadly, research has shown that many men become infected with HPV through prostitutes, and they infect their wives shortly after marriage. Years later, many of these innocent wives and mothers develop cervical cancer.[16]

Hepatitis

Six types of hepatitis have been discovered so far: A, B, C, D, E, and G. They all infect and damage the liver. Types A and E are usually spread through consuming food or water contaminated with infected fecal material. All other types are spread through contaminated bodily fluids.

Upon infection, these viruses cause serious illness for up to four months. Patients usually exhibit jaundice, which indicates some degree of liver failure, but many people become carriers of the virus after having initial symptoms that are so mild they just think they had a case of the flu. Any infection with types B–E may become chronic and eventually result in cirrhosis and liver cancer over the course of a lifetime.

Hepatitis B (HBV)

Hepatitis B is second only to the AIDS virus in the number of people it kills annually. Each year, more than 300,000 Americans, mostly young adults, contract it. It is estimated that the U.S. currently has one million people who are infectious carriers of hepatitis B. Worldwide, it is a major cause of liver cirrhosis and liver cancer. It is transmitted through contact with contaminated body fluids. Intimate sexual contact is not even required. People who are in frequent contact with carriers can contract it.[17] There is now a vaccine available, but few people take advantage of it.[18]

Hepatitis D (HDV) is a variant of hepatitis B and is often found along with HBV.

Hepatitis C (HCV)

Hepatitis C was first identified in 1990. Before that time, it was classified as non-A, non-B hepatitis because the tests for HAV and HBV failed to detect it. Of those who received blood transfusions before 1992—when the HCV blood test became available—it is believed that as many as 20% were infected through contaminated blood. Recent surveys now estimate that *four million* Americans are chronic carriers of HCV.[19] Eighty to ninety percent of intravenous drug users show signs of infection with HVC. This disease kills 8,000–10,000 Americans annually, and *some expect the number of deaths attributable to it will exceed deaths from AIDS within a few years.*

HCV is believed to be passed on primarily through contact with contaminated bodily fluids, including intimate sexual contact. However, there is some evidence that people living in the same household are at some risk for contracting HCV from infected family members.[20] Those who frequently work with HCV carriers, such as health care professionals, are also at increased risk for contracting it. It is estimated that 1% of health care workers are currently infected.[21]

HCV eventually causes liver cirrhosis and liver cancer in those infected by it, but symptoms may not appear until ten to thirty years after infection. There is currently no vaccine to prevent infection. Active cases of the disease can be somewhat relieved with drug therapy, but there is no known cure. Once infected, you will carry the virus for the remainder of your life.

Hepatitis G has been discovered only recently, but it seems similar to hepatitis C in its destructive activity. It is quite likely that there are still more undiscovered forms of hepatitis in the blood supply. The risk for contracting hepatitis G and other still-undiscovered types of hepatitis is estimated at around 4% for those who receive transfusions or blood products.

Epstein-Barr Virus (EBV)

It is estimated that most of the population of industrialized countries have been infected with this virus by adulthood. Teenagers frequently contract this disease when they start dating. All it takes is kissing an infected person on the mouth and you will come down with mononucleosis (the "kissing disease"). Our culture views this lightly as a "rite of passage," but it is much more serious than most people realize. Mononucleosis makes you sick and weak for several months. During that time your liver is being damaged and your spleen swells. It can easily burst, which is a life-threatening event. Meanwhile, the EBV virus is busy infecting white blood cells, which can cause anemia and several other blood abnormalities. It can also infect the brain, causing encephalitis and paralysis.

Once infected, you remain contagious for the next year and a half, long after recovering from the initial symptoms. But even worse, EBV infects your white blood cells and remains in your body for the rest of your life. As you grow older, the virus can break out again and cause several types of *lymphoma*, which is cancer of the immune system (two possible types are Burkitt's and non-Hodgkin's).[22] All this from kissing one person too many!

Cytomegalovirus (CMV)

This is one of the most common STDs. Studies have shown that nearly 100% of prostitutes and sexually active homosexual men have been infected with this virus. It is estimated that 1% of newborns are infected by their mothers while still in the womb, and many show birth defects as a result. One of the effects in newborns can be life-threatening pneumonia.

In adults CMV can cause mononucleosis, similar to EBV. Once you are infected, CMV remains in your body for life, infecting many different organs and all bodily fluids. If your immune system ever becomes weakened—through severe illness, receiving an organ transplant, or contracting AIDS—CMV goes on a rampage, causing widespread destruction of many organs. This is a major cause of death in AIDS patients and the leading cause of blindness in them.[23]

There is also a growing body of evidence that CMV plays a significant role in causing heart disease—as significant a role as high cholesterol, some researchers believe. CMV has been found in many plaques recovered from clogged arteries. CMV-infected heart patients who have had their arteries reamed out through angioplasty are five times more likely to have them close up again within six months, when compared with similar patients who are not CMV-infected. CMV-infected heart transplant patients are twice as likely to die of heart disease within five years than similar uninfected patients.[24]

HTLV-I

This virus is a relative of HIV, the AIDS virus. It is found in many parts of the world, and is particularly common in Africa, Jamaica, and Japan. It causes adult T-cell leukemia, a disease that is not easily treatable and is usually fatal. The leukemia may not appear until years after the initial infection. This virus can be passed in bodily fluids between sex partners and from mother to child.[25]

HTLV-II

This virus is related to HTLV-I and also to HIV. It causes hairy cell leukemia, which may not appear until years after the initial infection and is usually fatal. This virus can be passed in bodily fluids between sex partners and from mother to child.[26]

HHV-6

Human herpes virus 6 is a newly discovered virus. It is spread through saliva and other body fluids. HHV-6 is believed to cause oral cancer, many types of lymphoma, brain cancer, liver failure, and chronic fatigue syndrome (CFS). It destroys immune system cells, infects all organs of the body, causes blood-clotting disorders, and causes the bodies of transplant patients to reject their new organ.[27] Recent research presented to the American Neurological Society provides strong evidence that HHV-6 is the cause of multiple sclerosis.[28]

HHV-8

Human herpes virus 8 is now known to be the cause of Kaposi's sarcoma, a formerly rare type of cancer of the blood vessels that occurs frequently in people with AIDS. This virus can be passed on through body fluids independently of HIV, and it is believed that a high percentage of sexually active gay men are currently infected. When the immune system of anyone infected with HHV-8 becomes weakened—whether through ill health, chemotherapy, an organ transplant, or AIDS—the virus then produces the ugly tumors that are the calling card of Kaposi's sarcoma.[29] There is also evidence to implicate HHV-8 in causing the chronic disease sarcoidosis.[30]

Human Immunodeficiency Virus (HIV), Which Causes Acquired Immune Deficiency Syndrome (AIDS)

There are two recognized HIV viruses (HIV-1, HIV-2), each with many variants. All gradually destroy the immune system, perhaps with the help of certain other viruses, like CMV and herpes, that may already be in the infected person's body. Once the immune system has been destroyed, an HIV-infected person is considered to have AIDS. More than 33 million people worldwide are infected with HIV, and 6 million new cases are expected this year. In some countries, approximately 1 out of every 4 adults is infected. It is believed that HIV is ultimately fatal in all who are infected, except for a very small number of people who receive a weakened version of the virus. So far, 64% of all people ever diagnosed with AIDS have died.[31]

Current estimates are that up to 50,000 new HIV infections occur each year in the United States. According to the U.S. Centers for Disease Control, 1 out of every 300 Americans (one-third of 1% of the population) is already infected. However, infection rates are drastically different for each sex, since 1 in 160 males aged 13 and older are infected versus only 1 in 800 females aged 13 and older.[32] Among American men 17–22 years old who have had same-gender sex, it is estimated that *around 10% are already infected with HIV*.[33] Nearly one-fifth of all HIV cases occur among young people between the ages of 13 and 29.[34]

However, shocking new evidence indicates that *2 out of 3 people who are currently infected with HIV do not even know it and may be infecting others*, since their infection is not yet detectable by current blood tests.[35] These results confirm other research that has shown that HIV can persist in the genital tracts of men and women, enabling them to pass the virus on to sex partners, even though their bloodstreams are free of the virus.[36]

HIV has been found in all bodily fluids, including saliva and mothers' milk. It is most often transmitted sexually but can be transmitted through nonsexual means, such as leakage from skin wounds or contact with contaminated blood. **The U.S. Centers for Disease Control even warns that open-mouth kissing, where saliva is exchanged, is a potential means of infection.**

Having any other additional STD puts a promiscuous person at a 3–5 times greater risk for catching HIV because other STDs cause sores and inflammation that allow the HIV virus to enter the body more easily.[37] (This includes STDs like chlamydia that cause few symptoms.)

Once the immune system has been destroyed by HIV, any other viruses, fungi, or bacteria in the body are free to grow unhindered, consuming all bodily tissues and organs until death ensues. Some of the most frequent infections are bacterial and viral pneumonia; Kaposi's sarcoma (caused by HHV-8 infection); brain infections, which result in dementia; herpes infections; and eye infections of CMV, which result in blindness.[38]

HIV May Not Be the Only Factor Destroying the Immune System, Resulting in AIDS.

There is a small, but respected, group of scientists (Peter Duesberg, Kary Mullis, and others) who have found evidence that HIV is not the only cause of AIDS.[39] HIV may require a "helping hand" from other factors to produce full-blown AIDS. These other factors may even be able to produce some cases of AIDS without HIV being present. The other factors that seem to work together in destroying the immune system are various other viruses and bacteria, drug abuse, and contact with the immune system components (antigens) from other people's blood and bodily fluids.

To summarize, researchers have found cases where people died of full-blown AIDS with Kaposi's sarcoma, pneumocystis carinii pneumonia (PCP), and AIDS dementia, but *never tested positive for HIV*. There is some evidence that the following factors may work with or without HIV to cause AIDS symptoms:

- Human herpes virus 6 (HHV-6) infects a considerable portion of the population. But when someone with HHV-6 acquires

HIV, HHV-6 becomes deadly, causing widespread destruction of T cells and most organs of the body.[40]
- *Mycoplasma fermentans*, a bacterium, has been found to work with HIV to help kill T cells.
- Kaposi's sarcoma is now known to be caused by a different virus, HHV-8; it can occur in people infected with HHV-8, even if they do not have AIDS.[41]
- "Poppers" (amyl and butyl nitrite inhalants often used by many gay men to increase their sexual pleasure) and other abused drugs, such as heroin, have shown the ability to suppress the immune system even without HIV being present.
- Hemophiliacs in the 1960s and 1970s came down with AIDS-like illnesses before HIV is known to have arrived in this country. It is believed that the clotting factor they were given was contaminated with foreign proteins that suppressed their immune systems. Other studies have shown that just receiving a transfusion of another person's blood can temporarily suppress the immune system.
- Some researchers believe that the proteins found in semen can suppress the immune system. Gay men who have had many partners and been recipients of anal sex have shown evidence of a suppressed immune system without having HIV.

At the very least, all of these additional factors illustrate just how harmful a lifestyle of drug abuse and promiscuity can be.

Can AIDS Be Cured?

Researchers no longer talk about a "cure" for AIDS. They have discovered that the virus is just too cunning in its ability to hide within the body's longest-lived cells. Some researchers have estimated that if an infected person could take drugs to suppress the virus continuously *for 60 years*, only then might it be cleared from the body. The only hope they now offer for infected people is "management" of the disease to prolong life with expensive and complex "drug cocktails."

However, a new threat is on the horizon. The drug cocktails that many hoped would cure AIDS are now showing their limitations. The first AIDS cases that are resistant to these drugs, and thus untreatable, have already been found. Researchers traced the origins of these cases to gay men who were taking the drug cocktail and still having unprotected sex. By doing this, they passed on to their sex partners a mutated version of the virus that is resistant to all known drugs. They have essentially created a "super-AIDS." It is estimated that 20-30% of all new HIV infections are now resistant to at least one commonly used drug, while 10% show resistance to two or more drugs.[42]

Even if HIV is eventually made controllable with drugs, only relatively rich countries will be able to afford them. The poorest countries, which have the highest rates of infection, will continue to suffer and the epidemic will continue to spread *unless people stop being promiscuous.* Simply following God's laws of sexual purity would virtually eliminate this terrible plague within a decade.

Bacterial STDs

STDs caused by bacteria are just as serious and as deadly as those caused by viruses, but most can be treated with antibiotics. The only problem is that many of these bacterial STDs have so few symptoms that the infected person does not seek treatment until after much internal damage has been done. Many of these bacteria are also becoming resistant to known antibiotics and may eventually be untreatable.

Chlamydia

Chlamydia is one of the most common STDs. There are 4 million new cases in the U.S. each year. Almost half (46%) of all new cases occur in young women 15-19 years old. An astounding 80% of all cases have been found to occur in women 15-24 years old. The total estimate of infections would be higher if men were tested for this, but they rarely are, even though they are often carriers.

The symptoms of chlamydia are so mild that 50% of men and 75% of women never realize they have been infected. Sadly, when untreated, it causes permanent damage to the female reproductive organs through pelvic inflammatory disease (PID), an infection of the ovaries, fallopian tubes, and abdomen.[43] PID scars the Fallopian tubes, which carry eggs from the ovaries to the uterus, either making the woman sterile or causing a future ectopic pregnancy (where the embryo implants somewhere in the abdomen besides the uterus). Ectopic pregnancy is the primary cause of first trimester pregnancy-related deaths in American women. Over 100,000 cases of ectopic pregnancy occur in the United States each year, and the number is steadily increasing. It is estimated that at least 50% of these ectopic pregnancies are caused by STD-related damage.[44]

Chlamydia can also lead to chronic abdominal pain[45] and can eventually cause arthritis. Babies born to infected mothers can suffer from eye infections and pneumonia. The cost of untreated chlamydia and its complications is over two billion dollars a year.[46]

Based on the statistics above, nearly 2 million girls between the ages of 15–19 each year put themselves at risk for becoming sterile or for having abnormal, life-threatening pregnancies. The CDC recommends that all women who are sexually active be tested for chlamydia annually.[47]

Gonorrhea

There are 800,000 new cases of gonorrhea diagnosed every year in the U.S.[48] It is often a "silent disease" in women—98% of infected women have no symptoms. This means that they do not get treatment and eventually suffer permanent damage to their reproductive organs. Like chlamydia, gonorrhea leads to pelvic inflammatory disease (PID). This results in sterility, ectopic pregnancies, and chronic abdominal pain.

Gonorrhea can also infect the throat, anus, skin, and eyes, and can even lead to death.[49] It can also infect the joints and cause arthritis. Gonorrhea causes serious infections and even blindness in infants who are born to infected mothers. Because gonorrhea is so common in America, all newborns are routinely given eye drops to prevent blindness just in case the mother was infected.[50]

Some strains of gonorrhea have now developed resistance to penicillin and must be treated with other drugs. It is likely that some strains will eventually develop resistance to all known antibiotics and thus become incurable.

Syphilis

It is estimated that there are 100,000 new syphilis infections in the U.S. each year.[51] Syphilis can cause heart disease, brain damage, blindness, and death.[52] For women who are infected while pregnant, 40% of their babies die before birth, and 40% of the babies who survive have permanent damage.[53]

The law requires doctors to report the names of those infected with gonorrhea and syphilis to the local health department so workers can follow up and make sure that all sex partners of the patient get treatment. This is a reasonable measure designed to maintain public health by preventing the spread of disease. Yet this procedure is not followed for those infected with HIV, which is far more of a threat to public health. Incredibly, current law says that only those infected with HIV have the right to decide whether or not to inform their sex partners so they can receive testing and treatment. This is yet another example of the power of the gay political lobby. Tragically, a recent survey reveals that two-thirds of HIV-infected people continue to have sex without always using a condom, and 40% never tell their sex partners that they are infected.[54]

Bacterial Vaginosis

It has recently been discovered that when women have multiple sex partners, their sexual organs become infected with many different types of bacteria. The full effects of all these bacteria are not yet known, but it has been shown that such infections increase a pregnant woman's chance of delivering a premature infant by 40%. These bacteria also cause PID, which leads to sterility; they can infect the fetus if the woman is pregnant, and they give her a 50-times greater risk of contracting HIV from an infected partner.[55]

3. As if these STDS were not bad enough, scientists are now discovering many more infectious agents in the human bloodstream that may be responsible for most, if not all, of the major chronic and degenerative diseases. It is likely that all these disease agents can be transmitted sexually.

Hundreds of New Viruses Have Been Discovered

During their search for the cause of AIDS, researchers found hundreds of unidentified viruses in the blood supply. They have not yet determined what diseases they cause, but some researchers suspect they could be "slow viruses"—that is, it may take many years of infection before they cause noticeable damage. These slow viruses could be responsible for many types of cancers and degenerative diseases—such as multiple sclerosis,

Parkinson's, Alzheimer's, chronic fatigue syndrome, arthritis—that may not show up until many years later. These viruses may even be handed down in families from one generation to the next, causing the same disease in many generations. (HTLV-I and HTLV-II, described earlier, are examples of slow viruses known to run in families.)

"Stealth" Bacteria Are Believed to Cause Atherosclerosis (Heart Disease)

Surprisingly, a bacterial infection in blood vessel walls is now believed to be a leading contributor to America's number one killer, atherosclerosis (heart disease). These bacteria are able to evade our immune system and actually *live in* the white blood cells that fight disease. As these infected white blood cells try to clean up cholesterol deposits in the arteries, the bacteria inside them invade the blood vessel walls and cause inflammation. This inflammation is what eventually leads to a clogged artery and a heart attack or stroke.

New "Stealth" Viruses Are Being Discovered

Dr. John Martin has discovered a new family of viruses called stealth viruses. The term "stealth" is used because these viruses are able to evade the human immune system—your body never knows it's infected. These viruses move from cell to cell, destroying them as they go. They primarily infect the brain. These viruses were first identified in the brains and spinal fluid of people suffering from chronic fatigue syndrome. They have since been isolated in people suffering from cancer, depression, dementia, fibromyalgia, multiple sclerosis, schizophrenia, and even autism. It seems likely that stealth viruses play a role in causing some types of brain disorders or mental illnesses. It is not yet known how contagious these viruses are, but it is likely that they can be transmitted sexually, as are most bloodborne viruses.[56]

Newly Discovered Infectious Proteins (Prions) Can Cause Terrible Diseases

Because of the outbreak of "Mad Cow" disease in Great Britain, scientists now know that certain proteins called *prions* can cause diseases. These prions can be spread from one person to another or from an animal to a person, but the disease may not show up for decades. The fear in Great Britain is that over a million people may have eaten beef contaminated with these prions (since they cannot be destroyed by cooking) and will eventually contract the human version of the disease, called *Creutzfeldt-Jakob* disease, which is incurable and gradually destroys the brain.

An FDA advisory panel is now recommending that Americans who lived in Great Britain for more than six months between 1980 and 1996 be permanently barred from donating blood, since they might have become infected during that time and the disease is believed to be transmittable through blood transfusions. The American Red Cross reports that 23 percent of U.S. blood donors visited Great Britain between 1980 and 1996.[57] It is not yet known whether prions can be transmitted sexually, but since they are blood-borne, there seems to be a potential risk.

Animal Viruses: Why God Prohibited Consuming Animal Blood

We can now better understand God's Old Testament prohibition of consuming animal blood. As the Scripture says, "For the life of the flesh is in the blood" (Leviticus 17:11 NKJV). For over a hundred years, scientists have known of many animal viruses that can be passed to humans through blood and bodily fluids. These viruses are usually quite harmless to the animals, but are often quite harmful to us.

Unfortunately, in their zeal to prevent disease, medical research transgressed God's principle for keeping the human bloodstream pure. Over the past fifty years, the process of vaccine manufacturing has used living animal tissues, some of which were ultimately discovered to have been infected with animal viruses. This contaminated some batches of vaccines, particularly the smallpox vaccines. Though these vaccines were effective in preventing many deaths from disease, they have also now infected millions of people worldwide with little understood animal viruses. This problem was first discovered by researchers in the 1960s, but the U.S. government kept the information from the public. Incredibly, the FDA has still not required any changes in the vaccine development process. So this viral contamination of vaccines is still occurring today. For example, in 1995 a patient was found to be infected with a monkey virus (SCMV), evidently from a polio vaccination. This was reported to the FDA, but no new testing of polio vaccines has been required.

If you were ever given the injected polio vaccine instead of the oral vaccine, it is possible that you have been infected with a monkey virus.

Monkey cell cultures were used to create that vaccine. Some batches were found to be contaminated with SIV-9, which is the monkey version of HIV. Another monkey virus, SV-40, was detected in polio vaccines beginning in the 1960s. Recent tests have shown that 23% of Americans are now infected with this virus, most likely through contaminated polio vaccines. This virus has been found in human seminal fluid, so it is believed that the virus will be passed on to sex partners and to future generations. SV-40 is particularly disturbing because it has already been found in many brain, lung, and bone tumors and is believed to have been the cause of those tumors.[58]

These animal viruses have added to the number of viruses that can be sexually transmitted. As yet, people are rarely tested for these viruses, so we do not really know how many Americans are infected. We also do not know what these animal viruses will ultimately do to those who are infected.[59] HIV started out as a harmless monkey virus that was passed to humans and eventually became a deadly plague.

Many Unknown Infectious Agents Are in the Bloodstreams of the General Population

We need to realize that, despite the advances of modern medicine, there are still many unknown or unstudied infectious agents in the bloodstreams of the general population. It is quite likely that most of these agents will ultimately have harmful effects. Since these unknown viruses, bacteria, or prions exist in the bloodstream, they can permeate all bodily fluids, such as saliva, tears, semen, and vaginal fluids. When you exchange bodily fluids with another person through intercourse or even kissing, you are mingling your bloodstreams. You are exchanging all the infectious agents that are present in each person's body.

For example, a one-time sex partner could infect you with a virus that has been handed down in his family for generations and causes some type of cancer or degenerative disease. Because the disease does not show up until decades after the initial infection, no one ever realizes the connection. But once infected, you are doomed to pass that disease on to *your* children and your children's children and all their descendants. *This is not a hypothetical situation.* HTLV-I and HTLV-II are just two known examples of viral diseases that work in this manner. There are likely to be many more not yet discovered.

It is beginning to look like the ancient concept of a "generational curse" has a basis in medical fact. If your ancestors obeyed God's laws of sexual purity, then they have passed on to you a pure bloodstream. But if any of them transgressed His law of sexual purity, then they may have contaminated their blood, and that of all their descendants, with illnesses that can cause much suffering and even early death.

Can you see now how serious sexual sin is? Through having sex with only one person who is not a virgin, you can permanently contaminate your own body and bring the curse of a disease on all your descendants. But even worse, the more people you have sex with, the more of these infectious agents you will collect in your bloodstream.

Most people do not think about this, but when you have sex with someone, as far as STDs are concerned, you are having sex with every sex partner they have ever had, and every sex partner their sex partners' ever had, and so on. Researchers have calculated the statistics on this. For example, if you have had six sexual partners and each of them had an equal number of partners, then you have been exposed to the STDs, not just of your six partners, *but of a total of 63 people*. If you have had nine sexual partners, then you have been exposed to the STDs of *511 people*.[60] The numbers grow exponentially. It is not just simple multiplication.

These numbers are very realistic and, when combined with the statistics on teen promiscuity, show that teenagers are particularly at risk for having their lives ruined or destroyed by STDs. In 1993, it was estimated that 53% of all high school students had had sexual intercourse at least once, but only half of these said they had used a condom.[61] Among sexually active teenagers 18–19 years old, nearly 25% of girls report having 6 or more partners, and nearly 20% of boys report having 6–10 partners.[62]

The sad truth is that people who have had sex with many partners are doomed to a shortened, disease-ridden life, since they accumulate so many different blood-borne diseases from all of their partners and their partners' partners. Such a lifestyle results in literally hundreds of different disease organisms floating around in a promiscuous person's bloodstream—they become walking septic tanks. Even if HIV can be eventually suppressed through drugs (for those who can afford them), promiscuous people will always be afflicted with many diseases that cause suffering and shorten the life span.

American blood banks have learned an important lesson from a terrible tragedy: blood testing is just not enough. Since blood banks can only test for diseases that are already known and for which tests have been developed, they were unable to prevent millions of innocent people from becoming infected with hepatitis C and HIV through blood transfusions before those diseases were recognized. As a result of this tragedy, American blood banks have instituted a policy to reduce the future risk of contaminated blood by refusing to accept blood from people they consider most likely to be carriers of new and unknown diseases. *They include in this category any man who has had sex with another man since 1977 or has injected drugs of abuse.*

These medical professionals realize that intravenous drug abuse and homosexual sex practices have created a pool of men infected with huge numbers of as-yet-unknown disease agents that will likely spawn the new plagues of the coming decades. However, gay political groups see this policy not as a reasonable medical decision designed to protect public health, but as a violation of their "right" to donate blood and an insult to their chosen lifestyle. So some are actually fighting to overturn this policy through legal means.[63]

In any case, many surgeons now recommend that those undergoing surgery have blood donated specifically for their surgery by trusted family members. The risk of contracting unknown viruses from the public blood banks is just too great.

4. Virologists now believe that rampant promiscuity in any society actually creates new and more deadly STDS.

Here is the reason that the above statement is true: Most viruses and bacteria mutate over time so that new generations of these viruses and bacteria are different from their ancestors in some way. This explains why we catch several colds each year and perhaps the flu. Our bodies learn to recognize and fight off each cold or flu virus we contract, but there is always a new mutated version on the way that our bodies have never seen before. Some mutations make a virus more deadly and some make it less deadly. (Recall the great flu epidemics of the past that killed hundreds of thousands worldwide in 1918 and 1957. These were examples of how the flu virus can mutate in ways that make it more likely to kill.) When a virus kills quickly—like the Ebola virus, which kills its victims within 48 hours—it does not have a chance to spread very far, so it dies out with its last victim. If a virus kills very slowly—say, it causes liver cancer 30 years after infection—it will obviously have many more chances to be passed on to many more people.

Based on this fact, many virologists now believe that when a society begins to pass viruses around more rapidly—such as through increased promiscuity and intravenous drug use—they are actually helping viruses mutate into more and more deadly forms. This is what seems to have happened with HIV. This virus has been found in African blood samples dating back to 1959 and is believed to have been widespread there for perhaps hundreds of years. It was passed from monkeys to humans through eating undercooked monkey meat. Yet, the first AIDS cases were not reported until the early 1980s and first occurred in the larger African cities. What happened to make HIV deadly?

The most likely explanation seems to be this: In the 1960s, as Africans began to move in large numbers to the cities, rates of promiscuity and STD infections skyrocketed. Also, anal sex became commonly practiced as a means of birth control, and this practice provides a direct path into the bloodstream for infection. Such conditions allowed HIV to be passed around faster than it ever had before, so it could keep mutating—growing more and more deadly—until a new mutation produced the first AIDS case in the early 1980s.[64]

Another contributing factor is that HIV is the most rapidly mutating virus scientists have ever seen. This explains why researchers have had such difficulty finding drugs to fight it and so far have failed to produce a vaccine. HIV constantly mutates in an infected person, so that there are several different versions present at any one time. A drug may kill one version of the virus but not the others, which then continue to grow and mutate. This also explains why some HIV-positive individuals get full-blown AIDS and die rapidly, while others continue for years without any symptoms. In some people the virus randomly mutates into a more deadly form, while in others it mutates into a less deadly form.

A study published in 1997 showed that HIV is becoming more deadly worldwide. It found that those infected in the early 1990s developed full-blown AIDS much more rapidly than those infected in the early 1980s. Another study revealed that the HIV strain passed around by intravenous drug users has become more deadly and now kills people more quickly than the strains passed on by homosexual men. Researchers believe this difference has developed because intravenous drug users share contaminated needles with each other more frequently than most gay men have sex.[65]

Bottom Line

Even if HIV is eventually controlled by drugs or even wiped out by a vaccination program, it will not really matter as long as sexual promiscuity continues to be widely practiced. Already hundreds more viruses are being passed around among promiscuous people. These viruses are growing more deadly all the time and are destined to take HIV's place as major plagues. Those people who have many sex partners or who abuse intravenous drugs may not realize it, but they are the ones responsible for breeding these killer diseases, enabling them to become even more deadly and then unleashing them on the rest of society. In this way all of us end up paying the price for the sins of a minority.

Notes.

1. "The Challenge of STD Prevention in the United States," *AIDS Weekly Plus*, 10 February 1997, 25. Also, a summary of a report by the Institute of Medicine, "The Hidden Epidemic: Confronting Sexually Transmitted Diseases" (Washington, DC: National Academy Press, 1977).

2. Ibid.

3. Debora L. Shelton, "Sex Turns Dangerous," *American Medical News*, 3 February 1997, 11.

4. "The Challenge of STD Prevention in the United States," 25 (see note 1).

5. Ibid.

6. "Sexually Transmitted Diseases Which Strike Millions Each Year," Knight-Ridder/Tribune News Service, 16 March 1994.

7. E. O. Laumann et al., *The Social Organization of Sexuality: Sexual Practices in the United States* (Chicago: University of Chicago Press, 1994), 383.

8. Deborah L. Shelton, "STDs: A 'Hidden Epidemic,'" *American Medical News*, 9 December 1996, 1. Also, a summary of a report by the Institute of Medicine, "The Hidden Epidemic: Confronting Sexually Transmitted Diseases" (see note 1).

9. "The Challenge of STD Prevention in the United States," 25 (see note 1).

10. Shelton, "STDs: A 'Hidden Epidemic'" (see note 8).

11. *Harrison's Principles of Internal Medicine*, 11th ed. (New York: McGraw-Hill, 1987), 693-696.

12. Ibid.

13. "The Challenge of STD Prevention in the United States," 25 (see note 1).

14. Lynn Borgatta, Edward W. Hook, III, Julius Schachter, and Judith N. Wasserheit, "A Contemporary Approach to Curbing STDS," *Patient Care*, 15 December 1996, 30.

15. Christopher P. Crum and Gary R. Newkirk, "Abnormal Pap Smears, Cancer Risk, and HPV," *Patient Care*, 15 June 1995, 35.

16. Shyman S. Agarwal, Ashok Sehgal, Sarita Sardana, Anil Kumar, and Usha K. Luthra, "Role of Male Behavior in Cervical Carcinogenesis among Women with One Lifetime Sexual Partner," *Cancer*, 1 September 1993, 1666.

17. "Public Health Service Inter-Agency Guidelines for Screening Donors of Blood, Plasma, Organs, Tissues, and Semen for Evidence of Hepatitis B and Hepatitis C," Morbidity and Mortality Weekly Report (MMWR), 19 April 1991, 1-17.

18. Shelton, "Sex Turns Dangerous," 11 (see note 3).

19. Seroprevalence data from the *Third National Health and Nutrition Examination Survey, 1988-94* (NHANES III), National Center for Health Statistics, Centers for Disease Control and Prevention.

20. "Public Health Service Inter-Agency Guidelines for Screening Donors of Blood, Plasma, Organs, Tissues, and Semen for Evidence of Hepatitis B and Hepatitis C," 19 April 1991, 1-17 (see note 17).

21. *Hepatitis Surveillance - Issues and Answers Report Number 56*, April 1996, Centers for Disease Control and Prevention.

22. *Harrison's Principles of Internal Medicine*, 699-703, 1555 (see note 11).

23. Ibid., 697-699.

24. Geoffrey Cowley, "The Heart Attackers," *Newsweek*, 11 August 1997.

25. Kazunari Yamaguchi, "Human T-lymphotropic Virus Type I in Japan," *The Lancet*, 22 January 1994, 213.

26. "New Venereal Diseases Strengthen Case for Safer Sex," *AIDS Weekly Plus*, 24 February 1997, 24.

27. "Peter Jennings Breaks the HHV-6 Story. Gallo Affirms to ABC That Treating 'HHV-6 Disease' Could Save Lives," *New York Native*, 18 December 1995, 32-33.

28. John McKenzie, "The Key to Multiple Sclerosis?" *ABC News*, ABCNEWS.com, 19 October 1998.

29. "New Venereal Diseases Strengthen Case for Safer Sex," 24 (see note 26).

30. Luca Di Alberti, Adriano Piattelli, Luciano Artese et al., "Human Herpesvirus-8 Variants in Sarcoid Tissues," *The Lancet*, 6 December 1997, 1655.

31. Harrison's Principles of Internal Medicine, 11th ed., 697-699 (see note 11).

32. "Statistical Projections/Trends," National Center for HIV, STD, and TB Prevention, Centers for Disease Control and Prevention, 13 May 1999.

33. Juarlyn L. Gaiter and Scott M. Berman, "Risky Sexual Behavior Imperils Teens," *The Brown University Child and Adolescent Behavior Letter*, 10 (10): 1 (1994).

34. "Sexually Transmitted Diseases and Adolescents," *State Legislatures* 22 (4): 7 (1996).

35. Maggie Fox, "Urine Test Shows Hidden HIV: One in 1,000 May Be Infected but Not Know It," Reuters, 3 December 1998.

36. Charlene Laino, "HIV Can Hide in Semen, Study Says: Finding Suggests Some Who Test Negative Could Still Infect Others," MSNBC, 16 December 1998.

37. "Chlamydia Causes Infertility and Increases Risk of HIV Transmission," *AIDS Weekly Plus*, 20 November 1995, 20.

38. Harold C. Neu and Glenda Garvey, "Acquired Immune Deficiency Syndrome (AIDS)," in *The Columbia University College of Physicians and Surgeons Complete Home Medical Guide*, 3rd ed. (New York: Crown Publishing, 1995), 492.

39. Peter H. Duesberg, *Inventing the AIDS Virus* (Washington, DC: Regnery Publishing, 1996).

40. "Peter Jennings Breaks the HHV-6 Story. Gallo Affirms to ABC That Treating 'HHV-6 Disease' Could Save Lives," 32-33 (see note 27).

41. "New Venereal Diseases Strengthen Case for Safer Sex," 24 (see note 26).

42. Charlene Laino, "Drug-proof HIV Strain Transmitted. Potent Protease Inhibitors Found Powerless," MSNBC, 29 July 1998. Also, Michael Waldholz, "Drug-resistant HIV Becomes More Widespread," *Wall Street Journal*, 5 February 1999, B5.

43. "Chlamydia Causes Infertility and Increases Risk of HIV Transmission," 20 (see note 37).

44. "Chlamydia Trachomatis Genital Infections - United States, 1995," *The Journal of the American Medical Association*, 26 March 1997, 952.

45. Ibid.

46. Ibid.

47. Ibid.

48. "The Challenge of STD Prevention in the United States," 25 (see note 1).

49. David S. Sobel and Tom Ferguson, "Gonorrhea Tests. (Sexually Transmitted Disease Tests)," in *The People's Book of Medical Tests,* 1st ed. (Boston: Simon and Schuster, 1985), 140.

50. Ibid.

51. "The Challenge of STD Prevention in the United States," 25 (see note 1).

52. "Sexually Transmitted Diseases Which Strike Millions Each Year," Knight-Ridder/Tribune News Service, 16 March 1994.

53. Ibid.

54. "Many with HIV Don't Tell Partners," Associated Press, 8 February 1999.

55. Lynn Borgatta, Edward W. Hook, III, Julius Schachter, and Judith N. Wasserheit, "A Contemporary Approach to Curbing STDs," *Patient Care*, 15 December 1996, 30.

56. W. J. Martin, "Viral Infection in CFS Patients," in *The Clinical and Scientific Basis of Myalgic Encephalomyelitis Chronic Fatigue Syndrome* (Ottawa: Nightingdale Research Foundation Press, 1992), 325-327. Also, see Daniel H. Fylstra, "Dr. Martin's Stealth Virus Research: A Closer Look," available at the web site of the Center for Complex Infectious Diseases, Rosemead, CA 91770, http://www.ccid.org.

57. "Mad-Cow Fears Lead Panel to Urge Barring Some Blood Donors," *Wall Street Journal*, 3 June 1999, B16.

58. "SV-40," available at the web site of the Center for Complex Infectious Diseases (see note 56). Original research published in Martin et al., "SV-40: Early Region and Large T Antigen in Human Brain Tumors, Peripheral Blood Cells, and Sperm Fluids from Healthy Individuals," *Cancer Research* 56 (1996): 4820-4825.

59. John Martin, foreword to *Emerging Viruses: AIDS and Ebola: Nature, Accident or Intentional?* by Leonard G. Horowitz and W. John Martin (Rockport, MA: Tetrahedron, 1996).

60. "Most People Underestimate AIDS Risk from 'Phantom' Sex Partners," *AIDS Weekly*, 18 July 1994, 7.

61. "Sexually Transmitted Diseases and Adolescents," *State Legislatures*, April 1996, 7.

62. Gaiter and Berman, "Risky Sexual Behavior Imperils Teens," 1 (see note 33).

63. *Culture Facts*, Family Research Council, www.frc.com, 10 February 1999.

64. Geoffrey Cowley, "New Research Suggests HIV Is Not a New Virus but an Old One That Grew Deadly," *Newsweek*, 22 March 1993.

65. "A More 'Virulent' Strain of HIV?" MSNBC, 1997.

About the Author

Terry Wier, co-pastor of the Isaiah Worship Center, in Dallas, Texas, is at the forefront of groundbreaking ministry to street people and those caught up in destructive sexual practices. He was born in Odessa, Texas, in 1948 to parents who were both actively involved in Christian ministry. Wier graduated from East Texas State University with a degree in journalism and worked for a time at a television station in Waco, Texas. He has been married for twenty-seven years to Phyllis Cuington, who was an internationally known beauty and fashion photographer, the first black woman photographer for Vogue magazine, and and the first black woman to impact the modeling agency business in New York City. They have two children and one grandchild.

Wier and his wife were members of Brooklyn Tabernacle Church in New York City for eight years. While they were there, Wier led several outreaches before founding West Side Ministries, which continues to operate out of Brooklyn Tabernacle. For years he and Phyllis ministered weekly in the 14th Street garbage dump to a congregation of street dwellers. He also established ministries in New Orleans and Miami through the original staff of West Side Ministries.

In 1993, Wier and his family moved to Dallas and attended Covenant Church, where pastor Mike Hayes ordained Wier to the ministry. Two years later, Isaiah Ministries (an outgrowth of West Side Ministries that Wier founded) was given the property that now houses the Therapeutic Living Center, where people can go to recover from sexual problems and addictions. In 1996, he began a bilingual, nondenominational church, the Isaiah Worship Center, in Dallas, Texas, which he co-pastors with Phyllis. The following year, he began Internet counseling for those with sexual problems. In 1998, he began work in Guadalajara, Mexico, with the street prostitutes and transsexuals.

Wier has also taught the topic of holy sex to students at Oral Roberts University, the Wesleyan Foundation at Southern Methodist University, and Criswell Bible College. *Holy Sex* is Wier's first book.